Deep Learning

(A Practical Approach)

(Using Python)

Second Edition

Dr. Rajiv Chopra
Associate Professor
Guru Tegh Bahadur Institute of Information Technology,
CSE Department,
GGSIPU Delhi

KHANNA BOOK PUBLISHING CO. (P) LTD.
Publisher of Engineering and Computer Books
4C/4344, Ansari Road, Darya Ganj, New Delhi-110002
Phone : 011-23244447-48 **Mobile:** +91-9910909320
E-mail : contact@khannabooks.com
Website : www.khannabooks.com

Dear Readers,

To prevent the piracy, this book is secured with HIGH SECURITY HOLOGRAM on the front title cover. In case you don't find the hologram on the front cover title, please write us to at contact@khannabooks.com or whatsapp us at +91-99109 09320 and avail special gift voucher for yourself.

Specimen of Hologram on front Cover title:

Moreover, there is a SPECIAL DISCOUNT COUPON for you with EVERY HOLOGRAM.

How to avail this SPECIAL DISCOUNT:

Step 1: Scratch the hologram
Step 2: Under the scratch area, your "coupon code" is available
Step 3: Logon to www.khannabooks.com
Step 4: Use your "coupon code" in the shopping cart and get your copy at a special discount
Step 5: Enjoy your reading!

Price: ₹ 450.00

ISBN: 978-93-86173-41-6

Deep Learning
by Dr. Rajiv Chopra

First Edition: 2017
Second Edition: 2020
Reprint: 2021, 2022, 2023, 2024, **2026**

To view complete list of books, Please scan the QR Code:

Published by:
Khanna Book Publishing Co. (P) Ltd.
CIN: U22110DL1998PTC095547

Visit us at: **www.khannabooks.com**
Write us at: **contact@khannabooks.com**

Printed in India.

PREFACE TO SECOND EDITION

In 1980's deep learning was a science. But in 2019, it has become a technology. Artificial Intelligence contains Machine Learning and Deep Learning. Deep Learning applications range from simple applications like image classification to complex real-time applications like autonomous car driving.

Many industry giants like Google, MS, Amazon and Facebook have been using and supporting deep learning as they have found extensive usage of neural networks in their products and solutions. Business data analytics has a lot to do with these improvements.

Deep learning using Python is the need today. It is possible to solve AI problems using Neural Networks and deep learning architectures.

PREFACE TO FIRST EDITION

It is indeed a matter of great pride and inspiration to write this book entitled Deep Learning. The study of deep learning is sub-field of machine learning which comes under Artificial Intelligence only. It is the current area of research. So, this text is bolstered with several examples, case studies and case tools. With the reinvigoration of neural networks (2000s), deep learning has resulted in modern machine learning. Industry giants like MS, Google, Facebook, Deloitte etc. have formed in-house deep learning teams for the same. Present day research papers in this field of deep learning are very rare, scattered and less supportive for deep learning. There seems to be a symbiotic association between Big Data and Deep Learning. The rise of data is exponential. So, the need is to go in for Big Data Analytics and Web Analytics. We define deep learning as a set of machine learning techniques that learn multiple levels of representations in deep architectures. A deep architecture is capable of learning feature representations from both the labelled data and unlabelled data available. We need to do deep learning from this sea of data. Several applications like speech recognition, collaborative filtering, computer vision, Robotics etc use deep learning. Companies giants like Apple, Google, Facebook, Amazon etc. who collect and analyze Big Data on daily basis, have now jumped to deep learning related projects only. Even IBM has used deep learning to make use of Big Data for their company's advantage.

A brief overview of the chapters is as follows:

Chapter-1 deals with the traditional, basic neural network architecture and its working. This chapter depicts that there is a symbiotic association between big data and deep learning.

Chapter-2 focuses on the concepts on machine learning and various algorithms for machine learning. It also discusses on unsupervised and supervised learning approaches and methods.

Chapter-3 talks about deep feed-forward networks and their usage. It discusses about the training sets, their divisions as testing sets and various hyperparameters related to the deep model. It also discusses about overtraining or overfitting of data and how can it be avoided.

Chapter-4 delineates on the various methods of deep learning optimization by making use of hyperparameters.

Chapter-5 explains the new Convolutional Neural Networks [CNNs]. It also explains the architecture of CNNs and their working.

Chapter-6 discusses about sequence analysis meaning that there exists some sequence in the given input of the data available. It also discusses about Recurrent Neural Networks [RNNs], stateful deep learning networks, bidirectional RNNs and Neural Turing machines.

Chapter-7 focuses on CASE TOOLS like H2O and TensorFlow. Also shown are the steps followed to install these tools that are used to design and analyze deep neural networks.

Chapter-8 gives the application areas of deep learning. Deep learning is still in its infancy and needs to be applied further.

Chapter-9 traverses to give a survey on deep neural networks like on structured and unstructured modelling. Also discussed are Boltzmann machines and also discusses on representational and transfer learning.

ਦਿੱਲੀ ਸਿੱਖ ਗੁਰਦੁਆਰਾ ਪ੍ਰਬੰਧਕ ਕਮੇਟੀ

(ਦਿੱਲੀ ਸਿੱਖ ਗੁਰਦੁਆਰਾ ਅਧਿਨਿਯਮ, 1971 ਭਾਰਤ ਸਰਕਾਰ ਦੁਆਰਾ ਪਾਰਿਤ ਅਧੀਨ ਸਥਾਪਿਤ ਸੰਸਥਾ)

ਗੁਰੂ ਗੋਬਿੰਦ ਸਿੰਘ ਭਵਨ, ਗੁਰਦੁਆਰਾ ਰਕਾਬ ਗੰਜ ਸਾਹਿਬ, ਨਵੀਂ ਦਿੱਲੀ-੧੧੦੦੦੧

DELHI SIKH GURDWARA MANAGEMENT COMMITTEE

(Statutory Body Estd. under the Delhi Sikh Gurdwaras Act, 1971 of the Govt. of India)

Guru Gobind Singh Bhawan, Gurdwara Rakab Ganj Sahib, New Delhi-110001

Date : 18-12-2017

FOREWORD

Process of Education is perfect only when the teachers and students keep abreast of International developments in the areas of their specializations.

It is a matter of great pride to notice that Dr. Rajiv Chopra, Associate Professor in Computer Science Engineering, of Guru Tegh Bahadur Institute of Technology (Aff. To GGSIPU, Delhi) has come out with a book on such a hot topic on "Deep Learning-A Practical Approach" under the publication of M/s Khanna Book Publishing Co. (P) Ltd. headed by Mr. Mukul Seth.

Sharing of the knowledge acquired is a sacred mission and it enhances the vision for further research work. I am sure that this book will create new horizons for further innovative thoughts and fruitful discussions among the Professors and student community. I am proud to know that the author and the publishers have reached to commendable acme in the field of their specializations in a very short time span, exhibiting their versatile knowledge, leadership and administrative competence.

Deep learning is one of the most powerful and fastest growing fields of Technology and Computer Science. There is a dearth of books on deep learning today. I hope that the Indian Engineers as well as Engineers abroad would be benefitted from this book.

I also congratulate the team behind in the making of this excellence performance. My best wishes to the author for future endeavours.

Manjit Singh

(MANJIT SINGH G.K.)
PRESIDENT

Phones : +91 11 23712580, 23712581, 23712582, 23737328, 23737329 Fax : +91 11 23317511

Website : www.dsgmc.in Email : info@dsgmc.in

ACKNOWLEDGEMENTS

The blessings showered by the almighty GOD cannot be ignored. So, first of all I would like to thank the omnipresent GOD. I would like to thank the entire staff of Guru Tegh Bahadur Institute of Technology, Delhi. Thanks are also due for the **Director (Dr. Rominder Kaur), Manager (Gurmeet Singh Bhatia)** and **Chairman (S. Avtaar Singh Hit)** of my college of GTBIT, Delhi. Also, acknowledgements would be incomplete if I do not thank my colleague and administrative officer, **Mr. Harjeet Singh** who motivated me while writing of this book.

Also thanks are reserved for Mr. Mukul Seth, Director of M/s Khanna Publishing House, who despite his busy schedule got the book printed in a nice format. Thanks to the entire team of Khanna publishing for getting the work done on time.

Finally, I would like to thank my parents-Dr. J. R. Chopra and Mrs. Sushma Chopra along with my spouse Shakti Chopra and my twin babies-Arjeesh Chopra and Arshitha Chopra, who cooperated for this project.

Dr. Rajiv Chopra
Ph. D. (Computer Science); M. Tech. (IT); MIT; BE(CSE)
Associate Professor (CSE Dept.)
Guru Tegh Bahadur Institute of Information Technology
G-8 Area Rajouri Garden, Delhi-64.
raj_74chopra2004@yahoo.com

CONTENTS

1 The Neural Network

1.0 Introduction

Deep Learning and **Big Data** are inter-related. Big data refers to the pools of data being generated every second while deep learning is an active research area in the field of **machine learning.** But as the data is growing at an exponential rate, deep learning is providing big data predictive analytical solutions. According to the report of National Security Agency (NSA), the Internet itself is processing 1,826 Petabytes of data per day [1]. By 2020, the figure will reach 35 Trillion gigabytes. This leads to a remarkable paradigm shift in computer science literature towards data-driven discovery. Today machine learning techniques and newer software, hardware and computational power help in big data as well as web data analytics.

We need to define **Deep Learning** now.

Deep learning is defined as the machine learning techniques that use supervised and/or unsupervised methods to automatically learn hierarchical representations in deep architectures for classification.

Or

Deep learning is a subset of artificial intelligence field called as machine learning which is predicted on the basic idea of learning from example.

Or

Deep Learning is a new area of machine research that moves machine learning objectives to one of its original goals.

Or

Deep Learning is about learning multiple levels of representation and abstraction that help to make sense of data like images, sound and text.

Or

Deep learning emplasizes the network architecture to today's most successful machine learning approaches. These methods are based on "deep" multilayer neural network with many hidden layers.

Challenges in Deep Learning

1. Need is to find and process **massive datasets** for training.
2. Large number of interconnected neurons or **free parameters** makes deep learning better. This allows to capture subtle nuances and **variations in data**.
3. Due to sheer number of layers, nodes and connections, it is difficult to understand how deep learning networks arrive at insights.
4. Deep learning networks are highly susceptible to the **butterfly effect**–Small variations in input data can lead to different results, making them inherently unstable.

Applications of Deep Learning

1. Image caption generation.
2. Automatic game playing.
3. Coloriozation of black and white images.
4. Adding sound to silent movies.
5. Automatic machine translation.
6. Object classification in photographs.
7. Automatic handwriting generation.
8. Character text generation.

In machine learning, instead of teaching a computer a massive list of rules to solve the complex problem, we give it a **model** with which it can evaluate examples. Also we give it a small set of instructions to modify the model when it makes a mistake. **Please note that we have an expectation that as the time passes, a well suited model would be able to solve the problem more accurately.**

For example, say our model is defined by a function $f(x, \theta)$. The input x is an example expressed in vector form. Like, if x were a gray-scale image, the vector's components would be pixel intensities at each position. The input θ is a vector of the parameters that our model uses. **Also note now that it is our machine learning program that tries to perfect the values of these parameters as it is exposed to more and more examples.**

The conventional learning methods are shallow-structured learning architectures while deep learning is deep-hierarchical levelled learning architecture. It is based on the biological neurons within human brain. Several research domains like speech recognition, Natural Language Processing (NLP), collaborative filtering and computer vision. Big industry giants like Google, Apple and Facebook who work on sheer size of data lakes today have also given vital importance to Big Data Analytics and Web Data Analytics. Google applies deep learning algorithms to massive chunks of messy data obtained from Internet. IBMs brain-like computer uses techniques like deep learning to make available big data available for its betterment. **Please note that as the data keeps increasing at an exponential rate, deep learning is playing a key role in providing** in big data and web analytics. **Also note that deep learning refers to a set of machine learning techniques that learn multiple levels of representations in deep architectures.** Deep learning is the new name for neural networks. Deep learning algorithms have best performance as far as complex problems like pattern recognition are concerned. Practically speaking, even machine learning approaches find it difficult to solve. Theoretically, they can solve any problem. Several libraries also exist for neural nets or deep learning.

But deep learning algorithms such as an auto-encoder i.e. unsupervised deep learning, several parameters and slower deep learning grids are some of the issues to be discussed in this text. These programs may need more hardware.

The information that is available on the web and is searched using search engines like Google is called as the **surface web.** On the other hand, **deep web** consists of data hidden behind web-based services. Theoretically, the deluge (flood) of data within deep web is exponentially high. Practically, useful information hidden in deep web is finite but very large. Each web form can give rise to thousands of results, each of which qualifies as a **deep web page.** Similarly, every Facebook or Twitter post might be considered as a **deep web page.** Finally, if one considers all possible pages of search results then the size of deep web is infinite. As per the survey report (2007), roughly 2.5% of random sample of web pages were forms that should be considered as part of deep web. **Please understand that deep web is huge, far larger than the indexed web of 50 billion pages.** Searching the deep web is current research area today.

Let us explore this and many more interesting topics in this book.

1.1 Neurons

We define a neuron first of all. **A neuron is a function that takes multiple numeric inputs and gives out one numeric output. These neurons are organized in layers and the outputs from all of the neurons in one layer become the inputs for each neuron in the next layer.**

The functional unit of a normal human brain is the **neuron.** The **objective of this** book is to use this natural brain concept to build machine learning models that solve problems in a similar fashion. A neuron is optimized to receive information from other neurons, process this information and send its results to other cells. This is shown in figure-1.1.

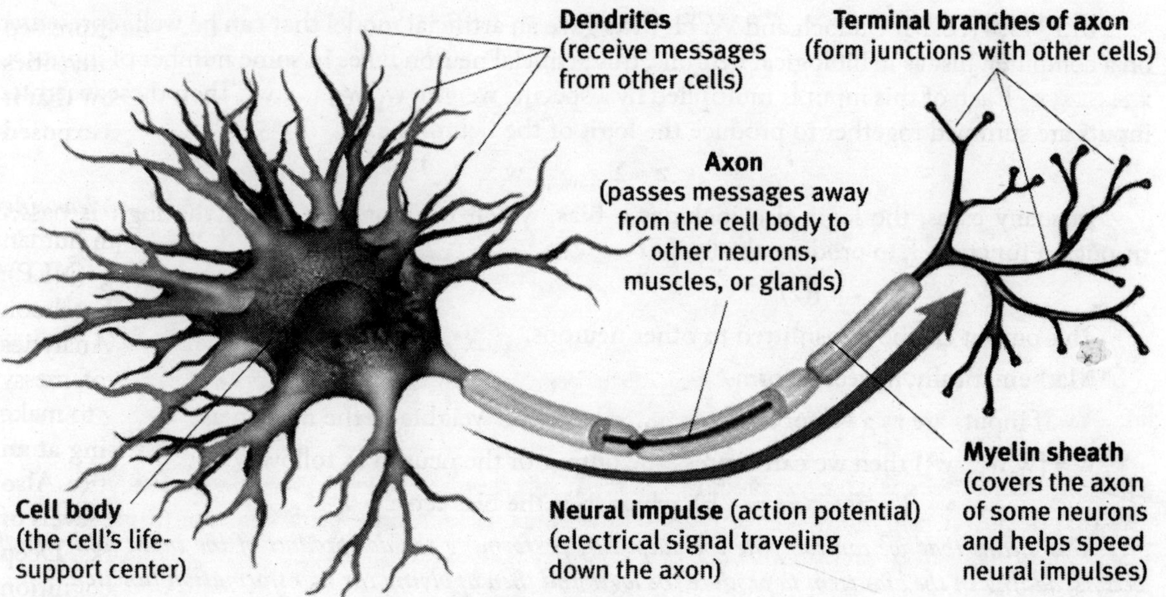

Fig.1.1: A Neuron

The neuron receives its inputs along antennae-like structures called **dendrites.** Each of these incoming connections is dynamically strengthened or weakened based on how often it is used. **Please understand that it is the strength of each connection that determines the contribution of the input to the neuron's output.** After being weighted by the strength of their respective connections, the inputs are summed together in the **cell body. Also understand that this sum is then transformed into a new signal that is propagated along the cell's axon and sent to other neurons.**

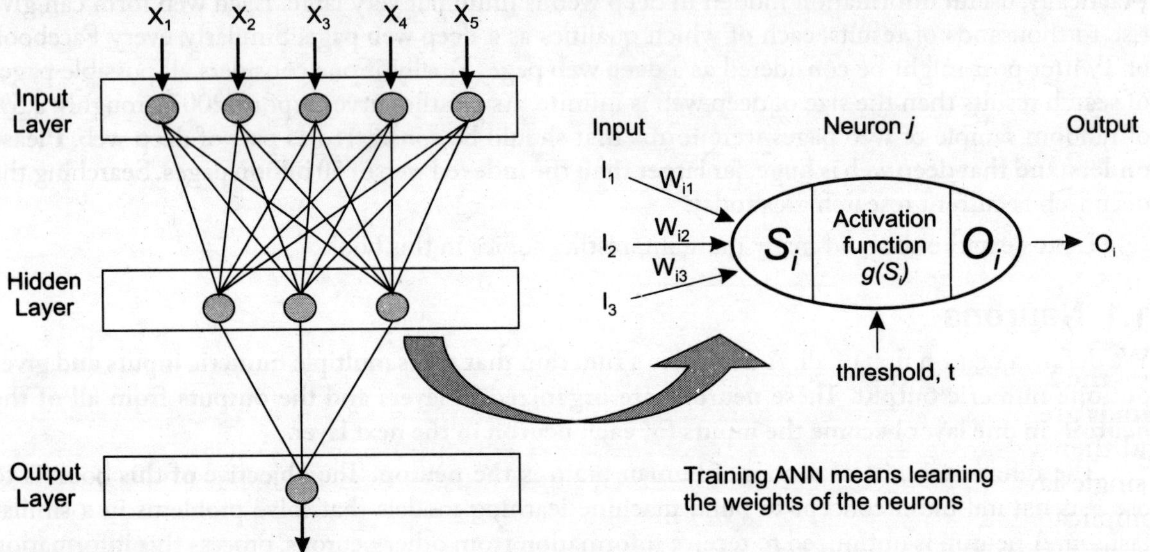

Fig.1.2: A Neuron

In 1943, W. S. McCulloch and W. H. Pitts gave an artificial model that can be well represented on a computer. Just as in biological neurons, this artificial neuron takes in some number of inputs, x_1, x_2, ..., x_n. Each of this input is multiplied by a specific weight, w_1, w_2,......,w_n. Then these weighted inputs are summed together to produce the **logit** of the neuron i.e.

$$z = \Sigma_{(i=0 \text{ to } n)} \; w_i x_i$$

In many cases, the logit also includes a **bias,** which is a constant. Then the logit is passed through a function, f, to produce the output-

$$y = f(z)$$

This output can be transmitted to other neurons.

Mathematically, in vector form-

If inputs are as a vector $x = [x_1 x_2......x_n]$ and the weights of the neuron as $w = [w_1 w_2 ...... w_n]$ then we can express the output of the neuron as follows:

$$y = f(x \,.\, w + b)\text{, where 'b' is the bias term.}$$

This means that we can compute the output by performing the dot product of the input and weight vectors, adding in the bias term to produce the logit and then applying the transformation function.

1.2 Linear Perceptrons as Neurons

Much of the work of McCulloch and Pitts in 1943 and subsequentiy in 1947 was based on a simple neuron model. It is shown in figure-1.3.

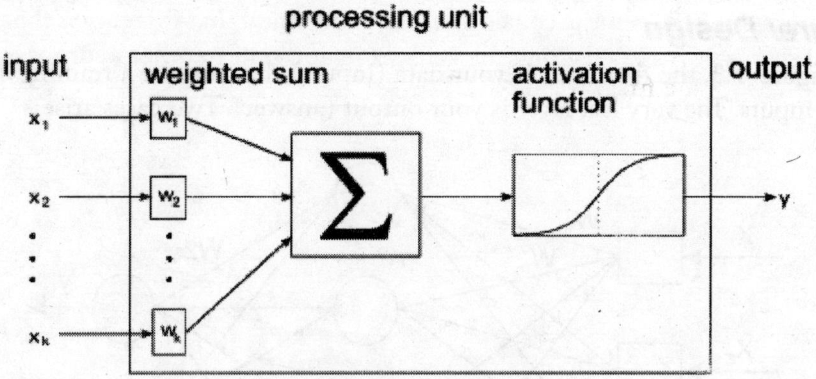

processing unit

input	weighted sum		activation function	output
x_1	w_1	Σ		y
x_2	w_2			
x_k	w_k			

Fig.1.3: Perceptron Neuron

The Σ unit multiplies each input, x, by a weight ,w, and sums the weighted inputs. **If this sum is greater than a predetermined threshold, the output =1 else it is zero.** These systems and their variants collectively have been called as **perceptrons.** In general, they consist of a single layer of artificial neurons connected by weights to a set of inputs although more complicated networks bear the same.

The **PERCEPTRON LEARNING THEOREM** states that-**"A perceptron could learn anything it could represent." Rosenblatt, in 1962, proved that a perceptron can be trained to any function it can represent.** The difference between **representation** and **learning** lies in the point of reference. **Representation means** the ability of a perceptron to simulate a specified function while **learning** requires the existence of a systematic procedure for adjusting the network weights to produce that function.

Note: A neuron with n binary inputs can have 2^n different input patterns, consisting of 1s and 0s. Because each input pattern can produce two different binary output, one and zero, there are 2^{2n} different functions of n variables.

Learning is of two types- Supervised and Unsupervised. **Supervised learning** needs an external "teacher" that evaluates the behaviour of the system and directs the subsequent modifications. On the other hand, **unsupervised learning** needs "no teacher" as the network **self-organizes** to produce the desired changes. **Please note here that the Perceptron learning is of the supervised type.** The perceptron training algorithm can be implemented on a system and the network becomes **self adjusting.** This is reason as to why adjusting of weights is called as **training** and the network is said to **learn.**

Rosenblatt's proof was a major milestone and it provided a great impetus to the research field. **Also note that a perceptron is trained by representing a set of patterns to its input, one at a time and adjusting the weights until the desired output occurs for each of them.**

Linear perceptron and the neuron model are somewhat equivalent. But the point to ponder is that **every linear perceptron can be expressed as a single neuron but single neurons can also express models that cannot be expressed by any linear perceptron.**

1.3 Neural Nets

We have already defined what a neuron is. These neurons are organized into layers. The outputs from all the neurons in one layer become the inputs for each neuron in the next layer.

Architecture/ Design

As shown in figure-1.3, the first layer is your data (inputs) that may be a training sample or a test sample or real inputs. The very last layer is your output (answer). Two cases arise:-

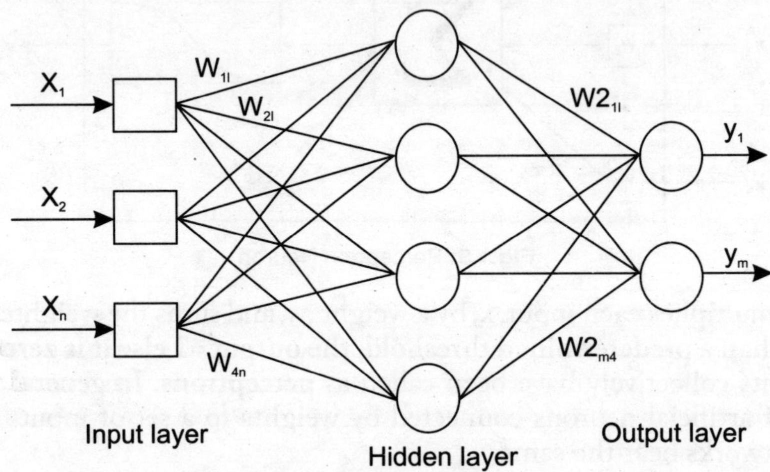

Fig.1.4: Neural Nets

Case-1: If you are doing a **regression** i.e. learning a single value then the output layer will have **one neuron.**

Case-2: If you are doing **classification,** then the output layer will have one neuron for each possible answer. Here, the output (answer) with the highest probability for the set of inputs is chosen.

The layers between the input layers and the output layers are called as the hidden layers.

Rule: "Each neuron in each hidden layer has a weight for each of its inputs and modifying those weights is how the network learns. There is a bias input to each neuron, (a weight only) connected to a constant input and is also tuned during the training process."

1.4 Working of Neural Nets

As shown in figure 1.4, we start with random weights. Then we give it the first training sample and the correct answer (also called as **supervised learning),** calculate the error and then use that to go back and tweak each of the weights so that there is a bit less error. **This process is called as backpropagation.** Then we take the second training sample and repeat the process. **This process of taking each and every training data is called as an epoch. Also note that we specify the number of epochs in the algorithm that we develop. Also note that even fractional epochs are allowed. For example,** requesting 20.5 epochs means all training data samples are processed 20 times while the first half of the training data is also processed an 11th time.

Many deep learning libraries use the concept of **mini batches.** A mini-batch of say, size 20 means that it will process 20 training samples then go back and update the weights in one batch. But deep learning libraries like H2O does not use mini-batch concept in H2O the weights get updated after every single sample.

If it is a **multimode cluster** then each node in the cluster works independently for one iteration. At the end of each iteration, the network weights are averaged with those on every node. **Also note that one iteration can be larger or smaller than an epoch.**

Note: Everything is a number in neural net. For example, in digit recognition problem there will be one neuron per pixel and the value will be the intensity of that pixel.

1.5 Layers of Neural Networks and Deep learning

In theory, one hidden layer is sufficient to represent all of our data whether linear or non-linear relationships but practically speaking it is not enough to have entire data in one layer.

Please understand that having many hidden layers is deep learning but more layers/neurons means longer training and slower usage. Many researchers say that it is not deep learning if we have just one hidden layer only.

How to choose the number of layers and neurons in a neural net?

There are six (rules) rules of thumb to select the number of layers and neurons:-

Rule-1: If the problem is non-linear then we start with two (2) layers and observe how it performs on it.

Rule-2: More non-linear is the problem, the more layers you need. If you observe that the problem is not getting solved, then add another layer to it and try. You can also try with more epochs, more training data. It has been observed that if you have moved till 5-layers then the 6th layer probably will not help.

Rule-3: More are the number of neurons in a layer, the more clearly it will be able to understand the data. You can add more neurons or more epochs or more training data.

Rule-4: More data inputs you have, the more neurons are needed in the first hidden layer.

Rule-5: More output neurons you have, the more neurons you are likely to need in the final hidden layer.

Rule-6: More are the layers, more will be the benefit from activation functions (to be discussed).

The time spent in training a deep learning model is given by the formula:-

Training Time (TT) = [Number of training samples] * [Number of Epochs]

How much training is required depends on the weights in our model. **Please note that more are the weights, more can be learned from the model.**

The number of weights between two layers is given by the formula:-

Weights (W) = [Number of Neurons in layer-1] * [Number of Neurons in layer-2]

Also note that you will also have to count two more layers: the input layer and the output layer.

For example, in a 50*50 network, with 2 numeric inputs and 1 output, there are:-

(2*50) + (50 * 50) + (50 * 1) = 100 + 2500 + 50 = **2650 weights.**

Now, say, you add another 3rd layer with 50 neurons, then we can compute weights required as follows:-

(2 * 50) + (50 * 50) + (50 * 50) + (50 * 1) = 100 + 2500 + 2500 + 50 = **5150 weights.**

It has been observed that if more are the weights, slower is the training.

Researchers say that deep learning is a new AI that can tell whether our tweets are sarcastic (abusive) or not. Scientists at Massachusetts Institute of Technology (MIT) USA have developed a new artificial system that can detect sarcasm in tweets better than humans. It's developers say that this advancement may help computers automatically spot and remove online hate speech and abusive comments. Detecting the sentiments of social media posts can also help gauge attitudes towards brands and products and identify signals that might indicate trends in the financial markets. **Please note that they said that a deeper understanding of Twitter may also help understand how information and influence flows through the network.** The researchers originally aimed to develop a system capable of detecting racist posts on Twitter. However, the meaning of many messages could not be properly understood without some understanding of sarcasm. **Also note that the algorithm uses deep learning, a popular machine learning technique that relies on training a very large simulated neural network to recognise subtle patterns using a large amount of data.** Researchers took advantage of *emoji* to help the algorithm identify and label emotional content.

According to the report of "MIT Technology Review", 2017, once the system read tweets for emotions, the researchers taught it to recognise sarcasm. According to MIT, the neural network learned the connection between a certain kind of language and an emoji.

1.6 Activation Functions

We use activation functions to **propagate the output of one layer's nodes forward to the next layer**; upto and including the output layer. Activation functions are a scalar-to-scalar function, yielding the neuron's activation. We use activation functions for hidden neurons in a NN to introduce non-linearity into the network's modeling capabilities.

Many activation functions belong to a logistic class of transforms that when graphed resemble an S. This class of function is called **sigmoidal.** The sigmoid family of functions contains several variations, one of which is known as **the sigmoid function**.

Depending on the activation function you pick, you will find that some objective functions are more appropriate for different kinds of data eg. sparse data versus dense data. Depending on the architecture we are working, we tend to use certain subsets of layer activation functions.

In figure-1.1, it was observed that a neuron has many weighted inputs coming in and one output going out. The inputs are summed. The value of the output is decided by the **activation functions.**

For examples,

Rectifier, outputs the sum of its weighted inputs but clips all negative values to zero. This implies that it will be generating quite a few zeros as zeros are good for training deeper networks but also means that positive values are unbounded.

Tanh, takes as input range of negative infinity to positive infinity. It converts that to an output range of -1 to +1. **Note that it varies more rapidly when the sum of inputs is closer to zero.**

Maxout, gives the maximum of the inputs. It means that the weighted inputs are used directly and not summed up.

1.7 Feed Forward Neural Networks

Single neurons are better and more powerful than linear perceptrons yet they are not very effective to solve complex problems. Just as our brain is made of many neurons so should be artificial neurons. In normal human brain, there are six layers. The information flows from one layer to another layer. The sensory input is converted into conceptual understanding. **For instance,** the bottommost layer of our brain receives raw data from our eyes. This information is the processed by each layer and passed on to the next layer and finally to the 6th layer. It is then we conclude that whether we are looking at a car or a bike. Our **artificial neural network** is analogous to this. A neural network is formed when we start attaching neurons to each other, the input data and to the output nodes. This corresponds to the network's answer to a learning problem. A simple three layer (or 3-tier) feed forward network is shown in figure 1.5:

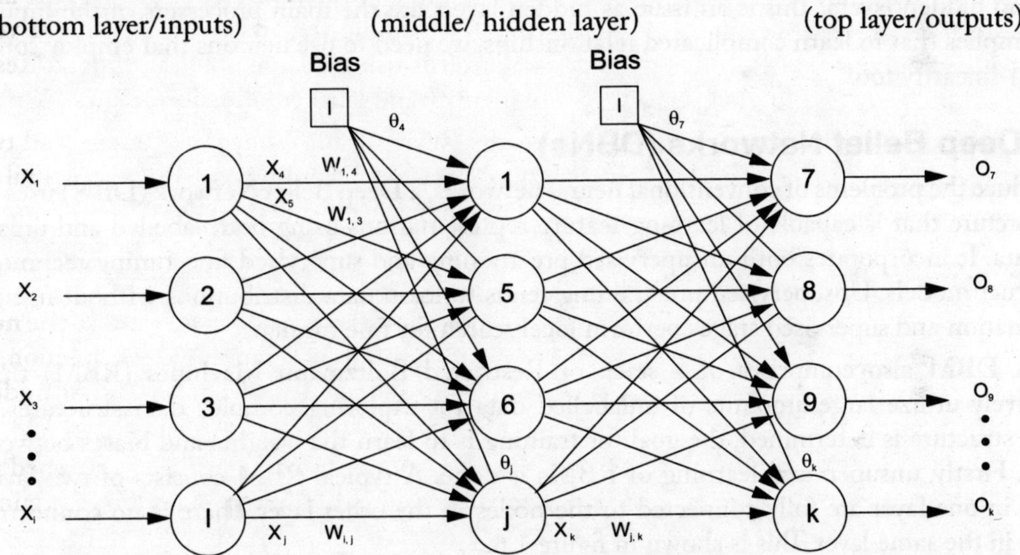

Fig.1.5: Three-layer Feed- Forward Neural Network with inputs, 3 Hidden Layers, Outputs and Bias.

Explanation: The network of neurons as shown in figure 1.5 is similar to the architecture given by McCulloch and Pitt in 1943. The bottom layer of the network takes the input data. The top layer of neurons or output nodes computes the final answer. The middle layer(s) of neurons are called as **hidden layers.** Now, if $W_{ij}^{(k)}$ is the weight of connection between the ith neuron in the kth layer with the jth neuron in the $k+1^{st}$ layer; then these weights constitute a parameter vector, θ. And our ability to solve the problem with neural networks concept will depend on finding the optimal values of this parameter θ. **Please note that the connections traverse from a lower layer to a higher layer and there are no connections between neurons in the same layer. Also note that there are no connections that transmit data from a higher layer to a lower layer. These types of neural networks are called as feed-forward networks.** These networks are simple to analyze.

Before we discuss further, note down the following points:-

1. It is the **hidden layer** where actually the problem is being solved by our neural network. Hidden layers automate the process.
2. **Hidden layers have fewer neurons than the input layer.** Although input is taken from bottom layers yet hidden layers come up with better presentations for everything in output.
3. Every layer **may or may not have the same number of neurons.**
4. It is not mandatory that every neuron has its output connected to the inputs of all neurons in the next layer. It comes from experience only.
5. The inputs and outputs here are **vectorized** representations.

1.8 Limitations of Neurons

Any feed-forward neural network consisting of only linear neurons can be represented as a network with no hidden layers. This is an issue as hidden layers are the main processers of the input data. This implies that to learn complicated relationships, we need to use neurons that employ some sort of non-linearity too.

1.9 Deep Belief Networks (DBNs)

To reduce the problems of conventional neural networks, a Deep Belief Network (DBN) uses a deep architecture that is capable of learning feature representations using both labelled and unlabelled big data. It incorporates both unsupervised pre-training and supervised fine-tuning techniques to construct models. Unsupervised pre-training tends to learn data distributions without using label information and supervised stages perform local search for fine tuning.

A DBM also comprises of a stack of Restricted Boltzmann Machines (RBM) that can effectively utilize large amounts of unlabelled data for exploring complex data structures. After DBN structure is determined, the goal for training is to learn the weights and biases between the layers. Firstly, unsupervised learning of RBMs is done. A typical RBM consists of two layers i.e. nodes in one layer are fully connected to the nodes in the other layer. There is no connection for nodes in the same layer. This is shown in figure 1.6.

It is shown in figure 1.6 that nodes in one layer are fully connected to the nodes in the other layer. There are no connections for nodes in the same layer. The input layer and the first hidden layer H_1 form a RBM. Each node is independent of the nodes in the same layer. Before fine-tuning, a layer by layer pre-training of RBM is performed. The outputs of a RBM are fed as inputs to the next RBM and the process is repeated until all RBMs are pre-trained. This is layer by layer unsupervised learning. **Please note that after pre-training information about the input data is stored in weights between every adjacent layers. Also note that DBNs use a greedy and efficient layer by layer approach to learn the latent variables/weights in each hidden layer and a back propagation method for fine-tuning.** So this hybrid training method improves both the generative performance and the discriminative power of the network.

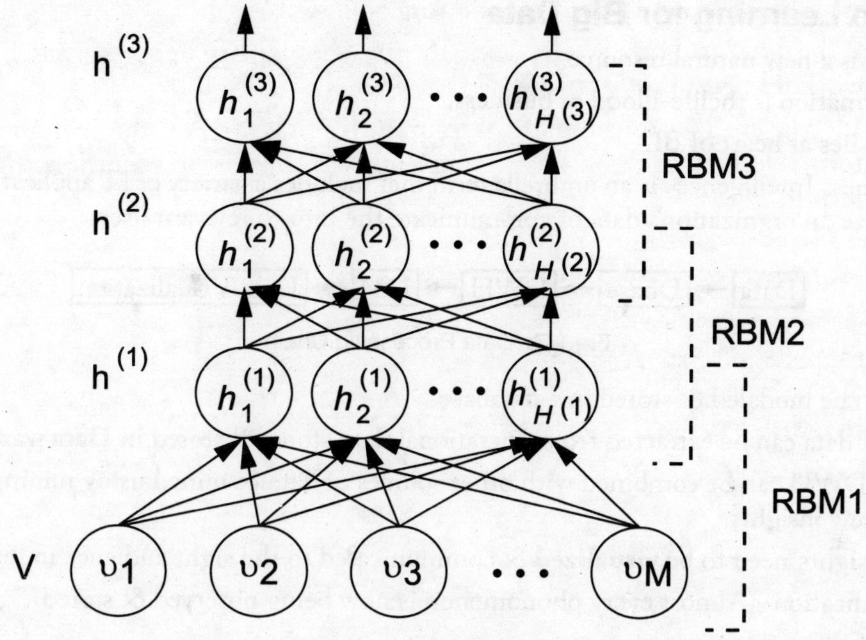

Fig.1.6: DBN and RBM

1.10 Large Scale DBNs

To reduce the data transfer times between host and global memory and to allow parameter updates, one technique is to store all parameters and a large chunk of training examples in **global memory** during training. This shows the reusing of large chunks of training examples.

1.11 Large Scale Convolutional Neural Networks

Locally connected deep learning method is **Convolutional Neural Networks (CNNs).** Large scale CNNs learning is implemented on parallel processors. CNN training involves both forward and backward propagation. For this one or more blocks are assigned for each feature map. Each thread in a block shows a single neuron in a map. The computation of each neuron with the neurons from the previous layers, activation and summation is then performed. Finally, the outputs are stored in the global memory. Also the weights are updated by back-propagation of errors. Parallelizing backward propagation can be implemented either by pulling or pushing. **Pulling error signals is the process of computing delta signals for each neuron in the previous layer by pulling the error signals from the current layer.** This is quite complex. On the other hand, pushing the error signals from the current layer to the previous layer is more efficient. That is, for each unit in the current layer, we update the related units in the previous layer.

Note: To implement data parallelism, we need to consider two things:-

- **a) The size of global memory.**
- **b) The feature map size.**

1.12 Deep Learning for Big Data

- Data is a new natural resource.
- Information is thelife-blood of business.
- Data lies at heart of BI.
- Business Intelligence : is an umbrella term that includes a variety of IT applications that are used to analyze an orgnization's data of communicate the into to relevant users.

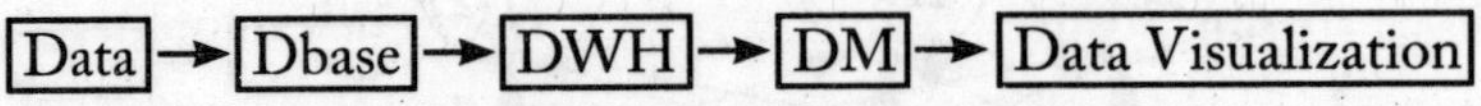

Fig.1.7: Data Processing Chain

Data can be modaled & stored in a database.

Relevant data can be extracted from operational data stores & stored in **Data ware house.**

Data in DWH can be combined with other sources of data & mined using mining techniques to generate new insights.

Then 'insights' need to be **visualized** & communicated to the sight audience in real-time.

- Datafication–"Almost every phonomenon is now being observed & stored".
- Machines are generating data.
- IOT is growing faster than Internet of People (IOT)
- Exponential data growth.

Kryders Law– "Density & capability of hard drive storage media will double every 18 months."

Big data is at the core of our society today. The need is to process yottabytes (a billion petabytes) of data. Traditional machine learning algorithms are not sufficient as they were designed for data that could be stored in memory. But today data is "big". So, algorithms that can learn from massive amount of data are required now. Large scale deep learning is still in its infancy.

1.13 Deep Learning from High Volumes of Data

The data pool available today is a major challenge for deep learning today. The sheer volume of data results in run –time complexity and model complexity. These data lakes often make it impossible to train a deep learning algorithm with a central processor and storage. Hence, distributed machines and parallel machines are preferred. In nutshell, in order to build the future deep learning system scalable to Big Data, we need to develop high performance computing infrastructure-based systems. Also we need **parallel learning algorithms** now.

Another problem with these data lakes is that it results in data incompleteness and noisy labels. One of the features of deep learning algorithms is that they have the ability to use unlabelled data during training. So, the presence of large unlabelled data presents many chances for deep learning methods. Advanced deep learning methods are required to handle noisy big data.

1.14 Deep Learning from High Variety of Data

One advantage of deep learning is its ability of representational learning with either supervised or unsupervised methods or their combinations. Deep learning can integrate data from different sources. Deep learning can utilize heterogeneous sources for better system performance. In nutshell, *deep learning seems to be well suited to integrate heterogeneous data with multiple modalities due to its capability of learning abstract representations.*

1.15 Deep Learning for High Velocity of Data

Conventional neural networks have been used for online learning but still the progress is insufficient. Data is non-stationary i.e. it changes over time. Deep learning algorithm for big data is the ability to learn the data as a stream. So, deep online learning is yet to be explored.

In nutshell, big data presents many challenges to deep learning including large scale, heterogeneity, noisy labels and non-stationary distribution etc.

1.16 Local Minima in Deep Networks

The main issue in optimizing deep learning models is that we are now compelled to use minimal local information to infer global structure of the error surface. But this is not easy because the correspondence between local and global structure is quite less.

The first source of local minima is related to the term **model identifiability. It has been observed that the error surface of deep neural networks is very large and sometimes infinite too.** So, they have many local minimas.

1.17 Rearranging Neurons in a layer of a Neural Network

It has been observed that within a layer of a **fully-connected feed-forward neural network, any rearrangement of neurons will still give us the same result (final output) at the end of the network. Also note that if a layer has n neurons then there are n! ways to rearrange the parameters.** But if it is a deep layered network, then with k layers, each with n neurons, we will have a total of $n!^k$ equivalent (similar) configurations.

Here, local minima is not a problem. Bit local minima are a problem if and only if they are spurious. We say that a local minima is spurious refers to those weights in neural network that incurs a higher error rate than at the global minima.

1.18 Spurious Local Minima in Deep Networks

Researchers of deep learning say that it is difficult to train deep networks on spurious local minima. The point is that in practical neural networks spurious local minima and global minima have higher error rates. Some researchers say that most local minima have error rates similar to the global minima.

Given any function, a point at which the gradient is a zero vector is known as a **critical point. Actually, local maxima** do not cause much of the problems. **The flat regions of the curve that are more trouble causing and informal are called as saddle points.** Research shows that as our function adds up more and more parameters i.e. we have more and more parameters in our model, then saddle points rise exponentially than local minima. In one dimensional subspace, a critical point can come in three different types and hence the probability that the random critical point is in a random function is $1/3^d$.

Note:

1. If we have a total of 'k' critical points, then we will have a total of k/3 local minima.
2. A random function with 'p' critical points has an expected number of $p/3^d$.

Summary

In biological organisms, knowledge is stored as complex structures of interconnected neurons. The structures correspond to symbolic representations of the knowledge possessed by the organism, the facts, the rules and so on. **Please note that an average human brain weighs about 3.3 pounds and contains an estimated number of 10^{12} neurons. Also note that these neurons and their interconnection capabilities provide about 10^{14} bits of potential storage capacity.** Artificial neural networks are not a panacea. They are unsuitable for tasks like payroll calculations. Backpropagation uses gradient descent to adjust the network weights. This is fine with convex error surfaces as they have a **unique minimum.** But it results in non-optimal solutions with non-convex surfaces. In some scenarios, a local minimum is acceptable as a solution but in some it is inadequate.

Even if the network is trained yet there is no way to depict that this backpropagation algorithm has found the global minimum. **Also understand that if the solution is unsatisfactory, we must re-initialize the weights to new random values and re-train the network.** But there is no guarantee that a global minima will be found. One has to take care as far as weight selection is concerned. This may result in **network paralysis.**

In this chapter we have seen the basic neuron structure and the working of feed-forward networks. Also observed is the problem of non-linearity in solving complex learning problems.

Multiple Choice Questions (MCQs)

1. Machine learning includes-
   (a) Narrow Learning. (b) Deep Learning.
   (c) Varied Learning. (d) None of the above.
2. A subset of artificial intelligence field called as machine learning which is predicted on the basic idea of learning from example is named as-
   (a) Learning by Examples. (b) Learning by Machine.
   (c) Deep Learning. (d) None of the above.
3. RBM stands for-
   (a) Restricted Boltzmann Machines. (b) Regular Boltzmann Memory.
   (c) Referred Boltzmann Machine. (d) None of the above.
4. Deep Belief Networks use-
   (a) RBM. (b) DBMS.
   (c) IBM. (d) None of the above.
5. The time spent in training a deep learning model is given by the formula:-
   (a) Training Time (TT) = [Number of training samples] + [Number of Epochs]
   (b) Training Time (TT) = [Number of training samples] - [Number of Epochs]
   (c) Training Time (TT) = [Number of training samples] * [Number of Epochs]
   (d) Training Time (TT) = [Number of training samples] / [Number of Epochs]

6. The more are the weights-
   (a) Slower will be the training. (b) Faster will be the training.
   (c) Lesser will be the training. (d) None of the above.
7. Which of the following is a rectification function-
   (a) Rectifier. (b) Amplifier.
   (c) Simplifier. (d) None of the above.
8. The working of ANNs is similar to-
   (a) A human brain. (b) A car working.
   (c) A human eye. (d) None of the above.
9. Even a tiny part of the brain that is about the size of a grain of rice has-
   (a) 5000 neurons. (b) 6000 neurons.
   (c) 10,000 neurons. (d) None of the above.
10. Connections traverse from-
    (a) Lower to higher layer. (b) Higher to lower layer.
    (c) At same layer. (d) None of the above.
11. As we make neural networks deep, which phenomenon is seen-
    (a) Overloading. (b) Overriding.
    (c) Overfitting. (d) None of the above.
12. A single iteration over the entire training set is called as an-
    (a) Epoch. (b) Clock.
    (c) Cycle. (d) None of the above.
13. The data is split up into two parts-
    (a) Training data and valid data. (b) Training data and test data.
    (c) Training data and big data. (d) None of the above.
14. At the end of each epoch, we must see that-
    (a) Error is increasing. (b) Error is decreasing.
    (c) Error is static. (d) None of the above.
15. One of the methods of overcoming 'overfitting' phenomenon is called as-
    (a) Regularization. (b) Segmentation.
    (c) Fragmentation. (d) None of the above.
16. Deep learning is also called as-
    (a) Feature learning. (b) Representation learning.
    (c) Example based learning. (d) Only 'a' and 'b'.

17. An artificial neural network used for learning efficient coding is-
    (a) Auto-encoder. (b) Decoder.
    (c) Encoder. (d) None of the above.
18. Deep learning is useful as-
    (a) Non-linear function can be represented in a better way.
    (b) Linear function can be represented in a better way.
    (c) Polynomial function can be represented in a better way.
    (d) None of the above.
19. A systematic method for training multilayer ANN is named as-
    (a) Forward-propagation. (b) Backpropagation.
    (c) Error propagation. (d) None of the above.
20. If we want to train the network to recognize all letters of the alphabet then we need-
    (a) 20 training pairs. (b) 26 training pairs.
    (c) 30 training pairs. (d) None of the above.
21. A group of training pairs is called as-
    (a) Training set. (b) Working set.
    (c) Logical set. (d) None of the above.
22. A neuron with n binary inputs can have-
    (a) 2n input patterns. (b) 2n input patterns.
    (c) n/2 input patterns. (d) None of the above.
23. Each input pattern can produce-
    (a) Two binary inputs (1s and 0s). (b) 2n inputs.
    (c) 2n inputs. (d) None of the above.
24. In a 50*50 network, with 2 numeric inputs and 1 output, there are:-
    (a) 2650 weights. (b) 3650 weights.
    (c) 4300 weights. (d) None of the above.
25. If we have a total of 'k' critical points, then we will have a total of-
    (a) k/3 local minima. (b) k/2 local minima.
    (c) k * 3 local minima. (d) None of the above.

Answers

1. b	6. a	11. c	16. d	21. a
2. c	7. a	12. a	17. a	22. a
3. a	8. a	13. b	18. a	23. a
4. a	9. c	14. b	19. b	24. a
5. c	10. a	15. a	20. b	25. a

Conceptual Short Questions with Answers

Q1. Define deep learning.

Ans. It is defined as a set of machine learning algorithms which attempt to learn multiple-layered models of inputs (neural networks). They are composed of multiple levels of non-linear operations. The core concept of deep learning is a greedy layerwise unsupervised pre-training that is to learn a hierarchy of features one level at a time.

Q2. What is an auto-encoder?

Ans. An auto-encoder is an artificial neural network used for learning efficient coding. The objective is to learn a compressed representation /encoding for a data set. This means that it was being used for dimensionality reduction or data compression.

Q3. What are the advantages of deep learning?

Ans. Deep learning has the following advantages:

1. Non-linear functions can be represented in a more efficient manner.
2. Deep representations may allow for a hierarchical representations that allow for combinatorial sharing of statistical strength.

Q4. Define transfer learning.

Ans. It is defined as the ability of a learning algorithm to explore commonalties between different learning tasks in order to transfer knowledge across different tasks.

Q5. Compare conventional learning methods with deep learning methods.

Ans. Conventional learning methods use shallow-structured learning architectures. On the other hand, deep learning refers to machine learning techniques that use supervised and/or unsupervised methods to learn hierarchical representations in deep architectures.

Q6. Big data presents many challenges to deep learning. List some of them.

Ans. Big data challenges to deep learning are as follows:-

- Large scale data.
- Heterogeneity of data.
- Noisy labels.
- Non-stationary distribution.

Q7. How are deep learning, AI and machine learning inter-related?

Ans. **Deep learning is a subset of** Artificial Intelligence (AI) branch called as machine learning. In machine learning, we do not teach a computer a huge list of rules to solve a problem rather we give it a **model** so that it can evaluate examples and a small set of instructions to modify the model when it makes mistakes. **Please understand here that we expect that as the time passes, a suitable model would be able to solve the problem more efficiently.**

Q8. Define what is training?

Ans. Training is the process in which we show the neural network large number of training examples and then iteratively modify the weights to minimize the errors we make on the training examples.

Q9. What causes the problem of overfitting?

Ans. In deep learning, our neural nets have large number of layers containing many neurons. The number of connections in these models is in millions (very high). This results in overfitting.

Q10. A machine learning engineer is always confronted with a delimma between overfitting and model complexity. What is this delimma?

Ans. The problem arises in both the cases i.e. when the model is simple or when the model is complex. If the model is simple then it may not be powerful to capture all of the useful information required to solve a problem. On the other hand, if the model is complex then it may result in overfitting problem. Hence, there is a need of a trade-off. To resolve this problem, deep learning solves complex problems with complex models but at the same time take additional steps to avoid overfitting.

Q11. What is TensorFlow?

Ans. An open source software (Python-based) library released by Google in 2015 that is used to design, build and train deep learning models is **TensorFlow.**

Exercise Questions

Q1. What do you mean by deep learning? Why is it required?

Q2. Compare human neuron with that of an Artificial Neuron?

Q3. How are big data and deep learning related?

Q4. Explain the three-layered neuron architecture.

Q5. Explain the design of neural network.

Q6. What are the rules that you follow to choose the number of layers and neurons in a neural net?

Q7. What are Feed Forward Neural Networks? Explain.

Q8. What are deep belief networks?

Q9. What are CNNs?

Q10. Throw some light on big data and deep learning with respect to the five V's of big data.

Q11. What is RBM? What is its role?

Q12. Define the following:

a. Pulling error signals.

b. Pushing error signals.

Q13. Describe the structure of an artificial neuron. Compare it with a biological neuron.

Q14. Use a simple perception with weights w_0, w_1 and w_2 as −1, 2 and 1 respectively, to classify data points (3, 4), (5, 2), (1, −3).

2 Machine Learning Retrospective

2.0 Introduction

Machine is a semi or fully automated device that intensifies human physical or mental competence in carrying out one or more operations. Learning is building up experience or enhancing one's abilities through analysis, taking into account happenings around us (experience) and being taught by the same. By the word 'experience' we mean the following:

- Finding out when the same situation was visited.
- What was the action taken?
- Did it worked or failed?

Present day data pool is in terabytes and petabytes. We want our machines to learn from the available giant stock of data through experience. Big data is growing exponentially every second. The objective is to use this data for some benefit. We have colossal data on computers related to hospitals, railways, Universities, banks etc. They are storing data constantly. Each of this organization maintains data in some way or the other. **Please understand that the ultimate aim is to do/extract something useful from this data** like treatments that do not work on a patient can be removed or discarded, Universities can put invalid admissions on hold and so on. **Also understand here that it implies that we can conclude a human or animal with the label of being intelligent only when they exhibit act of learning from experience.**

So, we define machine learning as a powerful AI tool that allows us to crunch petabytes of data. Arthur Samuel, in 1959, defined machine learning as **a field of study that gives computers the ability to learn without being explicitly programmed.** When exposed to new data the main focus is on developing computer programs that can **teach themselves** to grow and change. Software tends to learn from the previous encountered computations in order to produce decisions and results which are **reliable and repeatable in nature.** This field is quite vast and expanding at a faster rate. When we say machine learning we actually mean building and studying of those algorithms which can learn from data and make predictions (analytics) on it. The final aim is to get more accurate actions that were chosen to be taken in a particular situation by computers, thus making it intelligent in making predictions.

Searching the deep web is the current research area today. This is shown in figure 2.1.

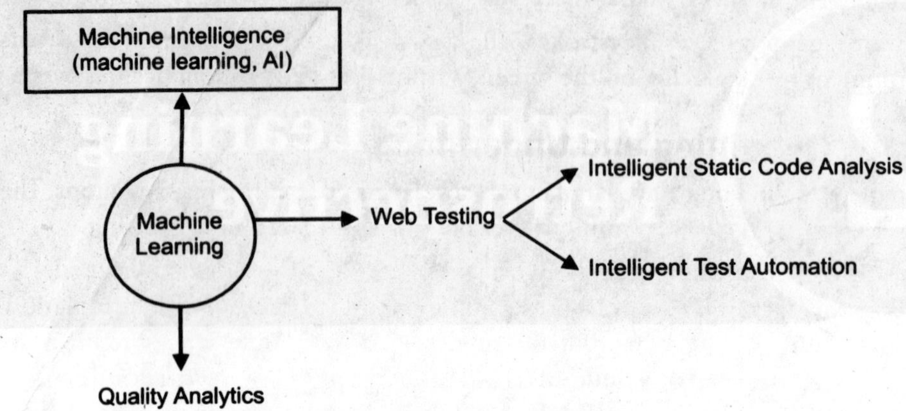

Fig.2.1: Machine Learning, Machine Intelligence and Web Testing

Machine tool like Test Rail are useful here.

PowerSet Company used deep NLP technology to improve basic web search. Web uses the power of-

(a) Information Theory.

(b) Statistical Inference.

(c) NLP (Natural Language Processing).

2.1 Learning Algorithms

We need to define a learning system first of all. It is defined as an interaction of a learning agent / intelligent agent with its environment by perceiving an input and doing actions accordingly. An agent is one who can perceive its environment with the help of sensors and acts upon its environment through actuators.

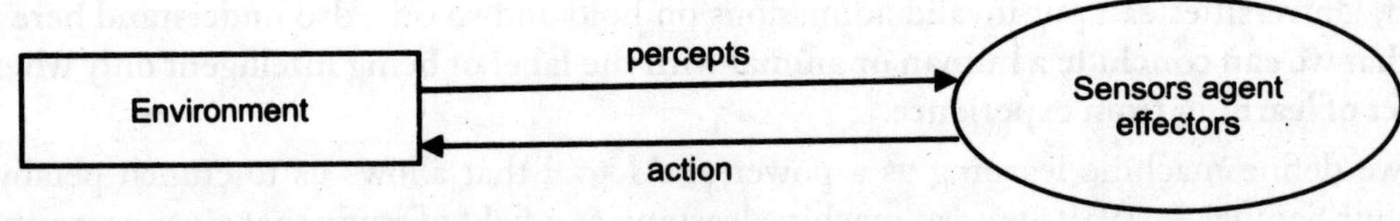

Fig.2.2: A Learning System

An intelligent agent is a software entity which senses its environment and then carries out some set of operations on behalf of a user with some amount of autonomy and to do so it employs some knowledge or representation of the end-user's goal. Note that an agent is different from a program. An agent need not be a program at all. It may be a robot or a college professor. Software agents are by definition programs but a program must measure up to several marks to be an agent. **For example,** humans, animals, autonomous mobile robots or softbots calculators are **real-world agents. Software agents live in the systems OS.**

As shown in figure 2.1, an **agent** perceives its environment through sensors. It then acts upon that environment through **actuators. For example,**

- Human agent has eyes, ears, nose etc. as sensors while hands, legs, mouth are actuators.
- Software agent receives keystrokes, files, packets are sensory inputs and acts on the environment by displaying on the screen, writing files and sending packets over a network.

2.2 Capacity, Overfitting and Underfitting

In deep learning, our neural nets have large number of layers containing many neurons. The number of connections in these models is in millions (very high). This results in **overfitting.**

The problem arises in both the cases i.e. when the model is simple or when the model is complex. If the model is simple then it may not be powerful to capture all of the useful information required to solve a problem. On the other hand, if the model is complex then it may result in **overfitting problem.** Hence, there is a need of a trade-off. To resolve this problem, deep learning solves complex problems with complex models but at the same time take additional steps to avoid overfitting.

Generalization is defined as the ability of machine to learn on being introduced with sets of data during training so that when it is introduced to new and unseen examples then it can perform accurately. To ensure that a network generalizes well, we tend to use a neural network in order to generalize from the training examples to all possible inputs. Whether it is training or overtraining of the network, troubles do arise. We can change the weight in a neural network. Thus, the degree of variability is quite high.

In machine learning, overfitting occurs when a statistical model defines random error or noise rather than underlying relationship. When a model is extremely complex, overfitting is observed because of having too many parameters relating to the number of training data types. The model exhibits poor performance which has been overfit. The risk of overfittting exists as the standards used for training the model is not the same as the standards used to judge the effectiveness of a model.

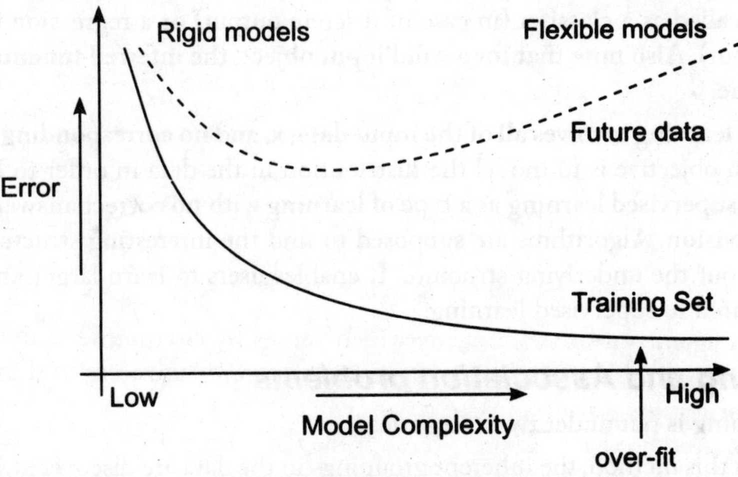

Fig.2.3: Underfitting & overfitting

By means of loads of data, overfitting can be avoided. Overfitting occurs when you have a smaller data set and you make effort to learn from it. **Note that if you have a small database and it is desired**

to build a model based on that then in such a situation a technique known as cross validation can be used. In this method, the dataset is is divided into two segments-testing and training datasets. The testing dataset will only test the model while in training dataset, the data points will come up with the model. In this method, a model is generally provided with a dataset of a known data on which training data-set is run and a dataset of unknown data against which the model is tested. The purpose of cross validation is to define a dataset to test the model in the training phase.

When we try to reduce the problem of under-fitting the data (by giving it more data), it rather results in a risk of over-fitting. The graph of fig 2.3 above shows the overfit and under-fit condition when model complexity and errors increases.

2.3 Supervised Learning Algorithms

Machine learning algorithms, based on the basis of desired outcome is put under two categories:

- Supervised learning.
- Unsupervised learning.

Let us discuss these types first.

Supervised learning is the machine learning task of applying inference function on supervised training data. Training data comprises of a set of training examples. We try to infer a function from the training data. A supervised learning algorithm takes a known set of input data and known responses to the data/output and further training a model to generate reasonable predictions for the response to new data. The main **objective is to learn an unknown function f(x) = y where x is an input example (a vector) and y is the desired output (also known as supervisory signal).** The model used in this type of learning describes the effect of one set of observations on the other set of observations. So, we can say that the user tries to find the connection between the sets of inputs and outputs. In nutshell, this algorithm analyzes the training data and produces an inferred function which is called as a **classifer** (in case of discrete output) or a **regression function** (in case of continuous output). **Also note that for a valid input object, the inferred function should predict correct output value.**

Unsupervised learning involves all of the input data, x, and no corresponding output data, y, is available. The main objective is to model the distribution in the data in order to learn more about data. **We define unsupervised learning as a type of learning with no correct answers and no teacher available for supervision.** Algorithms are supposed to find the interesting structure present in the data thus figuring out the underlying structure. It enables users to learn larger and more complex problems as compared to supervised learning.

2.3.1 Clustering and Association problems

Unsupervised learning is put under two categories:-

1. **Clustering:** In this method, the inherent groupings in the data are discovered. The organization of unlabeled data into similar groups known as **clusters. And the process of partitioning of a set of observations into subsets (or clusters) so that observation in the same cluster is similar is called as clustering.** So, a cluster consists of data items which are similar in comparison to other clusters which contain dissimilar items. **Please understand that the aim of unsupervised**

learning is to find clusters of similar inputs in the data without knowing that these data points belong to one class and those to different class. Rather the algorithm has to uncover similarities for itself. **For example,** there is a collection of 30,000 essays on voting process. These essays can be automatically grouped into small number on the basis of word frequency, page count, word limit etc.

2. **Association:** In this method, we discover a set of rules that describes large portions of data. **For example,** a doctor observes same set of symptoms in several patients suffering from some disease. Then based on his experience the doctor can conclude that the patient is suffering from the same disease.

Dendrograms

1. The visual representation of the compound correlation data is known as a **dendrograms.**
2. The individual compounds are arranged along the bottom of the dendrogram. These are called as **leaf nodes.**

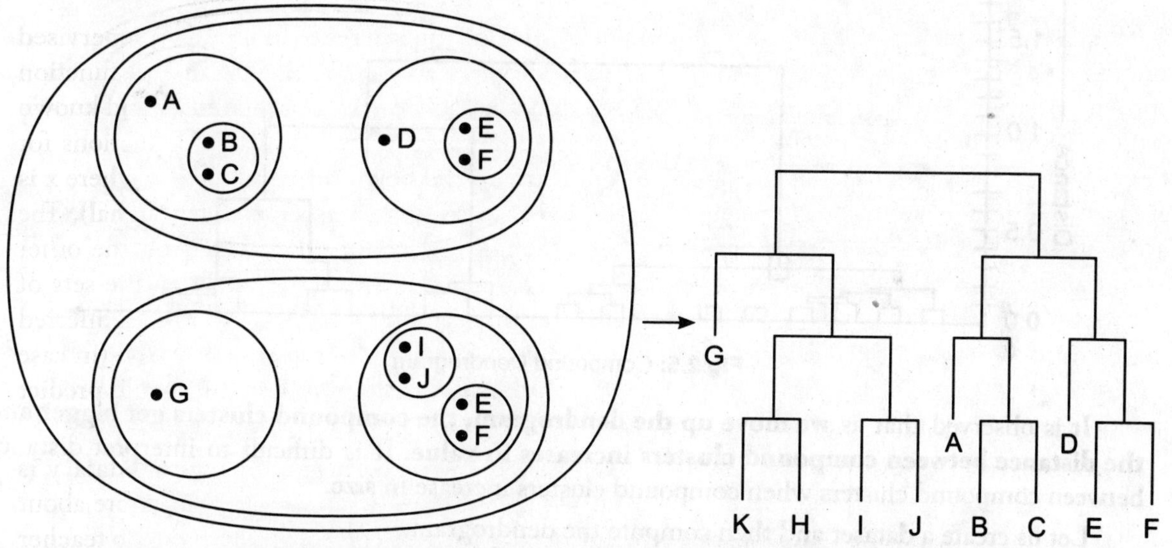

Fig.2.4: Fig. Dendogram (onright) shows rested clusters (on left)

3. **Compound clusters** are formed by joining individual compounds or existing compound clusters with the join point named as a **node.**

   As shown in figure 2.4 above, at each dendogram node we have a right and a left sub-branch of clustered compounds. In the following discussion, compound clusters can refer to a single compound or a group of compounds.
4. The vertical axis is labelled distance and it refers to a **distance measure** between compounds or compound clusters.
5. The **height** of the node can be thought of as the distance value between the right and left sub-branch clusters.

6. The distance meaure between two clusters is calculated by the formula.

$$D = 1 - C$$

Where D = Distance,

C = Correlation between compound clusters.

7. **Note that if compounds are correlated**, they will have a **correlation value close to 1**. So, D = 1 – C will **have a value close to zero.**

∴ highly correlated clusters are nearer to the bottom of the dendrogram. **Compound clusters that are not correlated** have a correlation value of zero and a corresponding distance value of 1.

8. **Compound that are negatively correlated** i.e., showing opposite abundance behaviour, will have a correlation value of – 1 and D = 1 – (– 1) = 1 + 1 = 2

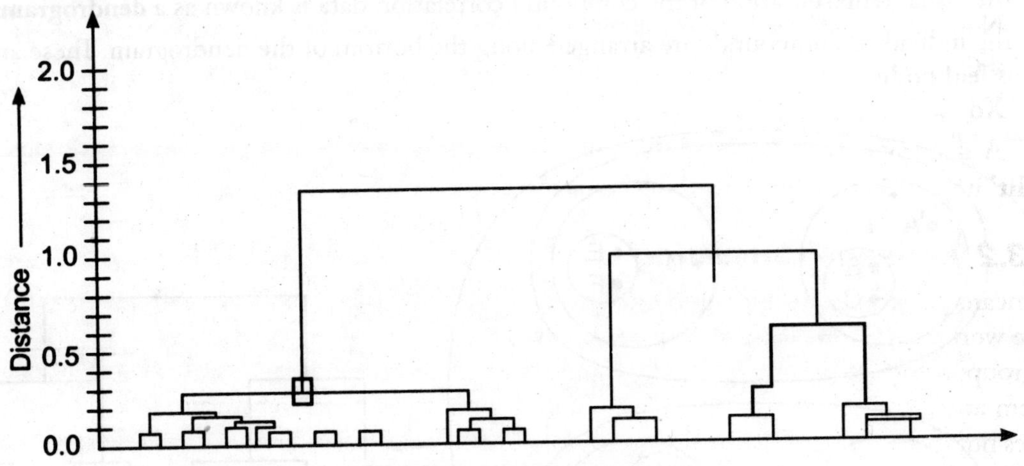

Fig.2.5: Compound Dendrogram

It is observed that as **we move up the dendrogram, the compound clusters get bigger and the distance between compound clusters increases in value**. It is difficult to interpret distance between compound clusters when compound clusters increase in size.

Let us create a dataset and then compute the dendrogram.

```
# Dendrogram
import numpy as np
import matplotlib. pyplot as plt
from sklearn. datasets import make–blobs
from scipy. spatial. distance import pdist
from scipy. cluster. hierarchy import linkage
from scipy. cluster. hierarchy import dendrogram
# for reproducibility
np. randam. seed (1000)
nb _ samples = 25
```

```
# create the dataset
X, Y = make _ blobs (n _ samples = nb _ samples,
n _ features = 2, centers = 3,
cluster _ std = 1.5)
```

keep the number of samples very low to avoid complexity in the resulting plot.

Let us now compute the dendrogram.

Firstly, we compute a distance matrix as follows :

```
# Compute the distance matrix
Xdist = pdist (X, metric = 'euclidean')
# Compute the linkage
Xl = linkage (Xdist, method = 'ward')
```

Now it is possible to create and visualize a dendrogram–

```
# Compute and show the dendorgram–
Xd = dendrogram (Xl)
```

A dendrogram shows how the clusters are **'merged'** iteratively (agglomerative clustering) or **'split'** iteratively (divisive clustering) to arrive at the **optimal clustering** solution.

2.3.2 k-means Clustering

k-means is a simple unsupervised learning algorithm that solves the well known clustering problems. The working of k-means is similar to that of a real life situation in which we have observed that in a group of tourists with a few tourists guides who hold the umbrella up so that everybody can see them and follow them. On the other hand, in static k-means algorithm the data (i.e. the tourists) does not move rather only the tour guide (s) move. Analogous is the situation in k-means clustering.

Basic Principle of k-means

"Divide your data into k groups (you have to specify what 'k' is) such that each data item is closer to the center of its cluster than to the centre of any other cluster."

Explanation of k-means: We classify a given data-set into k number of clusters which is fixed in advance. Now the task is to define 'k' centres (middle point) one for each cluster. But we do not know where their centres are. So, we need an algorithm that will find the middle points. The centre of a set of points is based on two parameters:-

(a) **Distance Measure:** It measures the distance between a set of points. We may use Euclidean distance but other options are also available.

(b) **Mean Average:** After we compute the distance measure (as stated above) we finally compute the **central point of the set of data points which is the mean average.**

Please note that this is valid in Euclidean space where everything is flat and easily measured. Now the need is to place cluster centres properly. We compute the mean of each cluster, μ_i (i) and position the cluster centre right there. **Also note that this is similar to minimizing the Euclidean distance** (i.e. sum-of-squares again) **from each data point to the centre of cluster.**

Now we would like to find out that which point belongs to which cluster. This is mandatory as it lets us know the position of cluster centres. It is crystal clear to associate closest point with the cluster centre. This might change as the algorithm iterates on. In the input space we start positioning the cluster centres randomly as we do not know where to put them exactly and further update their positions in accordance with the data. Now we start picking up the data points and find out which cluster, particular data point belongs to depending on the distance between each data point and all of the cluster centres and assigning it to cluster that is closest.

The purpose of the hidden layer is to summarize the data and compress it. The multidimensional data is to be reduced to either 2 or 3 dimensions only as then we can plot the graphs too. If we use the PYTHON LANGUAGE then note that layers and column indices are counted from zero while in R they are counted from one.

With auto-encoding neural networks we do learning one layer at a time.

For example, a model, m1, say, has the following-

- 5 hidden layers
- 11 neurons (in middle layer)

It is trained on the raw data. Then that third hidden layer is extracted into a transformation, f1 with still 100 rows but only 11 columns. Model-2 (m2) uses this f1 as its input and builds up a much simpler model, reducing 11 input nodes to 2 hidden nodes then back out to 11 output nodes. At the end, results are put in f2. f2 now has 2 columns but still 100 rows.

2.3.3 Algorithm

k-means clustering involves the following steps:-

Step-1: **Randomly** select 'c' cluster centres.

Step-2: Compute the **distance** between each data point and cluster centres.

Step-3: Assign the data point to the cluster whose distance from the cluster centre is **minimum** in the value of cluster centres.

Step-4: Calculate the **new cluster centre** using the following formula:-

$$v = 1/\ c_i\ \Sigma\ (j=1 \text{ to } c_i)\ x_i$$

where c_i represents the number of data points in the ith cluster.

Step-5: New **cluster centres** are computed.

Step-6: If no data point is reassigned then stop else repeat from step-3.

As we know that H2O is software for machine learning and data analysis. H2O algorithm has been developed keeping in mind clustering only. But clusters in H2O have some limitations:-

(a) Each H2O node on the cluster must be of the same size. It implies that if the smallest machine in our cluster has 2GB free, then every node must be given 2GB even if some of them have 32GB.

(b) You cannot add the machines once the cluster has started.

(c) In case a machine dies then the whole of the cluster must be rebuilt. **Please note that the whole cluster becomes unusable if a single node gets removed. In such a case, you cannot even export data or models from the left over clusters.**

(d) Each node must run the same API version of h2o.jar.

(e) To reduce the network latency, the nodes should be physically close.

You can also give your cluster a name and specify this name when starting on each node. In H2O, the cluster can be created in two ways:-

1. **Flat-file:** A simple text file giving the IP address and port number of each node in the cluster. **Note that you must prepare this file identically on each machine.**
2. **Auto-discovery:** When you specify the network address then it searches through that subnet to find all nodes and join them together in a cluster. This is slower than the flat file.

Python code for K-means

Consider a dummy dataset. Python code for K-means is as follows :

```
# K-means on dummy dataset
import numpy as np
import matplotlib.pyplot as plt
from sklearn. cluster import kmeans
# for reproducibility
np. random. seed (1000)
nb_samples = 1000
X, _ = make _ blobs (n_samples = nb_samples,
n _ features = 2,
centers = 3,
cluster_std = 1.5,
random_state = 1000)
```

2.3.4 Expectation Maximization (EM) Algorithm

Many a times the presence of unobserved variables is observed as a problem of learning. In case of some variable that can be observed sometimes and cannot be observed at other times then the time when it was observed can be used to learn its values when it was not observed. So, EM is an algorithm for maximizing a likelihood function when some of the variables in your model are unobserved. **A variable that is not directly observed is called as a latent variable/ hidden / unobserved variable / missing data.**

Statement of EM algorithm: EM is applied where we are required to estimate a set of parameters θ that represents an underlying probability distribution, given only the observed portion of full data. In general, let X = {x_1, x_2,......,x_m} denote the observed data in a set of m independently drawn data items. Let Z = {z_1,......, z_m } mark the unobserved data in these same data items and let Y = X U Z; thus marks the full data.

The EM algorithm searches for the maximum likelihood hypothesis h' by seeking the h' that maximizes E [ln P (Y| h')],

where, P (Y| h') is the likelihood of the full data Y given hypothesis h'

ln P (Y| h')- maximizing logarithm value of this quantity further maximizes P (Y| h')

E [ln P (Y| h')] –expected value of full data is introduced as Y is a random variable.

We need to know that what is the probability distribution governing Y. In general, we will not know this distribution as it is determined by the parameters, θ, that is to be estimated. So, EM algorithm uses its current hypothesis, h, in place of θ to estimate the distribution governing, Y.

If we assume that θ = h, then, we define a function Q (h'| h) as follows:-

$$Q(h'|\ h) = E\ [\ln P\ (Y|\ h')\ |\ h, X]$$

In general form of an EM algorithm, two steps are repeated until convergence:-

S1: Estimation (E) step: Calculate Q (h'| h) using the current hypothesis, h and the observed data X to estimate the probability distribution over Y. So,

$$Q(h'|\ h) = E\ [\ln P\ (Y|\ h')\ |\ h, X]$$

S2: Maximization (M) step: Replace h by h' that maximizes this Q function-

$$H \leftarrow \textbf{argmax}\ Q(h'\ |\ h)$$

Please note that when the function, Q, is continuous, the EM algorithm converges to a fixed point of the probable function P(Y | h'). **Also note that when this probable function has a single maximum, EM will converge to this global maximum probable estimate for h'.**

Example : Consider an experiment of tossing of a coin-say, 5 experiments were done and in each experiment 10 tosses were made using two coins. This is shown below :

1. H T T T H H T H T H
2. H H H H T H H H H H
3. H T H H H H H T H H
4. H T H T T T H H T T
5. T H H H T H H H T H.

Given that coins are equally likely to be chosen, how will you extimate the unknown parameters 'p' and 'q'? Apply EM algorithm.

Solution : EM involves two steps as follows :

SI : "E" Step (Expectation)

We start with some initial guess for the unknown parameters p = 0.6 and q = 0.5. Let us take the first experiment. Call this observation 'S', we want to estimate what is the likelihood that the observation 'S' is coming from coin A i.e. P(A/S). Remember your Baye's theorem that—

$$P(A/S) = \frac{P(S/A) \times P(A)}{P(S)}$$

P(A) is the probability of choosing coin A, it is 0.5 (so is P(B)) as we know that each coin has equal probability of being picked. P(S/A) is the probability of observation given that it has come from coin A, i.e., using bionomial distribution, we infer that it is—

$$P(S/A) = p^5 * (1 - p)^5$$

&

$$P(S/B) = q^5 * (1 - q)^5$$

P (S) is the probability of the observation. Since the observation can come from either coin A or coin B or both.

Hence, $P(S) = P(S, A) + P(S, B)$

$= P(S/A) * P(A) + P(S/B) * P(B)$

Thus, we now get :

$$P(A/S) = \frac{0.5*(p^5 \times (1-p)^5)}{0.5*(p^5*(1-p)^5)+0.5*(q^5*(1-q^5))}$$

Substituting the values of our initial guesses for p = 0.6 and q = 0.5, we get :

$P(A/S) = 0.45.$

$\therefore$ $P(B/S) = 1 - P(A/S) = 1 - 0.45 = 0.55.$

Thus, given the observation 1, the probability of it coming from coin A is 0.45 and from coin B is 0.55. Thus, the expected number of heads coming from **coin** A = 5 * 0.45 and tails = 5 * 0.45. Similarly, the expected number of heads coming from coin B = 5* 0.55 and tails = 0.5 + 0.55.

Repeating the same Expectation (E) steps for the other four experiments, we get the total number of extected heads from coin A = 21.3 and tails = 8.6.

Similarly, for coin B, the total number of expected heads = 11.7 and tails = 8.4

S2 : "M" step (Maximization)

The new estimates for the unknown parameters, p and q are as follows :

$$p = \frac{21.3}{21.3+8.6} = 0.71$$

&

$$q = \frac{11.7}{11.7+8.4} = 0.58$$

This step is 'M' step or maximization step. We repeat above EM-steps until the values 'p' and 'q' **converges**. In this example, the values of 'p' and 'q' converge to the final values of p = 0.8 and q = 0.52 in about 10-steps.

Conclusions : This example shows that given a parameter estimation problem with missing data, EM algorithm can iteratively solve the problem by generating likely guesses for the missing data and then maximizing the likelihood of the observations by using those guesses. EM has also been applied successfully in training HMM for hidden states, in clustering applications and in semi-supervised learning

2.3.5 Mixture of Gaussians

A very popular continuous probability distribution is **Gaussian distribution / Normal Distribution.** It is also called as a **bell curve since it has a bell shaped curve.** The equation in one dimension is as follows:-

$$p(x) = 1/\sqrt{2\Pi}\sigma \exp[-(x-\mu)^2/2\sigma^2] \quad ......(1)$$

where μ = mean

σ = standard deviation

Please note that it is useful because of its Central Limit Theorem which tells us that lots of random numbers will add up to something Gaussian.

In Gaussian Mixture Models (GMM), we assume that there are **number of different classes.** *Each class comes from its own Gaussian distribution.* **And such type of data is known as multi-model data as there are number of modes or distribution for each particular class.** We are unable to accommodate Gaussian to the data in totality as it does not appear to be Gaussian overall.

If we know the number of classes that are there in the data then we can put effort to estimate the parameters for that many number of Gaussians and that too all at the same time.

On the other hand, **if we do not the number of classes then we can attempt for different numbers and finds out which one works best.** Then the output for any specific data point which has already been an input to the algorithm will be the sum of the values expected by all of the 'M' Gaussians. That is,

$$f(x) = \Sigma\,(m=1 \text{ to } M)\ \alpha_m\ \phi\,(x;\mu_m, \Sigma_m) \quad \text{........(2)}$$

where $\phi\,(x;\mu_m, \Sigma_m)$ = Gaussian function with mean μ_m and covariance matrix and the α_m are the weights with the constraints i.e. $\Sigma\,(m=1 \text{ to } M)\ \alpha_m = 1$.

The task is to choose the weights $\alpha_{m.}$ The target is for Maximum likelihood solution. **Note that likelihood refers to the conditional probability and Maximum Likelihood solution refers to maximizing the conditional probability.**

2.3.6 Factor Analysis and its applications

Factor Analysis (FA) is a method for modelling observed variables and their covariance structure in terms of a smaller number of underlying unobservable/ latent factors. These 'factors' are typically observed as broad concepts or ideas that may describe an observed phenomenon. This method is quite comprehensive but is similar to principal components. **Please understand that in factor analysis the observed variables are modelled as linear functions of the factors.** On the other hand, **principal components analysis (PCA) involves the creation of new variables that are linear combinations of the observed variables.** But in both the methods, the dimensions of the data are reduced.

FA involves using of a data reduction tool to-

(a) Remove **redundancy** from a set of correlated variables.

(b) Represent correlated variables with a smaller set of **derived variables.**

(c) Form **factors** that are independent of each other.

(d) Two types of variables are used- latent variables (factors) and the observed variables.

Notations used:

Say, there is a vector X consisting of variables X's for each individual subject. Let X_i denote observable trait, i. This is the data of each subject and will be collected into a vector of traits.

That is,

$$X = \begin{pmatrix} X_1 \\ X_2 \\ \vdots \\ X_p \end{pmatrix} = \textbf{vector of traits}$$

This will be a **random vector** with a population mean. We assume that sampling of vector of traits X is done from a population with population mean vector:

$$\mu = \begin{pmatrix} \mu_1 \\ \mu_2 \\ \vdots \\ \mu_p \end{pmatrix} = \textbf{population mean vector}$$

Here, $E(X_i) = \mu_i$ denotes the population mean of variable i.

In general, consider 'm' unobservable common factors $f_1, f_2, ...f_m$.

The ith common factor is f_i. In general, m will be less than p.

The common factors will be collected into a vector only:-

$$F = \begin{pmatrix} f_1 \\ f_2 \\ \vdots \\ f_m \end{pmatrix} = \textbf{vector of common factors}$$

The Factor Model

Our factor model will be a collection of series of multiple regressions, predicting each of the observable variables, X_i from the values of the unobservable common factor, f_i. That is,

$$X_1 = \mu_1 + l_{11} f_1 + l_{12} f_2 + ...+ l_{1m} f_m + \varepsilon_1$$
$$X_2 = \mu_2 + l_{21} f_1 + l_{22} f_2 + ...+ l_{2m} f_m + \varepsilon_2$$
$$\vdots$$
$$\vdots$$
$$\vdots$$
$$X_p = \mu_p + l_{p1} f_1 + l_{p2} f_2 + ...+ l_{pm} f_m + \varepsilon_p$$

Here, the variable means μ_1 through μ_p can be explained as the intercept terms for the multiple regression models.

The regression coefficients l_{ij} (are the partial slopes) for all of these multiple regressions are called as factor loadings. The relationship of each variable to the underlying factor is expressed by factor loading. Here, l_{ij} = **loading of the ith variable on the jth factor.** These will be collected into a matrix as follows:-

$$L = \begin{pmatrix} l_{11} & l_{12} & ......l_{1m} \\ l_{21} & l_{22} & ......l_{2m} \\ \vdots & \vdots & \vdots \\ l_{p1} & l_{p2} & ......l_{pm} \end{pmatrix} = \textbf{matrix of factor loadings}$$

And that the errors, ε_i are called as the **specific factors.**

Here, ε_i = specific factor for variable i.

These **specific factors** are also collected in a vector:-

$$\varepsilon = \begin{pmatrix} \varepsilon_1 \\ \varepsilon_2 \\ \vdots \\ \varepsilon_m \end{pmatrix} = \textbf{vector of specific vectors}$$

In nutshell, the basic model is like a regression model only. Each of our response variables X is to be predicted as a linear function of the unobserved common factors f_1, f_2 through f_m. Thus, our explanatory variables are f_1, f_2 through f_m. Therefore, we conclude that we have m unobserved factors that control the variation among our data.

Generally, we can reduce this into a matrix notation as shown in this form below:-

$$X = \mu + Lf + \varepsilon$$

In general we want m << p.

Assumptions of the model

(a) Mean-

1. The **specific factors or random errors** all have mean zero: $E(\varepsilon_i) = 0$; i=1,2,.....p.
3. The **common factors,** the f's also have a mean zero: $E(f_i) = 0$; i = 1,2,...m.
4. A consequence of these assumptions is that the mean response of the ith trait is μ_i. that is,

$$E(X_i) = \mu_i$$

(b) Variance-

1. The **common factors** have variance one: $var(f_i)$ =1,2,...m.
2. **The variance of specific factor** i is ψ_i : $var(\varepsilon_i) = \psi_i$; i=1,2,...p. Here, ψ_i is called as the **specific variance.**

(c) Correlation-

1. **The common factors** are uncorrelated with one another: $cov(f_i, f_j) = 0$ for i != j.
2. The **specific factors** are uncorrelated with one another: $cov(\varepsilon_i, \varepsilon_j) = 0$ for i != j.
3. The specific factors are uncorrelated with the common factors: $cov((\varepsilon_i, \varepsilon_j)$ = cov; i=1,2,....p; j = 1,2,...,m.

To calculate the parameters these assumptions are necessary. **An infinite number of equally well-fitted models with different values for the parameters may be obtained unless these suppositions are done. Also note that under this model, the variance for the ith observed variable is equal to the sum of the squared loadings for that variable and specific variance:-**

The variance of trait is: $\sigma_i^2 = var(X_i) = \Sigma\,(j=1 \text{ to } m)\, l^2_{ij} + \psi_i$

Where $\Sigma\,(j=1 \text{ to } m)\, l^2_{ij}$ **is called as the communality for variable, i. Please note that the larger is the communality, the better is the model performance for the ith variable.**

The covariance between pairs of traits i and j is given by the formula-

$$\sigma_{ij} = \text{cov}(X_i, X_j) = \Sigma\,(k=1 \text{ to } m)\; l_{ik}\, l_{jk}$$

The covariance between trait i and factor j is: cov $(X_i, f_i) = l_{ij}$

In matrix form, our model for the variance-covariance matrix is going to be expressed as shown below:-

$$\Sigma = LL' + \psi$$

This is the matrix of factor loadings times its transpose plus a diagonal matrix containing the specific variances.

Here ψ is as follows:

$$\Psi = \begin{pmatrix} \Psi_1 & 0 & \ldots\ldots 0 \\ 0 & \Psi_2 & \ldots\ldots 0 \\ : & : & : \\ 0 & 0 & \ldots\ldots \Psi_p \end{pmatrix}$$

Hence, a simplified model for the variance-covariance matrix is obtained. This is used for estimation.

Notes:

1. The model assumes that the **data is a linear function of the common factors.** But since the common factors are not observable, there is no amount of data that can be used to check for linearity.
2. The **variance-covariance matrix is a symmetric matrix** that is, the variance between variables i and j is the same thing as the variance between j and i. For this model-

$$\Sigma = LL' + \psi$$

3. The **variance-covariance matrix** is going to have p (p+1)/2 unique elements of Σ that are approximated by mp factor loadings in the matrix L and p specific variances. **Also understand that this means that there is going to be mp plus p parameters in this model of the variance-covariance matrix.** Ideally, (mp + p) is to be substantially smaller than p (p + 1)/2. However, if mp is too small, the mp +p parameters may not be adequate to describe Σ. There may always be the case that perhaps this is not the right model. It may be the case that you cannot reduce the data to a linear combination of factors.
4. If we have more than one variable in our analysis, that is, if p > 1, the model is going to be inherently ambiguous. Say, T be any (m * m) orthogonal matrix. Note that a matrix is said to be orthogonal if its inverse is equal to the transpose of the original matrix i.e.

$$T'T = TT' = 1$$

Hence, we can write our factor model in the matrix notation as follows:-

Please note that this does not change the calculation since the identity matrix times any matrix just gives back the original matrix. This results in an alternative factor model where the relationship between the new factor loadings and the original factor loadings is given by:-

$$L^{\cdot} = LT$$

And the relationship between the new common factors and the original common factors is:-

$$f^{\cdot} = T'f$$

This gives a model that fits equally well. Moreover, since there are an infinite number of orthogonal matrices then there is an infinite number of alternative models. This model, as it turns out, satisfies all of the assumptions that we have discussed earlier.

1. $E(f^{\cdot}) = E(T'f) = T'E(f) = T'0 = 0$ and
   $var(f^{\cdot}) = var(T'f) = T' var(f) T = T'IT = T'T = 1$
2. $Cov(f^{\cdot}, \varepsilon) = cov(T'f, \varepsilon) = T' cov(f, \varepsilon) = T'0 = 0$

Thus, we can say that f satisfies all of the assumptions and hence f is an equally valid collection of common factors. So, there is a certain apparent ambiguity to these models. However, it is the same ambiguity that we are going to exploit. This ambiguity is going to be used to justify the factor notation that will be used to derive more parsimonious description of data.

Applications of FA

The following are some of the applications of FA:

1. **Identification of underlying factors:** It clusters variables into homogeneous sets, creates new variables/factors and allows us to gain insight to categories.
2. **Screening of Variables:** It identifies groupings to allow us to select one variable and is useful in regression/ recall collinearity applications of FA.
3. **Summary:** It allows us to describe many variables using few factors.
4. **Sampling of variables:** It helps us to select a small group of variables of representative variables from a larger set.
5. **Clustering of Object:** It helps us to put objects/people into categories depending on their factor scores.

2.3.7 Principal Component Analysis (PCA)

PCA refers to a **mathematical procedure that tends to transform a number of possibly correlated variables into a small number of uncorrelated variables which are called as the principal components.** The first PCA accounts for as much of the variability as possible in the data and the next following components takes into account possible remaining variability. **Please understand that PCA is a technique used to focus on variation and figure out strong patterns in a dataset.** The objective of PCA is to make data easy to explore and visualize.

Dimensionabilty reduction
→ Correlation
→ Compress orginal data X with correlations for PCA
(Very large, X)

Say, X (Data matrix)= $\begin{bmatrix} . & . & . \\ . & . & . \\ . & . & . \end{bmatrix}$ where n = samples
(n×m)

m = measurements.

When n $\geq$ 2 ; it becomes difficult to visualize data.

$\therefore$ PCA, will reduce higher dimension (By data) data to lower dimension for better understanding of data & its trends.

PCA–is Eigen decomposilion of (cov. matrix) :

$$\underbrace{(X^TX)}\longrightarrow \begin{matrix} W \leftarrow \text{eigen vector} \\ \lambda \leftarrow \text{eigen values} \end{matrix}$$

is also (nxm) matrix W & λ will describe our data

$$\underset{\substack{\uparrow \\ \text{"Scores"} \\ (\text{nxm})}}{T} = \overset{\substack{\text{Data} \\ \downarrow}}{X}\ \underset{\substack{\uparrow \\ \text{"Loadings"}}}{\underbrace{W}}\ (\text{m×m})$$

modify X by W & resultant is T matrix

What is W-size?

W is also m×m . Each col of W is a principal component.

$\therefore$ Cols. of W are principal component . T has same size as X (data)

$\therefore$ data has not changed. It's projected now. We have moved from measurement space to W-space now.

Cols of W are ® ordered cols by value of corresponding λ (eigen values)

$\therefore$ we can truncate them. We can take just a few cols. Let us take the Ist two.

Component of W i.e.,

principal component

$$W_r = \text{first r–cols of } W = \underbrace{\begin{bmatrix} | & | & | \\ W_1 & W_2 & W_n \\ . & . & . \end{bmatrix}}_{r}$$

Truncate & keep only say, 2 components

$\therefore$ r = 2

$$X\underbrace{W_r}_{(m \times r)} = \underset{(n \times r)}{T_r} \quad \text{(truncated data)}$$

We can throw other cols. of W i.e., ordered data & W_1, is better than W_2 and so on. Say, m = 2 i.e., 2D dimensional data–(cloud of points) (as i = 1)

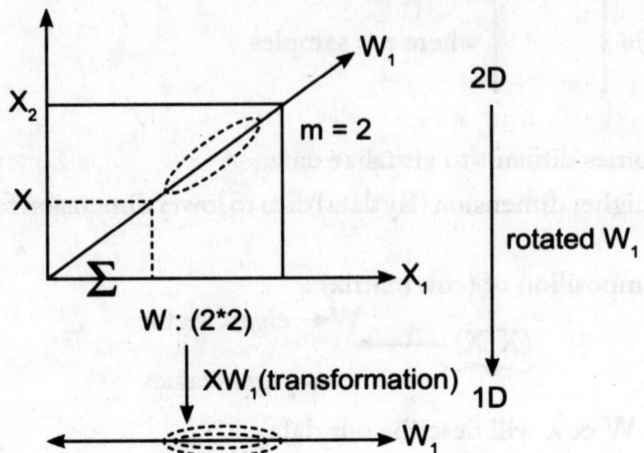

(PCA maximizes variance) (X_1 & X_2 are 2 features)

i.e.m rotated cloud of data above. Their rel. pos. have not changed. This is 1D data now. PCA has not changed data. Just another way data is being observed.

$\therefore$ PCA = eigen decomposition of (X^TX)

W : (mxm) matrix of PC. Xis data matrix as earlier

Better way of computing W is SVD (Singular Value Decomposition) This is more efficient (SVD).

$$X = \underbrace{U}\ \Sigma\ \underbrace{V^*} \quad (^*: \text{Conjugate transpose})$$

(data matrix same one) left singular vectors right singular vectors

Σ is matrix that contains singular values on its diagonal i.e.,

$$\begin{bmatrix} \sigma_1 & 0 & 0 \\ 0 & \sigma_2 & 0 \\ 0 & 0 & \sigma_3 \end{bmatrix} \text{ ordered}$$

W is identical to V

Each singular value (σ_1...... σ_n). λ's are not identical to these σ'_s. σ_1 corresponds to U_1 & V_1 & so on.

Also u & v are unitary is, $U^* u = I$

& $V^* v = I$ [Identity matrix only]

These are nice properties.

$$T = XW$$

or

$$XV = U\Sigma \underbrace{V^*V}_{I}$$

$\therefore \quad T = U\Sigma$

↑ Scores

(i) Similarly we can do truncation i.e.,

$\therefore \quad T_\gamma = U_\gamma \Sigma_r$ (truncated U & trunc. Σ matrices)

SVD is very-very fast & more efficient.

how to pick r?

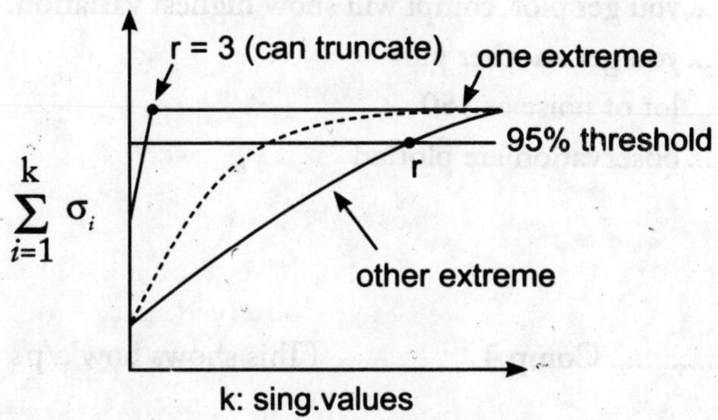

[after r = 3, adding any PCs will not affect. ∴ take r = 3]

Plotting (or Adding) Singular values (K) on graph gives curve above. Take threshold (say 95%) & where it crosses, take it as r.

PCA on Iris data (inbuilt dataset with R)

- several dimensions
- iris dataset

> head (iris)

sepal. length .... species

5.1 3.5 .... setosa

4.9 3.0 1.4 ...... setosa

(setosa) is to be removed as PCA workes on integers/numeric data only.

∴ Create a new dataset

> d ¬ iris [R, 1:4] keep R, take only 1:4 cols

> d ¬ iris [R, – 5]

> head (d)

∴ you get new dataset with last col. removed

sepal. length .... petal. width

5.1 .... 0.2

> pc ¬ princomp (d=data, cor = TRUE, score = TRUE)

> Summary (pc)

Importance of Components : There are PC_1, PC_2, PC_3, PC_4, as input data had 4 features as you passed. Cosider those comporents where reflection of var is more. Here (compl + comp2) would be best.

	Comp. 1	Comp. 2	Comp. 3	Comp. 4
Std. dev.	1.7083	0.95	0.38	0.1439
Prop. of var	...	...	...	...
Comm. prop	...	...	...	...

```
> plot (pc)          ... you get plot. compl will show highest variation.
> biplot (pc)        ... you get another plot
> dim (d)            ... lot of noise as 150
[1] 150 4            ... observation are plotted
> attributes (pc)
> pc $ loadings
Loadings:
Comp.1 ............................. Comp.4        (This shows how c/p's have bearings on PCs)
> pc $ scores
..................150 observations
> str (iris)
'data grave': 150 obs of 5 vars.
```

Aim of PCA

1. To discover or to reduce the dimensionality of the data set.
2. To identify new meaningful underlying variables.

Algorithm

Suppose that we have a random vector, X. That is,

$$X =: \begin{pmatrix} X_1 \\ X_2 \\ \vdots \\ X_p \end{pmatrix}$$

And with the population variance-covariance matrix as follows:-

$$\text{var}(X) = \Sigma = \begin{pmatrix} \sigma_1^2 & \sigma_{12} & \ldots\ldots\sigma_{1p} \\ \sigma_{21} & \sigma_2^2 & \ldots\ldots\sigma_{2p} \\ \vdots & \vdots & \vdots \\ \vdots & \vdots & \vdots \\ \sigma_{p1} & \sigma_{p2} & \sigma_p^2 \end{pmatrix}$$

Now consider the following linear combinations:-

$$Y_1 = e_{11} X_1 + e_{12} X_2 + \text{........} + e_{1p} X_p$$

$$Y_2 = e_{21} X_1 + e_{22} X_2 + \text{........} + e_{2p} X_p$$

$$\vdots$$

$$Y_p = e_{p1} X_1 + e_{p2} X_2 + \text{........} + e_{pp} X_p$$

Each of these is just like a linear regression, predicting Y_i from $X_1, X_2, \ldots, X_p$. There is no intercept but $e_{i1}, e_{i2}, \ldots e_{ip}$ may be considered as the **regression coefficients.**

Also note that Y_i is a function of our random data and hence it is also random. So, it has a population variance of-

$$Var(Y_i) = \Sigma(k=1 \text{ to } p)\ \Sigma(l=1 \text{ to } p)\ e_{ik}\, e_{il}\, \sigma_{kl} = e'_i \Sigma e_i$$

How to find 1st PCA, 2nd PCA and the ith PCA?

1. The 1st **Principal Component** i.e. PCA_1 means Y_1 and is computed as follows:-

   The 1st principal component is a linear combination of x-variables that has maximum variance (among all linear combinations). Thus, it accounts for as much possible variation in the data as possible. More specifically, we will define coefficients $e_{11}, e_{12}, \ldots, e_{1p}$ for that component in such a way that its variance is maximized, subject to the constraint that the sum of the squared coefficients is equal to one. This constraint is required to obtain a unique answer.

   Formally, we select $e_{11}, e_{12}, \ldots, e_{1p}$ that maximizes-

   $$Var(Y_1) = \Sigma(k=1 \text{ to } p)\ \Sigma(l=1 \text{ to } p)\ e_{1k}\, e_{1l}\, \sigma_{kl} = e'_1 \Sigma e_1$$

   Subject to the constraints:-

   $$e_1\, e_1 = \Sigma\,(j=1 \text{ to } p)\ e^2_{1j} = 1$$

2. The 2nd **Principal Component** i.e. PCA_2 means Y_2 and is computed as follows:-

   The 2nd principal component is a linear combination of x-variables that has maximum variance (among all linear combinations). Thus, it accounts for as much possible variation in the data as possible with the constraints that the correlation between the first and second component is 0. More specifically, we will define coefficients $e_{11}, e_{12}, \ldots, e_{1p}$ for that component in such a way that its variance is maximized, subject to the constraint that the sum of the squared coefficients is equal to one. This constraint is required to obtain a unique answer.

   Formally, we select $e_{21}, e_{22}, \ldots, e_{2p}$ that maximizes-

   $$var(Y_2) = \Sigma(k=1 \text{ to } p)\ \Sigma(l=1 \text{ to } p)\ e_{2k}\, e_{2l}\, \sigma_{kl} = e'_2 \Sigma e_2$$

   Subject to the constraints:-

   $$e'_2\, e_2 = \Sigma\,(j=1 \text{ to } p)\ e^2_{2j} = 1$$

Please note that all subsequent PCAs have this same property i.e. they are linear combinations that account for as much of the remaining variation as possible and they are not correlated with the other PCAs. Also note that we will do it the same way for each and every additional component.

So, in general, the ith **Principal Component** i.e. PCA_i means Y_i and is computed as follows:-

We select $e_{i1}, e_{i2}, \ldots, e_{ip}$ that maximizes-

$$var(Y_i) = \Sigma(k=1 \text{ to } p)\ \Sigma(l=1 \text{ to } p)\ e_{ik}\, e_{il}\, \sigma_{kl} = e'_i \Sigma e_i$$

This is subject to the constraints that the sums of squared coefficients add up to 1, along with the additional constraint that this new component will be uncorrelated with all the previously defined components. That is,

$$e'_i e_i = \Sigma \text{ (j=1 to p) } e^2_{ij} = 1$$

How to find these coefficients e_{ij} for a principal component?

To solve these coefficients we use Eigen values and Eigen vectors of the variance-covariance matrix, Σ. Let λ_1 through λ_p represent the Eigen values of the **variance-covariance matrix, Σ.** These are ordered so that λ_1 **has the largest Eigen value and** λ_p **is the smallest.** That is,

$$\lambda_1 \geq \lambda_2 \geq \ldots\ldots \geq \lambda_p$$

Also say vectors e_1 through e_p i.e. $(e_1, e_1, \ldots, e_p)$ denote the **corresponding Eigen vectors. Note that the elements for these Eigen vectors will be coefficients of our principal components.**

The variance for the i^{it} PC is equal to the i^{ith} Eigen value as follows:-

$$\text{var } (Y_i) = \text{var } (e_{i1} X_1 + e_{i2} X_2 + \ldots\ldots + e_{ip} X_p) = \lambda_i$$

Moreover, the principal components are uncorrelated with one another:-

$$\text{cov } (Y_{i,} Y_j) = 0$$

When we have correlations / multi-collinearity between the x-variables, the data may be more or less fall on a line or plane in a lower number of dimensions.

For example, consider a plot of two x-variables that have a nearly perfect correlation. The data **points will fall close to a straight line.** That line could be used as a new 1D axis to represent the variation among data points.

Let us define this now in terms of variance-covariance matrix, Σ, which is unknown. But we may estimate Σ by the sample variance-covariance matrix, Σ, which is given in the standard formula as follows:-

$$S = 1/(n-1)\, \Sigma \text{ (i=1 to n) } (X_i - x)(X_i - x)'$$

Algorithm followed:

We calculate the Eigen Values $\lambda_1', \lambda_2', \ldots\ldots, \lambda_p'$ of the sample variance-covariance matrix, S, and the corresponding Eigen Vectors $e_1', e_2', \ldots\ldots, e_p'$. Then we will define our estimated PCs using the Eigen Vectors as our coefficients:-

$$Y_1' = e_{11}' X_1 + e_{12}' X_2 + \ldots\ldots + e_{1p} X_p$$
$$Y_2' = e_{21}' X_1 + e_{22}' X_2 + \ldots\ldots + e_{2p} X_p$$
$$\vdots$$
$$Y_p' = e_{p1}' X_1 + e_{p2}' X_2 + \ldots\ldots + e_{pp} X_p$$

In general, we can retain only the first k principal component. But we need to balance two conflicting issues:-

1. To obtain the simplest possible interpretation, we want k to be as small as possible. If we can explain most of the variation just by 2 principal components then this would give us a much

simpler description of data. **The smaller is the k , the smaller amount of variation is explained by the first k component.**

2. To avoid loss of information, we want the proportion of variation explained by the first principal components to be large. That is, what we want is-

$$\frac{\lambda_1' + \lambda_2',+......,+\lambda_k'}{\lambda_1' + \lambda_2',+......, +\lambda_p'} = 1$$

So, we can say that all principal components are uncorrelated with one another.

PCA involves the following steps :

S1 : Import the necessary libraries.

eg. import numpy as np

S2 : Give the input dataset. Input x and y as an **array** of say, 20 values, for simplicity. Also compute the **mean** of the values.

eg. x = np. array ([2.5, 1.5, 3.3, 4.5, 2])

data = np. array (x)

print (x)

print (data)

x Mean = np. mean (x)

print (x mean)

S3 : Compute the mean adjusted values by subtracting each point from its mean. This is useful for normalizing the values.

eg. mean Adjusted = np. zeros ((2,5))

for i in range (len (data [0])) : mean Adjusted [0] [i] = data [0] [i] -xmean print (mean Adjusted)

S4 : Compute the covariance matrix of the mean adjusted data.

eg. cov_mat = np. cov (data)

S5 : Then, **compute** the eigen values and eigen vectors. Python does this easily.

S6 : Sort the eigenvalues in descending order and print them.

S7 : Retain those eigenvalues that have maximum values. Transform the data and print it.

S8 : Reconstruct and **transform** the original data.

2.3.8 *Independent Component Analysis (ICA)*

A method for finding the underlying factors or components from multi-variate or multi-dimensional statistical data is called as Independent Component Analysis (ICA). This method is somewhat different. It is so because it uses both statistically independent and non-Gaussian form.

For example, consider a scenario in which three people are speaking simultaneously in a room. There are 3 microphones that are present in different locations for the same. The microphones give us 3 recorded time signals which can be denoted by x1(t), x2(t) and x3(t) with x1, x2 and x3 referring to the amplitudes and t is basically the **time index.** Each of these recorded signals can be represented as a weighted sum of the speech signals produced by the three speakers which is denoted by s1(t), s2(t) and s3(t). In linear form we can represent it as follows:-

$$x_1(t) = a_{11}\, s_1 (t) + a_{12}\, s_2 (t) + a_{13}\, s_3 (t)$$
$$x_2(t) = a_{21}\, s_1 (t) + a_{22}\, s_2 (t) + a_{23}\, s_3 (t)$$
$$x_3(t) = a_{31}\, s_1 (t) + a_{32}\, s_2 (t) + a_{33}\, s_3 (t)$$

where a_{ij} with j=1...3, depend on the distances of the microphones from the speakers.

It is very innovative to estimate the original speech signals s1(t), s2(t) and s3(t) by making use of the recorded signals x_i (t). **And this problem is known as a cocktail-party problem.**

If we know the mixing parameter, a_{ij} value then we would have easily solved the linear equation by simply inverting the linear system. But the problem is that we neither have a_{ij} nor the $s_i(t)$. One of the ways of solving this problem is to use some information on the statistical properties of the signals, s_i (t). It is more than enough to assume that s_1 (t), s_2 (t) and s_3 (t) are **statistically independent at each time instant, t.** ICA can be used to estimate a_{ij} based on their information of their independence. This allows us to separate out the three original signals s_1 (t), s_2 (t) and s_3 (t) from their mixtures x_1 (t), x_2 (t) and x_3 (t). ICA was developed to deal with the variant forms of **cocktail-party problem.**

The Noise-free ICA Model

The ICA model is a generative model that means that it describes how the observed data are generated by a process of mixing the components, s_j.

To model ICA, the following points must be remembered:-

1. Use statistical **latent variables** in the system.
2. Use **random variable, s_k** instead of time signal.
3. $X_j = a_{j1}s_1 + a_{j2}s_2 + ... + a_{jn}s_{n,}$ for all jx = As
4. Task: Estimate A and S using only the observable random vector, x.
5. Assuming that number of Independent Components = number of observable mixtures and A is square and invertible, we can estimate A. Then we can calculate $W=A^{-1}$ and thus $s = Wx = A^{-1}\, x$.

Limitations in ICA

The following are some of the limitations of ICA:

1. The independent components are assumed statistically independent.
2. The independent components must have non-Gaussian distributions.
3. The joint density of unit variances, s_1 and s_2 is symmetric. So, it does not contain any information about the directions of the columns of the mixing matrix, A. So, A can't be estimated.
4. If only one Independent component is Gaussian then the estimation is still possible.

Ambiguities in ICA

The following are some of the ambiguities in ICA:

1. It cannot determine the variances /energies of the independent components (ICs). Both s and A are unknowns and that any scalar multiple in one of the sources can always be cancelled by dividing the corresponding column of A by it. Also because of the fixed magnitudes of IC's assuming unit variance i.e. $E\{S_i^2\} = 1$.

2. It cannot determine the order of Independent components. The terms can be easily changed as both a and A are unknown, so, we call any IC as the first one.

How to centre the variables?

We can assume that both the mixture variables and the independent components have **zero mean without any loss of generality.** This assumption simplifies the theory and algorithms further. **If the assumption of zero mean is not true, some pre-processing is done to make it hold.** This is possible by centering the observable variables i.e. subtracting their sample mean. This means that the original mixtures, say x', are pre-processed by $x = x' - E\{x'\}$, before doing ICA. Thus, the independent components are also made zero mean because-

$$E\{s\} = A^{-1} E\{x\}$$

On the other hand, the **mixing matrix** remains intact after this pre-processing. So this can always be done without affecting the estimation of the **mixing matrix.** After estimating the mixing matrix and the independent components for the zero-mean data, the subtracted mean can be simply reconstructed by adding $E\{s\} = A^{-1} E\{x\}$to the zero-mean independent components.

2.3.9 Latent Semantic Indexing (LSI)

Latent Semantic Indexing (LSI) is a retrieval method that makes use of a mathematical technique called as Singular Value Decomposition (SVD) which in turn is used to figure out patterns in connection to terms and concepts included in unstructured collection of data. This process acts as an add-on to document indexing process. In addition to keeping track of keywords that are there in the document , this method analyzes the document entirely to find out which other document contains the same words. **Please note that LSI considers documents to be semantically close if they have many words in common and semantically distant if few words are there in common.** LSI algorithm is unable to understand the words as it does not know the meanings but still it is able to figure out the pattern that makes it look **intelligent.**

The LSI Algorithm

Step-1: Convert each document in your index in a **vector-form** of word occurrences. Here,

Number of dimensions in vector = Number of unique words in the entire document set.

Most document vectors will have large empty patches, some will be quite full. It is recommended that common words like 'this', 'him', 'the' etc. should be removed.

Step-2: Scale each vector so that every term reflects the frequency of its occurrence in context.

Step-3: Combine these column vectors into a large **term-document matrix.** Here, *rows represent terms and columns represent document.*

Step-4: Perform **Singular Value Decomposition** (SVD) on the term-document matrix. This will result in three matrices commonly called U, S and V. S, is a diagonal matrix of singular values for your document system. It is of use to us.

Step-5: Set all but the k-highest singular values to 0. K is a parameter that needs to be tuned based on your space. **Very low values of k** are very lossy and lands up with net poor results. **But very high values of k** do not change the results much from simple vector search. This gets a new matrix, S'.

Step-6: Recombine the terms to form the original matrix-

U * S'* V(t) = M'

Where (t) signifies transpose.

Step-7: Break this reduced rank term-document matrix back into column vectors. Associate these with their corresponding documents.

Step-8: Now you get the LSI i.e., **Latent Semantic Index.**

Advantages of LSI

1. **LSI** is used to analyze the similarity between the bodies of the text. This can be used in dozens of ways, from finding related documents in a group to doing paragraph-wise LSI to find site summaries.
2. It can also be used to assist **search** in a smarter way of your **document space.**
3. To do **document categorization.**
4. You can take the inner product (dot product) of two of the LSI vectors and perform operations with that information. Sometimes you may do this operation on your unit LSI vectors, particularly when you are searching on a vector that is a search term. It will never have the magnitude that a full document would have.

2.3.10 Spectral or Sub-space Clustering

It is one of the most modern and simple clustering algorithms. It can be solved efficiently by standard linear algebra software. Sometimes it is better than traditional k-means algorithm. **Please understand that the objective of spectral clustering is to cluster connected data but not certainly compact or clustered within convex boundaries.**

When we talk of compactness then k-means model is useful while when we talk of connectivity then spectral clustering is used.

Algorithm

Step-1: **Project** your data into R^n.

Step-2: Define an **Affinity matrix,** A, using a Gaussian Kernel, K, or say just an adjacency matrix i.e. $A_{ij} = \delta_{ij}$.

Step-3: Construct the **Laplacian Graph** from A i.e. decide on a normalization.

Step-4: Solve an **Eigen value problem** such as $Lv = \lambda v$ or a Generalized Eigen Value problem i.e., $Lv = \lambda Dv$.

Step-5: Select **k Eigen Vectors** $\{v_i, i = 1, k\}$ corresponding to the k-lowest or highest Eigen values, to define a k-dimensional subspace $P^t LP$.

Step-6: Form clusters in this subspace using, say, k-means.

Metrics

A metric that computes the similarity or closeness of two points in space is called as an affinity. We either guess the metric or learn the metric. Now we will guess the metric. **Please note that it is not the standard Euclidean metric.** The next simplest one is Guassian Kernel.

Given 2 data points, x_i, x_j that is projected in R^n, we define an Affinity A_{ij} that is positive, symmetric and depends on the Euclidian distance $||x_i - x_j|$ between the data points:-

$$A_{ij} = \exp(-\alpha ||x_i - x_j||^2)$$

We might provide a hard cut-off R so that $A_{ij} = 0$ if $||x_i - x_j||^2 \geq R$ and in some applications we pre-multiply A_{ij} with a feature Affinity Kernal. Just note that-

$A_{ij} = 1$ when the points are close in R^n and $A_{ij} \rightarrow 0$ if the points x_i, x_j are far apart. **Please note that close data points are in the same cluster while data points in different clusters are far away. Also note that data points in the same cluster may also be far away in comparison to the points in different clusters.**

Objective: Our task is now to transform the space so that when the 2 points x_i and x_j are close enough so that they are always in the same cluster and when they are far apart, they are in different clusters.

Many types of Laplacians (L) are given in the literature like Normalized, Generalized, Relaxed etc. they all share the degree matrix, D. We define a **degree matrix as a diagonal matrix that measures the degree at each node as follows:-**

$$D_{i,j} = \Sigma \text{ (j to n) } a_{i,j}$$

This is known as a **local nearest neighbour mean-field average** of the Affinity. D is a normalization factor for A so that the Cluster Affinities are balanced across different clusters.

2.3.11 Hidden Markov Model

A tool used for representing probability distributions over a sequence of observations is Hidden Markov Model (HMM). The observation is denoted at a particular instance time, t, by variable Y_t. As long as we can define **a probability distribution,** this symbol can vary from discrete alphabet to a real valued variable or to an integer. Here, we assume that 't' can be an integer valued time index as the observation are sampled at discrete equally spaced time intervals. This model assumes that the observation at time, t, was generated by the same process whose state S_i is concealed or hidden from the observer. This model has two defining properties as follows:-

1. This process conforms the Markov Property i.e. given the value of S_{i-1}, the current state S_i is independent of all the states prior to t-1.
2. The outputs also conforms a Markov property in accordance to the states given S_i, Y_i is independent of the states and observation at other times indexes.

Markov properties signifies joint distribution of a sequence of states and observations. The **factorization** of joint distribution given in equation can be represented graphically as shown in figure 2.6:

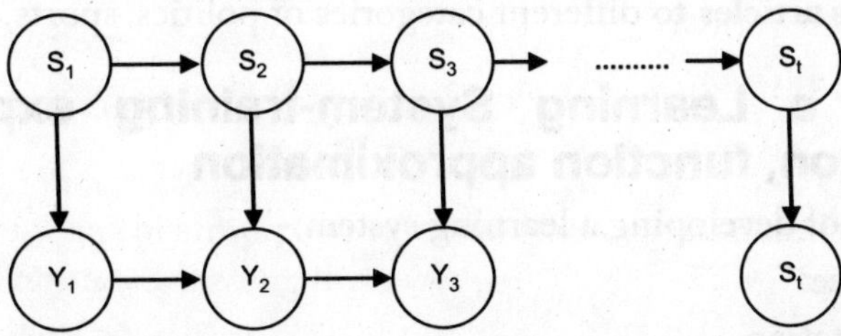

Fig.2.6: Bayesian Network specifying Conditional Independence relation for a Hidden Markov Model

Each variable is denoted by a node in the graph of figure 2.6. each node receives a directed graph from the nodes that is conditionally dependent on, in the factorization of joint distribution. It also assumes that hidden variable is discrete i.e. s_i can take on k values which will be denoted by the integers {1.....k}.

To define a probability distribution over sequences of observations:-

$P(S_i)$ = probability distribution over initial state.

K X k = state transition matrix defining $P(S_i \mid S_{i-1})$

$P(Y_t \mid S_t)$ = Output Model.

Notes:

1. HMMs assume that the model is time invariant.
2. If the observables are in form of discrete symbols, taking one of L values, the pd model is represented by k X L emission matrix.
3. HMMs can be augmented to allow for input variables i.e. in such a way that there is an input dependent state transition probability. The system then steps ahead and models the conditional distribution of sequence of output distribution when you are provided with the input distributions.

2.4 Goals and Applications of Machine Learning

Our objective is to devise such algorithms that does learning naturally without human interference. So, **we can say that machine learning model can be considered in the form of programming by example.** The following are some of the goals and applications of machine learning:-

1. To improve the **image classification** in apps like Google photos, deep learning is required.
2. To improve **detection of malicious software,** machine learning is used in anti-virus software.
3. **Anti-spam software** are trained better by machine learning. Identify e-mail messages as spam or non-spam and if it happens to be spam then penalize them
4. **Tagging people** in photos like Facebook does it. It shows whether a face is present or not in a photograph.
5. To **diagnose patients' suffering** from a particular disease or Not.
6. For **speech recognition.**
7. **To predict a set of customers** who will respond to a particular type of advertisement or promotion like Amazon recommends products especially for you.
8. To identify **fraudulent credit card transactions.**
9. When machine learning is applied to **weather forecasting software** it enhances quality of software by resulting in accurate predictions for instance whether it will rain today or not.
10. To categorize **news articles** to different categories of politics, sports, entertainments etc.

2.5 Developing a Learning System-training experience, concept representation, function approximation

There are three aspects of developing a learning system:-

1. Training Experience.
2. Concept Representation.
3. Function Approximation.

Let us study these one by one now.

1. **Training Experience:** There are three (3) attributes for the selection of the design-
   (a) To make choice of the type of training experience from a set of experiences from which the system learns. The chosen training experience has a deep effect on learner's success or failure. Once the choice is made by the Performance System, the query of whether direct or indirect feedback regarding choices is provided by the training experience. **For example,** in case of a chess game, the system may learn from **direct training** (like board states, correct moves etc.) or **indirect training** (like move sequences, final outcomes of the games etc.). **It has been found that learning done from the direct training feedback is easier than learning from indirect feedback.**

   (b) To what extent sequence of training examples is controlled by the learner. **For example,** for the selection of board states and correct move for each, the learner might require teacher's assistance. On the other hand, learner can use a different approach i.e., the board states that seems confusing to the learner might itself be proposed by the learner. A learner can have an entire control over both the conditions i.e., of the board states as well as of training classifications (indirect) as it does when it learns by playing against itself without the assistance of a teacher.

   (c) How well it signifies the **distribution of examples over which the final system's performance is measured.** In chess game, the performance count metric, P_c is the number of games the system wins. The training experience, E_t , might not be fully illustrative of various situations over which it will be later on tested; if the games played against itself is only taken into account.

Please note here that the most of the theory of machine learning is dependent on the assumption that distribution of training examples is identical to distribution of test examples.

The training proceeds as follows. No external trainer will be present. Hence, the system gets trained by playing games against itself. *This results in generation of lot of training data with time.*

Keep in mind these 3 points when viewing a complete design of the learning system:-

1. Exact type of knowledge to be learned.
2. How this target knowledge is represented.
3. A learning means.

How to choose the target function?

The **performance program** will decide on what sort of knowledge will be learned and how will this program put it to use. **For example,** consider a chess program that can generate legal moves from any board state. The program needs to find out the best move, out of the large number of legal moves available. Now the type of function to be learned is a program or function that finds the best move from a lot of moves available for a particular board state.

2. **Concept Representation:** The learning task is narrowed down to the problem of finding an operational description of ideal target function, E, that is difficult to learn perfectly. **Note that we expect learning algorithms to attain some approximation to the target function and thus the process of learning the target function is called as function approximation.**

For example, in chess problem-

T_G is the task i.e., to play chess.

P_c is the percentage of games won against competitor.

E_T is practising against itself.

Target Function, E: Board à R

So, Target Function Representation is-

$$E'(s) = w_0 + w_1b_1 + w_2b_2 + w_3b_3 + w_4b_4 + w_5b_5 + w_6b_6$$

Note that the first three points relate to specification of learning task and last two items form design choices that are required for the implementation of the learning program.

3. Function Approximation

We need a set of training examples in order to learn target function, E', each describing a particular board states and training value E for s. Every training example is represented as an ordered pair of the form (s, E_{train} (s)). **For example,** consider the following training example that tells a board state in which red has won the game. Note that

$b_1 = 0$ = number of black pieces left for this target function value is E_{train} (s) + 100.

2.6 Estimating Training Values

The only **training information** available to a learner, in accordance to the formulation of learning problem is whether the game was last won or lost. Also **training instances** are required so that particular board states can be given specific scores. In guessing the training values for intermediate board states there are some uncertainty associated.

Rules for estimating Training Values

To assign the training value of E_{train}(s) for any intermediate board state (s) to be E' (successor(b)), where E' is the learner's current approximation to E and where successor (s) signifies the next board state following 's' for which it is again the program's turn to move i.e., the board state following the program's move and the opponents response. This is known as a **rule for estimating training values.** It can be represented as follows:-

$$E_{train}(s) = E'(successor(s))$$

Please note here that we are using the estimates of the value of the successor (s) to estimate the value of board state (s). This will make sense if E' tends to be more accurate for board states closer to the games end. **Also note that under certain situations the approach of iteratively estimating training values based on the estimates of successor state values can be proven to converge to perfect estimates of $E_{train.}$**

The learning algorithm for choosing the weights, w_i, to best fit the set of training examples {(s, E_{train} (s))}. We mean to say the best fit to the training data. One general approach is to define the best hypothesis or a set of weights, which in turn minimizes the squared error, E, between the training values and the values predicted by the hypothesis E'. That is,

$$E' = \Sigma_{(s,\, E_{train}(S))\ \varepsilon\ \text{training examples}} (E_{train}(s) - E'(s))^2$$

Thus, our objective is to seek the weights or equivalently E' that minimize E for the observed training examples.

Supervised and Unsupervised Learning- A CASE STUDY

According to Simon Haykin, **learning is the process by which free parameters of a neural network are adapted through a process of stimulation by the environment in which the network is embedded. The type of learning is determined by the manner in which the parameter changes take place."** This process of learning involves three steps:-

S1: The neural network is stimulated by the environment (excitatory or inhibitory).

S2: The free parameters of the network like the synaptic weights and the biases, undergo a change as a result of this stimulation.

S3: The response of the neural network to the environment changes as a result of the change in its internal free parameters.

The process of learning involves two things:

1. **The Learning Paradigms,** which determine the manner in which a neural network relates to the environment. Here a neural network represents a set of inter-connected neurons.
2. **The Learning Law,** which is a set of well defined rules called as the **learning algorithm.** There is no unique algorithm. One law differs from the other in the manner in which weights and biases are adjusted.

Artificial neural networks can modify their behaviour in response to their environment. Given as a set of inputs with desired outputs, they self-adjust to produce consistent responses. Different types of training algorithms have been developed. Learning algorithms like ANNs, in general, can be presented in either differential-equation or difference-equation form.

A network is trained so that application of a set of inputs produces the desired set of outputs. Each such input is known as a **vector.** Training is accomplished by sequentially applying input vectors while adjusting network weights according to a predetermined procedure. During training, *the network weighs gradually converge to values such that each input vector produces the desired output vector.* Training algorithms are put under two categories- supervised and unsupervised.

Supervised Training: A type of training that needs the pairing of each input vector with a target vector showing the desired output. Together these are called as a **training pair.** A network is trained over a number of such training pairs. **An input vector is applied, the output of the network is calculated and compared to the corresponding target vector and the difference (error) is fed back through the network and weights are changed according to an algorithm that tends to minimize the error.** The vectors of the training set are applied sequentially and errors are calculated and weights adjusted for each vector until the error for the entire training set is at an acceptably low level.

The knowledge is represented in form of input-output examples called as the **training data.** The training data consists of pairs of input samples in form of a vector and the corresponding output, which happens to be the desired output. The **teacher** provides the desired output for a given input vector by virtue of inbuilt knowledge as shown in figure 2.4.

The network computes the output called as the **actual output.** The **error signal is the difference between the desired output / response and the actual output/response.**

Please understand that the network parameters like the synaptic weights and biases are adjusted by means of the learning law, under the influence of the error signal and the input vector.

Also note that this is done iteratively until the actual response is close to the desired response. It is at this point that we can say that the network is trained. In nutshell, supervised learning involves the following steps:-

S1: Determine the type of **training examples and form the training set.** This is a set of **input vector** and the corresponding **output vectors.**

S2: The input vector must capture the features descriptive of the object. ***The number of features should not be too large but large enough to predict the output.***

S3: Determine the **learning law** and **train the network** with the input training data.

S4: After the training is completed, the network is **validated** with a subset of the training set.

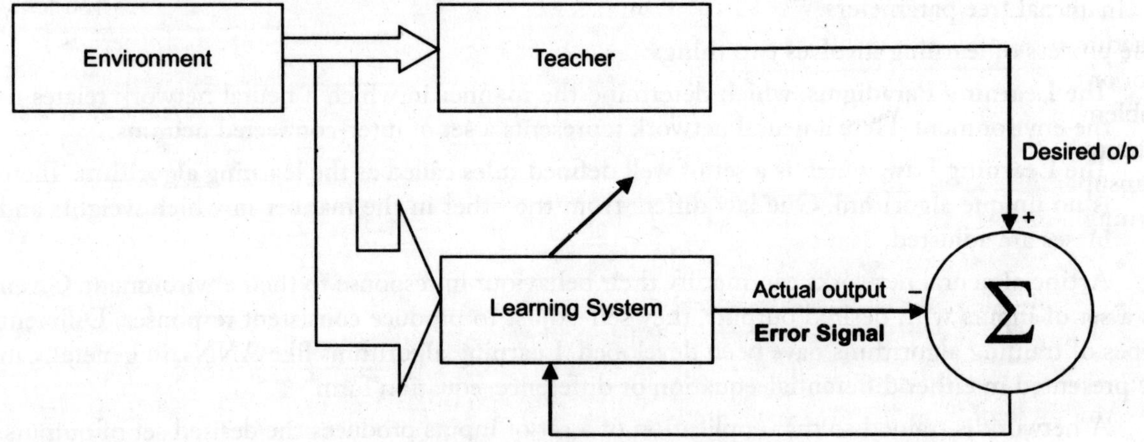

Fig.2.7: Supervised Learning

Please note that the mean-square error or the sum of squared errors over the training sample, defined as a function of the system parameters can be used as a performance measure for the system. Also note that for the system to improve the performance, the operating point must move towards a point of minimum error. Supervised learning is used in applications like pattern classification and function approximation.

Unsupervised Training: It is a more plausible model of learning in biological system. It was developed by Kohonen et. al. in 1984. It requires no target vector for the outputs. Hence no comparisons to pre-determined ideal responses can be made. **The training set solely consists of input vectors.** The training algorithm modifies the network weights to produce output vectors that are consistent. This means that both application of one of the training vectors or application of a vector that is similar to it, will produce the same pattern of outputs. **Please understand that the training process extracts the statistical properties of the training set and groups similar vectors into classes.** Applying a vector from a given class to the input will produce a specific output vector but there is no way to find out prior to training which specific output pattern will be produced by a given input vector class. **Also note that the outputs of such a network must generally be transformed into a more comprehensible form following a training process.** This is not difficult. It is so because it is simpler to identify the I/O relationships in a network.

In this type of learning, there is no teacher to see the process of learning. We deal with a class of problems to find out how data is organized. It is shown in figure 2.5.

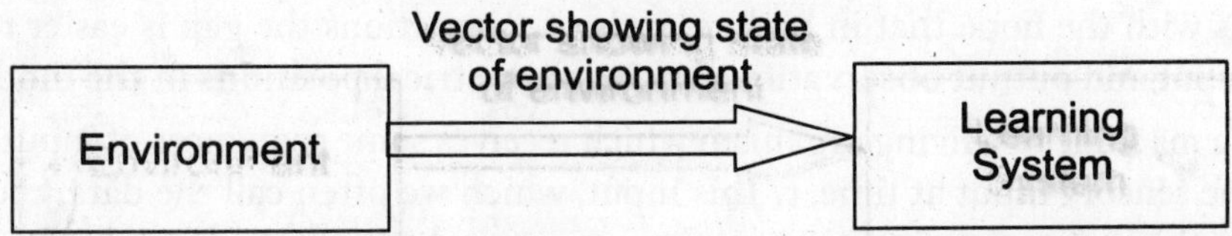

Fig.2.8: Unsupervised Learning

In machine learning, unsupervised learning refers to the problem of trying to find hidden structure in unlabeled data. Because the examples given to the learner are unlabeled, there is no error or reward signal to evaluate a potential solution. Unsupervised learning is closely related to the problem of **density estimation** in statistics. However, unsupervised learning also covers many other techniques that seek to summarize and explain key features of the data. Many methods employed in unsupervised learning are based on data mining methods used to pre-process data. Unsupervised learning includes several approaches as listed below:-

- Clustering like k-means, mixture models, hierarchical clustering;
- Blind signal separation using feature extraction techniques for dimensionality reduction like Principal Component Analysis, Independent Component Analysis, Non-negative matrix factorization, singular value decomposition.

Among neural networks models, the Self-organizing Map (SOM) and Adaptive Resonance Theory (ART) are commonly used unsupervised learning algorithms.

Differences between unsupervised and supervised learning

Supervised and unsupervised learning differ only in the casual structure of the model. In **supervised learning,** the model defines the effect one set of observations, called as **inputs,** has on another set of observations, called **outputs.** This means that the input are assumed to be at the beginning and outputs at the end of the causal chain. The models can include **mediating variables** between the inputs and outputs. In unsupervised learning, all observations are assumed to be caused by latent variables. This means that the observations are assumed to be at the end of the causal chain. On the other hand, the models for supervised learning often leave the probability for inputs undefined. This model is not needed as long as the inputs are available but if some of the input values are missing then it is not possible to infer anything about the outputs. If the inputs are also modelled then missing inputs cause no problem since they can be considered latent variables as in unsupervised learning. With unsupervised learning it is possible to learn larger and more complex models than with supervised learning. This is so because in supervised learning one is trying to find the connection between two sets of observations. **Please note that the difficulty of learning task increases exponentially in the number of steps between the two sets and that is why supervised learning cannot learn model with deep hierarchies.** In unsupervised learning, learning can proceed hierarchically from the observations into ever more abstract levels of representation. Each additional hierarchy needs to learn only one step and therefore, the learning time increases linearly in the number of levels in the model hierarchy. **Also note here that if the causal relation between the**

input and output observations is complex i.e. there is a large causal gap, it is often easier to bridge the gap using unsupervised learning instead of supervised learning. Instead of finding the casual pathway from the inputs to the outputs, one starts building the model upwards from both the sets of observations with the hope that in higher levels of abstractions the gap is easier to bridge. **Note also that the input and output observations are in symmetrical positions in the model.**

Consider a machine or a living organism which receives some sequences of inputs, $x_1, x_2, x_3, \ldots\ldots x_t$ where x_t is the sensory input at time, t. This input, which we often call the data, could correspond to an image on the retina, the pixels in a camera or a sound waveform. It could also correspond to less obviously sensory data like words in a news story or the list of items in a mall. So, now four types of machine learning are possible:

(a) In **supervised learning,** the machine is also given a sequence of desired outputs as $y_1, y_2, y_{3.....}y_t$ and the goal of the machine is to learn to produce the correct output given a new input. The output could be a class label (in classification) or a real number (in regression).

(b) In **reinforcement learning,** the machine interacts with its environment by producing actions $a_1, a_2, \ldots\ldots a_{n.}$ these actions affect the state of the environment which in turn results in the machine receiving some scalar rewards or punishments, $r_1, r_2 \ldots. r_{n.}$ **the goal of the machine is to learn to act in a way that maximizes the future rewards it receives or minimizes the punishments over its lifetime.** Reinforcement learning is closely related to the fields of decision theory and control theory.

(c) Another third type of machine learning is related to the game theory and it generalizes reinforcement learning. Here again the machine gets the *inputs, produces actions and receives rewards.* However, the environment that the machine interacts with is not some static world but rather it can contain other machines which can also sense, act, receive rewards and learn. So, **the goal of the machine is to act so as to maximize rewards in light of the other machines current and future actions.** Although there is a great deal of work in game theory for simple systems, the dynamic case with multiple adapting machines remains an active and challenging area of research.

(d) Finally, in unsupervised learning, the machine simply receives inputs $x_1, x_2, \ldots.,$ but obtains neither supervised target outputs nor rewards from its environment. It may seem somewhat mysterious to imagine what the machine could possibly learn that it doesn't get any feedback from its environment. However, it is possible to develop a formal framework for unsupervised learning based on the notion that the machine's goal is to build representations of the input that can be used for decision making, predicting future inputs, efficiently communicating the inputs to another machine etc. in a sense, unsupervised learning can be thought of as finding patterns in the data above and beyond what would be considered **pure unstructured noise.**

Unsupervised algorithms can be compared to a three months old baby. As 3 months old child receives the same visual stimuli as a newborn infant but can make much more sense of them and can recognize various patterns and features of visual input data. These abilities are not acquired from an external teacher and illustrate that a significant amount of learning is accomplished by biological facts, the artificial neural network discussed in this chapter attempt to discover special features and patterns from the available data without using external help.

Our learning starts from birth only. Observe how a baby learns to recognize its mother. The first act of learning of baby is **'to recognize'**. When a child is trained to recognize concepts by being provided with labels for each experienced instance then this is **supervised learning.** On the other hand, learning the features themselves is an example of **unsupervised learning.** In this the lower-level features are automatically grouped or clustered based on how similar they are across many observed instances. In computing terms, we may call these images i.e. collection of pixels. As a child sees many images of **'dogs' or 'cats', then those pixels that form 'legs'** are automatically grouped or clustered together. So, now we can say that the child has learned a new concept of **'legs** without any external supervision (or teacher) even though the baby does not know about **"leg"**. Furthermore, this concept of **'leg'** becomes a feature that takes a baby to the next higher level of learning.

Several types of learning do exist, like-

1. Learning how to **parse sentences.**
2. Learning to recognize whether a **tweet is positive or negative.**
3. **Learning the topic,** a particular web page is talking about or
4. **Discovering the topics** that are being discussed in a corpus of text.

In many cases, the machine needs to be trained using data labelled by humans like **parsing or sentiment mining.** These are the examples of **supervised learning.** On the other hand, **topic discovery** is an example of **unsupervised learning** wherein there is no pre-existing knowledge being provided by outside human intervention. Our computer observes a number of such instances. Its task is to learn the concepts from the **training set** so as to be able to recognize future instances.

A simple computer program for the above scenario of **'cat-dog'** may choose to store all of the observed instances, just as Google stores web pages and also creating an index of features as Google indexes documents using the words they contain. Then when presented with a new instance, our program merely looks up its fast experience very fast, using **binary searching.**

Case 1: If an exact match is found, the new observation is given the same animal label as the old one it matches with.

Case 2: If no match is found, we might use the closest match, in terms of the number of features that match exactly or use a small number of close matches and choose the label that occurs most often amongst these. **This is called as a k-nearest-neighbour (or KNN) classifier** as it classifies the instances given to it. **But please note that if the number of past observations is very large then the classification process may be slow.**

Google also uses classifiers to filter spam, learn user preferences or to classify tweets as **positive or negative. Also note that machine learning using classifiers is also at the heart of NLP wherein the computer is trained to parse sentences from a large corpora of human-parsed text.**

Google Translate that does automated translation between different languages also uses machine learning heavily. Now the objective is to find out whether a new sentence is expressing positive or negative opinion and to learn how to do so from the past observations of sentences that have been labelled correctly by humans. Instead of size and sound, now our features are the occurrences of words in sentences.

Actually, learning from a small number of examples cannot be perfect so the **accuracy** with which a concept is learned also needs to be considered. **Accuracy** *is usually measured in terms of the* *probability of the learned classifier making a mistake.* **Please note here that the larger the chance of a mistake, lower is the accuracy. Also note that the inverse of the mistake probability can be used a s a measure of accuracy.**

Clustering i.e. grouping items that are similar to each other is another basic technique of **unsupervised learning.** All that is needed is some way to compare two items.

Thus, we can say that machines can learn from examples, in case of supervised learning, such as for browsers versus surfers or dogs versus cats, a human-labelled set of training examples is needed. On the other hand, in unsupervised learning, machine learns from experiences as long as they can be clearly identified even if implicitly.

Web pages are mostly unstructured text. We know that text can be analyzed using NLP techniques. And that,

NLP + Machine Learning techniques → allows machine to learn larger number of General Knowledge facts from such large corpus as the entire web.

Whole of our machine learning is based on first being able to distinguish objects along with some of the features describing them. On the other hand, computers derive this ability directly through our programming. The classifiers can distinguish between different classes of objects like cats from dogs, buyers from browsers etc. provided they have been trained suitably. Unsupervised rule learning can discover important features and frequently observed associations between features, there by learning some structure of the world. Latent learning techniques can also discover infrequent correlations between objects based on their features. Finally, the computer can learn facts from vast volumes of text available on the web.

In nutshell, the learning algorithm uses a large number of labelled instances to learn its model. Then the learned model is used to assign labels to future instances. This is **supervised learning.** On the other hand, in **unsupervised learning, instances are grouped into clusters based on their mutual similarity.** There are no labels but only clusters characterized by a set of similar features.

2.7 Overview of Classification

In the field of machine learning, **classification is the problem of finding out to which category a newly encountered observation belongs, based on the training dataset containing observations.**

Before we discuss further, let us first of all define a multilayer perceptron and its training.

Multilayer Perceptron (MLP): It is a feed-forward ANN. It maps a set of input data to a set of output data. It consists of multiple layers of nodes represented in a directed graph with each layer being connected to the next layer completely. Apart from the input nodes, each node itself is a neuron or a processing element with a non-linear activation function. The activation function of a node in this context defines the output of that node given an input or set of inputs.

Activation Function: The problem to be considered here is that the jump should be in between firing and not firing to make it behave like neuron. So, we need an activation function that looks like a **threshold function** but it is differentiable so that gradient can be computed. If we look at the graph of the threshold function, it is similar to S-shaped functions whose mathematical form is called as a **sigmoid function.**

Error Function: The method that we are using is called back-propagation error which depicts that errors are sent backward through the network. It is a type of **gradient descent.** In perceptron, the weights are changed so that the neurons were fired only when the targets **indicate** and they did not fire when the targets did **not indicate.** It was time to choose an error function, E (t, o) and tried to make it as small as possible. Since there was only one set of weights available in the network, it was sufficient to train the same. We prepare to minimize the error so that neurons fire only when they should but on adding extra layers of weights it becomes difficult to arrange. Also when trying to adapt the weights of MLP it is difficult to find out which weights caused the error. This could be any of the weights i.e. the weights connecting inputs to the hidden layer or weights hidden layer to the output layer. We have so far used E = t-o for the perceptron. Say, we have two errors-

1. The target is bigger than the output.
2. The output is bigger than the target.

Please understand that if these two errors are of same size, then we assign them the resultant zero which depicts that no error was made and is incorrect. To get this in line, we need to make all errors to have a same sign. To cope with this problem, the best way is to find the sum of squares error function. **The sum of squares error function** basically calculates the difference between target (t) and output (o) for each node, squares them and adds them all together. That is,

$$\mathbf{E(t, o) = \frac{1}{2} \Sigma_{l=1 \text{ to } n} (t_l - o_l)^2}$$

2.8 MLP in Practice

Three steps are involved here:-

S1: Data Preparation.

S2: Training, Testing and Validation.

S3: Generalization and Overfitting.

Machine learning algorithms **tend to learn from data.** So, it is important that right data is fed for the problem to be solved. **Please note that the more disciplined the data is handled, more consistent and better are the results.**

Let us study these steps now.

S1: Data Preparation: It involves three sub-tasks-

1. **Select Data**- It involves the selection of subset of all available data that we will be dealing with. We need to take into consideration what data is needed to solve the problem that we are working on.
2. **Pre-process Data**- After you have selected the data, the next step is how you are going to use the data.

Steps for data pre-processing:

2.1 **Formatting:** The data should be in a suitable format that you want to work on like the data may be in relational database and you want to use it as a text file.

2.2 **Cleaning:** It is the removal or fixing of missing data.

2.3 **Sampling:** It is better to take smaller representative sample of data instead of more selected data which results in shorter running times for algorithms and smaller computational and memory requirements.

3. Transform Data

The final step is to transform the processed data. The specific algorithms that you are using and the knowledge of the problem domain will influence this step and you will very likely have to revisit different transformations of your pre-processed data as you work on your problem. Three common data transformations are *scaling, attribute decomposition and attribute aggregations.* This step is also called as **feature engineering.** It involves-

(a) Scaling: The pre-processed data may contain attributes with a mixtures of scales for various quantities like dollars, kgs and sales volume. Many machine learning methods like data attribute to have the same scale such as between 0 and 1 for the smallest and the largest value for a given feature. Consider any scaling feature that you may need to perform.

(b) Decomposition: There may be features that represent a complex concept that may be more useful to a machine learning method when split into the constituent parts. For example, a date that may have day and time components that in turn could split out further. Perhaps only the hour of the day is relevant to the problem being solved. Thus, consider what feature decompositions can be made performed.

(c) Aggregation: There may be features that can be aggregated into a single feature that would be more meaningful to the problem you are trying to solve. **For example,** there may be data instance for each time a customer logged into a system that could be aggregated into a count for the number of logins allowing the additional instances to be discarded. You have to consider the type of feature aggregations to be performed.

Note: One can spend a lot of time engineering features from your data and it can be very beneficial for the algorithm performance. Start small and build on the skills you learn.

How data preparation is done in MLP?

Every machine learning algorithm is likely to learn more effectively if some pre-processing of the data inputs and targets is performed before the network is trained. In the case of Perceptron, if sigmoidal activation function is used then possible target values should be 0 and 1. In fact, the targets are scaled to lie between 0 and 1, no matter what sort of activation function is used for the output layer neurons. This helps in avoiding the weights to get too large values. The most common approach to scaling the data for MLP is to look at each data dimension independently and further make each dimension have a zero mean and unit variance in each dimension or simply to scale them so that maximum value is 1 and minimum is -1. These scaling are basically data normalization (or standardization). In case of MLP, normalization is not mandatory but useful. In this, it is very easy to perform normalization by using in-built function mean( ) and var( ). But take care of which axis the mean and variance is to be computed. That is,

```
data = (data – data.mean (axix=0)) / data.var(axis=0)
targets = (targets – targets.mean(axis=0)) / targets.var(axis=0)
```

S2: Training, Testing and Validation

After MLP training is over, in next step we need to find out how well it performs. In case of trained network, the error can be computed by computing the sum of squares error between output and target. The next task is what data should be used to test the network. It is not intelligence to use the same data for training as well as testing. This is so because it would not tell us how well the network generalizes and whether or not overfitting has happened. Thus, we need to keep separate pairs in reserve for testset (input, target) which are not used for the training purpose. In this case, we have to adjust with the fact that the amount of data which is available for testing is reduced. It is more complex, scenario when we check how well the network is learning during training so that when to stop can be decided. Now to make such a decision we cannot use training data as we would not detect overfitting but we cannot use the testing data either as we are saving it for the final test.

So, a 3rd data set called as a **validation set** is required to validate the learning so far, in the field of statistics, it is called as **cross validation.**

The ratio of training to testing to validation data is-

50:25:25 if you have large amount of data and

60:20:20 if you have a lesser amount of data.

So, the input data set is split into three different sets-training set, testing set and validation set.

S3: Generalization and Overfitting

The ability of a machine to learn on being introduced with the sets of data during training so that when it is introduced to new and unseen examples, it can perform accurately is known as Generalization. To ensure that network generalizes well, we tend to use a neural network in order to generalize from the training examples to all possible inputs. Some troublesome situations also arise in both under training and over training the network. Every other weight can be changed in a neural network. Thus, **degree of variability** is quite high. This is certainly more than in variation than there is in the function we are learning. So, the care has to be taken if we are training for long. This implies that we will overfit the data which means that during the process we have also learnt about the **noise and inaccuracies** in the data along with the **actual function.** Overfitting makes the model quite complex by having too many parameters. By doing this it loses its generalization power which results in poor performance in new data.

LDA's objective is similar to that of PCA or SVD i.e., it intends to transform a dataset into a lower dimensional feature space. LDA (like PCA) will not capture the dataset variability rather LDA focuses on **class separability** i.e., separating the features based on class separability in order to avoid overfitting of the ML model.

PCA computes the eigen-values and eigen-vectors of the covariance matrix of the dataset. On the other hand, LDA computes eigenvalues and eigenvectors within a class. LDA follows 4 steps :

S1 : Compute the mean vectors for individual classes.

S2 : Calculate intra-class and inter-class scatter matrices.

S3 : Compute eigenvalues and eigen vectors for intra-class scatter matrix (S_W) and the inter-class scatter matrix (S_B).

S4 : Find out top 'K' eigenvectors having top 'K' eigenvalues.

LDA is very common dimensionality reduction technique. It involves finding the axis that maximize the separation between multiple classes. In, nutshell, LDA projects a feature space of size n onto a smaller subspace, K (where $K \leq (n - 1)$) while maintaining the class-discriminatory information.

2.9 Linear Discriminant Analysis (LDA)

A linear discriminant method that is used in the field of statistics, pattern recognition and machine learning is *Fisher's Linear Discriminant*. It is used to find the linear combination of features that divides two or more classes of objects or events. The combination that comes out in the form of result may be used later as a **linear classifier,** in general, for dimensionality reduction before later classification. So, we can say that **LDA is a supervised technique of feature extraction that is used to find a linear combination of the available features which separate the classes.**

Applying LDA: The core objective is to decrease the dimension of the data in order to reduce the computational cost of classification. After applying the LDA to a dataset, the **"new features" minimizes the dispersion between the samples of the same class and maximizes the dispersion between samples of different classes.**

For example, say you have a dataset of players who practice different sports like may be cricket, basketball, soccer, Golf etc.. Imagine that the available features taken into consideration for these sports are height, weight and body mass index. Now when the instances are plotted, there might be some regions of intersection of two or more classes. So, when you apply LDA to a data set, it will produce new features that might result in better separation of classes-lesser and smaller regions of intersection.

Limitations of LDA

1. LDA can generate only C (number of classes) or less number of features.
2. At times, one is dealing with datasets of 20 features, for example, and there are only 2 classes, so LDA have to be reduced to 2 axis. **Such reductions usually results in loss of information that further results in low classification accuracy.**

2.10 Probabilistic Models

We discuss two types of models here:-

1. Generative Model.
2. Conditional Model.

   i. **A generative model is a model that generates observable data values randomly, usually provided with some hidden parameters.** It states '*a joint probability distribution over observation and label sequences*'. As far as machine learning is concerned, these models are used for either modelling data directly or as an intermediary phase to form a conditional probability density function. A conditional distribution can be derived from a generative model with the help of Bayes Rule. **For example,** Gaussian mixture model, Hidden Markov model, Naive Bayes, Restricted Boltzmann Machine, generative adversial networks, probabilistic context-free Grammer etc.

   ii. **Conditional models or discriminative models are used in machine learning for demonstrating the dependence of an unobserved variable 'y' on an observed variable 'x'.** In terms of probability, this is prepared by modelling the conditional probability distribution P(y| x), which can be used for predicting from discriminative models, in contrast to generative models, that do not permit to generate samples from the joint distribution of x and y. **For example,** Logistic regression (a type of generalized linear regression) used for predicting binary or categorical outputs—called as **maximum entropy classifiers,** Support Vector Machines, Boosting-a meta-algorithm, conditional random fields, linear regression, neural networks etc.

Tasks like classification and regression do not require joint distribution. In fact, conditional models can return excellent performance. **Please understand that these generative models are more flexible than discriminative models in stating dependencies in complex learning tasks. Also note that most discriminative models are fundamentally supervised and cannot easily be stretched to unsupervised learning.** Application decides whether to go for generative or conditional model.

Say, the input data is 'x' and the set of labels for x is 'y'. Then,

1. Generative model learns the joint probability distribution p(x, y).
2. Discriminative model learns the conditional probability distribution p(x | y) i.e. the 'probability of y given x'.

2.11 Decision Trees

In decision trees, we break the classification down into a set of choices about each feature starting at the root of the tree and progressing down to leaves where we receive the final classification decision. The data structure, tree, is very easy to understand and implement.

In this approach, we have handy, if-then-else rules which are useful for use in a production system. This type of algorithm has been applied successfully to a broad range of tasks from learning to diagnose medical cases to learning to assess credit risk of loan applicants.

Decision trees classify instances by sorting them down the tree from the root to some leaf nodes which provides the classification of the instance. Each **node** in the tree specifies a test of some attribute of the instance and each **branch** descending from that node corresponds to one of the possible values for this attribute. **An instance is classified by starting at the root node of the tree, testing the attribute specified by this node then moving down the tree branch corresponding to the value of the attribute in the given example.** This process is then **repeated** for the subtree rooted at the new node.

This method is very popular because we can turn into a set of logical disjunctions (if-then-else rules) that fit into program code easily.

Limitations of Decision Trees

1. **Instances** are represented by **attribute-value pairs.**
2. Target function has discrete output values.
3. **Disjunctive descriptions** may be required.
4. **Training data** may contain **errors.**
5. Training data may contain **missing attribute values.**

This method of learning has been applied to problems like learning to classify medical patients on the basis of their disease, equipment breakdowns by their cause and loan applicants by their possibility of non-payment. Such problems, in which the task is to classify examples into one of a discrete set of possible categories, are often stated as **classification problems.**

For constructing a decision tree, the features that are required for the algorithm are as follows:-

1. The state of energy level.
2. The date of your nearest deadline.
3. Whether or not there is a party tonight.

Now the challenge is to construct a tree based on these features. Literature provides different types of decision tree algorithms that are based on the same principle but follow different approaches. **Principle: "The algorithm states that the algorithm built the tree in a greedy manner starting at the root and choosing the most informative feature (how the tree works) at each step".**

ALGORITHM ID3 {by Quinlan}

This algorithm learns decision trees by constructing them in top-down fashion i.e. starts with the question "at the root of the tree, which attribute is to be tested?" In order to answer this question, each **instance attribute** is assessed using a statistical test to find out how well it classifies the training examples. *The best attribute is selected to be used as the test, as the root node of the tree. Then a successor of the root node is produced for each possible value of this attribute and the training examples are sorted to the suitable successor node i.e. down the branch conforming to the example's value for this attribute. The complete process is then repeated using the training examples related with each descendant node to select the best attribute at test at that point in the tree.* This practices a greedy search for an acceptable decision tree, in which the algorithm never backtracks to review earlier options.

Now the question is **which attribute is the best classifier?**

Selecting which attribute that is to be tested at each node in the tree is the basic factor that is to be considered in ID3 algorithm. We would like to make choice of the attribute that is most beneficial for the classifying examples.

What is a good quantitative measure of the value of an attribute?

A statistical property called as an **information gain will compute how well a given attribute separates the training examples** in accordance to their target classification. ID3 uses up this information gain measure to make a choice amongst the candidate attributes at each step while the tree grows.

ID3 (Examples, Target-attribute, Attributes)

(where, **Examples** are the training examples, **Target-attribute** is the attribute whose value is to be predicted by the tree and **Attributes** is a list of other attributes that may be tested by the learned decision tree)

(this algo returns a decision tree that correctly classifies the given Examples)

Step-1: Create a root node for the tree.

Step-2: If all Examples are positive, return the single-node tree Root, with label = +

Step-3: If all Examples are negative, return the single-node tree Root, with label = -

Step-4: If Attributes is empty, return the single-node tree Root with label = most common value of Target-attribute in Examples.

Step-5: Otherwise Begin

5.1 A ← the attribute from Attributes that best classifies Examples.

5.2 The decision attribute for Root ← A.

5.3 For each possible value, v_i, of A,

5.3.1 Add a new tree branch below Root, corresponding to the test A = v_i.

5.3.2 Let Example, sv_i be the subset of Examples that have value v_i for A.

5.3.3 If Example sv_i is empty

5.3.3.1 then below this new branch, add a leaf node with label = most common value of Target-attribute in Examples.

5.3.3.2 Else below this new branch add the subtree ID3 (Examples v_i, Target-attribute, Attributes – (A))

Step-6: End

Step-7: Return Root

In nutshell, ID3 algorithm is dedicated to learning Boolean-valued functions. ID3 is a greedy algorithm that develops the tree in top-down fashion, at each node choosing the attribute that best classifies the local training examples. This process carries until the tree perfectly classifies the training examples or until all attributes have been taken into consideration.

2.12 K-nearest Neighbor Learning-distance weighted Nearest Neighbour Algorithm

It is an instance-based method.

Principle: "This algorithm assumes that all instances relate to points in the n-dimensional space, R^n. The nearest neighbours of an instance are defined in terms of the standard Euclidean distance."

Let feature vector describe an arbitrary instance, x. The feature vector is-

$$< a_1(x), a_2(x), \ldots\ldots a_n(x) >$$

Where $a_r(x)$ denotes the values of the rth attribute of instance, x. Then the distance between two instances, x_i and x_j is defined to be $d(x_i, x_j)$ and is calculated as follows:-

$$d(x_i, x_j) = \sqrt{\Sigma \ (r = 1 \text{ to } n) \ (a_r(x_i) - a_r(x_j))^2}$$

In nearest-neighbor learning, the target function may be either for discrete-valued or real-valued. Let us first of all study learning discrete valued target functions of the form-

$$f: R^n \rightarrow V$$

where V is the finite set $\{v_1, \ldots\ldots v_s\}$.

ALGORITHM k-nearest Neighbor { a discrete-valued target function }

Training algorithm:

For each training example (x, f (x)), add the example to the list of training examples.

Classification algorithm:

Given instance x_q is to be classified. Let x_1......x_k denote the k-instances from training examples that are nearest to x_q. Return

$$f'(x_q) \text{ ß } \arg\max (v \varepsilon V) \Sigma_{(i=1 \text{ to } k)} \delta(v, f(x_i))$$

where δ (a, b) = 1 if a=b and where δ (a, b) = 0 otherwise.

Explanation: The value f' (x), given back by the algorithm as its approximation of $f(x_i)$ is just the most common value of f amongst the k training examples which are nearest to x.

If we choose k=1, then the 1-nearest neighbour algorithm assigns the value $f'(x_i)$ to $f(x_i)$ where x_i is the training instance which is nearest to x_i.

For larger values of k, the algorithm allots the most common value among the k-nearest training examples.

Figure 2.9 explains the working of the k-nearest neighbour algorithm for the case where the instances are basically points in a 2D space. Also the target function is in form of Boolean. The **positive and negative** training examples are depicted by "+" and "-" respectively. **Please note that the 1-nearest neighbour algorithm classifies x, as a positive example in figure 2.5 whereas the 5-nearest neighbour algorithm classifies it as a negative example. Also note that k-nearest neighbour algorithm never forms a clear hypothesis regarding the target function, f.** It just works out for the classification of each new query instance encountered as needed.

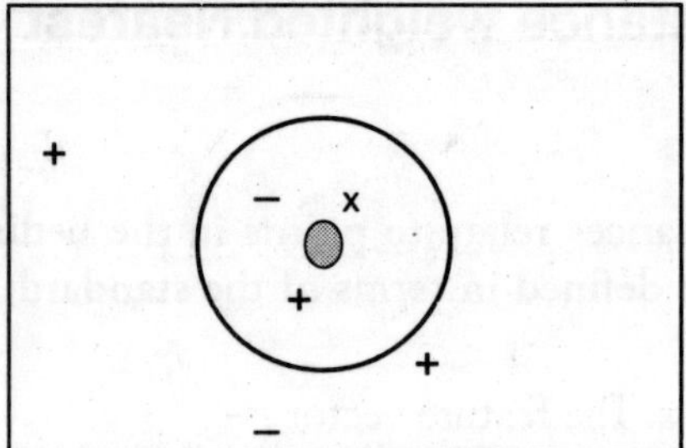

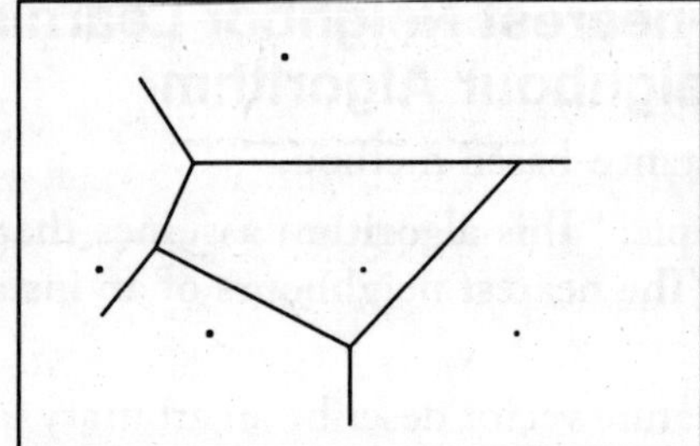

Fig.2.9: k-Nearest Neighbour

Explanation: A set of positive and negative training examples is shown on the left diagram of figure 2.9. The 1-nearest neighbour algorithm classifies x as positive whereas 5-nearest neighbour classifies it as negative. On the right hand side of the figure 2.6, is the decision surface induced by the 1-nearest neighbour algorithm for a typical set of training examples. **Please note that the convex polygon surrounding each training example indicates the region of instance space closest to that point.** This means that the instances for which the 1-nearest neighbour algorithm will assign the classification belonging to that training example. On the right side of the figure 2.9, is shown a shape of the **decision surface** made by 1-nearest neighbour over the complete instance space. *The decision surface is basically a grouping of convex polyhedral surrounding each of the training examples.* For every training example, the polyhedron shows the set of query points whose classification will be completely decided by that training example. **Also note that the query points that lie outside the polyhedron are closer to some other training example. And such a type of diagram is often called as the Voronoi diagram of the set of training examples.** The k-nearest neighbour algorithm is easily adapted to approximating continuous-valued target functions. To accomplish this, we need the algorithm to calculate the mean value of k-nearest training examples rather than calculate their most common value. Practically speaking, to estimate a real-valued target function f: $R^n \rightarrow R$, we replace the final line of the above algorithm by:

$$f'(x_q) = \Sigma \text{ (i=1 to k) } f(x_i) / k$$

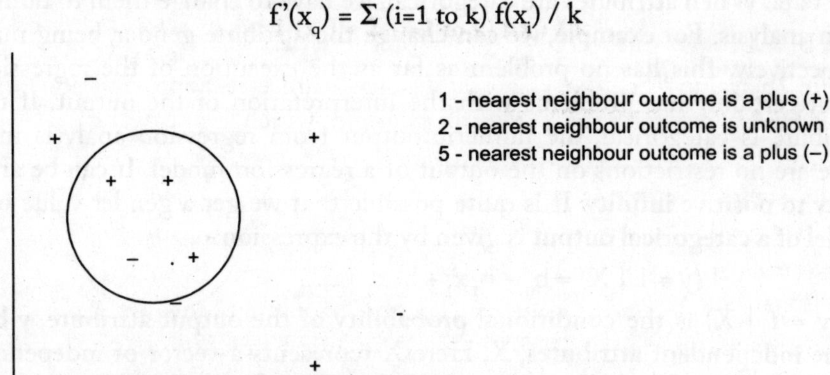

Fig.2.10: Accurate Estimate of Real-valued target Function

Distance weighted nearest-Neighbour Algorithm

This algorithm is an enhancement of k-nearest algorithm.

Principle: Weigh the contribution of each of the k-neighbours depending on their distance to query point, x, awarding greater weight to closer neighbours.

For example, in the algorithm of k-nearest above, that approximates discrete-valued target functions, we might weight the support of each neighbour corresponding to the inverse square of its distance from x_i. And this is done by interchanging the last line of the algorithm by:-

$$f'(x_q) \text{ ß argmax } (v \in V) \Sigma_{(i=1 \text{ to } k)} w_i \delta(v, f(x_i))$$

where $w_i = 1 / d(x_q, x_i)^2$

To consider the case where the query point, x, exactly matches one of the training instances, x_i and the denominator $d(x_q, x_i)^2$ is therefore zero, we assign $f'(x_q)$ to be $f'(x_i)$ in this particular case. We can distance-weight the instances for real-valued target functions in alike fashion, interchanging the final line in the algorithm in this case by-

$$f'(x_q) \text{ ß} \Sigma \text{ (i=1 to k) } w_i f(x_i) / k / \Sigma \text{ (i=1 to k) } w_i$$

where w_i is defined as above.

2.13 Curse of Dimensionality

Distance usually relates to all the attributes and assumes all of them have the same effects on the distance. The similarity metrics do not consider the relation of attributes which result in inaccurate distance and then impact on classification precision. **This wrong classification due to presence of many irrelevant attributes is often termed as the curse of dimensionality.**

For example, say each instance is described by 20 attributes out of which only 2 are relevant in determining the classification of the target function. In this case, instances that have identical values for the 2 relevant attributes may nevertheless be distant from one another in the 20 dimensional instance space.

2.14 Introduction to Logistic Regression

Logistics Regression was developed by statistician David Cox in 1958. Regression analysis needs always numeric data. When attributes are categorical, we have to change them to numeric values to apply regression analysis. **For example,** we can change the attribute gender, being male or female, to 0 and 1 respectively. This has no problem as far as the execution of the regression algorithm is concerned but certainly has problems with the interpretation of the output. If the output or dependent attribute is categorical, the numeric output from regression analysis may not make any sense. There are no restrictions on the output of a regression model. **It can be any value from negative infinity to positive infinity.** It is quite possible that we get a gender value of 0.5. So, the **regression model of a categorical output** is given by the expression:-

$$P(y = 1 \mid X) = b_0 + b_1 x_1 + b_2 x_2 + \ldots.. \quad (1)$$

Where, $P(y = 1 \mid X)$ is the **conditional probability of the output attribute, y being 1 given the values of the independent attributes, X.** Here X represents a vector of independent variables $x_1, x_2 \ldots..$ **Because** the value of probability lies within the range [0, 1], we can increase the range by considering the following ratio:-

$$\frac{P(y = 1 \mid X)}{1 - P(y = 1 \mid X)} \quad (2)$$

This can have the value between 0 and infinity. This is the **odds ratio, which can be interpreted as how often the class associated with y=1 is seen relative to other classes.** If we take the natural logarithm of this odds ratio, we will get an unbounded function from negative infinity to positive infinity since log 0 = -∞ and log ∞ = + ∞. So, we can write:-

$$\ln \frac{P(y = 1 \mid X)}{1 - P(y = 1 \mid X)} = b_0 + b_1 x_1 + b_2 x_2 + \ldots.. \quad (3)$$

Please note that this equation is also known as the ***logit*****.** On solving this equation we get:-

$$P(y = 1 \mid X) = \exp(b_0 + b_1 x_1 + b_2 x_2 + \ldots..) / 1 + \exp(b_0 + b_1 x_1 + b_2 x_2 + \ldots..) \quad (4)$$

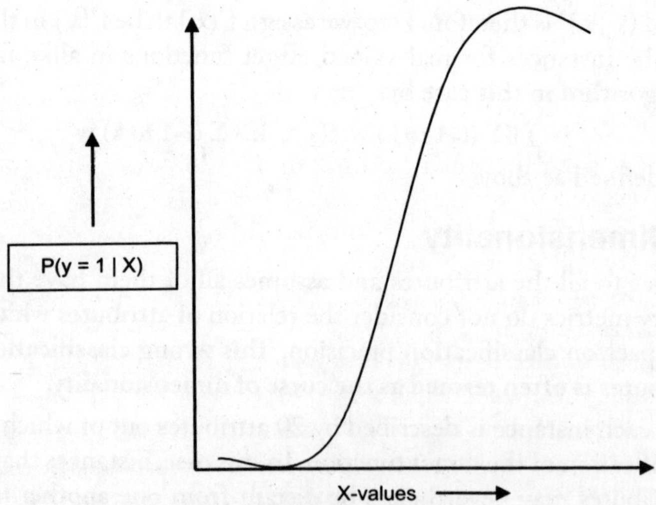

Fig.2.11: Graph of Logistic Regression Equation

This equation-4 is called as a **logistic regression model.** Here, the expression **exp** stands for the base of natural logarithm (e = 2.7182). If we plot this equation-4 then we will get an ***S-shaped curve*** as shown in figure 2.11.

To find the coefficients b_0, b_1, b_2, ... of equation-4, we use iterative method. The purpose of the method is to minimize the sum of logarithms of conditional probabilities. **Please understand that the aim of the method is to minimize the sum of logarithms of the conditional probabilities. Also note that convergence occurs when this value is close to zero or it does not change from one iteration to the next.**

Cases with more than two categories are called as **multinomial logistic regression.** If the multiple categories are ordered then it is **ordinal logistic regression.** The **binary logistic model** is used to estimate the probability of a binary response based on one or more predictor or independent variables features. It is also called as **qualitative response or discrete choice model** in economics field. Logistic regression measures the relationship between the categorical dependent variable and one or more independent variables by estimating probabilities using a logistice function, which is the **cumulative logistic distribution.**

Applications

Logistic regression is used in variious fields like machine learning, many medical fields and social sciences. **For example,** the Trauma and Injury Severity Score (TRISS), which is widely used to predict mortality in injured patients, was developed by Boyd et al. using Logistic regression only. It may be used to predict whether a patient has a given disease, based on observed characteristics of the patient.

Example 2, to predict whether an American voter will vote democratic or Republican, based on age, income, sex, race, previous votes etc.

Example 3, this technique can also be used in engineering field to predict the probability of failure of a given process, system or product.

Example 4, it is also used in marketing applications like prediction of a customer's propensity to purchase a product or halt a subscription etc.

Example 5, in economics, it can be used to predict the likelihood of a person's choosing to be in the labour force and a business application would be to predict the likelihood of a homeowner defaulting on a mortgage.

Example 6, conditional random fields that are an extension of logistic regression to sequential data, are used in NLP.

Logistic regression can be binomial, ordinal or multinomial. Binomial or binary logistic regression deals with situations in which the observed outcome for a dependent variable can have only two possible types like "win" or "loss". **Multinomial logistic regression** deals with situations where the outcome can have 3 or more possible types like disease A or disease B or disease C, that are not ordered. **Ordinal logistic regression deals** with dependent variables that are ordered. In **binary logistic regression,** the outcome is usually coded as "0" or "1", as this leads to the most straightforward interpretation. If a particular observed outcome for the dependent variable is the noteworthy possible outcome (referred to as a "success" or a "case") it is usually coded as "1" and the contrary outcome (referred to as a "failure" or a "noncase") as "0". **Please note that this** Logistic regression **is used to predict the odds of being a case based on the values of the independent variables/ predictors. Also note that the odds are defined as the probability that a particular outcome is a case divided by the probability that it is a noncase.**

Like other forms of Logistic regression analysis, Logistic regression makes use of one or more predictor variables that may be either continuous or categorical. However, unlike ordinary linear regression, logistic regression is used for predicting binary dependent variables rather than a continuous outcome. Given this difference, the assumptions of linear regression are violated. In particular, the residuals cannot be normally distributed. Also, linear regression may make non-sensical predictions for a binary dependent variable.

The aim is to find a way to convert a binary variable into a continuous one that can take on any real value (negative or positive). To do this, Logistic regression takes first takes the odd of the event happening for different levels of each independent variable then take the ratio of those odds (which is continuous but cannot be negative) and then takes the logarithm of that ratio. **This is referred to as logit or log-odds to create a continuous criterion as a transformed version of the dependent variable.** So, the logit transformation is referred to as the **link function in** Logistic regression although the dependent variable in logistic regression is binomial, the logit is the continuous criterion upon which linear regression is conducted. The logit of success is then fitted to the predictors using linear regression analysis. The predicted value of logit is converted back into predicted odds via the inverse of the natural logarithm, namely the **exponential function.** Although the observed dependent variable in logistic regression is a **zero-or-one variable,** the logistic regression estimates the odds as a continuous variable, that the dependent variable is a case. In some applications, the odds are all that are needed. In others, a specific yes-or-no prediction is needed for whether the dependent variable is or is not a case. This categorical prediction can be based on the computed odds on a success, with predicted odds above some chosen cut-off value being translated into a prediction of success.

Queries that can be answered here are like does body weight calorie intake, fat intake and age have an influence on heart attacks?

Assumptions made:

1. The outcome must be discrete.
2. The dependent variable should be dichotomous in nature like 'present' or 'absent'.
3. There should be no outliers in the data which can be assessed by converting the continuous predictors to standardized or z-scores and remove values below -5 or above 5.
4. There should be no high inter-correlations or multi-collinearity among the predictors. This can be assessed by a correlation matrix among the predictors.
5. Tabachnick et al. suggest that as long as correlation coefficients among independent variables are less than 0.90 the assumption is met.
6. Standard linear regression requires the dependent variable to be of metric (interval or ratio) scale.
7. Logistic regression assumes that the dependent variable is a stochastic event. For instance if we analyze a pesticide kill rate the outcome event is either killed or alive.
8. Since even the most resistant bug can only be either of these two states, logistic regression thinks in likelihoods of the bug getting killed. If the likelihood of killing the bug is > 0.5, it is assumed dead, if it is <0.5 then it is assumed alive.

2.15 Perceptron and Perceptron Learning Algorithm (PLA)

According to Minsky et al. a perceptron is defined as **"A machine which learns from examples, to assign input samples (vectors) to different classes using a linear function of inputs"**. Simply stated, it is a neural network used for pattern classification. It consists of a single neuron with adjustable synaptic weights. It is also possible to expand the output layer of perceptron to include more than one neuron. So, they are also called as **weighted networks.** There are two types of perceptions as follows:

(a) Single layer perception.

(b) Multi layer perception.

Single layer perception: A single layer perceptron is shown in figure 2.12. It consists up of an input layer and an output layer with **adjustable weights and a bias.** It is used for classification of patterns that are linearly separable. The perception algorithm converges and positions the **decision surface** in the form of a hyper plane between the two classes. The limitation of this network is that it performs pattern classification with only two classes which are linearly separable. **Please understand that the linearity and integrity learning makes the single layer perception network very simple. Also understand that the training in the perception continues till no error occurs.**

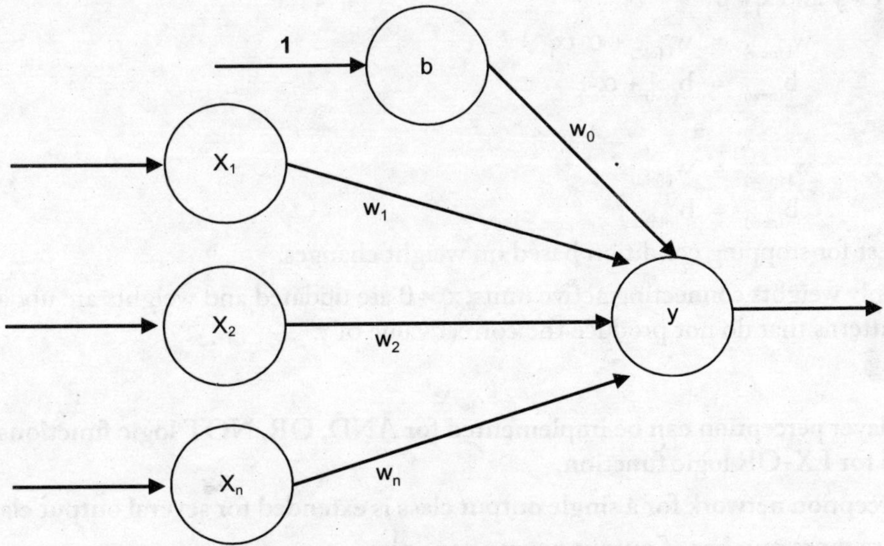

Fig.2.12: Single Layer Perceptron

In this network, only the weights between the **associator** and the **response unit** are adjusted. The input layer consists of input neurons from $x_1, x_2, ..., x_n$. **There always exists a common bias "1".** The output is compared with this target, if any difference occurs, update weights else stop training process.

In machine learning, the perceptron is an algorithm for supervised learning of binary classifiers i.e. functions that can decide whether an input represented by a vector of numbers, belongs to some specified class or not.

The Training Algorithm

Step-1: Initialize weights and bias to zero and set learning rate, $\alpha = 0$ to 1.

Step-2: While stopping condition is false do step-3 to step-7.

Step-3: For each training pair s: t do step-4 to step-6.

Step-4: Set activation of input units-

$$x_i = s_j \text{ for } i = 1 \text{ to } n.$$

Step-5: Determine the output unit response-

$$y_{in} = b + \Sigma\,(i = 1 \text{ to } n)\, x_i\, w_i$$

Where the activation function is-

$$y = f(y_{in}) = \begin{cases} = 1, \text{ if } y_{in} \geq \theta \\ = 0, \text{ if } y_{in} = -\theta \text{ to } \theta \\ = -1, \text{ if } y_{in} < -\theta \end{cases}$$

Step-6: Observe the match between the target and the output response. If they do not match, update the weights and bias. So,

if $t \neq y$ and $x_i \neq 0$

$$w_{i\,(new)} = w_{i\,(old)} + \alpha\, tx_i$$
$$b_{(new)} = b_{(old)} + \alpha_t$$

else

$$w_{i\,(new)} = w_{i\,(old)}$$
$$b_{(new)} = b_{(old)}$$

Step-7: Test for stopping condition based on weight changes.

Step-8: Only weights connecting active units, $x_i \neq 0$ are updated and weights are updated only for patterns that do not produce the correct value of y.

Notes:

1. **Single layer perception can be implemented for AND, OR, NOT logic functions but cannot be used for EX-OR logic function.**
2. **The perception network for a single output class is extended for several output classes.**
3. **There are more number of output neurons or units.**
4. **The weight updated in this case is also based on the perception learning rule.**

2.16 Exponential Family

In probability field, an exponential family is a set of probability distributions of a certain form. This special form is chosen for mathematical convenience, on account of some useful algebraic properties as well as for generality, as exponential families are in a sense of very natural sets of distributions to consider. In 1935, Pitman et al. gave this concept of **exponential families/exponential family.** The exponential families include many of the most common distributions including the normal, exponential, gamma, chi-squared, beta, Bernoulli, Poisson, Inverse Wishart etc. A number of common distributions are exponential families only when certain parameters are considered fixed and known e.g. binomial (with fixed number of trials), multinomial (with fixed number of trials) and negative bionomial (with fixed number of failures).

2.17 Generative Model and Generative Learning Algorithm (GLA)

A generative model is a model for randomly generating observable data values, typically given some hidden parameters. It specifies a joint probability distribution over observation and label sequences. **Note that generative models are used in machine learning for either modelling data directly** i.e. modelling observations drawn from a probability density function, or as an intermediate step to form a conditional probability density function. A conditional distribution can be formed from a generative model through Baye's rule. Generative learning is a theory that involves the active integration of new ideas with the learners existing schemata. **The main idea is that in order to learn with understanding, a learner has to construct meaning actively.** According to Wittrock, learners construct meaning by actively building relationships between stimuli and their stored information such as knowledge and their experiences. This construction of **semantic and distinctive idiosyncratic associations between stimuli and stored information is called as generation.** So, we can say that Generative Learning **is the process of constructing meaning through generating relationships and associations between stimuli and existing knowledge, beliefs and experiences.**

Shannon in 1948, gave an example of in which a table of frequencies of English word pairs is used to generate a sentence beginning with "representing and speedily is an good"; which is not proper English but which will increasingly approximate it as the table is moved from word pairs to word triplets etc.

Generative Models v/s Discriminative Models

A **Generative model** is a full probabilistic model of all variables while a discriminative model provides a model only for the target variables conditional on the observed variables **for example,** generative model can be used to simulate values of any variable in the model. On the other hand, **discriminative model** allows only the sampling of the target variables conditional on the observed quantities. Despite of the fact that descriptive model do not need to model the distribution of the observed variables, they cannot generally express more complex relationships between the observed and target variables. They do not necessarily perform better than generative models at classification and regression tasks. In modern applications, the two classes are complementary to each other.

Some examples of Generative models are:-

(a) Gaussian mixture model.

(b) Naive Baye's.

(c) Context-free Grammar.

(d) Hidden Markov Model.

(e) Restricted Boltzman Machine.

(f) Generative Adversial Networks.

Please note that if the observed data are truly samples from the generative model then fitting parameters of the generative model to maximize the data likelihood is a common method. But since most of the statistical models are only approximations to the true distributions, if the model's application is to infer about a subset of variables conditional on known values of others then it can be argued that the approximation makes more assumptions than are necessary to solve the problem at hand. In such cases, it can be more accurate to model the conditional density functions directly using a discriminative model. But the application-specific details will ultimately dictate which approach is most suitable in any particular case.

Generative model in context of Machine Learning

A generative algorithm models how the data was generated in order to categorize a signal. It answers to queries like 'based on my generation assumptions, which category is most likely to generate this signal? **A discriminative algorithm** does not care about how the data was generated, it simply categorizes a given signal.

Example: Say, the input data is x and the set of labels for x is y. A generative model learns the joint probability distribution p(x, y) while a discriminative model learns the conditional probability distribution p (y | x) i.e. the probability of y given x.

Discriminative algorithms tries to learn p (y | x) directly from the data and then tries to classify data. On the other hand, **generative algorithm** tries to learn p(x, y) which can be transformed into p (x | y) later to classify the data. One of the benefits of generative algorithms is that you can use p(x, y) to generate new data similar to the existing data. On the other hand, **discriminative algorithms** generally give better performance in classification tasks.

Some examples of **Discriminative models** are:-

(a) Logistic Regression.

(b) Support Vector Machines.

(c) Neural Networks.

(d) Conditional Random Fields.

2.18 Guassian Discriminant Analysis

Guassian Discriminant Analysis (GDA) is a method for data classification commonly used when data can be approximated with a normal distribution.

The first step needs a training set i.e. a bunch of data yet classified. These data are used to train your classifier and obtain a discriminant function that will tell you to which class a data has higher probability to belong. When you have your training set, you need to compute the mean and the standard deviation. These two variables allow us to compute normal distribution. Once you have computed the normal distribution for each class, to classify a data you will need to compute, for each one, the probability that the data belongs to. **Note that the class with the highest probability will be chosen as the affinity class.** GDA is a generative model for classification where the distribution of each class is modelled as a multivariate Gaussian. GDA is a generative learning algorithm. In this model, we will assume that P(x | y) is distributed according to a multivariate normal distribution.

Note: We make stronger assumptions in GDA. If we do not know where the data comes from then the logistic regression analysis would be more robust. But if we know then GDA may perform better.

2.19 Naive Bayes and its Algorithm

It is a supervised machine learning algorithm. It is often associated with NLP (Natural Language Processing) applications like spam recognition or sentiment analysis.

By the term **'naive'** we mean **"immature"**. A naive Bayes classifier is a simple probability-based algorithm. It uses Bayes theorem. It assumes that instances are independent of each other. They work very well in complex real world scenarios also. The naive Bayes algorithm offers a fast model building and scoring both for binary and multiclass situations for relatively low volumes of data. According to Hand et al., 2001, this algorithm makes predictions using Bayes theorem which includes evidence or prior knowledge in its prediction.

Tool like WEKA also uses this naive Bayes algorithm on the dataset provided to it. In WEKA, there is an option of naive Bayes classifier under **'bayes' subdirectory.** Then in next step we keep the **default settings** of the Weka environment and the classifiers parameters. Next, we click on the Start button and the program executes and we will get the needed analysis. Thus, this model is used for analysis of the input dataset. Naive Bayes is a simple technique for constructing classifiers-models that assign class labels to problem instances that are represented as vectors of feature values. The class labels are drawn from some finite set.

Principle: "All Naive Bayes classifiers assume that the value of a particular feature is independent of the value of any other feature, given the class variable."

For example, a rectangle may be considered to be a whiteboard if it has a length, breadth and some thickness. A **Naive Bayes classifier** considers each of these features to contribute independently to the probability that this rectangle is a whiteboard, regardless of any possible correlations between the color, its shape and its thickness.

Note that for some types of probability models, Naive Bayes classifiers can be trained very efficiently in a supervised learning setting. Practically, parameter estimation for **Naive Bayes models** uses the method of maximum likelihood. In other words, one can work with **Naive Bayes model** without accepting Bayesian methods. The advantage of this is that it requires only a small number of training data to estimate the parameters necessary for classification. As far as machine learning is concerned, Naive Bayes classifiers are a family of simple probabilistic classifiers based on applying Baye's theorem with strong independence assumptions between the features.

Naive Bayes classifiers have been studied extensively since 1950s. It forms the baseline for text catagorization. With suitable pre-processing, it is competitive in this domain with more advanced methods including support vector machines. Also it has some applications in automatic medical diagnosis. **Naive Bayes classifiers are highly scalable,** requiring a number of parameters linear in the number of variables (features/ predictors) in a learning problem. **Also note that maximum-likelihood training can be done by evaluating a closed-form expression, which takes linear time rather than by expensive iterative approximation as used for many other types of classifiers.**

Advantages of Naive Bayes Algorithm:

1. The algorithm as well as its implementation process is simple. Calculations do not involve any numerical optimization, no matrix algebra and no calculus.
2. The algorithm is efficient to train and use. It can be easily updated with new data. This algorithm is similar to linear classifier and hence is fast too.

3. From one dataset we can estimate content features from messages without headers.
4. Unlabelled data can be used in parameter estimation for other applications. This algorithm performs well with smaller training sets.

Disadvantages of Naive Bayes Algorithm:-

1. The independence assumption is a very strong inference and untrue for most real world problems.
2. The boundaries between classes have to be fine tuned and not to be set analytically.
3. It is not very effective algorithm as it is simple.

Applications of Naive Bayes Algorithm:

1. The classifiers used in text classification have higher success rate as compared to other algorithms. As a result, it is widely used in spam filtering i.e. identifying spam e-mail and sentiment analysis i.e. in social media analysis to identify positive and negative customer sentiments.
2. Naive Bayes classifier and collaborative filtering together builds a recommendation system that uses machine learning and data mining techniques to filter unseen information and predict whether a user would like a given resource or not.
3. It is an eager learning classifier and is thus fast. It could be used for making predictions in real-time too.
4. It can be used to do parameter estimation for any model application.
5. It can be used for document classification also.
6. In medical diagnosis field, it has been used for localization of primary tumour, thyroid diseases etc.

2.20 Support Vector Machines (SVMs)

SVM belongs to the type of **supervised learning** methods used for **classification and regression.** **SVM were developed by Vladimir Vapnik et al. in 1998 at UK.** Statistical learning became important after its introduction.

Basic idea: Construct a hyper plane that best separates classes. If this is not feasible in the input space then the goal is achieved in a higher dimensional space called as a **feature space,** reached by mapping the input vector through a non-linear function.

This mapping has a property that will linearly separate the data sets in the feature space. The hyper plane in the feature space will maximally separate the data set classes. The method is based on **statistical learning theory** and is successfully used in a number of applications like particle identification, face detection, text categorization. Technically speaking, it is mathematically intuitive, reproducible and does not have problems of **local minima** as the optimization function is **convex** and is robust to new classification data tasks.

In machine learning, SVMs or Support Vector Networks are supervised learning models with associated learning algorithms that analyze data used for classification and regression analysis. Given a set of training examples, each marked as belonging to one or the other of two categories, an SVM training algorithm builds a model that assigns new examples to one category or the other, making it a non-probabilistic **binary linear classifier.** An SVM model is a representation of the examples as points in space, mapped so that the examples of the separate categories are divided by a clear gap that is as wide as possible. Then new examples are mapped into that same space and predicted to belong to a category based on which side of the gap they fall. SVMs can also perform a non-linear classification using what is called the kernel trick i.e. implicitly mapping their inputs into high dimensional feature spaces. When data are not labelled, supervised learning is not possible and an unsupervised learning approach is required, which attempts to find natural clustering of the data to groups and then map new data to these formed groups. The clustering algorithm which provides an improvement to SVM is called **support vector clustering.** It is often used in industrial applications either when data are not labelled or when only some data are labelled as a pre-processing for a classification pass.

This is shown in figure 2.10.

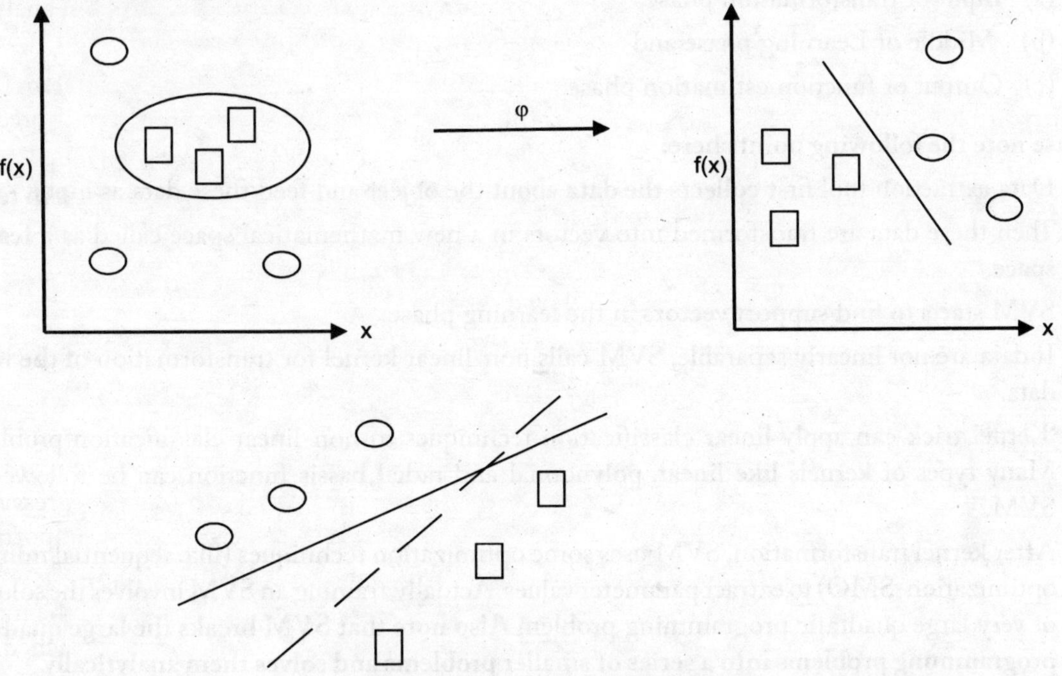

Fig.2.13: Data sets and their Separation

The upper part of the figure 2.10 shows the mapping of the training data non-linearly into a higher dimensional feature space and constructs a hyperplane with maximum margins. The lower part of the figure 2.10 shows two potential hyperplanes that separate data sets. A hyperplane is a concept in geometry. **Please note that hyperplane is a generalization of the concept of a plane which is used in SVM implementation for object separation. Also note that a hyperplane that separates the data points in the feature space with maximum distances among the classes in SVM is called as a maximum-margin hyperplane or optimal hyperplane.** The data points on the outer margins/ outside ovals and the inner margins/ inside ovals that are on the boundary lines are called as **support vectors.**

Support vectors or SVs are transformed training patterns that are always placed at the optimal hyperplane in the feature space during SVM LEARNING. SVM is a statistical based learning algorithm that has been widely used by researchers in various fields like business, text categorization, pattern recognition abd protein function prediction. Recently, researchers added a new dimension to SVM in cancer classification through its ability to deal with high dimensional data. SVM can handle any classification, clustering, regression and even novelty detection problems. The attractiveness of SVM algorithm lies in the fact that we do not have to consider all instances i.e. we can focus on the support vectors to do the analysis.

Algorithm: SVM

SVM architecture is analogous to neural network architecture. Like we have three layers of neural networks, similarly we have three phases of SVM-

(a) Input or transformation phase,
(b) Middle or Learning phase and
(c) Output or function estimation phase.

Please note the following points here:

1. Data extraction tool first **collects the data** about the object and feed these data as input.
2. Then these data are transformed into vectors in a new mathematical space called as a **feature space.**
3. SVM starts to find **support vectors** in the learning phase.
4. If data are not linearly separable, SVM calls non-linear kernel for transformation of the input data.
5. 'Kernel trick' can apply linear classification techniques to non-linear classification problems. Many types of kernels like linear, polynomial and radial bassis function can be followed by SVM.
6. After kernel transformation, SVM uses some optimization techniques (like sequential minimal optimization-SMO) to extract parameter values. Actually, training an SVM involves the solution of very large quadratic programming problem **Also note that SVM breaks the large quadratic programming problems into a series of smaller problems and solves them analytically.**
7. **Large quadratic programming problems have only one minimum.** So, SVMs do not suffer from finding local minima problems as they are in neural networks.
8. **The amount of memory required for SMO is linear with the training set size, which allows it to handle very larger training sets also.**
9. The time taken by SMO depends on the SVM's evaluation only. So, SMO is faster for linear SVMs and sparse datasets.
10. During optimization, SVM will try to find the support vectors for prediction.
11. SVM model can be constructed through WEKA tool. **Please note that SVM's default kernel is polynomial in WEKA.**

Advantages of SVM

Some of the advantages of SVM are as follows:

1. They can not only solve binary class pattern recognition problems but also for multiclass classification, regression estimation, feature selection etc.
2. Lesser chances of information loss as SVM kernel considers the dot product of the feature vectors in high dimensional space to construct the optimal hyperplane rather than clustering or interpolating in input space. SVM can handle a large number of attributes of a data set unlike neural nets **as these traditional algorithms need reduction of dimensionality i.e. the number of attributes, before they can be applied to a high dimensional problem.**
3. Even in the field of bioinformatics, it has proven to be useful as there we have more than 20,000 attributes.
4. They are very versatile as they have many extensions too like Support Vector Decision Tree, neural network based SVM, fuzzy SVM etc.

Disadvantages of SVM

Some of the disadvantages of SVM are as follows:-

1. The best choice of kernel for a given problem is still an issue in research work.
2. Its speed and size during training and testing is still an issue. Training for very large datasets / millions of support vectors is still an unsolved problem.
3. It lacks efficiency in solving of multi-class problems. It is still an active research area.

Applications of SVM

Some of the applications of SVMs are listed below.

1. They have been used to study financial forecasting.
2. Spatial and temporal environmental data can be analysed to find patterns and trends using SVMs.
3. In field of biology also SVMs have proven to be very useful, particularly for remote homology detection.
4. They have been used for face expression classification.
5. They have been used for e-learning.
6. They have been used to control traffic congestion problems.

2.21 Combining Classifiers

When designing any pattern recognition systems, the objective is to achieve the best possible classification performance for the task in hand. So, different classification schemes are developed. Based on the results, one of the possible classifiers can be used as a final solution to the problem. **Please note here that although one of the designs would yield the best performance, the sets of patterns misclassified by the different classifiers would not necessarily overlap.** This suggested that different classifier designs potentially offered complementary information about the patterns to be classified which could be harnessed to improve the performance of the selected classifier. These observations motivated in combining of classifiers. One should not rely on single decision making scheme. In fact, all the designs or their subsets are used for decision making by combining their individual opinions. **Also note that it has been found that better results are achieved if classifiers are combined rather than single classifier.**

There are two reasons as to why should we combine classifiers-

(a) Efficiency.

(b) Accuracy.

Now to get efficiency, we can use **multistage combination rules** wherein objects are classified by a simple classifier using a small set of cheap features in combination with a reject option. **Note that for more difficult objects, more complex procedures based on different features are used.** Classifiers are useful when they are different. And this can be done by using different feature sets and different training sets. There are two types of classifier combinations:

Case 1: All classifiers use the same representation of the input pattern. **For example,** a set of k-nearest neighbour classifiers, each using the same measurement vector but different classifier parameters.

Case 2: Each classifier uses its own representation of the input pattern i.e. the measurements extracted from the pattern are unique to each classifier.

Application of combining classifiers: Integrate physically different types of features. It is no longer possible to consider the computed aposteriori probabilities to be the estimates of the same functional value as the classification systems operate in different measurement spaces.

2.22 Evaluating Machine Learning Algorithms

The standard approach followed is that we divide data into training set and testing sets, train method on training set and report results on the training set. **But please understand that the testing set is not the same as the validation test.**

Procedure to evaluate ML algorithm

S1: Break all of the data into training/ testing sets.

S2: Break training set into training or validation set.

S3: Choose hyper-parameters using validation set.

S4: (optional step) Once we have selected the hyper-parameters, retrain using whole of the training set.

S5: Evaluate performance on the testing set.

2.23 Classification Errors

The classification error, E_i of an individual program, i, depends on the number of samples incorrectly classified (false positives and false negatives) and is computed by the formula:-

$$E_i = f / n * 100$$

Where,

'f' is the number of sample cases incorrectly classified.

'n' is the total number of sample cases.

In supervised learning applications in machine learning and statistical learning theory, **generalization error/out-of-sample error, is a measure of how accurately an algorithm is able to predict outcome values for previously unseen data.** The evaluation of a learning algorithm may be sensitive to the sampling error because learning algorithms are evaluated on finite samples. So, the measurements of prediction error on the current data may not provide much information about the predictive ability on new data. **Please note that this generalization error can be mitigated by avoiding overfitting in the learning algorithm. Also note that the performance of a machine learning algorithm is measured by plots of the generalization error values through the learning process, that are called as the learning curves.**

Summary

We have studied in this chapter that in machine learning instead of teaching a computer a massive list of rules to solve a problem, we give it a model with which it can evaluate examples. Also we give a small set of instructions to modify this model if it makes a mistake. We find that as the time passes by, well suited model will be able to solve the problems in a better and efficient way. The machine learning algorithm should be such that it tries to make the values of the parameters more and more accurate as it is exposed to more and more examples. But this is just a tip of an iceberg. Recently, scientists have developed the models that resemble the structures as used by a human brain. This involves deep learning only.

MULTIPLE CHOICE QUESTIONS (MCQs)

1. Predicting the price of a house given its size is an example of-
   (a) Supervised learning. (b) Unsupervised learning.
   (c) Remote learning. (d) None of the above.
2. The inherent groupings in the data discovered is known as-
   (a) Association. (b) Clustering.
   (c) Classifying. (d) None of the above.
3. Discovering rules that describes large portions of data is called as-
   (a) Association. (b) Clustering.
   (c) Classifiers. (d) None of the above.
4. Conditional models are also known as-
   (a) Demand models. (b) Discriminative models.
   (c) Generative models. (d) None of the above.
5. Logistic regression is also named as-
   (a) Login regression. (b) Logit regression.
   (c) Logout regression. (d) None of the above.
6. Naive Bayes is an example of-
   (a) Generative model. (b) Discriminative model.
   (c) SVM. (d) None of the above.

7. A common task in machine learning is-
   (a) Common data. (b) Classifying data.
   (c) Global data. (d) None of the above.
8. The classification error, E_i of an individual program, i, depends on the number of samples incorrectly classified (false positives and false negatives) and is computed by the formula:-
   (a) Ei = f / n * 100 (b) Ei = f* n * 100
   (c) Ei = f + n * 100 (d) None of the above.
9. PCA stands for-
   (a) Peer Component Analysis. (b) Principal Component Analysis.
   (c) Power Component Analysis. (d) None of the above.
10. Singular Value Decomposition is used in-
    (a) Latent Semantic Indexing. (b) Lateral Simple Indexing.
    (c) Lower Simple Indexing. (d) None of the above.
11. SVM stands for-
    (a) Support Vector Machine. (b) Simple Vector Machine.
    (c) Super Vector Machine. (d) None of the above.
12. A generalization of the concept of a plane which is used in SVM implementation for object separation is known as-
    (a) Hyperplane. (b) Airplane.
    (c) Aeroplane. (d) None of the above.
13. A model evaluation technique which is collection of methods used to examine the underlying constructs influence of the response of variables is-
    (a) Factor Analysis. (b) ICA.
    (c) PCA. (d) Singular Value Composition.

Answers

a	2. b	3. b	4. b	5. b
6. a	7. b	8. a	9. b	10. a
11. a	12. a	13. a		

Conceptual Short Questions with Answers

Q1. What are the differences between data mining and machine learning?

Ans. **Data mining** is the process in which the unstructured data puts efforts to extract knowledge or unfamiliar interesting patterns. On the other hand, **machine learning** relates to the study, design and development of the algorithms that give systems the ability to learn without being clearly programmed.

Q2. Give functions supervised and unsupervised learning.

Ans. **Supervised learning** involves-

(a) Classifications.

(b) Speech recognition.

(c) Regression.

(d) Predict time series.

(e) Annotate strings.

On the other hand, **unsupervised learning** involves-

(a) Finding the clusters of data.

(b) Finding low dimensional representations of data.

(c) Finding interesting coordinates and correlations.

(d) Finding novel observations or cleaning databases.

Q3. What is inductive machine learning?

Ans. **Inductive machine learning covers the process of learning by examples** where a system, from a set of perceived instances, tries to encourage a general rule.

Q4. List at least five common machine learning algorithms.

Ans. Some of the popular ML algorithms are as follows:-

(a) Decision Trees.

(b) Neural Networks.

(c) Probabilistic Networks.

(d) Nearest Neighbour.

(e) Support Vector Machines (SVM).

Q5. Name different algorithm techniques in ML.

Ans. Different types of techniques in ML are as follows:-

(a) Supervised learning.

(b) Unsupervised learning.

(c) Semi-supervised learning.

(d) Reinforcement learning.

(e) Transduction.

(f) Learning to learn.

Q6. Name three stages to build the models (or hypotheses) in machine learning.

Ans. Three stages to build the models in machine learning (ML) are as follows:-

(a) Model building.

(b) Model testing.

(c) Applying the model.

Q7. What is the standard approach to supervised learning?

Ans. The standard approach to supervised learning is to break the data set of example into training set and the test set.

Q8. Differentiate between 'training set' and 'test set'.

Ans. In different fields of data science like machine learning, a set of data is used to determine the potentially predictive relationship identified as **training set.** Training set is the example provided to the learner while test set is used to test the exactness of the hypotheses produced by the learner and it is the set of illustration weighed down from the learner. So, training sets are different from test sets.

Q9. What are the different approaches of machine learning?

Ans. Different approaches of machine learning are as follows:-

(a) Concept versus Classification Learning.

(b) Symbolic versus Statistical Learning.

(c) Inductive versus Analytical Learning.

Q10. Define Overfitting during machine learning. Why it happens?

Ans. In ML, overfitting occurs when a statistical model defines a random error or noise rather than underlying relationship. When a model is extremely complex, overfitting is usually observed because of having too many parameters relating to the number of training data types. The model exihibits poor performance which has to be overfit. The risk of overfitting exists as the standards used for training the model is not the same as the standards used to judge the effectiveness of a model.

Q11. How can overfitting be avoided?

Ans. By means of loads of data, overfitting can be avoided. **Overfitting** happens when comparatively you have a small dataset and you make effort to learn from it. But if you have a small database and it is necessary to come with a model based on that then in such a scenario, **cross validation** method may be used. In this method, the dataset is divided into two segments, testing and training datasets. The testing dataset will only test the model while in training dataset, the data-points will come up with a model. In this method, a model is generally provided with a dataset of known data on which training data set is run and a dataset of unknown data against which the model is tested. **The basic idea of cross validation is to define a dataset to test the model in the training phase.**

Q12. What is algorithm independent machine learning?

Ans. A type of machine learning in which mathematical foundations is independent of any particular classifier or learning algorithm is known as **algorithm independent machine learning.**

Q13. Distinguish between AI and machine learning.

Ans. Designing and developing algorithms according to the behaviours based on empirical data is known as machine learning. On the other hand, artificial intelligence, in addition to machine learning, also covers other aspects like knowledge representation, natural language processing (NLP), planning, robotics etc.

Q14. Define classifier as used in machine learning.

Ans. A classifier is a system that inputs a vector of discrete or continuous feature vales and outputs a single discrete value, the class.

Q15. Where is pattern recognition used?

Ans. It is used in computer vision, speech recognition, data mining, statistics, information retrieval and bio-informatics.

Q16. What is model selection in ML?

Ans. **The process of selecting the models from different mathematical models that refer to the same data set is called as model selection. It is applied to the fields of statistics, machine learning and data mining.**

Q17. Name the method that is frequently used to prevent overfitting.

Ans. 'Isotonic Regression' is used to prevent overfiting when the data is sufficient.

Q18. Why instance-based learning algorithm is sometimes also referred to as lazy-learning algorithm?

Ans. Instance-based learning algorithm is sometimes also referred to as lazy-learning algorithm because they delay the induction or generalization process until classification is performed.

Q19. What are the 2 classification methods that SVM handle?

Ans. The two classification methods that SVM can handle are as follows:-

(a) Combining binary classifiers.

(b) Modifying binary to incorporate multiclass learning.

Q20. For what purpose PCA and ICA are used?

Ans. PCA and ICA are used to extract features of data to reduce dimensions of data. They are important feature extraction techniques used for dimensionality reduction.

Q21. What do you mean by dimension reduction?

Ans. It is the process of reducing the number of random variables under considerations and can be divided into feature selection and feature extraction.

Q22. What are SVMs?

Ans. SVMs or Support Vector Machines are supervised learning algorithms that are used for classification and regression analysis.

Q23. What are the different methods to solve sequential supervised learning problems?

Ans. The different methods to solve sequential supervised learning problems are:-

(a) Sliding window methods.

(b) Recurrent sliding windows.

(c) Hidden Makov Models.

(d) Maximum entropy Markov Models.
(e) Conditional random fields.
(f) Graph transformer networks.

Q24. Name two techniques of ML. Give a very popular application of ML that you see everyday.

Ans. Genetic programming and inductive learning are the two methods of ML.

The recommendation engine implemented by major ecommerce websites uses machine learning (ML).

Q25. How is KNN different from k-means clustering?

Ans. k-nearest neighbours is a supervised classification algorithm. On the other hand, k-means clustering is an unsupervised clustering algorithm. In order for k-nearest neighbours to work, labelled data is needed that we want to classify an unlabeled point. In case of k-means clustering only a set of unlabelled points and a threshold is required. The algorithm will take unlabelled points in consideration and slowly learn how to cluster them into groups by computing the mean of the distance between different points. In nutshell, KNN needs labelled points and is thus supervised learning while k-means doesn't need labelled points and is thus unsupervised learning.

Q26. Why is "Naive" Bayes naive?

Ans. Even though it has practical applications, specially in text mining, Naive Bayes is still considered as **Naive** because the assumption that it makes becomes virtually impossible to be seen in real-life data. The conditional probability is computed as purely the product of the individual probabilities of different components. This denotes the absolute independence of features i.e. a condition that is probably never met in real life.

Q27. Differentiate between a generative and discriminative model.

Ans. A generative model learns categories of data while a discriminative model merely learns the distinction between different categories of data. Discriminative models will leave behind generative models on the basis of classification tasks.

Q28. Name at least three methods of reducing dimensionality.

Ans. The three methods of reducing dimensionality are as follows:-

(a) Removing collinear features.
(b) Performing PCA, ICA or other forms of algorithmic dimensionality reduction.
(c) Combining features with feature engineering.

Q29. What is the EM technique? How this algorithm works?

Ans. EM is an algorithm for maximizing a likelihood function when some of the variables in the model are unobserved i.e. when there are latent variables with you. To solve for our model parameters you need to know **the distribution of your unobserved data** but the **distribution of your unobserved data is a function of your model parameters.** EEM tries to get around this by guessing repeatedly about the distribution for the unobserved data then further estimating the model parameters by maximizing something that is lower bound on the actual likelihood function and repeating until convergence.

The EM algorithm starts with a guess for values of your model parameters as follows:-

The E-step: For each data point that has some missing values to solve for the distribution of the missing data, use your model equation, provided with your current guess of the model parameters and given the observed data. **Please note that you are solving for a distribution for each missing value and not for the expected value. Also note that now we have available with us a distribution for each missing value, we can calculate the expectation of the likelihood function with respect to the unobserved variables.** If our guess for the model parameter was correct, this expected likelihood will be the actual likelihood of our observed data. If the parameters were not correct, it will just be a lower bound.

The M-step: Now that we have got an expected likelihood function with no unobserved variables in it, maximize the function as you would in the fully observed case, to get a new estimate of your model parameters.

Repeat till convergence.

Q30. What do you mean by curse of dimensionality?

Ans. The curse of dimensionality refers to the tendency of a state space to grow exponentially in its dimension i.e. in the number of state variables.

Q31. What is H2O? What is prcomp?

Ans. H2O is software for machine learning and data analysis. PCA is named as **prcomp** in H2O and R system.

Q32. What is the principle of operation of the back-propagation algorithm?

Ans. Firstly, the inputs from the training data are propagated through the network to the output. Then the model outputs are compared with the actual outputs. The difference is the error. This error is then fed into the network backwards and connections weights are adjusted.

Q33. Define the following:-

(a) **Learning rate.**

(b) **Momentum.**

Ans. (a) **Learning rate:** A higher value of learning rate will make the algorithm converge more rapidly towards the desired values but it will reduce the stability of the algorithm.

(b) **Momentum:** It is used to control oscillations in weights which could be caused by alternately signed error signals.

Q34. WEKA tool may be used to construct neural network. Can it do the parameter value selection also for neural networks?

Ans. A neural network trains by repeated passes of the data. Each pass is called an **epoch. With each epoch, the connecting weights are adjusted until a satisfactory level of performance is reached.** We can ponder that if 50 epochs are good then 80 epochs should be better. But this argument does not hold with neural networks. With too many passes the network may over-train also. **Please understand that a well trained neural network model would show similar performance levels with both test and training data. Also understand that keeping this in mind we can change the parameter values of the algorithm.** We should not assume that default parameters are the best. We can change the parameters too. As the number of epochs increases we need more time for training. If we compare the outputs from the two different epochs, we can see the accuracy remains at the same level of 97.2%. that is why we say that higher the number of epochs has not improved the model performance. **Just keep in mind that we should restrict ourselves to the lower number of epochs as it not only involves less computing time but also lowers the danger of over-fitting.**

Q35. Define the following terms:

(a) Activation function.

(b) Back-propagation learning.

(c) Delta rule.

(d) Epoch.

(e) Feedforward neural networks.

(f) Genetic algorithm.

(g) Hyperplane.

(h) Kernel.

Ans.

(a) **Activation function:** A function that describes the output behaviours of a neuron in neural network.

(b) **Back-propagation learning:** It is a form of supervised learning used to train mainly, feedforward neural networks, that works by making modifications in weights values, starting at the output layer and then moving backwards through the hidden layer.

(c) **Delta Rule:** The delta rule changes the weight vector for a neural network in such a way that the error is reduced.

(d) **Epoch:** It is one complete pass of the entire training set through the neural network. The learning process is repeated epoch-by-epoch until the averaged square error converges to a minimum value.

(e) **Feedforward neural network:** It is a sort of ANN where connections between the units do not form a directed cycle.

(f) **Genetic algorithm:** It is an adaptive heuristic search algorithm premised on the evolutionary ideas of natural selection theory.

(g) **Hyperplane:** A plane (as in geometry) that is used to do object separation during SVM implementation.

(h) **Kernel:** Linear, polynomial and rbf are some of the kernels of SVM that allows SVM to fit the maximum margin hyperplane in the transformed feature space.

Q36. Tabulate the differences between supervised and unsupervised learning.

Ans. The following are the points of differences:

Supervised Learning	Unsupervised Learning
It incorporates **an external teacher** so that each output unit is told what should be the desired response to that input signal.	Uses no **external teacher.**
Global error signals govern learning.	**Local information** is used for learning.
Uses pattern class information of each training pattern.	Adaptively clusters patterns to generate decision codes.
Paradigms are error correction learning, reinforcement learning and stochastic learning.	Paradigms are Hebbian learning and competitive learning.
Learning is usually **off line.** It means that learning and operation phases are different. In off-line learning, all of the given patterns are used together.	Learning is **online.** It means that the agent learns and operates at the same time. Here, the information in each new pattern is incorporated into the agent.
All learning data are stored and can be accessed repeatedly. So, we can see whether we are making progress in training or not.	Locality allows learning in **real time.** So, the progress cannot be monitored.
Inputs and outputs are defined.	Only inputs are defined.
Uses pattern class information of each training pattern.	Adaptively clusters patterns to generate decision class without any prior pattern class information.
Global error signal governs learning.	Local information/ rules are used for learning.
Learning is offline usually.	Locality allows **synapses** to learn in real-time.

Q37. Explain different nets classes.

Ans. It is put under 2 main categories as follows:

I. **Unsupervised learning (i.e. without a teacher):**

1. Feedback Nets:
   (a) Binary Adaptive Resonance Theory (ART1).
   (b) Analog adaptive Resonance Theory (ART2).
   (c) Discrete Hopfield (DH).
   (d) Continuous Hopfield (CH).
   (e) Discrete Bi-directional Associative Memory (BAM).
   (f) Temporal Associative Memory (TAM).
   (g) Adaptive Bi-directional Associative Memory (ABAM).
   (h) Kohonen Self-Organizing Map/ Topology Preserving Map (SOM/TPM).

(i) Competitive learning.

2. Feed-forward only Nets:

(a) Learning Matrix (LM).

(b) Driver-reinforcement Learning (DR).

(c) Counter Propagation (CPN).

II. Supervised learning (i.e. with a teacher):

1. Feedback Nets:

(a) Boltzmann Machine. (BM).

(b) Mean Field Annealing (MFT).

(c) Recurrent Cascade Correlation (RCC).

(d) Learning Vector Quantization (LVQ).

(e) Back progpagation through time (BPTT).

(f) Real-time Recurrent Learning (RTRL).

2. Feed-forward only Nets:

(a) Perceptron.

(b) Adaline, Madaline.

(c) Backpropagation (BP).

(d) Cauchy Machine (CM).

(e) Artmap.

(f) Cascade Correlation (CasCor).

Q. 38. Given the following 2D datsets, apply K-means clustering :

Sample Data #	X	Y
1	185	72
2	170	56
3	168	60
4	179	68
5	182	72
6	188	77

Ans.

Sample Data #	X	Y	Assigriment
1	185	72	C1 (cluster-1)
2	170	56	C2 (cluster-2)

Centroid is : C1 = (185, 72) & C2 = (170, 56)

I[st] step :

Distance from C1 = Euclidean distance between (185, 72) and (168, 60) = 20.80

Distance from C2 = Euclidean distance between (170, 56) and (168, 60) = 4.47

∴ C2 is closer to (168, 60). So, sample belongs to C2. Hance, we get :

Sample Data #	X	Y	Assignment
1	185	72	C1
2	170	56	C2
3	168	60	C2
4	179	68	
5	182	72	
6	188	77	

Similarly, we compute as follows :

1. Distance from C1 for (179, 68) = 7.21

   Distance from C2 for (179, 68) = 15

∴ C1 < C2 (in terms of distance)

∴ C1 is closer to (179, 68).

So, the sample belongs to C1

2. Distance from C1 for (182, 72) = 3

   Distance from C2 for (182, 72) = 20

As C1 is closer to (182, 72), so the sample belongs to C1.

3. Distance from C1 for (188, 77) = 5.83

   Distance from C2 for (188, 77) = 27.6

As C1 is closer to (188, 77), the sample belongs to C1.

Hence, we get :

Sample Data #	X	Y	Assignment
1	185	72	C1
2	170	56	C2
3	168	60	C2
4	179	68	C1
5	182	72	C1
6	188	77	C1

∴ The new centroid for C1 is :

$$\left(\frac{185+179+182+188}{4}, \frac{72+68+72+77}{4}\right) = \left(\frac{734}{4}, \frac{289}{4}\right) = (183.5, 73)$$

and the new centroid for C2 is :

$$\left(\frac{170+168}{2}, \frac{56+60}{2}\right) = \left(\frac{338}{2}, \frac{116}{2}\right) = (169,58)$$

2nd step :

Distance from C1 is Euclidean distance between (183.5, 73) and (168, 60) = 20.2

Distance from C2 is Euclidean distance between (169, 58) and (168, 60) = 2.24.

∴ C2 is closer to (168, 60), the sample belongs to C2.

In same fashion, we get :

1. Distance from C1 for (179, 68) = 6.73
   Distance from C2 for (179, 68) = 14.14

∴ C1 is closer to (179, 68), the sample belongs to C1.

2. Distance from C1 for (182, 72) = 1.80
   Distance from C2 for (182, 72) = 19.10

∴ C1 is closer to (182, 72), the sample belongs to C1.

3. Distance from C1 for (188, 77) = 6.02
   Distance from C2 for (188, 77) = 26.87

∴ C1 is closer to (188, 77), the sample belongs to C1.

Hence, we get :

Sample Data #	X	Y	Assignment
1	185	72	C1
2	170	56	C2
3	168	60	C2
4	179	68	C1
5	182	72	C1
6	188	77	C1

Even after 2nd step, the assignment has NOT changed. So, we stop the algorithm & the points have been clustered now.

Exercise Questions

Q1. Define machine learning. Discuss the applications of Machine Learning.

Q2. Difference between training dataset and testing data set.

Q3. What are support vectors and margins?

Q4. Differences between supervised and unsupervised learning.

Q5. Explain Perceptron training algorithm for linear classification.

Q6. Explain PCA and ICA.

Q7. What are learning laws?

[Hint: Learning laws provide a set of well-defined rules that determine how the network learns. The laws are as follows:-

1. The learning algorithm/law must lead to convergence of weights.
2. The learning time or training time should be small.
3. The learning should make use of only the local information available. When the synaptic weight linking two neurons is changed, it should depend only on the states of these two units. In such a case, the learning process can be made parallel by changing weights parallel.
4. Online training may be done wherein the weights are changed based on the inputs.
5. Non-linear mapping between I/O pairs must be captured by the learning law.
6. Pattern information storage capacity should be as large as possible for a given network.]

Q8. Explain delta rule of learning.

Q9. Explain convergence rule for learning.

Q10. Explain the back-propagation neural network principles.

Q11. Using WEKA tool, how will you construct a fully connected feed-forward ANN that has three input nodes, one output node and four internal nodes in the hidden layer?

Q12. Explain SVMs in detail.

Q13 Apply K-means to form clusters on following data set:

Instance	X	Y
1	7	8
2	2	4
3	6	4
4	3	2
5	6	5
6	5	7
7	3	3
8	1	4
9	5	4
10	7	7
11	7	6
12	2	1

Find the optimal clusters out of data.

3 Deep Feedforward Networks

3.0 Introduction

There are two types of networks- with and without feedbacks. In networks **with feedback,** the output values can be traced back to the input values. On the other hand, in networks **without feedback,** for every input vector laid on the network, an output vector is calculated and this can be read from the output neurons. **There is no feedback.** So, only a forward flow of information is present. **Such networks having this type of structure are called as feed forward networks. For example,** Back Propagation Network.

3.1 Training Neurons

Managing the weights in a neural network is a challenge today. We do this by the process called as training. During training, we show a neural network a large number of training examples. Then we iteratively modify the weights to minimize the errors that we make on the training examples. We should be **intelligent** when we pick our training sets. Researchers say that intelligently selecting the training examples is what needs to be pondered around.

Assume that we have a set of several training examples. We need to calculate what the neural networks will output on the ith training example. **Please note that the objective is to train the neuron so that we select the optimal/ minimum weights possible.** That is, the weights that minimize the errors we make on the training examples. We want to minimize errors we make on the training examples. Mathematically,

If we know that t(i) is the true answer for the ith training example and y(i) is the value calculated by the neural network then we want to reduce the value of the error function (E) as follows:-

$$E = \frac{1}{2} \Sigma i \, (t(i) - y(i))^2$$

Please note that this squared-error value is zero when our model makes a perfect prediction on every training example. Also note that closer is E to 0, the better is our model. So, our objective is to select our parameter vector, θ, so that E is as close as possible to 0 (zero).

We have a set of equations and a bunch/set of unknown weights, for each training example. This would automatically give an error of 0 (zero). This is intelligent decision. This is true as far as we have linear neurons but as we talk about non-linear neurons like sigmoidal, tanh neurons then we get complex equations and hence we need a better method to tackle the training process.

The training set is a set of examples that are randomly drawn from the dataset for the purpose of training the model. **Training data** is the data set on which you train the model. It can also be said that the data from which the model has learned the experiences. The **test set** is a set of examples drawn from the data set for the purpose of evaluating the performance of the model. This is kept separate from the training and tuning data and cannot be used in the training or tuning stages of the learning process. Doing this would only bias the model to the data and affect performance. **Test data** is the data which is used to check if the model has learnt good enough from the experiences it got in the trained data sets. In machine learning a set of data is used to determine the potentially predictive relationship called as the **training set.** Training set is an example provided to the learner. On the other hand, test set is used to test the exactness of the hypotheses produced by the learner and it is the set of illustrations weighed down from the learner. Hence, training sets are different from test set.

3.2 Some Common Terminologies

3.2.1 Gradient Descent and Gradient-based Learning

It has been observed that as the weights increase, so does the error. If we are discussing about a linear neuron with 2 inputs only and thus 2 weights only then we are actually working in a 2 dimensional plane where the dimensions correspond to the two weights. We define them as contours that correspond to these two weights. **Please note here that contours correspond to the settings of two weights, w_1 and w_2 that evaluate to the same value of E. Also note that the closer are the contours to each other, the steeper is the slope.** It is observed that the direction of the steepest descent is always perpendicular to the contours. This direction is expressed in form of a vector called as the **gradient.**

This can be extended to non-linear neurons also and try to find out the weights that optimizes the error function. The purpose is to find the **point of minimum error. This algorithm is known as gradient descent.** This process is used to train individual neurons and hence the entire network.

When we try to train a neural network model using gradient-based optimization techniques, this problem of **Vanishing Gradient occurs.** When we do back-propagation i.e., process of moving backward in the network and calculating gradients of loss (error) with respect to the weight. **Please note that the gradients tend to get smaller and smaller as we keep on moving backward in the network. This means that the neurons in the earlier layers learn very slowly as compared to the neurons in the later layers in the hierarchy**. The earlier layers in the network are slowest to train. Gradient based methods learn a parameter's value by understanding how a small change in the parameter's value will affect the network's output. If a change in the parameter's value causes very small change in the network's output then the network can't learn the parameter effectively, which is a problem. This is what is happening in this vanishing gradient problem, the gradients of the network's output with respect to the parameters in the early layers become extrenaly small. **This means that even a large change in the value of parameters for the early layers doesn't have a big effect on the output.**

Why this problem occurs?

Vanishing gradient problem depends on the choice of the **activation function**. Most common activation function "squash" their input into a very small output range in a very non-linear fashion.

For **eg. Sig moid** maps the real number line onto a "small" range of [0, 1]. As a result, there are large regions of the input space which are mapped to an extremely small range. In these regions of the input space, even a large change in the input will produce a small change in the output. Hence, the gradient is small.

3.2.2 The Delta Rule

The delta rule changes the weight vector for a neural network in such a way that the error is reduced. We need this rule to train our linear neuron. To find out, how to change each weight, we need to evaluate gradient which is the partial derivative of the error function with respect to each of the weights. It is also called as **Widrow-Hoff rule.** It controls the change in the synaptic weight with respect to the learning rate. **Please note that this rule is local in nature as the change in the synaptic weight depends only on the error of the neuron and the input to it.** The weight in the next iteration is also computed here. **Also note that the error correction learning rule is a closed-loop feed back system.** This is also a type of learning only and is known as error-correction learning. This rule is predecessor of the back propagation rule only. **The total square error of the output computed by the net is minimized by a gradient descent method known as back propagation or generalized delta rule.**

3.2.3 The Rate of learning *(η)*

Rate of learning has a direct effect on change in synaptic weights. The back propagation algorithm is an approximation to the trajectory in weight space calculated by steepest descent method. **Please note that if we choose a small, parameter, η, the trajectory will be smoother in the weight space but the rate of learning will be very slow. Also note that a large learning rate parameter, η, will result in large changes in the synaptic weights and the network may show oscillatory response and may become unstable.** We can even add a momentum constant as an improvement to this delta rule as its inclusion stabilizes the weights which tend to oscillate.

3.2.4 The Backpropagation Algorithm

Back Propagation (BP) (Learning algo.)

Single-layer perception is NOT capable of representing all problems i.e., those problems that are very complex (i.e., are not linear seperable)

∴ **Multi-layer networks can** be trained to solve difficult & diverse problems by the **back-propagation algorithm** (or generalized gradient descant), Multilayer network trained with back-propagation are today the most widely used NN.

Principle–BP algo. is based on the error–**correction learning rule** i.e., the error-signal, e_i (n) is the difference between desired response, d_i (n) and the output signal, y_i (n) where i is the neuron whose synaptic weights are adjusted at discrete time, n.

∴ $$\text{Error, } e_i(n) = d_i(n) - y_i(n)$$

The corrective adjustments are designed to make the output signal, y_i (n) closer to the desired response, d_i (n).

Training of network is done?

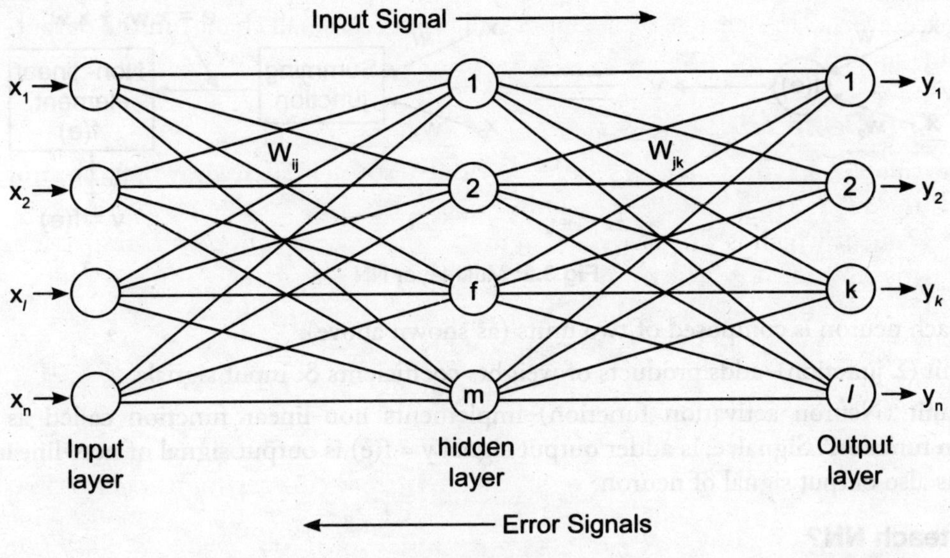

Fig.3.1: BP-NN

S1 : "The network is firstly initialized by setting up all its weights to the small random numbers in between – 1 and + 1."

S2 : Input pattern is applied and the output is calculated. This is called as the **forward pass.** This calculation gives an output which may or may not match the desired (Target output) as all weight are random.

S3 : Then calculate the error of each neuron i.e.,

Error = Target – Actual Output

or (what you want – what you actualy get)

S4 : Then this error is used mathematically to change the weight in such a way that the error will get smaller i.e., the output of each neuron will get closer to its target. This pass is called the **reverse pass.**

S5 : Repeat this process again and again until the error is minimal.

S6 : Once the network is trained, it will provide the desired output for any of the input patterns.

Training Multi-layered NN using BP

Consider the network :

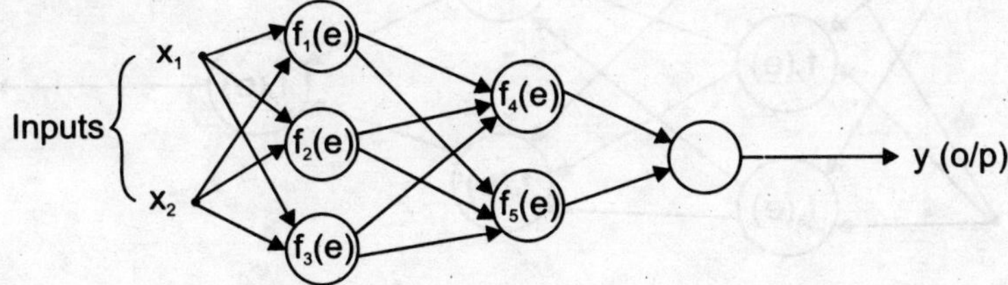

Convention:

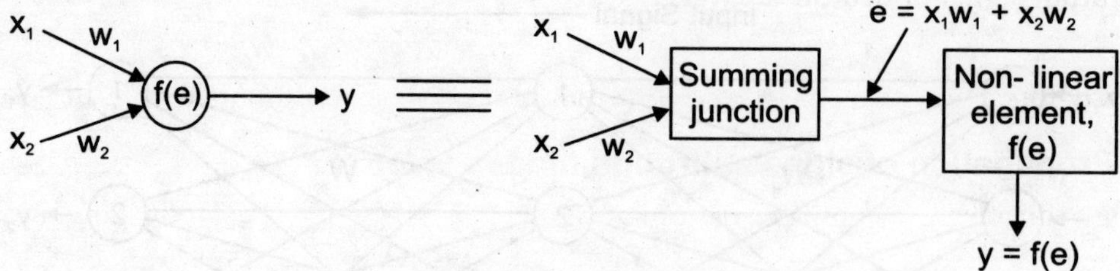

Fig.3.2: Multi-layer NN

∴ Each neuron is composed of two units (as shown above).

I[st] unit (Σ junction)–adds products of weights coefficients & input signals

2nd unit (Neuron activation function)–implements non-linear function called as **'Neuron activation function'**. Signal, e, is adder output signal y = f(e) is output signal of non-linear element signal, y is also output signal of neuron.

How to teach NN?

We need **training data set**. This t_r data set consists of input signals (x_1 and x_2) assigned with corresponding target (desired output), z. This network **training is an iterative process**. In each iteration, weights coeffs. of nodes are modified using new data from training data set.

3 cases arise—

I Propagation of signals through the input layer.

II Propagation of signals through the hidden layer.

III Propagation of signals through the output layer.

Sign Conventions

$W_{(xm)n}$ – represents weights of connections between n/w input, x_m & neuron, n in input layer.

y_n – represents output signal of neuron, n.

Case I : Propagation of signals through input layer

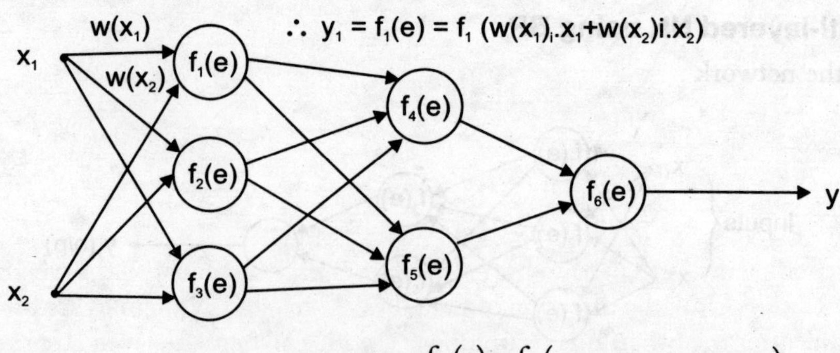

∴ $y_1 = f_1\ (e) = f_1\ (w_{(x1)\ 1}\ x_1 + w_{(x2)1} \cdot x_2)$

i.e., $w_{(x1)1}$ shows weight of connection between network input, x_1 & neuron, n in input layer-1

y_1 – Output signal of neuron-1, layer-1.

$\therefore$ $y_1 = f_1(e) = f_1(w_{(x1)1}\, x_1 + w_{(x2)1} \cdot x_2)$

Similarly for $f_2(e)$ and $f_3(e)$, we can compute y_2 & y_3 at layer-1.

Case II : Propagation of signals through hidden layer

In above fig., consider $f_4(e)$ now i.e., neuron at hidden layer.

$\therefore$ $y_4 = f_4(w_{14}y_1 + w_{24}y_2 + w_{34}y_3)$

Similarly, for y_5, we can compute $f_5(e)$.

Case III : Propagation of signals through output layer

Similarly, now $y = f_6(w_{46}\, y_4 + w_{56}\, y_5)$

where w_{46} means weight, w_4 and 6 means neuron-6, in input layer

Then, the **output signal of the n/w**, y, is **compared with** the **desired output** value (the target), which is found in training data set. The difference is called as an **error signal**, δ, of output layer neuron i.e.

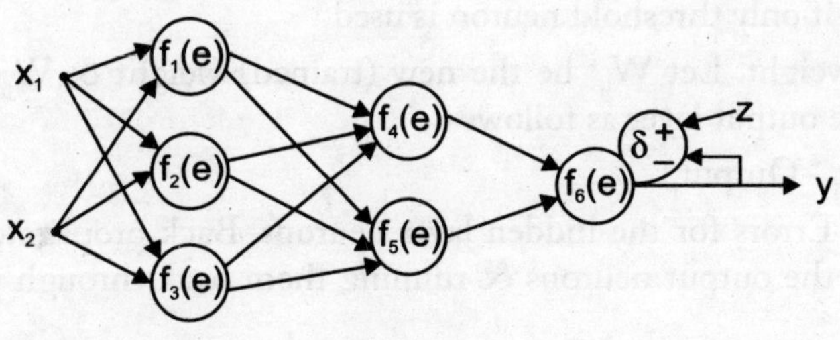

i.e., $\delta = z - y$

But it is impossible to compute error (δ) signal for internal neurons directly as output values of these neurons are unknown.

$\therefore$ BP algo is applied to propagate error signal, δ, back to all neurons i.e.,

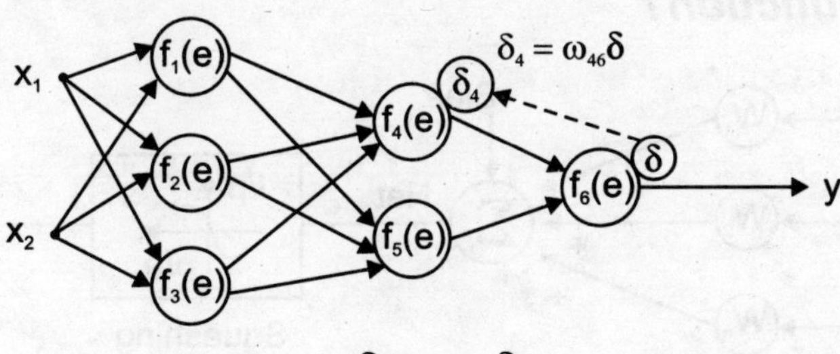

i.e., $\delta_4 = w_{46}\,\delta$

(i) Similarly, $\delta_5 = w_{56}\,\delta$

The weight coefficients, w_{mn}, used to propagate errors back are equal to the weight used during computing output value. Only the direction of data flow is changed i.e., signals are propagated from output to input one after the other. This technique is used for all network layers. If propagated errors came from few neurons, they are added.

Algorithm-BP

Consider a connection between a neuron in output layer & one in hidden layer as follows–

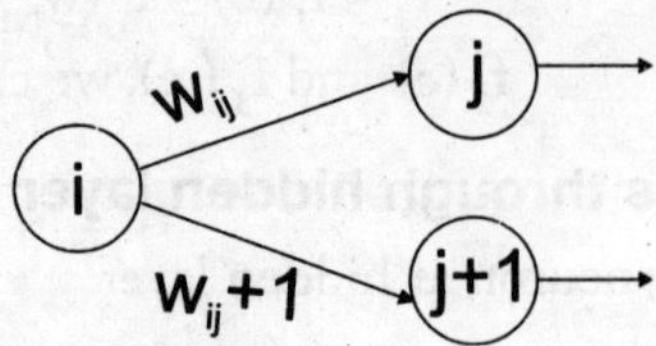

Given : A set of input-output vector pairs.

Compute : A set of weight for a network that maps inputs onto corresponding outputs.

Algorithm :

S1 : Apply the inputs to the network and work out the output. This initial output could be anything as the initial weight were random numbers.

S2 : Next find out the error for output neuron, j, i.e.,

$$\text{Error}_j = \text{Output}_j\ (1 - \text{Output}_j)\ (\text{Target}_j - \text{Output}_j)$$

Here, the term "Output (1 – output)" is mandatory if it is a sigmoid function else it would be just (Target – Output), if only threshold neuron is used.

S3 : Change the weight. Let W_{ij}^+ be the new (trained) weight & W_{ij} be the initial weight. Update all height in the output layer as follows–

$W_{ij}^+ = W_{ij} + (\text{Error}_j * \text{Output}_i)$

S4 : Calculate the Errors for the hidden layer neurons. Back propagate now. This is done by taking the errors from the output neurons & running them back through the weights to get the hidden layer errors i.e.,

$$\text{Error}_i = \text{Output}_i\ (1\text{-Output}_i)\ (\text{Error}_j W_{ij} + \text{Error}_{j+1} W_{ij+1})$$

Again, the factor "Output (1 - Output)" is present because of the sigmoid squashing function.

S5 : Go to step 3.

What is signoid function?

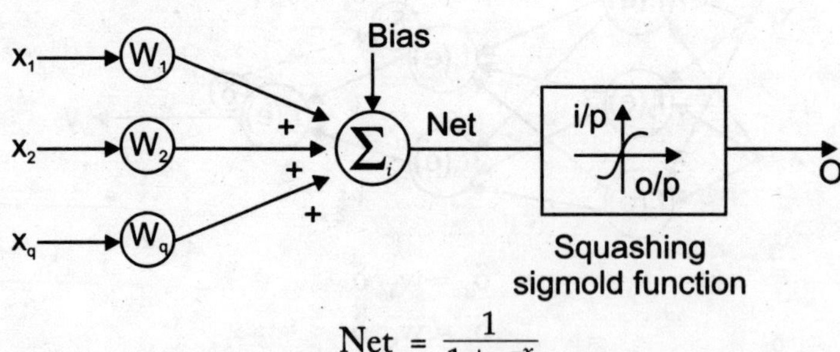

Now,
$$\text{Net} = \frac{1}{1+e^{-x}}$$

$$\therefore \quad \frac{d}{dx}\left(\frac{1}{1+e^{-x}}\right) = \frac{d}{dx}(1+e^{-x})^{-1}$$

$$= -1\,(1+e^{-x})^{-2}.\,(0-e^{-x})$$

$$= \frac{e^{-x}}{(1+e^{-x})^2} = \frac{1-1+e^{-x}}{(1+e^{-x})^2} \qquad \left[\because \frac{d}{dx}y^n = ny^{n-1}.\frac{dy}{dx}\right]$$

$$= \frac{1+e^{-x}}{(1+e^{-x})^2} - \frac{1}{(1+e^{-x})^2}$$

$$= \frac{1}{1+e^{-x}} - \frac{1}{(1+e^{-x})^2}$$

$$= \frac{1}{1+e^{-x}}\left[1 - \frac{1}{(1+e^{-x})}\right]$$

$$= O_i - (1 - O_i)$$

ML Algorithms

Gradient Descent

Imagine there is a ball inside a bucket the **goal** is to get is as low as possible. This requires **optimisation.**

Here, the ball is optimising its position (i.e., left to right or right to left, based on the condition) to find the lowest point in the bucket.

Information that is available to us is only the slope of the side of the bucket at its current position (Shown by a line in Fig-3.3)

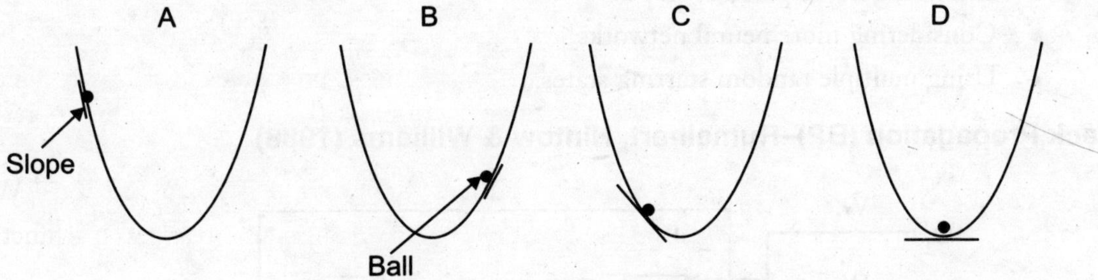

Fig.3.3: Gradient Descent (even surface)

In fig-3.3 **when slope is negative** Fig A (downward from left to right), the ball should move to right.

When slope is positive, the ball should move to left (Fig 1B)

So, this is more than enough information

Gradient Descent Learning

1. It is based on minimization of Error, E, defined in terms of weights & the activation function of the network.
2. Also, it is required that the activation function employed by the network is differentiable as the weight update is dependent on the gradient of the error, E.
3. $\therefore$ if ΔW_{ij} is the weight update of link connecting the ith & j^{th} neuron of the two neighbouring layers then ΔW_{ij} is defined as —

$$\Delta W_{ij} = \frac{\eta \delta E}{\delta W_{ij}}$$

Where η is learning rate parameter & $\eta\delta E/\delta W_{ij}$ error gradient w.r.t. weight W_{ij}

eg. Back Propagation learning rule is its eg. to find the bottom of the bucket in a few iterations. This is a sub-field of optimisation called **gradient optimisation,** (or slope)

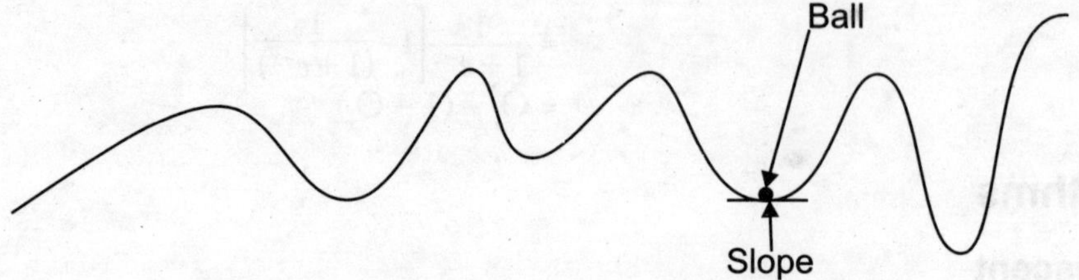

Fig.3.4: Gradient descent on an uneven surface.

Consider a surface that is uneven now like the surface of the moon or Mars. Now, the problem of calculating the slope is more complex & hence challenging. Getting the ball to the lowest position in this scenario needs a lot of mathematical calculations & also more data sets.

Modifications to Gradient Descent

- Increasing no. of possible slopes.
- Considering more neural networks.
- Using multiple random starting states.

Back Propagation (BP)–Rumelhart, Hintow & Williams (1986)

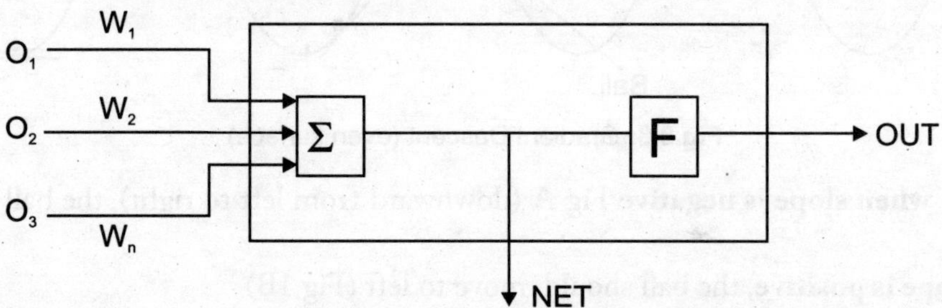

A neuron is used as a fundamental building block for BP networks. **A set of inputs** is either supplied from outside or from a previous layer. Each of those is multiplied by a weight and the products are summed. This summation of products is termed as NET & must be calculated for each neuron inthe network. After NET is calculated, an activation fuction, F is applied to modify it, thereby producing the signal OUT.

$\therefore$ NET = $O_1 W_1 + O_2 W_2 + \ldots\ldots + O_n W_n = \sum_{i=0}^{n} O_i W_i$ & OUT = F (NET)

OUT = $1/(1 + e^{-NET})$

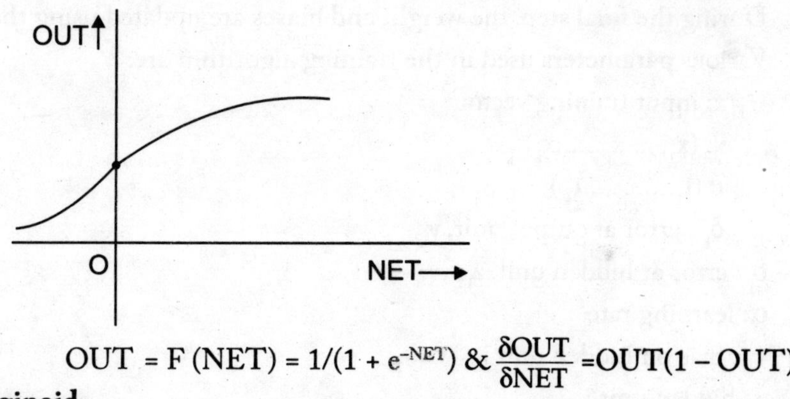

$$OUT = F(NET) = 1/(1 + e^{-NET}) \ \& \ \frac{\delta OUT}{\delta NET} = OUT(1 - OUT)$$

This function is called **siginoid.**

Sometimes called logistic or a squashing function, the sigmoid compresses the range of NET so that OUT lies between 0 & 1.

It is a system method for **training multi-layer ANNs.** It is a **multi-layer forward network** using extended gradient-descent based delta learning rule that is commonly known as **back propagation of errors rule.** Back propagation or BP is an efficient method for changing the weights in a feed forward network with differentiable activation function units, to learn a training set of input-output examples. Hinton, Rumelhart et al. first introduced it in 1986. We do not know what the hidden layers may be doing but we can compute how fast the error changes as we change a hidden activity. So, we can find out how fast the error changes when we change the weight of an individual connection. Being a **gradient descent method,** it minimizes the total square error of the output computed by the net. The network is trained by the supervised learning method. The **aim** of this network is to train the network to achieve a balance between the ability to respond correctly to the input parameters that are used for training and the ability to provide good responses to the input that are similar. Each hidden unit can affect many output units.

The training algorithm for back propagation involves four steps:-

(a) Initialization of weights.

(b) Feed forward.

(c) Back propagation of errors.

(d) Updation of weights and biases.

Explanation: During the **first step/stage,** weights are initialized with some random values. During **feed-forward stage,** each input unit (x_i) receives an input signal and transmits this signal to each of the hidden units, z_i ....z_p. Then each **hidden unit** calculates the activation function and sends its signal z_j to each output unit. The **output unit** calculates the activation function from the response of the net for the given input pattern. During **back propagation of errors,** each output compares its computed activation, y_k with its target value, t_k to determine the associated error for that pattern with that unit. Based on the error, the factor, δ_k (k =1,...,m) is computed and is used to distribute the error at the output unit, y_k back to all the units in the previous layer. Similarly, the factor δ_j (j =1,...,p) is computed for each hidden unit, z_j.

During the **final step**, the **weight and biases** are updated using the δ factor and activation.

Various **parameters** used in the training algorithm are:

x: input training vector

x: $(x_1, \ldots x_i, \ldots, x_n)$

t: $(t_1 \ldots t_k \ldots t_m)$

δ_k : error at output unit, y_k

δ_j : error at hidden unit, z_j

α: learning rate

v_{oj} : bias on hidden unit j

z_j: hidden unit j

w_{ok} : bias on output unit k

y_k : output unit, k.

ALGORITHM: BACK PROPAGATION

S1: Initialize weights.

S2: If **stopping conditions** are false, do steps 3 to 10.

S3: For each **training pair**, do steps 4 to 9.

S4: Apply input, x_i, and **transmit** thesc signals to the hidden units.

S5: Each **hidden unit sums its weighted input signals** and sends the signals to the output units.

S6: Each **output unit sums its weighted input signals** and applies its **activation function** to calculate the output signals.

S7: Each output unit receives a **target pattern** corresponding to an input pattern and **error** information is calculated.

S8: Each **hidden unit sums its delta inputs.** The error information is calculated.

S9. Each **output unit** updates its **bias and weights.**

S10: **Test the stopping condition** based on minimum error.

Properties of back-propagation (BP)

Some of the main properties of BP are as follows:

1. **Learning and NOT programming:** Any neural net can be converted into software like JAVA2 but at the level of neural network, the concepts are very different from conventional software.
2. **Generalization:** BP networks can generalize too. **For example,** the NETTalk network can pronounce words that it has not yet encountered. This is an essential property of intelligent systems that have to function in the real world. **Please note that it implies that not every potential situation has to be predefined in the system.** Generalization here means that, similar inputs leads to similar outputs. **Also note that this is the reason as to why parity is not a good candidate problem for generalization.** Like in XOR problem, change one bit in the input and the output has to change maximally say from 0 to 1.

3. **Noise and fault tolerance:** As we know that a network is noise and fault tolerant. The weights of NETTalk have been disturbed by adding random noise but the performance degradation was only gradual. **Note that this property is not explicitly programmed into the model.** It is the result of massive parallelism, in a sense, it comes for free.
4. **Re-learning:** The network shows fast re-learning. If the network is distorted to a particular performance level, it re-learns faster than a new network starting at the same performance level. So, despite of low performance, the network has retained something about its past.
5. **Emergent properties:** The consonant-vowel distinction that the nodes at the hidden layer pick-up has not been programmed into the system. Certain nodes can pick up these distinctions, which depends on how the examples are encoded. Secondly, since the net can pronounce words that it has not encountered, it has somehow learned the rules of English pronunciation. There are no rules in the network, only weights and activation levels. **Note that it is these emergent properties that make the neural network not only attractive for applications but also to the researchers working in the field of deep learning.**
6. **Universality:** According to Hornik et al. Machine language Programs are **universal approximators.** So we can say that with a 2-layer feed-forward network, every set of discrete function values can be represented or in a particular interval a continuous function can be approximated to any degree of accuracy. This is still a simplification but it is sufficient for our purposes. **Please note that again there is a difference between what can be represented and what can be learned.** Something that can be represented cannot be learned by BP algorithm. **For example,** BP might get stuck in local minima and we do not know whether the global minima will ever be reached. On one side, there are performance problems and on the other side, there are doubts whether supervised learning schemes like BP have a biological or psychological reality. Machine language Programs with BP have been tried on many different types of classification problems because:-
   (a) They are universal function approximators,
   (b) They are easy to use.

   Most of these experiments remained in the **prototype** stage only. The entire knowledge in a NN is in the **connection matrix.** There are no explicit rules. But there are a number of steps to extract rules from NN especially for **Self-Organizing Maps (SOMs).**

Advantages of BP

1. The mathematical formula can be applied to any network.
2. The computing time is less.
3. The batch update of weights is possible.

Disadvantages of BP

1. More number of learning steps.
2. Many calculations are involved.
3. For complex problems, more time is required.
4. The network may get stuck.
5. Quite unstable too.

Applications of BP

1. Optical Character Recognition (OCR).
2. Image and Data Compression.
3. Control systems.
4. Power systems.
5. Fault detection.
6. Non-linear simulation.
7. To train the multi-layer neural networks.

3.2.5 Stochastic and Minibatch Gradient Descent

We have already discussed about batch gradient descent. But the problem arises when our error surface tends to be more complex. So, to solve this problem we use stochastic and mini-batch gradient descent methods.

In Stochastic Gradient Descent (SGD), in each iteration, our error surface is estimated only with respect to a single example. Instead of single and static error surface, our **error surface is dynamic** now. The stochastic error surface fluctuates with respect to the batch error surface, thus enabling saddle point avoidance. As a result, descending on this stochastic surface significantly improves our ability to **navigate flat regions.**

The major drawback of this method is that looking at the error incurred, one example at a time may not be a good approximation of the error surface. So, gradient descent takes more time. To overcome this problem, we use mini-batch gradient descent method.

In Minibatch Gradient Descent method, at every iteration, we compute the error surface with respect to some subset of the total dataset instead of just a single example. **This subset is called as a mini-batch.** So, mini-batch size is another hyper-parameter just as we had learning rate earlier. **Please note here that these mini-batches strike a balance between the efficiency of batch gradient descent and the local minima avoidance afforded by stochastic gradient descent. Also note that here instead of summing over all the examples in the dataset, we sum over the examples in the current mini-batch.**

3.2.6 Test Sets and Validation Sets, Overfitting Phenomenon, Epoch, Training Data, Test Data

As already discussed, a linear fit is always better than a polynomial of higher degree. But for complex problems, linear fit may not be possible. So, we never train our model on the entire dataset. Instead we split up our data into two parts:-

(a) A training set.

(b) A test set.

Thus, now we can do better evaluation of our model by generalizing it. **But please remember that if our test data is not well constructed then we cannot draw any meaningful results about our model. Also note that this may prompt us to reuse the training data for testing.**

A complex model will perfectly fit our training dataset but it performs poorly if it it a new data set. So, the complex model does not generalize well. This is known as **overfitting. This phenomenon is very significant in case of deep learning where our neural networks have large number of layers consisting of many neurons.** It has been observed that as the number of connections increases, so is our problem of overfitting increases. The same problem can be seen when we make our neural networks deep. So, a machine learning engineer has three trade-offs in hand:

1. Overfitting and model complexity must be dealt with.
2. Both simple model and a complex model may not be the **silver bullet.**
3. It is very misleading if we evaluate the model using training data.
4. A stage is reached where instead of learning we start overfitting only.

Also note that deep learning takes the approach of solving complex problems with complex models and taking additional steps to prevent overfitting problem.

That is why we divide our training process into epochs. It is a single iteration over the entire data set. At the end of each epoch, we want to measure how well our model is generalizing. For this we use another **validation set.** At the end of each epoch, the validation set will tell us how the model does on data on the unseen data. **Just remember that if the accuracy on the training set still increases and the accuracy on the validation set remains the same or decreases then it is a good sign to stop training as then otherwise we would be overfitting.**

In deep learning, however we also include this validation data along with training data and test data to prevent overfitting during the training process.

For example, if we have 70,000 rows of training data and we randomly select 10,000 rows to be test data then randomly select another 10000 from the remaining 60,000 rows to be my validation data, leaves us with 50,000 as my training data set.

We train our models with the training data and score it on the validation data. Then we change the models and score again on the validation data. This is also called as **tweaking of the models.** Finally, we choose our model and try to test it on the test set. It is shown in figure 3.6.

The query is now how to **split the data**? There is no rule but unbalanced data is a problem with small datasets. This is so because we do not see any pattern in small data. When data is large/big then **the law of big numbers** tends to make sure that the data is evenly distributed. CASE TOOL like H2O provides a split( ) function for the same.

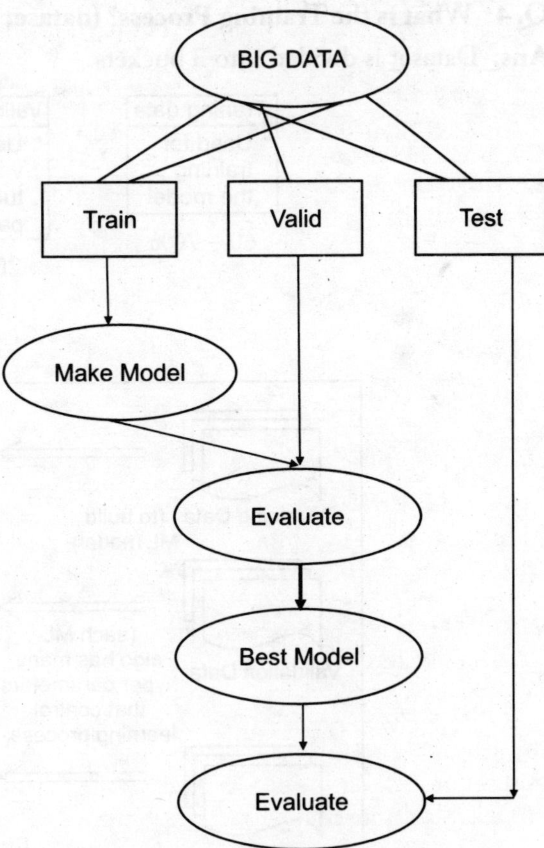

Fig.3.6: Train, valid and test data sets

Q.1 Why divide data set into 3 parts?

Ans. 1. ∴ If not done that we may end up in concluding that a 12 degree polynomical is better than a linear fit.

2. By including 'validation set' (see fig) we prevent over fitting during the training process

Q.2 What is Over fitting for over training and Under fitting?

Ans. Over fitting : Occurs when model or algorithm fits data too well.

Under fitting : Occurs when ML algo. cannot capture underlying trend of data.

Q.3 How is NVIDIA GPU-accelerated computing to train better than traditional CPUs?

Ans.

- A deep learning system with NVIDIA GPUS **encourages parallel** execution.
- It speeds up networks by 10 to 75 times over using traditional CPUs.
- It reduces the time of training iterations from several weeks to just days.
- NVIDIA claims that GPUs can acieve a 12-times improvement in training deep neural networks (DNNs) over use of CPUs.
- Your can quickly design & deploy Deep learning applications with real-time responses.
- Today, even **"GPU clouds"** have appeared in Amazon, IBM & MS cloud plattorms.

Q. 4 What is the Training Process? (dataset is divided into 3 buckets)

Ans. Dataset is divided into 3 buckets.

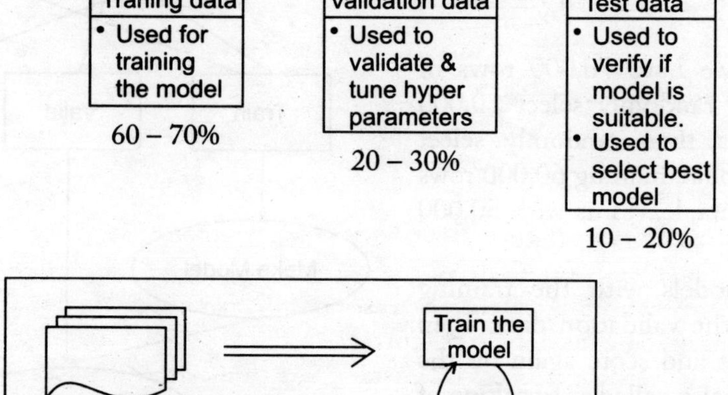

Q. 5 Why healthy dataset?

Ans. Prediction using **same** datasets over a period of time will have **diminishing returns.** So, look for alternate data sources & datasets that can strengthen the models and predictions.

eg. testing accuracy in Image Net 2015 has been improved to 95% by using DL methods.

– Training these large DL n/w's is more time consuming. So, parallelism is needed.

– Move from **"Multi-CPUs"** to **"Multi-GPUs"**.

– CUDA = CPU + GPU = GPGPU (by NVIDIA) (Compute Unified Device Architecture) Co-processor

– (Model parallelism + Data parallelism) by our approach

Parallelism, Within m/c's (by multithreading) to different replicas of a model & across m/c's (by message passing).

– **Data Parallelism**–Each GPU uses that same model to train on different data subset.

Model Parallelism–More communication delay than data parallelism.

CNNs trains on big data sets & Training deep model on huge no. of training data is time consuming & needs large amount of **compute cycles.**

3.2.7 Hyperparameter Optimization

Several hyperparameters like learning rate, mini-batch size etc., have been dealt with in previous sections. But the need is to find a framework for how to find the optimal values for these hyeperparameters. One method of finding the optimal parameters values is named as a **grid search.** In this method, we select a value for each hyperparameter from a finite set of options and batch size and train the model with every possible permutation of hyperparameter choices. The objective is to find out the accuracy of the model trained with the best set on the test set.

3.2.8 Critical Point

As studied earlier, in back propagation learning the network is trained with a number of input patterns. **The training involves adaptation of the synaptic weights of a multilayer perceptron.** For this we need to present the training patterns. **Please note that a network is said to generalize when the I/O mapping computed by the network is correct for the test data not used in the training. Also understand here that the learning process is considered to be a curve-fitting problem that involves some sort of interpolation.** By the term 'interpolation' we mean taking values outside the give range or near the range so as to fit the curve. **And this process in which a neural network learns too many input-output samples, the network may end up memorizing the training set without trying to find the underlying function to be modelled is known as over-fitting or over training.** In such a case, the network losses its ability to generalize. When you use more number of neurons that needed, it results in unwanted input domain due to the noise in the synaptic weights of the network.

Now given an arbitrary function, a point at which the gradient is zero vector is called as a **critical point.** Critical points are of various types like local minima, local maxima and saddle points. Both local minima and local maxima (discussed earlier) do not pose much of the problems but there are some strange critical points that lie somewhere in between. **And these flat regions that are potentially critical, problem-causing regions and are called as saddle points.**

Just remember the following points regarding critical points:-

1. As the number of parameters in our model / as our function gets **more and more dimensions,** the saddle points rise **exponentially** than local minima.
2. If we have a total of k-critical points then we will have a total of **k/3 local minima.**
3. In higher dimensional space, say of size'd', we need to slice the surface (called as **slicing**) then the critical points look like either local maxima or local minima. But the situation is different. They are in fact more complex and are called as **saddle points.**
4. **In general, in a d-dimensional parameter space, we can slice through a critical point on d different axis.**
5. A critical point can be a **local minimum** if it appears as if a local minima in every single one of the done dimensional sub-spaces.
6. In 1D space, critical points can come in three variants. They are all computed on the **error surface.** It is found that a probability that a random critical point is in a random function is $1/3^d$.
7. So, a **random function with k critical points** has an expected will have $k/3^d$ local minima.
8. As the dimensionality of our parameter space increases, local minima becomes **exponentially** more rare.
9. In case of more than 1D, we **slice the error surface.**
10. As far as **deep learning** is concerned, these flat areas of the curve (of error surface) are an issue but finally they do not prevent it from converging to a better answer. The problem does occur when it tries to solve for a point where the gradient is zero. This is a great challenge in deep learning field.
11. **In deep learning yet another challenge** is to find the correct trajectory.
12. In case of **deep networks, the contours** are very much **elliptical** and thus the gradient can be as inaccurate as 90 degrees away from the right direction.
13. If **contours are circular** then we move ahead with a big step in the direction of the steepest descent because the gradient does not change the direction we move on. But this is not true in case of elliptical contours of **deep networks.**
14. We use simple derivation concept of mathematics here to find out how the gradient changes as we move on. That is, **we can model this change of gradient with our derivatives.**
15. We compile this entire information into a matrix form called as **Hessian Matrix (H).**
16. This matrix is said to be **ill-conditioned** when we describe an error surface when the gradient changes.
17. We can even take the 2nd derivative of the error function to find out the **learning rate** at each step that maximizes the reduction in the error function.

3.2.9 Learning Rate Adaptation

The constant that is used in Artificial Neural Networks (ANNs) learning algorithms to affect the speed of learning is called as the **learning rate.**

One of the major challenges of training deep networks is to get the **correct learning rate.** *This* *is so because it has a lot of impact on the network's performance.* It has been observed that a learning rate that is too small does not learn quickly but a learning rate that is too large may have difficulty in converging as we approach the region of local minima. Modern deep network optimization provides a facility of **learning rate adaption. We define the learning rate adaptation as the process of suitably modifying the optimal learning rate over the period of learning to get good convergence properties.** Some of the learning rate algorithms are AdaGrad, RMSProp and Adam.

The deep learning practitioners must ponder on the point that their aim is not to build more and more advanced optimizers rather to discover the architectures that are simpler to train. They need not be busy on complex error surfaces only.

3.3 Flowchart for Training a Deep Learning Model

The following are the steps followed to train and evaluate a deep learning model:

S1: Define the Problem: It involves finding out the inputs, outputs and their vector representations. Say, we want to train a deep learning model to identify severe fever in a patient. Then our input will be the patient image that will be stored in form of a vector of pixel values. And the output will be the probability of it being viral, dengue or malaria.

S2: Building a Neural Network to solve it: The input layer will be of suitable size so as to accept the raw data from the image. And our output will be the type of the fever. Also we will have to define the internal architecture of the network i.e., the number of hidden layers, the connectives used etc.

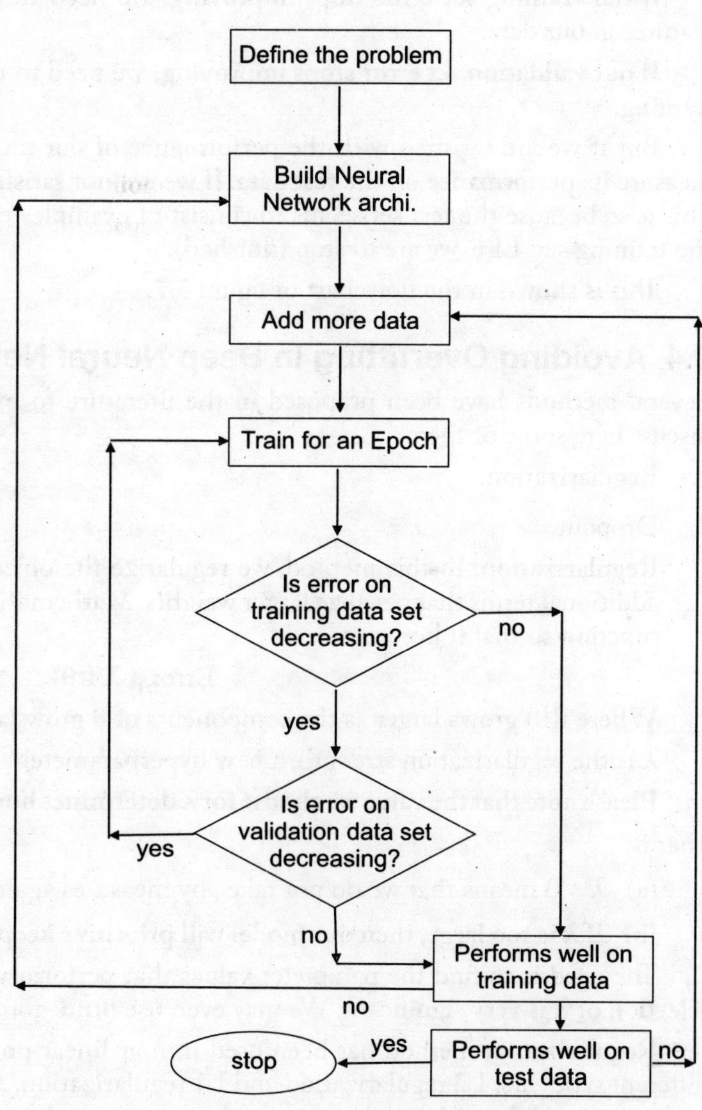

Fig.3.7: Flowchart to show Training and Evaluation of Deep Learning Model

S3: **Train for an epoch:** Now we want to collect a significant amount of data for training or modelling. Now we need the images of all with a uniform size.

S4: **Divide this Data:** Now we shuffle and divide this data as needed for training, validation and test sets.

S5: **Train the model on the training set:** We now train the model on our training set for an epoch at a time. At the end of each Epoch, **we ensure that our error on the training set and validation set is decreasing.** When one of this stops to improve, we terminate and check that our model performs well on the test data. If not, we need to design architecture again or check the data collected.

If our training set error stops improving, we need to do better by capturing the important features in our data.

If our validation set error stops improving, we need to take steps to prevent over-fitting/ over training.

But if we are satisfied with the performance of our model on the training data then we can measure its performance on the test data. If we are not satisfied, we need more data in our data set. This is so because the test set seems to consist of examples types that were not well represented in the training set. Else, we are to stop (finished).

This is shown in the flowchart of figure 3.7.

3.4 Avoiding Overfitting in Deep Neural Networks

Several methods have been proposed in the literature to prevent overfitting or overtraining. We discuss here some of them.

1. Regularization.
2. Dropout.

i. **Regularization:** In this method, we regularize the objective function. This is done by adding additional terms that penalize larger weights. Mathematically speaking, we modify the objective function so that it becomes-

$$\text{Error} + \lambda\, f(\theta)$$

Where $f(\theta)$ grows larger as the components of θ grow larger,

λ is the regularization strength, a new hyperparameter .

Please note that the value we choose for λ determines how much we want to prevent overfitting.

That is,

(a) $\lambda = 0$ means that we do not take any measures against the possibility of overfitting.

(b) If λ is too large, then our model will prioritize keeping θ as small as possible.

The need is to find the parameter values that perform well on the training set we choose. So, selection of λ is very significant. We may even use brute-force method here.

Regularization method has been used in non-linear problems by the researchers. It is also of different types like L2 regularization and L1 regularization. **Also note that during gradient descent update, using L2 regularization means that every weight is decayed linearly to zero. That is why, this phenomenon is also known as weight decay.**

ii. **Dropout:** It is the most popular method used today to prevent overfitting or overtraining in deep neural networks. During the training process, a dropout is implemented by only keeping a neuron active with some probability, p (a hyperparameter) or setting it to zero. This forces the network from becoming too much dependent on any one of the neurons or their small combinations. This method prevents overfitting by approximately combining exponentially many different neural network architectures and that too efficiently. So, dropouts sets each neuron in the network as inactive. This is done with some random probability during mini-batch training. Again we need to consider some complexities here. For example, we would like the outputs of neurons during test time to be equivalent to their expected outputs at the training time. We can fix this by scaling the output at test time. For example, if p= 1/4 then neurons must $3/4^{th}$ their outputs at the test time to be equivalent to their expected outputs at the training time. **Please note that this is easy as a neuron's output is set to 0 with the probability 1-p. Also note that this means that if a neuron's output prior to drop-out was x, then after dropout, the expected output would be –**

$$\mathbf{E[output] = px + (1 - p).0 = px} \qquad \text{.........(1)}$$

However, this implementation of dropout method is not very suitable as it needs scaling of neuron outputs at the test time. And that test-time performance is very critical to model evaluation. So we suggest the use of **inverted dropout method** here. This is so because here scaling occurs at the training time instead of at test time. In this new method, any neuron whose activation has not been silenced has its output divided by p before the value is propagated to the next layer. So, with this modification we have:-

$$E[output] = p.\,x/p + (1 - p).0 = x \qquad \text{.........(2)}$$

So, we can avoid any random scaling neuronal output during the test time.

In nutshell, for deep learning, there are two methods:

(a) Regularization.

(b) Drop connections when connecting one layer to the next.

3.5 Deep Reinforcement Learning

The process of learning from the interaction with an environment from the consequences of action (rather than explicit teaching) is known as reinforcement learning.

Or

It is defined as the branch of machine learning that deals with learning via interactions and feedback. [Nicholas et al.]

In 2014, deep neural networks were applied to reinforcement learning.

The learning process includes **an actor, an environment and a reward signal.** The actor takes an action in the environment and gets points. The method in which an actor chooses the actions is known as a **policy.** Since the actor wants to maximize its points (rewards) so it must learn an optimal policy for environmental interactions. This is shown in figure 3.5.

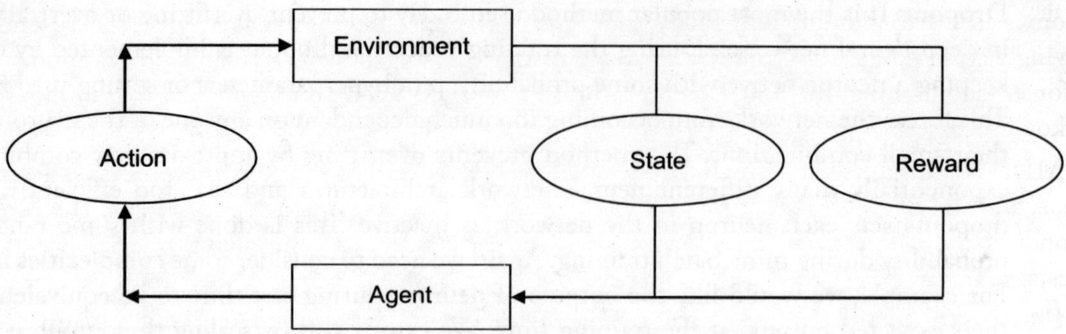

Fig.3.5: Reinforced Learning Framework

This type of learning is different from supervised or unsupervised learning as discussed earlier. Reinforcement learning is a general purpose framework for creating intelligent agents. The agent learns to interact with that environment to maximize its total reward. This type of learning has been found to be very useful in applications like self-driving cars, robotics, game playing, air conditioner control, stock markets, autonomous helicopter, mobile network routing, factory control and efficient web page indexing.

In reinforcement learning framework we will provide our algorithms only a reward function that indicates to the learning agent when it is doing well and when it is doing poorly. For example, in a four-legged robot walking case, the reward function might give the robot positive rewards for moving forwards and negative rewards for either moving backwards or falling over. Then it will be the task of the learning algorithm to find out how to choose actions overtime so as to obtain large rewards.

3.5.1 Markov Decision Processes [MDP]

The study of this type of reinforcement learning begins with Markov Decision Process (MDP) which provides the formalism in which reinforcement learning problems are usually posed.

Considering the reinforced learning framework of figure 3.5 we say that:

(a) **States:** These can refer to, for example, grid maps in robotics or like an open door and closed door scenario.

(b) **Actions:** A fixed set of actions like going north, south, east etc for a robot.

(c) **Transition Probabilities:** It is defined as the probability of going from one state to another given an action. **For instance,** what is the probability of an open door if the action is open.

(d) **Rewards:** These are used to guide the planning. For example, in case of a grid, we may like to go to a certain cell. The reward will be higher if we get closer. Like in case of a door example, an open door might give a high reward.

Please understand that once the MDP is defined, a policy can be learned by doing Value Iteration or Policy Iteration which calculates the expected reward for each of the states. Then the policy gives per state the best action to perform. **Also note that MDP is useful when you want to have an efficient sequence of actions in which your actions can not always be 100% effective.**

MDP provides a mathematical framework for modelling decisions making in situations where outcomes are partly random and partly under the control of a decision maker. MDPs are useful for studying a wide range of optimization problems that are solved using dynamic programming and reinforcement learning. In 1960, Ronald Howard published a book on Dynamic Programming and Markov Processes.

MDP is a discrete time **stochastic control process.** at each time step, the process is in some state, s, and the decision maker may choose any action, a, that is available in state, s. The process responds at the next time by randomly moving into a new state, s', and giving a decision maker a corresponding reward R_a (s, s').

Please note here that the probability that the process moves into its new state s' is influenced by the chosen action only. This is given by the state transition function, P_a (s, s'). So, the next state s' depends on the current state, s, and the decision maker's action, a. But given s and a, it is conditionally independent of all previous states and actions. **Just note here that the state transitions of an MDP process satisfies the Markov property. And MDPs are an extension of Markov chains.** The difference is the addition of actions and rewards. Conversely, if only one action exists for each state (e.g. 'wait') and all rewards are the same (e.g. 'zero'), a Markov decision process reduces to a Markov chain.

A Markov decision process is defined:

- S, a finite set of possible states.
- A, a finite set of actions.
- P(r, s' | s, a), a state transition function.
- R, a reward function.

When an agent takes an action in an MDP framework, it forms an episode. **We define an episode as a series of tuples of states, actions and rewards. These episodes run till the environment reaches a terminal state.** We can show the variables in an episode as follows:-

$$(s_0, a_0, r_0), (s_1, a_1, r_1) \ldots\ldots\ldots (s_n, a_n, r_n)$$

Objective: MDPs task is to find an optimal policy for our agent. We define policies as the ways in which our agent acts based on its current state. The aim is to find a policy to maximize the expected future return.

3.5.2 BELLMAN Equations

Richard Bellman, gave a dynamic programming equation known as BELLMAN equation. It is the necessary condition for optimality related to dynamic programming. It writes the value of a decision problem at a certain point in time in terms of the payoff from some initial choices and the value of the remaining decision problem that result from those initial choices. This breaks a dynamic optimization problem into simpler sub-problems. **This is known as "Principle of Optimality".**

The Bellman equation was first applied to engineering control theory and to applied mathematics and in economic theory. The basic concepts of dynamic programming have been given in John Von Neumann and Oskar's **theory of Games and Economic behaviour. It has been observed that any problem that can be solved using optimal control theory can also be solved by analyzing a suitable Bellman equation.** Bellman equation refers to the dynamic programming equation related to

discrete-time optimization problems. In continuous-time optimization problems, the analogous equation is a partial differential equation which is usually called as the **Hamilton-Jacobi-Bellman equation.** Given a fixed policy, Π, its value function, V^{Π}, satisfies the Bellman equations:

$$V^{\Pi}(s) = R(s) + \gamma \Sigma (s' \varepsilon S) P_{s\Pi(s)}(s') V^{\Pi}(s') \quad ......(3)$$

This expression shows that **the expected sum of discounted rewards, $V^{\Pi}(s)$, for starting, s, consists of two terms-**

(a) Firstly, the immediate reward R(s) that we get right away simply for starting in state, s.

(b) 2nd is the expected sum of future discounted rewards.

The 2nd term of the equation-3, shows the expected sum of discounted rewards for starting in state s', where s' is distributed according to $P_{s\Pi(s)}$, which is the distribution over where we will end up taking the first action in the MDP from state, s. So, the 2nd term gives the expected sum of discounted rewards obtained after the first step in the MDP.

These Bellman's equations can be used to efficiently solve V^{Π}. Specifically in a finite-state MDP (|S| < ∞), we can write down such equation for $V^{\Pi}(s)$ for every state, s. This gives us a set of |S| linear equations in |S| variables that can be then solved.

3.5.3 Value Iteration and Policy Iteration

Both value iteration and policy iteration are standard algorithms for solving MDPs. For small MDPs, policy iteration is often very fast and converges with very little iteration. On the other hand, for MDPs with large state spaces, solving for V^{Π} explicitly would involve solving a large system of linear equations and could be difficult. In these problems, value iteration may be preferred. This is the reason as to why practically, **value iteration seems to be used more often than policy iteration.**

3.5.4 Linear Quadratic Regulation (LQR)

The theory of optimal control is related to the operation of a dynamic system at a minimum cost. **And the case where the system dynamics are described by a set of linear differential equations and the cost is described by a quadratic function is called as the LQ problem.** One of the main results in the theory is that the solution is provided by the linear-quadratic regulator (LQR), a feedback controller whose equations are given here. LQR is an important part of the solution to the LQG (LINEAR QUADRATIC GAUSSIAN) PROBLEM. Like the LQR problem, the LQG problem is one of the most fundamental problems in control theory. The settings of a regulating controller governing either a machine or process like an airplane or chemical reactor, are found by using a mathematical algorithm that minimizes a cost function with weighting factors supplied by an engineer. **The cost function is defined as the sum of the deviations of key measurements, desired altitude or process temperature, from their desired values.** Thus the algorithm finds those controller settings that minimize undesired deviations. The magnitude of the control action also may be included in the cost function.

The LQR algorithm reduces the amount of work done by the control system engineer to optimize the controller. However, the engineer still needs to specify the cost function parameters and compare the results with the specified design goals. **Please note that this often means that the controller construction will be an iterative process in which an engineer judges the optimal controllers produced through simulation and then adjusts the parameters to produce a controller more consistent with the design goals.**

The LQR algorithm is an automated way of finding an appropriate state-feedback controller. As such, it is not uncommon for control engineers to prefer alternative methods like full state feedback, **also known as pole placement, wherein there is a clear relationship between the controller parameters and controller behaviour. Also note that difficulty in finding the right weighting factors limits the application of the LQR based controller synthesis.**

3.6 Explore versus Exploit

Consider a very famous mouse-maze problem. The mouse must either get the water or it may reach a poison container that is red in colour. Our agent must control the mouse to maximize reward. If the mouse gets water, it receives a reward of +1, if it reaches the poison container then it receives a reward of -10 and if the mouse gets the cheese, it receives a reward of +100. After receiving of the reward, the episode is over. **Please note that the optimal policy involves the mouse successfully navigating to the cheese and eating it.** The mouse may go left or right but the aim of mouse is to follow from its movements that if it goes left, it gets water and if it goes right it gets poison container. May be after 2 episodes the mouse may have found an optimal policy. It continues to follow its learned policy on subsequent episodes and gets the moderate reward. So, we can say that our agent uses a greedy method i.e. always it chooses a model's best action. Therefore, it gets struck in a policy that is a **local maximum.** To avoid this problem, our agent should deviate from the model's recommendation and take a suboptimal action in order to **explore more of the environment.** So, instead of taking the immediate right turn to exploit the environment to get water, our agent may choose a left turn and may enter into more dangerous areas in search of a more optimal policy. **Also note here that too much of exploration and our agent fails to optimize any reward. Not enough exploration can result in our agent getting stuck in local minima.** This balance of **explore versus exploit is vital to learn a successful policy.**

3.7 Policy versus Value Learning

To maximize the rewards we have to teach an agent. And for this teaching there are 2 methods:-

(a) Policy learning.

(b) Value learning.

In policy learning, we directly learn a policy that maximizes reward.

In value learning, we are learning the value of every state and action (a pair).

For example, say you are trying to learn 'how to ride a bike'. Then a policy learning method would be to think about how pressing the right pedal would correct you, if you are falling on to the left. On the other hand, with a value learning approach, you would assign a score to different bike orientations and actions that you can take in those positions.

3.8 Q-Learning and Deep Q-Networks

Q-learning comes under the catgory of reinforcement learning and is called as **value learning.** Here, instead of directly learning a policy, we will be learning the value of **states and actions.** It involves learning a function named as Q-function, that represents the quality of a state, action pair. We define Q-function as follows:-

"Q-function, Q(s, a) is a function that calculates the maximum discounted future return when action, a, is performed in state, s".

Q-value represents our expected long-term rewards. Given that we are at a state and take an action. Then take every subsequent action perfectly to maximize expected future reward. **Please understand that it is very difficult to know whether the action is good or not as you need to know how you are going to act in the future. Our future returns will depend on what our long-term methods are going to be. Also note here that in order to value a (state, action) pair you need to know all of the perfect subsequent actions.** And to know the best actions, you need to have accurate values for a state and action.

Q-learning is an alternative Temporal Difference (TD) method. It learns action-value representation instead of utilities. Q (a, s) denotes value of doing action, a, in state, s.

$$U(s) = \max Q(a, s)$$

A TD agent that learns a Q-function does not need a model for either learning or action selection. That is, it is model free.

Note: Q-learning agent learns optimal policy but much slower than ADP agent.

TD does not enforce consistency among values via a model.

According to Watkins and Dayan in 1992, the convergence results for Q-learning assumes a discrete time, finite-state system and requires the use of lookup-tables to represent Q-function. This is not suitable for the LQR domain where the states and actions are vectors of real numbers. We will use a parameterized representation of the Q-function and adjust the parameters through a learning process.

For instance, Jordan and Jacobs in 1990, Lin in 1992, used MLPs training using backpropagation to approximate the Q-function. **Please note that the function, Q_U, is a quadratic function of its arguments, the state and control action but it is a linear function of the quadratic combinations from the vector [z, u].**

For example, if $x = [x_1, x_2]$ and $u = [u_1]$, then $Q_U(x, u)$ is a linear function of the vector $[x_1^2, x_2^2, u_1^2, x_1 x_2, x_1u_1, x_2u_1]$. This fact allows us to use **Linear Recursive Least Squares (RLS) to implement Q-learning in the LQR domain.**

We must relate the Q-values of past and future. This forms a **new update rule i.e. we can update past Q-values to be based on future Q-values.** This is useful as we know that there exists a Q-value that we know is correct i.e. the Q-value of the very last action before the episode is over. For this last state, we know that the next action resulted in the next reward. So we can perfectly set the Q-values for that state. Then we can use this update-rule to propagate that Q-value to the previous time step as follows:

$$\hat{Q}_j \rightarrow Q_{j+1} \rightarrow Q_{j+2} \rightarrow \dots \rightarrow Q^*$$

And this process of updating of the Q-value is known as value iteration.

Our 1st Q-value may be wrong but it is fine as with the next iteration, we can update our Q-value via the correct one from the future. After 1st iteration, the last Q-value is accurate as it is just a reward from the last state and action before episode termination. Then we update our Q-value. This sets the 2nd to last Q-value. In next iteration, we can assure that the last two Q-values are correct and so on. Through this process of value iteration, we will be assured the convergence on the ultimate optimal Q-value.

There are two types of Q-learning as follows:-

(a) **Watkins Q-learning rule/ optimizing Q-learning** as it learn the Q-function of the optimal policy directly.

(b) The 2nd form of Q-learning tries to learn Q_U, the Q-function for some designated policy, U. U may or may not be the policy that is actually followed during training.

Bradtke et al. show in one of their papers that a linear RLS representation of the policy-based learning rule will converge to **Q_U, for LQR problems.**

Deep Q-Network (DQN)

DQN uses a deep neural network that takes an image (the state) in to estimate the Q-value for all possible actions. The aim is to train our network to estimate the Q-function. We know that Q-learning is a **value-learning algorithm.** We are not learning a policy directly rather we are learning the values of each state, action pair. They may or may not be good.

Value iteration produces a mapping between state and action pairs with corresponding Q-values and we are constructing a table of these mappings called as **Q-TABLE.**

What will be the size of this Q-TABLE?

As studied, value iteration is an exhaustive process that requires a full traversal of the entire space of state, action pairs. In stochastic environments, the space of our Q-TABLE would even be larger and possibly infinite. With such a large space, it will be intractable for us to find all of the Q-values for every state, action pair.

Note: If we approximate the Q-function then we need not perform an exhaustive and extensive search through all possible values of Q (Q-values) to learn a Q-function.

Deep Q Network is a Markov decision process that works on the Markov assumption. **This assumption sates that "the next state (s_i + 1) depends only on the current state s_i and action a_i and not on any previous states or actions."** This Markov assumption makes modelling decision processes simple and reliable too but at a loss of modelling power. DQN solves this problem by reusing the **state history i.e.** DQN considers the past four game frames instead of using only one game frame. This makes DQN to utilize time-dependent information.

Two types of Q-networks are available in literature-

(a) The prediction network.

(b) The target Q-network.

It is observed in these two Q-networks that they have the same architecture definition as they are the same network with the target Q just having delayed parameter updates.

Limitations of DQN

It takes long to train. It does not work well on some games and needs re-training for every new game.

Deep Recurrent Q-Networks (DRQN)

Let us recall the Markov's assumption. **It states that the next state relies only on the previous state and the action taken by the agent.** Using this on DQN has some limitations like why should there be only 4 frames, why not 8 or 10 or 12? This is an imposed frames history parameter that limits the model's generality. For this purpose we use DQRN.

DQRN uses a recurrent layer to transfer a latent knowledge of state from one time step to the next. Thus, the model itself can learn how many frames are informative that must be included in its state. DQRN has also been extended to include neural nets. The point to understand is that since DQRN deals with sequences of data, **it can attend only certain parts of the sequence. And this ability to learn just parts of the image will improve performance as well as it provides model interpretability.**

DQRN has been found to be better than DQN as far as the playing of certain games is concerned like DOOM, Atari games etc.

3.9 POMDPS

POMDPS stands for PARTIALLY OBSERVABLE MARKOV DECISION PROCESS. It is a generalization of a Markov decision process (MDP). A POMDP models an agent decision process in which it is assumed that the system dynamics are determined by an MDP but the agent cannot directly observer the underlying state. Instead, it must maintain a probability distribution over the set of possible states based on a set of observations and observation probabilities and the underlying MDP. A POMDP framework is general enough to model a variety of real-world sequential decision process. Applications like Robot navigation problems, machine maintenance and planning uncertainity are included here.

An exact solution to a POMDP yields the optimal action for each possible belief over the world states. **The optimal action maximizes or minimizes the expected reward or cost of the agent over a possibly infinite horizon. The sequence of optimal actions is known as the optimal policy of the agent for interacting with its environment.**

MDP assumes that the complete state of the world is visible to the agent. This is quite unrealistic. POMDPS models the information available to the agent by specifying a function from the hidden state to the observables. The **goal** now is to find a mapping from observations (not states) to actions. But the observations are not Markov because two different states might look the same, which invalidates all of the MDP solution techniques. **The optimal solution to this problem is to construct a belief state MDP, where a belief state is a probability distribution over states.**

Control theory is concerned with solving POMDPs. Practically speaking, control theory scientists make a strong assumption about the nature of the model (linear-Gaussian) and reward function (negative quadratic loss) in order to be able to make theoretical guarantees of optimality. Solving a generic discrete POMDP is wildly intractable. Finding tractable special cases like structured models is the current area of research today.

Limitations of POMDPs

They model the world in terms of a fixed size set of state variables, each of which can take on specific values, say true or false. **These are called as propositional models.**

3.10 Applications of POMDPs

POMDPs can be used to model real-life problems. It has been used in management of patients with ischemic heart disease, assistive technology for persons with dementia, the conservation of the critically endangered and difficult to detect Sumatran tigers and aircraft collision avoidance.

Summary

We have studied the concept of reinforcement learning like MDPs, maximum rewards problem. Different approaches to deep reinforcement learning like policy gradients, deep-Q networks etc have also been studied in this chapter. Deep reinforcement learning is a step in this direction that has produced agents capable of mastering Atari games, driverless cars, robotics etc.

MULTIPLE CHOICE QUESTIONS (MCQs)

1. MDP stands for-
   (a) Many Decision Problems.　(b) Markov Decision Process.
   (c) Markov Dynamic Problem.　(d) None of the above.
2. A branch of machine learning that deals with learning with interaction and feedback is called as-
   (a) Leaning by Example.　(b) Reinforcement Learning.
   (c) Deep Learning　(d) None of the above.
3. An application of reinforcement learning using deep networks is-
   (a) DQN.　(b) AQN.
   (c) PQN.　(d) None of the above.
4. Reinforcement learning involves-
   (a) An actor.　(b) An environment.
   (c) A reward signal.　(d) All of the above.
5. The ways in which our agent acts based on its current state is-
   (a) Policy.　(b) Learning.
   (c) Testing.　(d) None of the above.
6. Reinforcement learning is basically a-
   (a) Trial and error process.　(b) Algorithmic process.
   (c) Dynamic process.　(d) None of the above.
7. In which type of learning we learn the value of every (state+ action) pair-
   (a) Policy learning.　(b) Value learning.
   (c) Machine learning.　(d) None of the above.
8. Q-learning is put under-
   (a) Policy learning.　(b) Value learning.
   (c) Machine learning.　(d) None of the above.

9. The process of updating of the Q-value is known as-
   (a) Policy iteration. (b) Value iteration.
   (c) Research iteration. (d) None of the above.
10. DQN uses-
   (a) Life history. (b) State history.
   (c) Indian history. (d) None of the above.
11. Which of the following is a Q-network-
   (a) The prediction network. (b) The computer network.
   (c) LAN. (d) None of the above.
12. DQRN stands for-
   (a) Deep Recurrent Q-Network. (b) Direct Recursive Q-Network.
   (c) Prediction network. (d) None of the above.
13. Deep reinforcement learning has produced-
   (a) Agents. (b) Letters.
   (c) Messages. (d) None of the above.

Answers

1. b	2. b	3. a	4. d	5. a	6. a
7. b	8. b	9. b	10. b	11. a	12. a
13. a					

Conceptual Short Questions (with Answers)

Q1. Distinguish between a perceptron and delta rule.

Ans. The following are the points of differences between the two:

A Perceptron	Delta Rule
It uses threshold unit.	It uses unthreshold linear unit.
It converges after a finite number of iterations.	It converges asymptotically toward a minimum error hypothesis.
Output hypothesis classifies training data perfectly.	Termination is not guaranteed.
Linear separability is mandatory.	Linear separability is not mandatory.

Q2. List some applications of back propagation perceptrons.

Ans. The following are some of the applications:

1. Optical character recognition.
5. Data compression.
2. Image compression.

3. Load forecasting problems in power systems.
4. Speech synthesis.
5. Content problem.
6. Pattern recognition.
7. Fault detection problems.
8. Aircraft navigation.
9. Non-linear simulation

Q3. Write a short note on SOMs.

Ans. SOMs stands for Self Organizing Feature Maps or Kohonen Network **is a data visualization technique proposed by Kohonen, which provides a way of representing multidimensional data in much lower dimensional spaces. And this process of reducing the dimensionality of vectors is a data compression technique known as vector quantization.** This technique creates a network that stores information in such a way that any topological relationships within the training set are maintained. So they are also called as **topology-preserving maps.** The topological structure property is observed in our brain and is not found in any other ANN except SOM. **Please note that the self-organizing map as developed by Kohonen, groups the input data into clusters which are commonly used for unsupervised learning.**

In SOM, there are 'm' cluster units that are arranged in a 1D or 2d array, an input vector of n-tuples and a weight vector associated with the cluster unit. In self-organizing process, the cluster unit whose weight vector matches the input pattern closely is selected as a winner. The winning and the neighbouring unit update their weights. The neighbouring unit's weight vectors are not close to the input pattern but differ in some extent. That is why the connection weights do not multiply the signal sent from the input units to cluster units.

In SOM, all units in the neighbourhood that receive positive feedback from the winning unit participate in the learning process. Even if a neighbouring unit's weight is **orthogonal** to the input vector, its weight vector will still change in response to the input vector. This is required to maintain the order mapping.

Q4. Differentiate between PCA and LDA.

Ans. The following are the points of differences:-

1. PCA does more of feature classification whereas LDA does data classification.
2. In PCA, the shape and the location of the original data sets changes when transformed to a different space. LDA does not change the location but only tries to provide more class separability and draw a decision region between the given classes. As such, LDA also helps in better understanding the distribution of the feature data.
3. PCA deals with unlabelled data and tries to maximize variance. PCA deals with unlabeled data and tries to maximize variance. PCA deals with unlabeled data and tries to maximize the discrimination between the classes.
4. If the discriminating information lies within the variances, then PCA works better than the LDA.

5. PCA is an unsupervised linear feature extraction method. LDA uses the category information associated with each pattern for extracting the most discriminatory features.

Q5. List the three steps of PCA.

Ans. The summary of PCA steps is:-

1. Organize a data set as m*n matrix, where m is the number of measurement types and n is the number of trials.
2. Subtract off the mean for each measurement type or row.
3. Calculate the Eigen vectors of the covariance.

Q6. Define EBL. What are its advantages?

Ans. **EBL extracts general rules from single examples by explaining the examples and generalizing the explanation.** It provides a deductive method turning first-principles knowledge into useful, efficient and special purpose expertise. Some of its advantages are as follows:-

1. Training examples often contains irrelevant information. The domain theory allows the learner to select he relevant aspects of the training example.
2. EBL forms generalizations that are known to be relevant to specific goals that are logically guaranteed to be logically consistent with the domain theory.
3. By using domain knowledge, EBL allows learning from a single training instance.
4. Construction of an explanation allows the learner to hypothesize unstated relationships between its goals and its experiences.

Q7. What do you mean by gap filling by EBL?

Ans. EBL or Explanation Based Learning makes up for small number of examples by using extensive domain knowledge. **If the explanation is complete,** then one can guarantee that the description is correct. But there are some problems as there might be instances where explanations may use reasoning steps that are not sound. **When such gaps are found in the explanation, an EBL system may use abduction or induction to fill them.**

Q8. Why do we disparage the term Q-value?

Ans. Researchers in the field of reinforcement learning discuss about Q-values, Q-tables and Q-functions. Such usage almost always seem like jargon i.e. like apparently precise technical terms that are off-putting to new comers but really adds nothing. In this case, the Q-prefix means only that the values, tables or functions pertain to (state + action) pairs. In most of the cases, we give these functions different notations, all of which involve the letter, Q. The name Q-function appears to be technical but is in fact imprecise and undesirable.

Q9. Which algorithm to use-actor critic method or Q-learning?

Ans. In 1980s, actor critic methods were very popular but in 1990s these were dominated by value-function methods like Q-learning and Sarsa. But Q-learning is instable with function approximation. So, it is not very useful for long run.

Q10. Give some limitations of Multilayer perceptrons.

Ans. Limitations of multilayer perceptrons are as follows:-

1. It requires large number of iterations for learning that is unsuitable for real-time learning.
2. It gives no guaranteed solution.

3. They do not scale up well from small research systems to larger real systems.
4. It is very difficult to determine all of the weights and thresholds theoretically.
5. It is very difficult to decide which input pattern should be represented by hidden layer.

Q11. What are the characteristics of delta learning rule?

Ans. The characteristics of delta learning rule are as follows:-

1. It uses output of activation function to generate error signal.
2. It can only be used with continuous activation functions.
3. It is a gradient based method e.g. the least mean square algorithm.
4. It can be generalized to multi-layer networks.
5. It gives continuous output so can be used for function approximation.

Q12. Show how a multi-layered perceptron solves a non-linear separable class problem.

Ans. Logical XOR Function is as follows:-

X_1	X_2	Output (Y)
0	0	0
0	1	1
1	0	1
1	1	0

The output from a neuron is calculated as follows:

$$Y = X_1 * W_1 + X_2 * W_2$$

In form of a graph, we can draw:

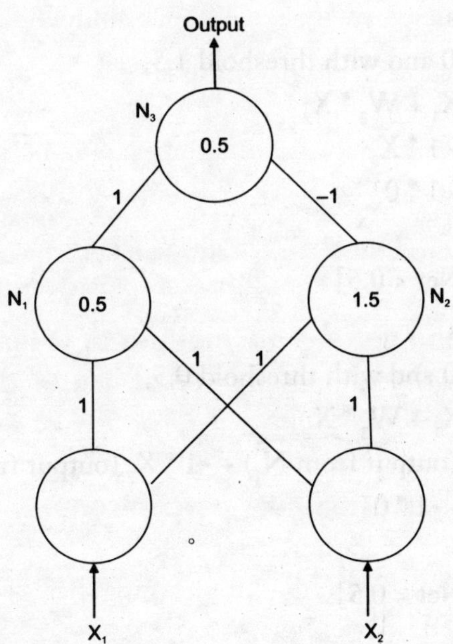

From this graph, the activations of output neuron can be formed:

Neuron, N_1 uses the activation function-

$$O = f(Net) = \begin{cases} 1 \text{ if } Net \geq 0.5 \\ 0 \text{ if } Net < 0.5 \end{cases}$$

Neuron, N_2 uses the activation function-

$$O = f(Net) = \begin{cases} 1 \text{ if } Net \geq 1.5 \\ 0 \text{ if } Net < 1.5 \end{cases}$$

Neuron, N_3 uses the activation function-

$$O = f(Net) = \begin{cases} 1 \text{ if } Net \geq 0.5 \\ 0 \text{ if } Net < 0.5 \end{cases}$$

Now the network learns as follows:

1. **Output from neuron, N_1 is**

   For input $X_1 = 0$ and $X_2 = 0$ and with threshold 0.5,

   $$\begin{aligned} Net &= W_1 * X_1 + W_2 * X_2 \\ &= 1.X_1 + 1 * X_2 \\ &= 1 * 0 + 1 * 0 \\ &= 0 \end{aligned}$$

   So, O= f (Net) = 0 [as Net < 0.5]

2. **Output from neuron, N_2 is**

   For input $X_1 = 0$ and $X_2 = 0$ and with threshold 1.5,

   $$\begin{aligned} Net &= W_1 * X_1 + W_2 * X_2 \\ &= 1.X_1 + 1 * X_2 \\ &= 1 * 0 + 1 * 0 \\ &= 0 \end{aligned}$$

   So, O= f (Net) = 0 [as Net < 0.5]

3. **Output from neuron, N_3 is**

   For input $X_1 = 0$ and $X_2 = 0$ and with threshold 0.5,

   $$\begin{aligned} Net &= W_1 * X_1 + W_2 * X_2 \\ &= 1.X_1 \text{ (output from } N_1) + -1 * X_2 \text{ (output from } N_2) \\ &= 1 * 0 + -1 * 0 \\ &= 0 \end{aligned}$$

   So, O= f (Net) = 0 [as Net < 0.5]

Output from Neuron, N_1

For input $X_1 = 0$ and $X_2 = 1$ and with threshold 0.5,

$$\begin{aligned} Net &= W_1 * X_1 + W_2 * X_2 \\ &= 1.X_1 + 1 * X_2 \\ &= 1 * 0 + 1 * 1 \\ &= 1 \\ \text{So, } O = f(Net) &= 1 \text{ [as Net} \geq 0.5] \end{aligned}$$

Output from neuron, N_2 is

For input $X_1 = 0$ and $X_2 = 1$ and with threshold 1.5,

$$\begin{aligned} Net &= W_1 * X_1 + W_2 * X_2 \\ &= 1.X_1 + 1 * X_2 \\ &= 1 * 0 + 1 * 1 \\ &= 1 \\ \text{So, } O = f(Net) &= 0 \text{ [as Net} < 1.5] \end{aligned}$$

Output from neuron, N_3 is

For input $X_1 = 0$ and $X_2 = 1$ and with threshold 0.5,

$$\begin{aligned} Net &= W_1 * X_1 + W_2 * X_2 \\ &= 1.X_1 \text{ (output from } N_1) + -1 * X_2 \text{(output from } N_2) \\ &= 1 * 1 + -1 * 0 \\ &= 1 \end{aligned}$$

So, O= f(Net) = 1 [as Net $\geq$ 0.5]

Output from neuron N_1

For input $X_1 = 1$ and $X_2 = 0$ and with threshold 0.5,

$$\begin{aligned} Net &= W_1 * X_1 + W_2 * X_2 \\ &= 1.X_1 + 1 * X_2 \\ &= 1 * 1 + 1 * 0 \\ &= 1 \end{aligned}$$

So, O= f (Net) = 1 [as Net $\geq$ 0.5]

Output from neuron, N_2 is

For input $X_1 = 1$ and $X_2 = 0$ and with threshold 1.5,

$$\begin{aligned} Net &= W_1 * X_1 + W_2 * X_2 \\ &= 1.X_1 + 1 * X_2 \\ &= 1 * 1 + 1 * 0 \\ &= 1 \end{aligned}$$

So, O= f (Net) = 0 [as Net < 1.5]

Output from neuron, N_3 is

- For input $X_1 = 1$ and $X_2 = 0$ and with threshold 0.5,

$$\begin{aligned} \text{Net} &= W_1 * X_1 + W_2 * X_2 \\ &= 1.X_1 \text{ (output from } N_1) + -1 * X_2 \text{ (output from } N_2) \\ &= 1 * 1 + -1 * 0 \\ &= 1 \end{aligned}$$

So, O= f(Net) = 1 [as Net ≥ 0.5]

Output from neuron, N_1 is

For input $X_1 = 1$ and $X_2 = 1$ and with threshold 0.5,

$$\begin{aligned} \text{Net} &= W_1 * X_1 + W_2 * X_2 \\ &= 1.X_1 + 1 * X_2 \\ &= 1 * 1 + 1 * 1 \\ &= 2 \end{aligned}$$

So, O= f (Net) = 1 [as Net > 0.5]

Output from neuron, N_2 is

For input $X_1 = 1$ and $X_2 = 1$ and with threshold 1.5,

$$\begin{aligned} \text{Net} &= W_1 * X_1 + W_2 * X_2 \\ &= 1.X_1 + 1 * X_2 \\ &= 1 * 1 + 1 * 1 \\ &= 2 \end{aligned}$$

So, O= f(Net) = 1 [as Net ≥ 1.5]

Output from neuron, N_3 is

For input $X_1 = 1$ and $X_2 = 1$ and with threshold 0.5,

$$\begin{aligned} \text{Net} &= W_1 * X_1 + W_2 * X_2 \\ &= 1.X_1 \text{ (output from } N_1) + -1 * X_2 \text{ (output from } N_2) \\ &= 1 * 1 + -1 * 1 = 1 - 1 \\ &= 0 \end{aligned}$$

So, O= f(Net) = 0 [as Net < 0.5]

Q13. Define the following:

(a) Pulling error signals.

(b) Pushing error signals.

Ans.

(a) **Pulling error signals:** The process of computing delta signals for each neuron in the previous layer by pulling the error signals from the current layer is called as pulling error signals.

(b) **Pushing error signals:** The process of pushing the error signals from the current layer to the previous layer i.e. for each unit in the current layer, we update the related units in the previous layer.

Q14. What is a confusion matrix or contingency table? What is its use?

Ans. In machine learning, a **confusion matrix/contingency matrix** is also known as an **error matrix.** It is a specific table layout that allows visualization of the performance of an algorithm, typically a supervised learning. The one in unsupervised learning is known as a **matching matrix.** Each column of the matrix represents the instances in a predicted class while each row represents the instances in an actual class or vice versa. **Please note that the name stems from the fact that it makes it easy to see if the system is confusing two classes i.e. commonly mislabelling one as another.** It is a special type of table with two dimensions-actual and predicted and identical set of classes in both the dimensions. So, each combination of dimension and class is a variable in the contingency table.

Q15. Define the following terms:

(a) Confusion matrix.

(b) False positive rate.

(c) True positive rate.

Ans. (a) **Confusion matrix:** A confusion matrix contains information about actual and predicted classifications done by a classification system. Performance of such systems is commonly evaluated using the data in the matrix. The following table shows the confusion matrix for a two class classifier. The entries in the confusion matrix have the following meaning in the context of our study:

- a is the number of **correct predictions** that an instance is **negative,**
- b is the number of **incorrect predictions** that an instance is **positive,**
- c is the number of **incorrect predictions** that an instance is **negative,**
- d is the number of **correct predictions** that an instance is **positive.**

Exercise Questions

Q1. Explain Q learning.

Q2. Explain value function in the context of reinforcement learning.

Q3. Explain Hidden Markov Model in detail.

Q4. Explain the back propagation algorithm of Multilayer Neural Network. Also explain the factor influencing back propagation training.

Q5. Explain SOMs.

Q6. What is delta rule?

Q7. Distinguish between perceptron and delta rule.

Q8. Why self organizing neural net is called as the topology preserving maps?

Q9. Distinguish between classification and regression.

Q10. State 'Universal Approximation Theorem'.

Q11. Define curse of dimensionality.

Q12. Define overfitting / overtraining.

Q13. Define cross validation.

Q14. Explain how optimization is achieved in neural networks.

Q15. 'Q learning agent learns optimal policy but much slower than ADP agent'. Explain this statement.

Q16. Draw flowchart to explain —Training a Deep Learning Model.

Q17. Explain the following- Test Sets and Validation Sets, Overfitting Phenomenon, Epoch, Training Data, Test Data, Hyperparameter Optimization, Critical Point, Local Maxima, Saddle Points, Learning Rate Adaptation.

Q18. Explain the following:
 (a) Markov Decision Processes [MDP].
 (b) BELLMAN Equations.
 (c) Value Iteration and Policy Iteration.
 (d) Linear Quadratic Regulation (LQR).

Q19. Draw a fully connected feedforward ANN that has three input nodes, one output node and four internal nodes in a hidden layer.

Q20. Explain how would you represent the ages of a group of people ranging from 20 to 50 years as input into an ANN.

4 Deep Learning Optimization

4.0 Introduction

The purpose of any optimization problem is to either maximize or minimize the objective function with some constraints. Some of these problems can be solved using complex ANNs too. It is an art and science of allocating limited resources in a best possible way. Pattern classification is a very common example of optimization. Here, the objective is to classify or recognize a pattern. In machine learning, an optimizer is used to maximize the performance of a machine learning model iteratively. The parameters are adjusted till the error is minimized.

4.1 Learning versus Pure Optimization

The main challenge in optimizing deep learning models is that **we are compelled to use minimal local information to infer the global structure of the error surface.** During training of deep networks, several challenges are observed like having complex error surfaces. The objective today is not to build a better optimizer rather it is to discover the architectures that are simple to train. Literature also describes the evolution of adaptive learning rate optimizers that tune the learning rate during the training process so as to get a better convergence.

Several hyperparameters like learning rate, mini-batch size etc., have been dealt with in previous sections. But the need is to find a framework for how to find the optimal values for these hyeperparameters. One method of finding the optimal parameters values is named as a **grid search.** In this method, we select a value for each hyperparameter from a finite set of options and batch size and train the model with every possible permutation of hyperparameter choices. The objective is to find out the accuracy of the model trained with the best set on the test set. This is **pure optimization.**

A MLP neural network trained by back propagation with 4026 input neurons and two hidden layers of 20 and 10 neurons each and with a single output neuron to say 'Yes' or 'No' was designed to classify the tissue data as cancerous or normal. A part of the available data i.e. 72 sets were used for training and 22 were kept for testing the network for generality. After training for 1000 iterations, the network predicted correctly on 91% of the test patterns.

Present day research is being done on the adaptation of neurocomputing, fuzzy logic and evolutionary search to overcome limitations found in the use of traditional optimization methods in problems of multi-disciplinary analysis and design. The challenges include reducing the high computational cost associated with repetitive analysis, adapting emergent optimization methods for large scale design problems involving a mix of continuous, discrete and integer variables.

On the other hand, learning **is the process by which a free parameter of a neural network gets adapted through a process of simulation by the environment. And the set of rules defined for the solution of a learning problem is called as a learning algorithm.**

According to Simon, **"Learning denotes changes in the system that are adaptive in the sense that they enable the system to do the task or tasks drawn from the same population more efficiently and more effectively the next time."** Learning may be supervised, unsupervised/clustering, reinforcement learning and inductive learning. One of the simplest algorithms is decision tree learning. Explanation based learning extracts general rules from simple examples by explaining and generalizing them. Statistical learning includes data and hypothesis.

Learning may be done by complete data or hidden data. Let us differentiate between them.

Table-1: Differences between complete data and hidden data

Complete Data	Hidden Data
Parameters of the model can be estimated locally and independently.	Parameters cannot be estimated independently.
Local likelihood has a unique maximum.	There are many local maxima.
Closed-form solutions are obtained.	Closed-form solutions cannot be obtained.

4.2 Challenges in Neural Network Optimization

The main challenge in optimizing deep learning models is that we are compelled to use minimal local information to infer the global structure of the error surface. During training of deep networks, several challenges are observed like having complex error surfaces. The objective today is not to build a better optimizer rather it is to discover the architectures that are simple to train. Literature also describes the evolution of adaptive learning rate optimizers that tune the learning rate during the training process so as to get a better convergence.

Present day research is being done on the adaptation of neurocomputing, fuzzy logic and evolutionary search to overcome limitations found in the use of traditional optimization methods in problems of multi-disciplinary analysis and design. The challenges include reducing the high computational cost associated with repetitive analysis, adapting emergent optimization methods for large scale design problems involving a mix of continuous, discrete and integer variables.

4.3 Basic Optimization Algorithms

In 2011, Duchi et al. gave an algorithm named as **AdaGrad** that tries to adapt the global learning rate over time using an accumulation of the historical gradients. In this algorithm, we keep track of a learning rate for each parameter. This learning rate is inversely scaled with respect to the square root of the sum of squares (rms value) of all the parameter's historical gradients. In TensorFlow (a deep learning tool), it has been found that there is an inbuilt *optimizer* and that it allows us to easily utilize AdaGrad as a learning algorithm. **Please note that the parameters with the largest gradients experience a rapid decrease in their learning rates while parameters with smaller gradients will**

observe only a small decrease in their learning rates. The final result is that **AdaGrad** compels better progress in a more gently sloped directions on the error surface.

Also **AdaGrad** has a drawback too. It causes a premature drop in learning rate. So, it does not perform well for some deep models.

AdaGrad works well for complex functions but it is not designed to navigate the complex error surfaces of deep networks. **Also note that flat regions compel AdaGrad to decrease the learning rate before it reaches a minimum.**

A solution to this is another algorithm- **RMSProp.** As RMSProp performs well with momentum, so it has been found to be better optimizer for deep neural networks. This algorithm was given by Geoffrey Hinton.

Yet another algorithm was proposed by Kingma et al. It is a combination of RMSProp and momentum. Here, **we want to keep track of an exponentially weighted moving average of the gradient.** We try to find the *first moment of gradient, second moment of gradient* and so on. These are our estimations. But here these estimations are biased relative to the real moments as we start by initializing both vectors to the zero vector. To remedy this bias, we derive the correction factor for both of the estimations. Recently, Adam has become very popular because of its corrective measure against the zero initialization bias, which happens to be a weakness of RMSProp, and its ability to combine the core concepts behind RMSProp with momentum more effectively. Also, Adam is robust to choices in hyperparameters, the only point is that the learning rate may need to be modified in certain cases from the default value of 0.001.

In nutshell, the adaptive learning rate optimizers evolve. They tune to the learning rate during the training process for better convergence.

4.4 Parameter Initializations

A neural network trains by repeated passes of the data. Each pass is called as an **epoch.** With each epoch, the connecting weights are adjusted until a satisfactory level of performance is reached. We think that by increasing the number of epochs, the system will perform better. But this is not true with deep neural networks. **It has been found that with several passes, the network gets overtrained and needs more computing time. This has been called as overfitting or overtraining.**

We can change the parameter values of the algorithm. The default setting of hyperparameters may not always be good.

Several hyperparameters like learning rate, mini-batch size etc., have been dealt with in previous chapters. But the need is to find a framework for how to find the optimal values for these hyeperparameters. One method of finding the optimal parameters values is named as a **grid search.** In this method, we select a value for each hyperparameter from a finite set of options and batch size and train the model with every possible permutation of hyperparameter choices. The objective is to find out the accuracy of the model trained with the best set on the test set.

4.5 Meta-algorithms

The early stopping meta-algorithm for determining the best amount of time to train is discussed now. This meta-algorithm is a general strategy that works well with a variety of training algorithms. It gives ways of quantifying error on the validation set.

Let n be the number of steps between evaluations.

Let p be the "patience," the number of times to observe worsening validation set error before giving up.

Let θo be the initial parameters.

θ ← θo

i ← 0

j ← 0

v ← ∞

θ← θ

i ← i

while j < p **do**

//Update θ by running the training algorithm for n steps.

i ← i + n

v ← ValidationSetError(θ)

if v < v **then**

j ← 0

θ ← θ

i ← i

v ← v

else

j ← j + 1

end if

end while

Best parameters are θ and the best number of training steps is i.

This strategy is known as *early stopping*. It is probably the most commonly used form of regularization in deep learning. It is very popular as it is both effectiveness and its simplicity.

One way to think of early stopping is as a very efficient hyperparameter selection algorithm. So, the number of training steps is just another hyperparameter.

In the case of early stopping, we are controlling the effective capacity of the model by determining how many steps it can take to fit the training set. Most hyperparameters must be chosen using an expensive guess and check process, where we set a hyperparameter at the start of training, then run training for several steps to see its effect. The **"training time"** hyperparameter is unique in that by definition a single run of training tries out many values of the hyperparameter. The only significant cost to choosing this hyperparameter automatically via early stopping is running the validation set evaluation periodically during training. Ideally, this is done in parallel to the training process on a separate machine, separate CPU, or separate GPU from the main training process. If such resources are not available, then the cost of these periodic evaluations may be reduced by using a validation set that is small compared to the training set or by evaluating the validation set error less frequently and obtaining a lower resolution estimate of the optimal training time.

An additional cost to early stopping is the need to maintain a copy of the best parameters. This cost is generally negligible, because it is acceptable to store these parameters in a slower and larger form of memory (for example, training in GPU memory, but storing the optimal parameters in host memory or on a disk drive). Since the best parameters are written to infrequently and never read during training, these occasional slow writes have little effect on the total training time.

Early stopping is a very unobtrusive form of regularization, in that it requires almost no change in the underlying training procedure, the objective function, or the set of allowable parameter values. **Also note that this means that it is easy to use early stopping without damaging the learning dynamics.** This is in contrast to **weight decay**, where one must be careful not to use too much weight decay and trap the network in a **bad local minimum** corresponding to a solution with pathologically small weights.

Early stopping may be used either alone or in conjunction with other regularization strategies. Even when using regularization strategies that modify the objective function to encourage better generalization, it is rare for the best generalization to occur at a local minimum of the training objective.

Early stopping requires a validation set, which means some training data is not fed to the model. To best exploit this extra data, one can perform extra training after the initial training with early stopping has completed.

Summary

In this chapter, we have studied how learning is different from optimization. Optimization here refers to the optimization of deep learning networks. It also discusses about the best optimization algorithms and their parameters initializations. Also discussed is a meta-algorithm, namely early learning. In nutshell, the adaptive learning rate optimizers evolve. They tune to the learning rate during the training process for better convergence.

MULTIPLE CHOICE QUESTIONS [MCQs]

1. Pattern classification is an example of-
   (a) Classification.
   (b) Optimization.
   (c) Normalization.
   (d) None of the above.
2. An optimizer aims to-
   (a) Maximize the performance of machine learning model.
   (b) Minimize the performance of machine learning model.
   (c) Neutralize the performance of machine learning model.
   (d) None of the above.
3. Which one of the following is a popular adaptive learning rate algorithm-
   (a) AdaGrad.
   (b) RMSProp.

(c) Adam. (d) All of these.

4. Optimizers tune the learning rate during-
(a) Training. (b) Generalizations.
(c) Specializations. (d) None of the above.

5. Which of the following is a deep learning tool-
(a) TensorFlow. (b) DataFlow.
(c) Wtare Flow. (d) None of the above.

Answers

1. b 2. a 3. d 4. a 5. a

Conceptual Short Questions (with Answers)

Q1. Are deep learning algorithms slower than other algorithms?

Ans. Yes, deep learning models take more CPU time than other algorithms. So, we have to keep our grid searches as precise as possible.

Q2. What is early stopping? Explain.

Ans. A technique based on dividing data into three subsets. The first subset is the training set used for computing the gradient and updating the network weights and biases. The second subset is the validation set. When the validation error increases for a specified number of iterations, the training is stopped and the weights and biases at the minimum of the validation error are returned. The third subset is the test set. It is used to verify the network design.

Q3. Define what is an Epoch?

Ans. A neural network trains by repeated passes of the data. Each pass is called as an **epoch.**

Q4. 'Increasing the number of Epochs will make the system perform better'. Explain.

Ans. This is not true with deep neural networks. **It has been found that with several passes, the network gets overtrained and needs more computing time. This has been called as overfitting or overtraining.**

Q5. What is grid search?

Ans. In grid search, we select a value for each hyperparameter from a finite set of options and batch size and train the model with every possible permutation of hyperparameter choices. The objective is to find out the accuracy of the model trained with the best set on the test set.

Exercise Questions

Q1. Define optimization and an optimizer.

Q2. Define an Epoch. What is its role during training?

Q3. What are meta-algorithms? Give an example to explain.

Q4. Write short notes on basic optimization algorithms.

Q5. Define the following:

(a) Overfitting or overtraining.

(b) Grid Search.

(c) Hyperparameters.

(d) Early stopping.

(e) Training time.

(f) RMSProp.

5 Convolutional Neural Networks

5.0 Introduction

A typical CNN consists up of many layers of hierarchy with some layers for feature representations or feature maps and others as a type of conventional neural networks for classification. It starts with 2 layers:

(a) Convolutional layers.

(b) Subsampling layers.

The convolutional layers perform convolution operations with several filter maps of equal size. The subsampling layers reduce the sizes of the proceeding layers by averaging pixels within a small neighborhood or by max-pooling.

The key parameters to be decided are weights between layers that are normally trained by standard backpropagation procedures and a gradient descent algorithm with mean squared-error as the loss function. **Note that training deep CNN architectures can be unsupervised or supervised.**

Inspired by the biological processes, CNN algorithms learn a hierarchical feature representation by utilizing strategies like local receptive fields where the size of each filter is normally small, shared weights-using the same weights to construct all of the feature maps at the same level reduces the number of parameters and subsampling to further reduce the dimensionality. Each filter bank can be trained with either supervised or unsupervised methods. A CNN is capable of learning good feature hierarchies automatically and providing some degree of translational and distortional invariances.

5.1 Convolution

Consider the case of an image wherein the input to NN will be pixels. By looking at pixels, **the first hidden layer** units may learn to check for edges of various orientations, then the combining edges, **the second hidden layer** units can learn to check for combinations of edges like arcs, corners, line ends and then **combining them in upper layers**, the units can look for semi-circles, rectangles. **Please note that this is an example of a hierarchical cone where features get more complex, abstract and fewer in numbers as we go up the network until we get to the classes. Such an architecture is called as convolutional neural network where the work of each hidden unit is considered to be a convolution of its input with its weight vector. The process of taking a filter and then multiplying it over the entire area of an input image is called as convolution.**

5.2 The Convolutional Layer

It is also possible to further reduce the number of parameters by the process called as **weight sharing.** Like in case of visual recognition system, features like oriented edges may be present in different parts of the input space. So, instead of defining independent hidden units, learning different features in different parts of the input space, we can have copies of the same hidden units looking at different parts of the input space. This is shown in figure 5.1. During learning, we compute the gradients by taking different inputs and then we average these and make a single update. This implies a single parameter that defines the weight on multiple connections. As the update on a weight is based on gradients for several inputs, it is as if the training set is effectively multiplied.

Fig.5.1: Weight Sharing

In weight sharing, different units have connections to different inputs but share the same weight value (denoted by line type). Only one set of units is shown in figure 5.1. There should be multiple sets of units, each checking for different features.

5.3 The Convolution Operation

The process of taking a filter and then multiplying it over the entire area of an input image is called as convolution.

Let us show this operation in terms of neurons in a network. In this schema, layers of neurons in a feed-forward neural net represent either the **original image or a feature map. Filters represent combinations of connections that get replicated across the entirety of the input (**as shown in figure 5.2). As shown in figure 5.2, connections of the same type are restricted to always have the same weight. We can get this by initializing all the connections in a group with identical weights and by always averaging the weight updates of a group before applying them at the end of each of the iteration of backpropagation. **Please note that the output layer is the feature map generated by this filter. Also note that a neuron in a feature map is activated if the filter contributing to its activity detected an appropriate feature at the corresponding position in the previous layer.**

The point is that the feature maps must be able to operate over volumes and not just areas. Each cell in the input volume is a neuron. A local portion is multiplied with a filter, corresponding to the weights in the convolutional layer, to produce a neuron in a filter map in the following volumetric layers of neurons. **Please understand that a convolutional layer that consists of a set of filters,**

converts one volume of values into another volume of values. The depth of the filter corresponds to the depth of the input volume. This is so that the filter can combine information from all the features that have been learned. The depth of the output volume of a convolutional layer is equivalent to the number of filters in that layer as each filter produces its own slice.

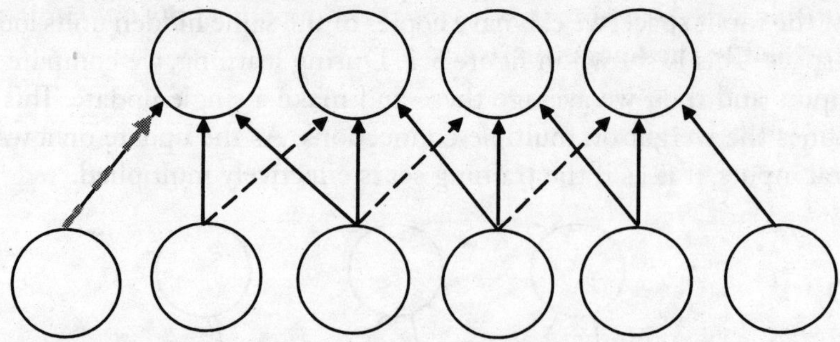

Fig.5.2: Showing Filters and Feature Maps as Neurons in a Convolutional Layer

Please remember the following points regarding Convolutional Layer:

1. A convolutional layer takes in an input volume.
2. This input volume has the following features- its width, its height, depth and zero padding.
3. This volume is processed by a total of k filters that represent the weights and connections in the convolutional network.
4. These filters have a number of hyperparameter as follows:
   (a) **Spatial extent (e):** It is equal to the filters height and width.
   (b) **Stride (s): The distance between consecutive applications of the filter on the input volume.** If we use a stride of 1, we get the full convolution.
   (c) **Bias (b):** A parameter learned like the values in the filter which is added to each component of the convolution.
5. This results in an output volume with the following features:-
   (a) The function, f, which is applied to the incoming logit of each neuron in the output volume to determine its final volume.
   (b) Its width;
   (c) Its height;
   (d) Its depth (= k)
6. The mth **depth-slice of the output volume corresponds to the function, f, applied to the sum of the mth filter convoluted over the input volume and the bias, b^m** where $1 \le m \le k$.
7. In general, the filter sizes should be kept in smaller sizes like 3 * 3 or 5 * 5.
8. But larger filter sizes like 8 * 8 may be used at the first convolutional layer only.
9. **Having more smaller filters will help us to achieve high representational power. Also the parameters will be smaller in number.**

10. We should use the stride of 1 to capture all useful information in the feature maps.
11. Use a zero padding to keep the output volume's height and width equivalent to the input volume's height and width.
12. Deep learning tool , **TensorFlow,** makes easier for us to perform a convolution on a mini-batch of input volumes. **Also note that we must choose and apply our choice of function, f, as it is not performed by the operation itself.**
13. The basic idea is to match patterns (like a 5 * 5 patterns) as sliding tiles, all over your image. This is alternated with a shrink layer where the maximum pixel value is chosen from each non-overlapping 2 * 2 block. This gives a 12 * 12 output per pattern. Then we might repeat with a 3 * 3 pattern and another round of 2 * 2 **shrinkage.**

5.4 Max Pooling

Pooling has been used in data mining field to determine and assign replacement values for missing, invalid or inconsistent data that have failed edits. The technique is known as **multiple imputation** that involves three steps- imputation, analysis and pooling. **Imputation** is about filling up of missing data and are drawn from the missing data (we get **m-complete data sets**). **Analysis** results in **m-analyses (analysing each of completed m-data sets).** And finally **pooling** involves **integration of these m-complete data sets into a final result.** The **point estimate** from multiple imputations is the average of the estimate from each analysis.

The process of reducing the dimensionality of feature maps by breaking up each feature map into equally sized tiles and sharpening the located features to create a condensed feature map is known as max-pooling. Specifically, we create a cell for each tile, compute the maximum value in the tile and propagate this maximum value into the corresponding cell of the condensed feature map. So, we can say that max pooling significantly reduces parameters as we move up the network. A pooling layer will have 2 parameters:

(a) Its spatial extent (e),

(b) Its stride (s).

Please note that only two major variations of the pooling layer are used as follows:

(a) Non-overlapping pooling layer with e=2 and s=2.

(b) Overlapping pooling layer with e=3 and s=2.

Also note that max pooling is locally invariant. This means that even if the inputs shift around a little bit, the output of the max pooling layer stays constant. This has an application in visual algorithms also. **Local invariance** is a very useful property but we need to think more whether some feature is present or not rather than where it is exactly. **But understand that compelling large amount of local invariance can destroy our networks ability to carry vital information. Also note that that is why we keep the spatial extent of our pooling layer smaller.**

Another variant of max pooling has been given by Graham and is named as fractional max pooling. He used a **pseudorandom number generator** to generate tilings with non-integer lengths for pooling. This also prevents **over-fitting or over-training.**

5.5 Various Convolutional Network Architectures

A typical CNN architecture is shown in figure 5.3.

Explanation: The **input** is a 2D image. This image **convolutes** with four different filters, f_1 to f_4. This is followed by non-linear activation, to form the four feature maps in the second layer (C_1). These **feature maps** are then **down-sampled** by a factor of 2 to create the feature maps in layer, S_1. *The sequence of convolution or non-linear activation or subsampling can be repeated many times.* But at C_2 layer, we need 8 different filters (f_{11} to f_{18}). The 1st, 3rd, 4th and 6th feature maps in layer C_2 are defined by one corresponding feature map in layer S_1, each convoluting with a different filter. And the 2nd and 5th maps in layer C_2 are formed by two maps in S_1 convoluting with two different filters. The last layer is an **output layer** to form a fully connected 1D neural network i.e. the 2D outputs from the last subsampling later (S_2) will be concatenated into one long input vector with each neuron fully connected with all neurons in the next layer i.e. a hidden layer.

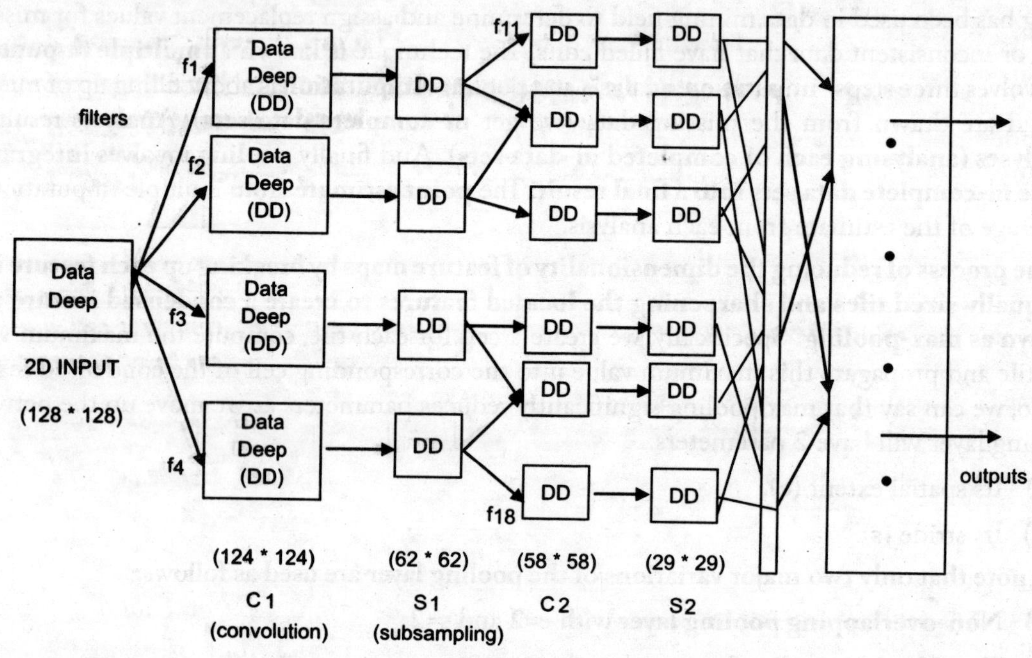

Fig.5.3: A Convolutional Neural Net Architecture

So, we find that the input is first convoluted with a set of filters (C layers). **These 2D filtered data are called as feature maps. Please note here that after a non-linear transformation, a subsampling is further performed to reduce the dimensionality (S layers).** The sequence of convolution and sampling can be repeated many times that is predetermined by the users. With local receptive fields, upper layer neurons extract some basic and complex visual features. Each convolutional layer consists of multiple feature maps that are constructed by convolving with inputs with different weight factors/ filters. So, the value of each unit in a feature map depends on a local receptive field in the previous layer and the filter. From figure 5.3, we observe that how a 2d input of size 128 * 128 is reduced to 124 * 124 at C_1 which is further reduced to 62 * 62 at S_1. By repeating this process again, we can further reduce the image to 58* 58 at layer C_2 and then to a 29 * 29 image at S_2.

The main factors to be decided are the **weights between these layers and that these are trained by standard back-propagation algorithm as discussed earlier.** Training deep CNN architectures can be unsupervised too.

Also note that as we build deeper networks, we reduce the number of pooling layers and instead stack multiple convolutional layers in tandem. This is better as pooling operations are **inherently destructive only.** So, *stacking several convolutional layers before each pooling layer gives better representations.* **Practically speaking,** deep convolutional networks may take significant amount of space. The bottleneck is the memory capacity. Many deep networks make a compromise by using strides and spatial extents at the 1st convolutional layer that reduces the amount of information that needs to propagate up the network.

Applications: CNN has been used to recognize handwritten digits. The feed-forward network was able to achieve an accuracy of 98.2% we can use Adam optimizer to train our network. The accuracy got further improved to 99.4%

Google scholars in 2015, gave another method of improving the training of feed-forward and CNNs by using a new technique named as **batch normalization. During the process of training of weights of the network, the output distribution of the neurons in the bottom layer also starts to shift. This means that the top layer has to learn now both – the appropriate predictions as well as to modify itself to accommodate the shifts in the incoming distribution. This will slow down the training process.**

But this process of batch normalization-

(a) Will normalize the inputs to every layer in our neural network to speed up the training process.

(b) Will increase the learning rate.

(c) Acts as a regularizer.

(d) Removes the need for dropout and regularizations.

(e) Removes the need for photometric distortions. We can expose the network to more real images during the training process.

Summary

As inspired by the biological neurons, CNN algorithms learn a hierarchical feature representation by using methods like local receptive fields, shared weights and subsampling. The aim is to reduce multi-dimensionality of data. We get a filter bank only that can be trained by either supervised or unsupervised methods. Also studied in this chapter is that CNN is capable of learning good feature hierarchies automatically.

MULTIPLE CHOICE QUESTIONS [MCQs]

1. CNN stands for-

(a) Complex Neural Networks. (b) Common Neural Nets.

(c) Convolutional Neural Networks. (d) None of the above.

2. 2D filtered data are called as-

(a) Feature maps. (b) Political maps.

(c) Social maps. (d) Google maps.

3. Training deep CNNs can be-
   (a) Unsupervised. (b) Supervised.
   (c) Both 'a' and 'b'. (d) None of the above.
4. Convolution can be performed-
   (a) By threads in parallel. (b) By threads in sequence.
   (c) By processes only. (d) None of the above.
5. We can reduce the number of parameters by-
   (a) Resource sharing. (b) Weight sharing.
   (c) Time sharing. (d) None of the above.
6. Learning should follow-
   (a) Early stopping. (b) Late stopping.
   (c) Normal stopping. (d) None of the above.
7. The process of breaking each feature map into equally sized tiles is known as-
   (a) Min pooling. (b) Max pooling.
   (c) Data pooling. (d) Spooling.
8. Inherently pooling operations are-
   (a) Constructive. (b) Destructive.
   (c) Objective. (d) None of the above.
9. In fractional max pooling, we use-
   (a) A clock. (b) A monitor.
   (c) A pseudorandom number generator. (d) None of the above.
10. Before each pooling layer, we stack several-
   (a) Hidden layers. (b) Convolutional layers.
   (c) Output layers. (d) None of the above.

Answers

1. c	2. a	3. c	4. a	5. b	6. a
7. b	8. b	9. c	10. B		

Conceptual Short Questions (with Answers)

Q1. Define cross validation.

Ans. **It is defined as a re-sampling technique used to estimate a model's performance.** It is always preferable if the number of examples in a data set is less than 1000.

Q2. What is the optimal point of stopping training?

Ans. The optimal point of stopping training and the optimal number of hidden units depends on the process called as cross validation. Cross validation is the process of testing the network's performance on validation data that is not seen during training.

Q3. What is max pooling?

Ans. The process of reducing the dimensionality of feature maps by breaking up each feature map into equally sized tiles and sharpening the located features to create a condensed feature map is known as max-pooling.

Q4. Define a stride.

Ans. Stride (s): The distance between consecutive applications of the filter on the input volume. If we use a stride of 1, we get the full convolution.

Q5. What are the advantages of batch normalization?

Ans. Batch normalization-

(a) Will normalize the inputs to every layer in our neural network to speed up the training process.

(b) Will increase the learning rate.

(c) Acts as a regularizer.

(d) Removes the need for dropout and regularizations.

(e) Removes the need for photometric distortions. We can expose the network to more real images during the training process.

Exercise Questions

Q1. Define convolution.

Q2. Explain CNN architecture with a neat diagram.

Q3. What is max pooling in CNNs?

Q4. Explain any one method of convolution.

Q5. What is batch normalization? How is it done?

Q6. Explain the following:-

(a) The convolution layers.

(b) The convolution operation.

Q7. What is the role of filters and subsampling in CNN architectures?

Q8. Explain the hyperparameters of filters.

Q9. What is the role of s pseudorandom number generator?

Q10. Name some deep learning case tools that help in convolution.

Q.11 The following table shows the Iris data set for 2 species only :

ID-No.	Petal Length	Petal Width	Sepal Length	Sepal Width	Species
1.	5.1	3.5	1.4	0.2	1
2.	7.0	3.2	4.7	1.4	0
3.	5.2	3.4	1.6	0.3	1

It is possible to differentate these data items by their petal length, petal width, sepal length and sepal width. Design an ANN model to clssify the Iris flonver's using a clustering approach.

6 Sequence Analysis

6.0 Introduction

A data mining method that helps us to understand which time-based sequences are usually encountered together in a domain is called as a sequence detection method. These frequent event sequences are very important elements.

6.1 Variable –sized Inputs Analysis

Everyday interactions that we make need is deep understanding of sequences of patterns that appears, say, in a newspaper, listening to radio etc. Similarly, to adjust variable-length inputs, we have to be a bit clever when designing deep learning models. Our feed-forward neural networks break when analyzing sequences. **If the sequence is the same size as the input layer, the model can perform as we expect it to be. It is also possible to deal with smaller inputs by padding zeros at the end of the input until its suitable length. Also note that when the input size exceeds the size of the input layer, then this feed-forward network no longer works.** A popular method of tracing sequence-to-sequence of parts of speech (POS) is Neural N-Grams. A feed-forward neural network architecture is used to process a body of text. The aim is to convert an input sequence into a corresponding output sequence. We have to take a body of test all at once to predict the full sequence of POS tags. It is better to predict each POS tag one at a time by using a fixed-length subsequence. **We use the subsequence starting from the word of interest and extending n-words into the past. This is neural n-gram method.** In general, when we predict the POS tag for the ith word in the input, we will utilize the i-n+1st, i-n+2nd......,ith words as the input. **This is also called as a context window or sliding window as here the context window is moved one word at a time, predicting the POS tag of rightmost word till we reach the end of the input.** In order to process the entire text we start at the beginning of the text and then proceed as explained above.

6.2 Beam Search

It is a variation of best-first search. Here, only n most promising states are kept for future consideration. It is efficient in terms of memory but it is possible to miss the solution due to early pruning of the tree. **Please remember the following points regarding beam search-**

1. It is like bfs in that it progresses level by level.

2. It moves **downward** only through the best, W nodes at each level by applying heuristics, the other nodes are ignored.
3. The number of nodes explored remains manageable even if there is a great deal of branching and the search is **deep.**
4. Whenever beam search is used, there are only W nodes under consideration at any depth rather than the exponentially explosive number of nodes as is done in bfs.
5. **The width of the beam is fixed and whatever be the depth of the tree, the number of alternatives to be scanned is the product of the width of the beam and the depth.**
6. Basic Principle- **"Instead of greedily selecting the most probable prediction at each step, we maintain a beam of most likely hypothesis (up to a fixed beam size, b) for the sequence of first k actions and their associated probabilities".**
7. **Beam searching** has two steps- expansion and pruning.
8. During **the expansion step**, we take each hypothesis and consider it as a possible input. Then we calculate the probability of each of possible hypothesis for the sequence of the first k+1 actions.
9. During the **pruning step,** we keep only the b hypothesis out of the total options with the largest probabilities.
10. Attempt has been made to bring closer **the concept of beam searching to the process of training the network.**
11. Andor et al. explains in his paper that **global normalization** provides a stronger guarantee and clear performance gains as compared to the **local normalization.**
12. In a **locally normalized network**, our network is tasked with selecting the best action given a configuration. The network gives as output a score that is normalized using a **softmax layer.** This is done to model a probability distribution over all possible actions. The **loss function** tries to compel the probability distribution to the ideal output.
13. In **globally normalized networks,** the interpretation of scores is somewhat different. Herein, **we add up all of the scores for a hypothesis action sequence** rather than putting the scores through a softmax to generate a per-action probability distribution. The problem here is that there is a large number of possible hypothesis sequences.
14. To cope with these problems, we use **beam search, with a fixed beam size and reach the end of the sentence or the correct sequence of actions is no longer contained on the beam.** Then we derive a **loss function** that tries to push the best action sequence as high as possible on the beam by maximizing its score relative to other hypothesis.

6.3 Stateful Deep Learning Models

Beam search and global normalization was used to get better solution for sequence analysis. But still this was useful for the scenarios where there was a one-to-one mapping between the elements in the input sequence to the elements in the output sequence. But sometimes the task is more complex, not just this.

Example 1: We may want a system model that can consume the entire text of input sequence at once and then conclude if the sentiment of the entire input was positive or negative.

Example 2: we may want to develop a system model or an algorithm that consumes as input a complex image and generate a sentence, one word at a time, to describe that image (input).

Example 3: the task may be to translate the sentences from one language to another language, say from Hindi to English. In all these situations, there is no mapping direct between input tokens and output tokens.

An ideal model, for **sequence analysis can store information in memory** over longer periods of time, leading to coherent **'thought vector'** that it can use to generate an answer. We want our model to maintain some sort of memory while reading the input sequences. As the process of reading continues, the model should be able to modify this **memory bank** and store the information that it observes. As the end of the input sequence is reached, this internal memory contains a **'thought'** that shows the key pieces of information i.e. the meaning of the original input. Then we should be able to use this thought vector to either produce a label for the original sequence or an output sequence like translation, summaries etc. But this is in contradiction to the concept studied earlier. **Note that the feed-forward networks are inherently stateless. After it has been trained, the feed-forward network is a static structure.** It cannot maintain memories between inputs as in sequential circuits. So, we now need the deep learning models that are **stateful.**

The standard deep neural network is a static classifier with input vectors having a fixed dimensionality. But many pattern recognition and information processing problems like speech recognition, machine translation, NLP, video processing and bio-information processing, need **sequence recognition. In sequence recognition,** also called as classification with structured I/O, the dimensionality of both inputs and outputs are variable. One method of solving this problem is through HMM. HMM is a tool to model the sequence data with variable length and is based on dynamic programming. **Please note that by combining static classifiers and HMM, it is able to handle dynamic or sequential patterns. So, it is better to combine deep neural network and HMM to bridge the gap between the static and sequence pattern recognition.** Networks like CNNs, RNNs have been applied to music with an error improvement of between 5% and 30% on a standard benchmark of four different datasets.

So, next we discuss some stateful models.

6.4 Recurrent Neural Networks (RNN)

The networks in which in addition to feedforward connections, we also have self-connections or connections to the units in the previous layers are known as Recurrent Neural Networks (RNNs). They are also called as feedback networks. This recurrency acts as a *short-term memory.* So the network now remembers what happened in the past. If we use a limited number of recurrent connections to a multilayer perceptron then it is called as a **partially recurrent network.** Thus, now we have combined the advantages of both non-linear approximation ability of the multilayer perceptron with the temporal representation ability of the recurrency. Such a network can be used to implement any of the three temporal association tasks. **Please note that it is possible to have hidden units in the recurrent backward connections and these are known as context units. Also note that no formal results are known to determine how to choose the best architecture given a particular application.**

The process that is used to convert an arbitrary recurrent network to an equivalent feedforward network is called as unfolding in time. It is used when the sequences have small maximum length. A separate unit and connection is created for copies at different times. The resulting network can be trained with backpropagation but with a constraint that all copies of each connection should remain identical.

Solution: As in weight sharing process explained earlier, the solution is to add/sum up the different weight changes in real time and change the weight by the average. **Also note that this is known as backpropagation through time.**

Problems: The problem with this approach is that of the memory requirement is the length of the sequence is large.

Another variant is **real time recurrent learning algorithm** to train recurrent networks without unfolding. It has a benefit that it can use sequences of any arbitrary length.

When connections are allowed both ways between a pair of units and also from a unit back to itself then it is called as a recurrent network. These networks do not settle down to a stable state even with a constant input. Symmetric connections $w_{ij} = w_{ji}$ ensures stable state. For example, Boltzman's machine is a symmetric machine.

A fully connected recurrent network is perhaps the simplest of neural network architectures. All units are connected to all other units and every unit is both an input and an output. Typically, a set of patterns is instantiated on all of the units, one at a time. As each pattern is instantiated the weights are modified. When a degraded version of one of the patterns is presented, the network attempts to reconstruct the pattern.

Recurrent networks are also useful in that they allow networks to process sequential information. Processing in recurrent networks depends on the state of the network at the last time step. Consequently, the response to the current input depends on previous inputs. Figure 6.1 shows a simple recurrent network.

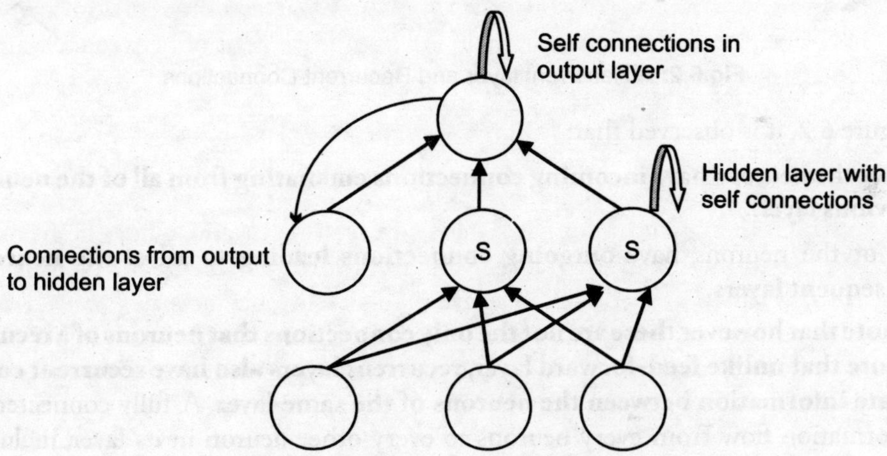

Fig.6.1: Simple Recurrent Network

Figure 6.1 shows three types of recurrent connections:-

(a) Self-connections in the hidden layer.

(b) Self-connections in the output layer and

(c) Connections from the output to the hidden layer.

Note that a combination of all these is also possible.

RNNs were introduced in 1980s. RNNs are different from feed-forward networks because they leverage a special type of neural layer known as **recurrent layers** that enable the network to maintain state between uses of the network.

Let us now study the neural architecture of a recurrent layer.

A recurrent layer contains recurrent connections i.e. the connections between neurons that are located in the same layer. Figure 6.2 shows recurrent layer and its connections.

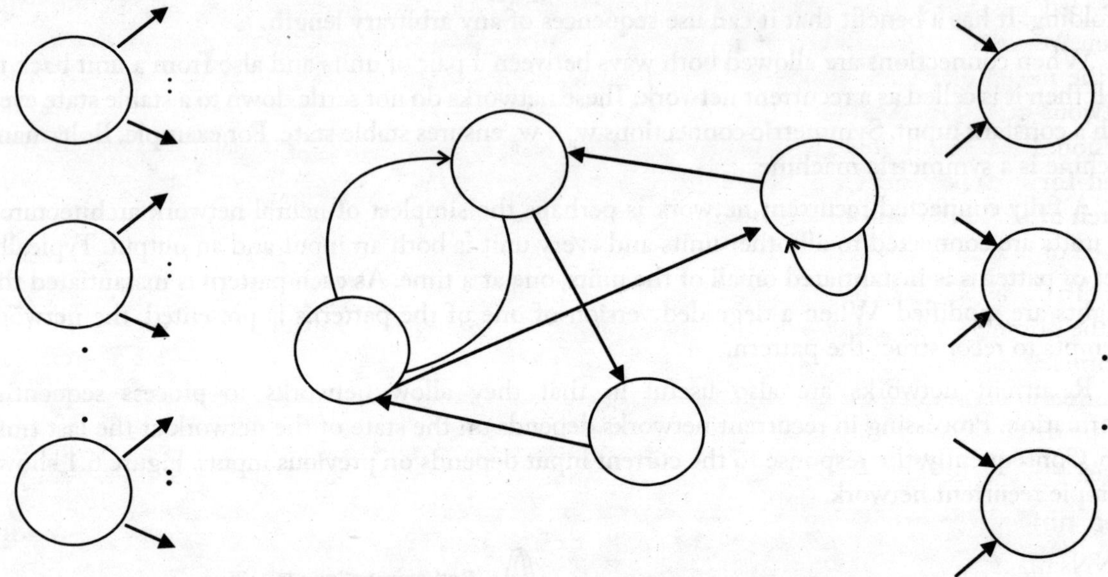

Fig.6.2: A Recurrent layer and Recurrent Connections

From figure 6.2, it is observed that:

(a) All of the neurons have **incoming connections emanating from all of the neurons of the previous layer.**

(b) All of the neurons have **outgoing connections leading to all of the neurons to the subsequent layers.**

Please note that however these are not the only connections that neurons of a recurrent layer have. Also note that unlike feed-forward layer, recurrent layers also have recurrent connections that propagate information between the neurons of the same layer, A fully connected recurrent layer has information flow from every neurons to every other neuron in its layer, including itself. **Thus, we can say that a recurrent layer with r neurons has a total of r^2 recurrent connections.**

Working of RNNs: Every time we want to process a new sequence, we create a fresh instance of our model. We can divide the life time of the network instance into discrete steps. At each time step, we feed the model the next element of the input. Feed-forward connections represent information flow from one neuron to another where the data being transferred is the computed neuronal activation from the current time step. **However, recurrent connections represent**

information flow where the data is stored neuronal activation from the previous time step. Thus, the activations of the neurons in a recurrent network represent the accumulating state of the network instance. The initial activations of neurons in the recurrent layer are parameters of our model. We determine the **optimal values** for them just like we determine the optimal values for weights of each connection during the process of training. **Note that given a fixed lifetime** (say, t time-steps) **of an RNN instance, we can actually express the instance as a feed-forward network. This process of mapping or transformation is known as unrolling the RNN through time.** The process performs the transformation by taking the neurons of the single recurrent layer and replicating them t-times, once for each step. Similarly, we **replicate the neurons** of the input and output layers. We redraw the feed-forward connections within each time replica just as they were in the original network. Then we draw the **recurrent connections as feed-forward connections** from each step replica to the next. This is so because the recurrent connections carry the neuronal activation from the previous time step. Also we can train this RNN by computing the gradient based on the unrolled version. **Please note that this means that all backpropagation techniques that we have used for feed-forward networks will also apply for training RNNs.** But there lies an issue now. We use **batch of training examples.** After every batch of training examples, we must modify the weights based on the error derivatives that we computed.

In the unrolled network, we have sets of connections that all correspond to the same connection in the original RNN. But the error derivatives so calculated for these unrolled connections are **not promised to be equal.** To solve this issue, we **average or sum up the error derivatives over all connections that belong to the same set.** This permits us to use error derivative that considers all of the dynamics acting on the weight of a connection as we try to compel the network to construct an accurate output.

Learning through RNNs

RNNs may use the **gradient descent** method to change each weight in proportion to the derivative of the error with respect to that weight. Several methods like back propagation through time (BPTT), real-time recurrent learning (RTRL) have been used in past literature. But gradient descent for RNNs has a problem that error gradients vanish exponentially.

At every point of time, t, RNN corresponds to an ANN with three layers. It uses **forward computation** as follows :

- The input at time, t, is x_t.
- The value h_t of the hidden layer is computed by the current input value, x_t and the value of h_{i-1} of the hidden layer at time, t – 1.
- The output value, y_t' is obtained while regarding h_t as the input of the output layer.

Most deep learning networks are **feedforward networks**. This means that the signal process flow in one layer is unidirectional from input to output. But RNN receives a sequence of input and also produces sequence values as output. RNN is a neural network that also includes 'temporal behavior'–i.e., the output of a sequence is fed as an input to the next input. The nodes between hidden layers are connected here and the inputs of the hidden layer includes the current input as well as the output of the hidden layer from the last time.

6.5 Bidirectional RNNs

All of the recurrent networks we have considered up to now have a **"causal" structure. This means that the state at time t only captures information from the past, x(1), . . . , x(t−1), and the present input x(t).** Some of the models we have discussed also allow information from past y values to affect the current state when the y-values are available. However, in many applications we want to output a prediction of y(t) which may depend on **the whole input sequence.**

For example, in speech recognition, the correct interpretation of the current sound as a phoneme may depend on the next few phonemes because of co-articulation and potentially may even depend on the next few words because of the linguistic dependencies between nearby words. This is also true of handwriting recognition and many other sequence-to-sequence learning tasks.

Bidirectional recurrent neural networks (or bidirectional RNNs) were invented to address that need. They have been extremely successful in applications where that need arises, such as handwriting recognition and bioinformatics. As the name suggests, bidirectional RNNs combine an RNN that moves forward through time beginning from the start of the sequence with another RNN that moves backward through time beginning from the end of the sequence.

A typical bidirectional RNN, with h(t) standing for the state of the sub-RNN that moves forward through time and g(t) standing for the state of the sub-RNN that moves backward through time. This allows the output units o(t) to compute a representation that depends on **both the past and the future** but is most sensitive to the input values around time t, without having to specify a fixed-size window around t (as one would have to do with a feedforward network, a convolutional network, or a regular RNN with a fixed-size look-ahead buffer).

This idea can be naturally extended to 2-dimensional input, such as images, by having **four** RNNs, each one going in one of the four directions: up, down, left, right. At each point (i, j) of a 2-D grid, an output O (i, j) could then compute a representation that would capture mostly local information but could also depend on long-range inputs, if the RNN is able to learn to carry that information.

Compared to a convolutional network, RNNs applied to images are typically more expensive but allow for long-range lateral interactions between features in the same feature map. Indeed, the forward propagation equations for such RNNs may be written in a form that shows they use a convolution that computes the bottom-up input to each layer, prior to the recurrent propagation across the feature map that incorporates the lateral interactions.

6.6 Deep Recurrent Networks

In most of the RNNs the calculations can be decomposed into three blocks of parameters and associated transformations:

1. from the input to the hidden state,
2. from the previous hidden state to the next hidden state, and
3. from the hidden state to the output.

When the network is unfolded, each of these corresponds to a shallow transformation. By a shallow transformation, we mean **a transformation that would be represented by a single layer within a deep MLP. Typically this is a transformation represented by a learned affine transformation followed by a fixed nonlinearity.**

Graves et al. were the first to show a significant benefit of decomposing the state of an RNN into multiple layers. The lower layers in the hierarchy are playing a role in transforming the raw input into a representation that is more appropriate, at the higher levels of the hidden state.

Considerations of representational capacity are to allocate enough capacity in each of these three steps, but doing so by adding depth may hurt learning by making optimization difficult. **In general, it is easier to optimize shallower architectures, and adding the extra depth makes the shortest path from a variable in time step t to a variable in time step t + 1 become longer.**

For example, if an MLP with a single hidden layer is used for the state-to-state transition, we have doubled the length of the shortest path between variables in any two different time steps, compared with the ordinary RNN.

6.7 Augmenting Recurrent Networks

The best way to make a machine learning model generalize better is to train it on more data. Of course, in practice, the amount of data we have is limited. One method to solve this problem is to create **fake data** and **add it to the training set.**

For some machine learning tasks, it is reasonably straightforward to create new fake data. This approach is easiest for classification. A classifier needs to take a complicated, high dimensional input x and summarize it with a single category identity.

This means that the main task facing a classifier is to be invariant to a wide variety of transformations. We can generate new (x, y) pairs easily just by transforming the x inputs in our training set. This approach is not as readily applicable to many other tasks.

For example, it is difficult to generate new fake data for a density estimation task unless we have already solved the density estimation problem.

Dataset augmentation has been a particularly effective technique for a specific classification problem: object recognition. Images are high dimensional and include an enormous variety of factors of variation, many of which can be easily simulated.

Operations like translating the training images a few pixels in each direction can often greatly improve generalization, even if the model has already been designed to be partially translation invariant by using the convolution and pooling techniques.

Many other operations such as rotating the image or scaling the image have also proven quite effective. One must be careful not to apply transformations that would change the correct class.

For example, optical character recognition tasks require recognizing the difference between 'b' and 'd' and the difference between '6' and '9', so horizontal flips and 180° rotations are not appropriate ways of augmenting datasets for these tasks.

There are also transformations that we would like our classifiers to be invariant to, but which are not easy to perform. For example, out-of-plane rotation can not be implemented as a simple geometric operation on the input pixels.

Dataset augmentation is effective for speech recognition tasks as well. Injecting noise in the input to a neural network can also be seen as a form of data augmentation. For many classification and even some regression tasks, the task should still be possible to solve even if small random noise is added to the input. Neural networks prove not to be very robust to noise. One way to improve the robustness of neural networks is simply to train them with random noise applied to their inputs. Input noise injection is part of some unsupervised learning algorithms such as the denoising autoencoder. Noise injection also works when the noise is applied to the hidden units, which can be seen as doing dataset augmentation at multiple levels of abstraction.

When comparing machine learning benchmark results, it is important to take the effect of dataset augmentation into account. Often, hand-designed dataset augmentation schemes can dramatically reduce the generalization error of a machine learning technique.

To compare the performance of one machine learning algorithm to another, it is necessary to perform controlled experiments. *When comparing machine learning algorithm A and machine learning algorithm B, it is necessary to make sure that both algorithms were valuated using the same hand-designed dataset augmentation schemes. Suppose that algorithm A performs poorly with no dataset augmentation and algorithm B performs well when combined with numerous synthetic transformations of the input. In such a case it is likely the synthetic transformations caused the improved performance, rather than the use of machine learning algorithm B. Sometimes deciding whether an experiment has been properly controlled requires subjective judgment.*

For example, machine learning algorithms that inject noise into the input are performing a form of dataset augmentation. Usually, operations that are generally applicable (such as adding Gaussian noise to the input) are considered part of the machine learning algorithm, while operations that are specific to one application domain (such as randomly cropping an image) are considered to be separate pre-processing steps.

6.8 Neural Turing Machines

We have already studied in the previous section, how RNNs are useful for solving complex problems like machine translation. It is said that RNN architecture is a **universal functional representer. This means that RNNs are Turing complete.** This implies that given proper wiring and adequate parameters, an RNN can learn to solve any computable problem. This is analogous to the fact that any problem can be solved by an algorithmic method or by a Turing Machine concept.

Graves et al. in 2014, from Google DeepMind coined this term of Neural Turing Machines (NTMs). **NTM according to them consists of a controller neural network i.e. an RNN only, with an external memory that is similar to our brain's working memory.**

NTM architecture-

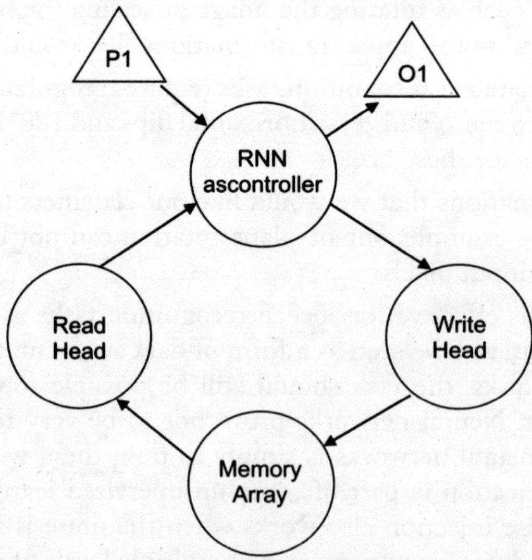

Fig.6.3: NTM Architecture

Comparing NTM of figure 6.3 with our modern day computer, we find that instead of RAM now we have an external memory, read/write heads instead of read/write buses and a controller of RNN instead of CPU. But the point of difference lies now in this point of reference. **The controller learns its program in NTMs whereas CPU does not.**

It is also possible to prune/ cut the search space as then we can further explore the potentials of RNNs. NTM can be used for doing reading comprehension tasks with gradient-based search (discussed earlier) only.

Limitations of NTMs

1. NTMs do not ensure that no interference or overlap between written data would occur.
2. NTMs are unable to free and reuse memory locations.
3. Read and write operations may become asynchronous. This is so because they involve new data being written to new memory locations that are contiguous. So, read/write head may jump to wrong locations.

Summary

In this chapter, we have seen how feed-forward networks fail when we do sequence analysis. This happens when the input exceeds the size of the input layer. Also we have seen in details the working and architectures of RNNs and NTMs.

MULTIPLE CHOICE QUESTIONS [MCQs]

1. During sequence processing, we make use of-
   (a) Context window. (b) Reference window.
   (c) MS WINDOWS. (d) None of the above.
2. Beam searching has two phases. One of them is expansion. The other phase is-
   (a) Searching. (b) Sorting.
   (c) Pruning. (d) None of the above.
3. Feed-forward networks are inherently-
   (a) Stateful. (b) Stateless.
   (c) Simple. (d) None of the above.
4. RNN stands for-
   (a) Recurrent Neural Networks. (b) Recursive Neural Networks.
   (c) Robust Neural Networks. (d) None of the above.
5. A special type of neural layer seen in RNNs is-
   (a) Recurrent Layer. (b) Transport Layer.
   (c) TCP/IP Layer. (d) None of the above.
6. RNNs are-
   (a) NP complete. (b) Turing complete.
   (c) Partially complete. (d) None of the above.

7. NTM stands for-
   (a) Natural Turing Machine.
   (b) Neural Turing Machine.
   (c) Natural Testing Machine.
   (d) None of the above.
8. A recurrent layer with r neurons has a total of –
   (a) r2 recurrent connections.
   (b) r/2r recurrent connections.
   (c) r recurrent connections.
   (d) None of the above.
9. One way to improve the robustness of neural networks is simply to train them with-
   (a) Random noise applied to their inputs.
   (b) Zero Noise at its inputs.
   (c) Maximum noise at its inputs.
   (d) None of the above.
10. A universal functional representer is-
   (a) ATM
   (b) ATN.
   (c) RNN.
   (d) None of the above.

Answers

a	2. c	3. b	4. a	5. a	6 .
b	7. b	8. a	9. a	10. C	

Conceptual Short Questions (with answers)

Q1. What is vanishing gradient phenomenon in RNNs?

Ans. It can be proved that a strong upper bound can be imposed on how much a change can be made in the input at time t-k that can impact the hidden state at time, t. As we know that the weights in our model are initialized to small values at the beginning of the training, the value of this derivative approaches zero as k increases. Thus, vanishing gradient problem arises. So, in this phenomenon, the gradient diminishes quickly when it is computed with respect to inputs several time steps into the past which limits our model's ability to learn long-term dependencies. This issue impacts the learning capabilities of RNNs.

Q2. Which tool can be used to draw RNN models?

Ans. **TensorFlow** can be used to build RNN models.

Q3. Write short note on 'Pipelines in Machine Learning'.

Ans. Pipeline used in training and hence in neural machine translation system is quite similar to most of the machine learning pipelines like gather data, prepare data, construct model, train the model, evaluate the model's performance and to train the model to get something fruitful.

Q4. How will you do 'Engilsh to French' data sequencing?

Ans. If we want to translate to or from different languages, we will have to train a model from scratch with the new data. Then we pre-process our data into a format that can be easily used by our models during training and inference time. We may also do cleaning and tokenizing too at this step. We start with parsing of strings. A process called as **tokenization.** Our

Engilsh or French sentence is now *discretized.* Then we do **optimization.** We use a concept called as **bucketing** here. It is a mechanism used basically in sequence-to-sequence tasks like machine translation that helps model efficiently handle sentences or phrases of different lengths. Finally, we reverse the source sequences.

Q5. What is a differentiable neural computer? Who gave it?

Ans. **Graves et al. in 2016,** from DeepMind, introduced a new memory-augmented neural architecture called differentiable neural computer (DNC) that improves on NTMs. DNCs keep other data structures along with memory itself to keep track of the state of the memory.

Exercise Questions

Q1. Explain the role of context window.
Q2. Compare feed-forward and RNN networks.
Q3. Explain with diagrams RNN architecture and its working.
Q4. Explain the role of pipelining in ML.
Q5. What are NTMs? Explain their architecture and working.
Q6. What are the limitations of NTM? How are they overcome?
Q7. Write short note on DNCs.
Q8. What do you mean by unfolding in time?
Q9. What are bidirectional RNNs?
Q10. What do you mean by augmenting RNNs?

7 Practical Deep Learning

7.0 Introduction

Several tools for analysis and design of deep neural networks have been developed and implemented by the researchers. Many more tools are in its infancy and yet a lot has to come. A very popular tool is H2O software for machine learning and data analysis. It is an open source, easy to use, scalable to big data, well documented, on its 3rd version and supports different operating systems and languages. As far as machine learning is concerned, H2O is not just a car rather a large truck for it!!!

Many industry giants are using H2O for big data processing. More than 5000 companies are currently using H2O. Unlike R and Python developers, H2O is easy to use. It is scalable too. H2O does not need clusters. It just compiles it to Java. There is no SVM algorithm. H2O algorithms are still in its infancy stage but are somewhat faster.

7.1 Tensor Flow Tool

A tool or software that is used to build and train deep learning models is named as **TensorFlow.** It is an open source software library. It was given by Google in 2015. It is used to design, build and train deep learning models.

Conventions used:

TensorFlow is a Python library. The computations are shown by the users in form of **a graph of data flows.**

Where, Nodes = mathematical operations.

Edges = data that is communicated from one node to another.

Data in **TensorFlow** is shown as tensors which are multidimensional arrays.

TensorFlow is used for deep learning, practically. We can think of deep neural networks as tensors and vice versa. If we show our deep neural networks like this gives us the advantage of making use of better speed-ups as available today. It also provides us cleaner and expressive ways of implementing models.

In **TensorFlow,** there are a number of libraries for developing deep neural networks. **For example,** Theano, Torch, Caffe, Neon and Keras. But we do not select these because-

(a) Theano has an additional step of **Graph Compilation** that is time consuming when we set certain types of deep learning architectures.

(b) **TensorFlow** has a much cleaner interface as compared to Theano.

(c) Many classes of models can be expressed with lesser number of LOC.

(d) **TensorFlow** was built with production in mind whereas Theano was designed by researcher purposes.

When we build a deep learning model in **TensorFlow,** certain variables are used to represent the parameters of the model.

Properties of Tensor Flow variables

The three properties discussed below make **TensorFlow** useful for building machine learning models:-

1. Variables must be explicity initialized before a graph is used.
2. Gradient methods can be used to modify variables, iteration wise.
3. These variables can be stored on disk for later use too.

When we say that the size of the tensor is 200 * 300 then we mean that the weights connect a layer with 200 neurons to a layer with 300 neurons. Also **TensorFlow** provides certain operations like abstract transformations that are applied to tensors in the computation graph. Attributes of these operations may be specified at runtime also. Operations are also named just as we name variables in **TensorFlow. Also note that a TensorFlow program will interact with a computation graph using a session.** It is the **TensorFlow session** that actually builds an initial graph. It can also be used to initialize all variables and to run the computational graph. **TensorFlow** can be used to train our machine learning model. Actually, building complex models requires **reusing and sharing of large data sets of variables that we want to instantiate together in one place.**

TensorFlow permits us to use multiple computing devices also in order to build and train our models.

Tensor Flow for Deep Learning

Tensors and Tensor Flow : Tensors are the data structures flowing among computation nodes in a data flow graph. They appear as multidimensional data arrays (or tables). Each tensor is defined by static rank, shape and type. Variables, on the other hand, are used to hold the dynamic information needed in graph execution. **For eg.** you treat the weights in a ANN–as variables stored in a tensor. **Note that in the training period, repeated use of the graph model is needed to update the weight tensors.**

The name Tensor Flow is derived from the **tensor flowing operations** which NN perform on multidimensional data arrays. These arrays are known as **tensors**. The **objective** is to train NNs to detect and decipher patterns and correlations. Classical Tensor flow implementation runs on single device. But present day, Tensor Flow can run on multiple CPUs and even GPUs, which can be easily built in big data centers/cloud clusters. Tensor Flow is a software platform that supports CUDA programming in general purpose computing on GPU.

System requirements:

- 64 bit LINUX or Mac OS
- Server Systems
- runs on mobile computing platforms like Android.

Tensor Flow Computations are denoted by a **state ful data flow graph** (SDG). Many companies like Google has moved from DistBe lief to Tensor Flow for research purposes.

Deep Neural Networks play a vital role in understanding of speech, images, NLP and vision aplications. **Note that both pretrained models and APIs must have lesser overhead so that they can be used in ML.**

DL applications include Gmail, Android apps. drugs discovery, image understanding, maps, NLP, photos, Robotics, Research, speech etc.

7.2 Deep Learning with H2O tool

When we use H2O all of the data is on cluster/ server and not on our client. This is done even when the client and cluster are on the same machine. So, whenever we want to train a model or make prediction, we have to get the data into the H2O cluster. We need to split the data into *training and test data so that overfitting or overtraining is prohibited.*

In the nustshell, **we are randomly choosing 80% of our data to train and then we will use our model on the remaining 20% to see its performance.** The split is decided randomly for each row. **The client has pointers that act as handlers to the actual data on the H2O cluster.** Our 'cluster is on local host. We can add machines to a cluster provided the total memory of the cluster is that much big that it can load and analyze billions of rows from a client. Next we go in for deep learning. As far as Python is concerned, there are two steps here:-

(a) Create an object for your machine learning algorithms and give parameters.

(b) Tell it to train and the data sets to use.

When we do not specify any parameters to the constructor, we mean that the model is built with all defaults i.e. with 2 hidden layers, each with 200 neurons and 10 epochs of training. **Also note that it is easy to train on default settings.**

Comparisons with R

In R, the machine learning is a single function call with parameters and training data being given at the same time.

In H2O, the command was:-

m ←h2o.deeplearning (x, y, train)

Just like data, the model is also stored on the H2O cluster and 'm' is a handle/pointer to it.

The command like-

h2o.mse (m) gives mean squared error (MSE).

Similarly, the command-

h2o.confusionMatrix (m) gives a confusion matrix on the training data set that you consider.

Also the command-

p ←h2o.predict(m, test) makes predictions using the model, m. Here, 'p' is a handle to a frame on the H2O server.

If the cluster is remote (far-off) or Big Data, then we also need to consider how much data is needed locally, how long will it take to download and will it fit on the machine or not.

Performance is different from prediction. In R, we use-

h2o.performance(m, test) and in Python we could use-

m.model_performance(test).

This will give us a lot of statistics.

The name of the web interface that is part of H2O is called as a Flow. It is another client written in CoffeScript (a javascript like scripting language). We can use this service to-

(a) View data.

(b) Upload data.

(c) View models created by user at client side.

(d) Create models easily.

(e) View predictions and run them.

We need to **import data** when using the H2O tool. You can select your files also. There are **buttons** to split the data into training sets and test frames or build a model.

Then click on **'train' option** and then on **'Build Model'**. From the **algorithms**, choose **Deep Learning.** A very large list of **parameters** also appears. You need to select only one as others are taken by default. They are considered to be good enough. Scroll down and click on **'Build Model'** option. Now click on the **View button.**

Also you can do full **load-model-predict cycle in flow.** From the model view, click on **'Predict'** option. Or you can also choose **Score** from the main menu and then click on **'Predict'** and choose a **model.** Then choose **'test data frame'** and click on Predict button.

Another beauty here is that the Flow commands can be saved as scripts for future use. In R and Python you can do merging of data sets that Flow cannot do.

Flow can be useful if you want to use only R or Python. **Please note that if you load data from R/Python, you can see it in Flow and if you load data in Flow, you can see it in R/Python.** You can start a long running model from Python or R, then go over to Flow and get immediate feedback on how training is being done.

7.3 Installation of Tools

Let us see how to install H2O with R.

Start R. Type install.packages("h2o"). If you want to install H2O in a way that it can be used by all of the users on that machine then run R as root and then type the command-

install.packages("h2o")

Then type-

library(h2o)

If everything goes Ok then type-

h2o.init ( ).

This will use only a quarter of the system memory.

You can use-

h2o.shutdown

To shut down, start again to check what it does.

Let us see how to install H2O with Python.

From the command line, we type-

pip install –U h2o

Start Python. Type the following-

import h2o and then

h2o.init( ).

By default, H2O instance is created that will be allowed to use all of your cores and will use 25% of your system memory. Also you need to include two libraries-

import h2o

and h2o.init( )

We get a complete script here. It downloads data, prepares it and creates a multi-layer neural net (deep learning).

7.4 Numpy

It is a **python library** which is used for scientific computing. It contains a powerful array object, mathematical and statistical functions and tools for integrating with C/C++ and FORTRAN code.

Numpy is designed for manipulating **homogeneous, multi dimensional arrays**. Which means that the elements in such arrays are all of the same type. Numpy refers to dimensions as **"axis"** and the number of axes is called as the **"rank"**.

For eg. [1, 2, 3] represents a point in 3D space that :

1. is an array of lenght 3.
2. has one axis.
3. is an array of rank 1.

Numpy provides the function array () for creating arrays with an option for specifying the type of each elements in the array as follows :

```
<<< from numpy import *
<<< arr 1 = array ([1, 2, 3)]
<<< arr 1
array ([1, 2, 3])
```

In Python, the Numpy package offers all functionality needed to create and manipulate matrices. The **ndarray** object allows the fast creation of an array such as a multidimensional matrix, by starting with data queued into lists. The term ndarray means 'n–dimensional array' implying that you can create arrays of multiple dimensions. Using a simple list, ndarrray can create a vector quickly as follows :

```
import numpy as np
y = np. array ([44, 21, 37])
print (y)
print (y. shape)
output : [44, 21, 37]
(3,)
```

The method 'shape' informs you about the shape of matrix. Here, it reports only three rows and no columns i.e., object is a vector.

Summary

In the field of computer science use of CASE TOOLS have always been emphasized. Machine learning with deep learning is not far off. Tools like H2O, TensorFlow are not far off as far as the design, implementation and analysis of neural networks is concerned. Tools make the job of deep engineer very simple, fast, efficient and effective. We have seen how to install H2O for R and Python. Also studied in this chapter are the ways to import data, make models and make predictions in either R, Python or Flow.

MULTIPLE CHOICE QUESTIONS [MCQs]

1. A software that is used for machine learning and data analysis is-
   (a) CO2 (b) H2O
   (c) CH4 (d) None of the above.
2. H2O has some code to call-
   (a) Google Docs. (b) Google Analytics.
   (c) Google Drive. (d) None of the above.
3. TensorFlow is a library of-
   (a) C (b) C++
   (c) Python (d) ADA
4. By splitting the data into training and test data , we avoid-
   (a) Overlapping. (b) Overfitting.
   (c) Overlays. (d) None of the above.
5. The command that gives a confusion matrix on the training data set that you consider is-
   (a) h2o.concocaveMatrix (m). (b) h2o.commonMatrix (m).
   (c) h2o.confusionMatrix (m). (d) None of the above.
6. The command h2o.mse (m) gives
   (a) Mean Squared Error. (b) Middle Squared Error.
   (c) Median Squared Error. (d) None of the above.

7. The command used to shut down is-
   (a) h2o.shutdown. (b) h2o.close.
   (c) h2o.click. (d) None of the above.

Answers

1. b 2. b 3. c 4. b 5. c 6. a
7. A

Conceptual Short Questions with Answers

Q1. What is a confusion matrix?

Ans. A confusion matrix contains information about actual and predicted classifications done by a classification system. Performance of such systems is commonly evaluated using the data in the matrix. It is also called as an **error matrix.**

In the field of machine learning, it is a specific table layout that allows visualization of the performance of an algorithm, typically a supervised learning. In unsupervised learning it is called as a **matching matrix**, however. Each column of the matrix represents the instances in a predicted class while each row represents the instances in an actual class or vice versa. The name stems from the fact that it makes it easy to see if the system is confusing two classes.

Q2. Distinguish between training dataset and testing dataset.

Ans. The training set is a set of examples that are randomly drawn from the dataset for the purposes of training the model. Training data is the data set on which you train the model or you can say the data from which the model has learned the experiences.

The test set is a set of examples drawn from the dataset for the purpose of evaluating the performance of the model. This cannot be used in training process.

Q. 3 It is desired to run a Tensor Flow program for classfying handwritten digits from the MNIST data set. Tensor Flow is basically a neural network library. Tensor Flow system can be appliled to any problem that can be expressed by a data flow graph. What steps will you follow to construct a four-layer ANN? Write code in python also.

Ans. The following four steps are followed for this problem :

S1 : Data Collection

We procure the MNIST data from LeCun's website. Tensor Flow has included some python code, as input-data. py. The data will be installed when running the downloaded files. We import it in **Python code** as follows :

```
# import tensor flow, numpy, input_data
import tensorflow as tf
import numpy as np
import input_data
# load the data
mnist = input_data. read_data_sets ("MNIST_data"/one_hot = True)
```

trX, trY, teX, teY = mnist. train. images,
mnist. train. labels,
mnist. test. images, mnist. test. labels.

S2 : The ANN model construction

We need a four-layered NN to construct this MNIST classifier. It must contain–**one input layer, two hidden layers and one output layer.**

// Weight initialization

def init_weights(shape): return tf. variable (tf. random_normal(shape, stddev = 0.01))

- tf. matmul ( ) function may be used to multiply.
- tf. nn. relu ( ) is a type of activation function.

S3 : Train the model

A comparison of the output of training data and its labels is done. The algorithm will adjust the parameters of the network.

S4 : Test the network

The algorithm compares the output of the test data and its corresponding label and calculate its accuracy. The training data is used to train the parameters of the model. Test data is, however, not used to train the hyper-parameters. Hence, we can use test data to get the accuracy of the train model as shown in graph :

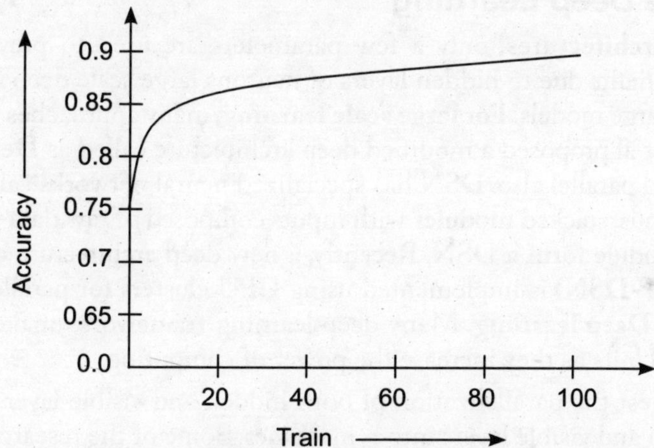

From the graph, it is clear that after each training, the accuracy becomes higher. Also it shows that after training the system multiple times, the accuracy of 0.985 was achieved.

Exercise Questions

Q1. Explain how Tensor tool helps in deep learning?

Q2. Why is H2O a good tool for deep learning?

Q3. Explain some of the commands of TensorFlow and H2O tool with their syntax and meaning.

Q4. How to install TensorFlow and H20 tools?

Q5. Give some properties of TensorFlow variables.

8 Applications of Deep Learning

8.0 Introduction

In today's world, deep learning has many applications. It is the current area of research too. During the past several years, the deep learning techniques have already been impacting a wide range of machine learning and AI. It has been applied in various fields like image processing, sounds, text and animations. Its success has been appreciated everywhere. The rapid increase in the field of deep learning has been appreciated by both academia and industry.

8.1 Large Scale Deep Learning

In case of shallow architectures, only a few parameters are used to prevent overfitting. Deep learning has many benefits due to hidden layers of neurons large scale deep learning involves large volumes of data and large models. **For large scale learning,** many approaches have been proposed in the literature. Deng et al proposed a modified deep architecture called as **Deep Stacking Network (DSN)**. It can be used parallel also. DSN has specialized neural networks called as **modules** with a single hidden layer. Thus, stacked modules with inputs composed of raw data vector and the outputs from the previous module form a DSN. Recently, a new deep architecture called as **Tensor Deep Stacking Network (T-DSN)** is implemented using CPU clusters for parallel processing. This has also led to **Big Data Deep learning.** Many deep learning frameworks make the use of GPUs i.e. Graphics Processors Units as they increase the power of computing.

Gibbs et al. suggest the parallelization of both hidden and visible layers. This they achieve by splitting these hidden and visible layers into n machines. Some of the researchers have also stressed on the reusing of the large chunks of training examples.

The following table 8.1 shows some recent works in the field of large scale deep learning:

Table-8.1: Recent Trends in Large-scale Deep Learning

Methods	Computing Power	No. of examples and parameters	Average running time
DBN	280 GPU, 1GB memory	1 million images and 100 million parameters	1 day (approx)
CNN	Two GTX 280 GPUs, 3GB memory	1.2 million high resolution images and 60 million parameters	5-6 days (approx.)

DisBelief	1000 CPUs	1.1 billion audio examples and 42 million model parameters	16 hours (approx.)
Sparse Autoencoder	1000 CPUs with 16,000 cores	10 million pixel images and 1 billion parameters	3 days (approx.)
COTS HPC	64 680 GPUs, each with 4GB memory	10 million images and 11 billion parameters	3 days (approx.)

It has been noticed that single CPU is not very practical for deep learning with large model. Deep learning is a big challenge for big data. The five Vs of big data are very significant here-Volume, Velocity, Veracity, Variety and Vulnerability of big data.

8.2 Computer Vision

1. A deep understanding of human vision is needed to develop better deep learning models for image related problems. To improve the **image classification** in apps like Google photos, deep learning is required.
2. It is difficult to teach a computer that an image is that of a face. Even traditional machine learning algorithms fail here. Now is needed a trade-off between traditional computer program and a machine learning technique.
3. In this trade-off, a program would choose the features (a lower dimensional representation of the same learning problem) while the machine learning algorithm would then use these **new feature vectors** to make classification decisions. **The machine learning algorithm will then use these new feature vectors to make classification decisions. Also note that this feature extraction process will improve the signal-to-noise ratio as compared to older algorithms of image processing.**
4. Jones et al. found that faces had certain patterns of light and dark patches that they could explore further. Like, there is a difference in the light intensity between the nose bridge and the eyes. The combined approach as explained in point no. 3 above, has proved to be very effective. Experimental results show that on a dataset of 130 images and 507 faces, the algorithm achieves a 91.4% detection rate with 50 false positives.
5. The basic goal of applying deep learning to computer vision is to remove the complex and limited process of feature selection.
6. One of the benchmarks in computer vision is ImageNet, that shows the power of deep learning.
7. An improvement on this was suggested in a deep learning architecture known as Convolutional Neural Network (CNN).

8.3 Speech Recognition

Speech recognition was one of the early applications of neural networks in CNNs or time delay neural neural networks. Both deep learning and representation learning had a strong impact in the field of speech recognition.

For example, MS (2002) has released a new version of their MAVIS-MICROSOFT AUDIO VIDEO INDEXING SERVICE, speech system based on deep learning.

The standard deep neural network is a static classifier with input vectors having a fixed dimensionality. But many pattern recognition and information processing problems like speech recognition, machine translation, NLP, video processing and bio-information processing, need **sequence recognition. In sequence recognition,** also called as classification with structured I/O, the dimensionality of both inputs and outputs are variable. One method of solving this problem is through HMM (Hidden Markov Model). HMM is a tool to model the sequence data with variable length and is based on dynamic programming. **Please note that by combining static classifiers and HMM, it is able to handle dynamic or sequential patterns. So, it is better to combine deep neural network and HMM to bridge the gap between the static and sequence pattern recognition.** Networks like CNNs, RNNs have been applied to music with an error improvement of between 5% and 30% on a standard benchmark of four different datasets.

8.4 Natural Language Processing (NLP)

One of the areas of NLP is **word embedding.** In this application, the concept is that the symbolic data can be represented with distributed representation. It was first developed by Bengio et al. in 2003, in the context of statistical language modelling. **And the learning of a distributed representation for each word is called as word embedding.** Later in 2008, Collobert and Weston applied **deep convolutional network** to implement this idea. Deep learning has the **transfer learning potential.** Deep learning approaches are better in this way. They propose that the learned features from deep learning can be shared by all NLP tasks. They also defined a unified architecture for NLP that learns features related to many well known NLP tasks including part-of-speech the basic idea behind deep learning approach is different from the traditional NLP approach. Not only standard deep neural networks, RNNs have also been applied to NLP. RNN was also applied to parsing. RNN has been applied for sentiment analysis too.

Collobert et al. also proposed general deep NN architecture for NLP. It was trained in an end-to-end fashion. It states that-

1. The input sentence is processed by several layers of feature extraction.
2. The features in deep layers of the network are automatically trained by backpropagation to be relevant to the task.
3. In this structure, the first layer extracts features for each word.
4. The second layer extracts features from the sentence.
5. The following layers are classical NN layers.

8.5 Other Applications

The study of deep learning is sub-field of machine learning which comes under Artificial Intelligence only. It is the current area of research. With the reinvigoration of neural networks (2000s), deep learning has resulted in modern machine learning. Industry giants like MS, Google, Facebook, Deloitte etc. have formed in-house deep learning teams for the same. Present day research papers in this field of deep learning are very rare, scattered and less supportive for deep learning. There seems to be a symbiotic association between Big Data and Deep Learning. The rise of data is exponential. So, the need is to go in for Big Data Analytics and Web Analytics. We define deep learning as a set of machine learning techniques that learn multiple levels of representations in deep architectures.

A deep architecture is capable of learning feature representations from both the labelled data and unlabelled data available. We need to do deep learning from this sea of data. Several applications like speech recognition, collaborative filtering, computer vision, Robotics etc use deep learning. Companies giants like Apple, Google, Facebook, Amazon etc. who collect and analyze Big Data on daily basis, have now jumped to deep learning related projects only. Even IBM has used deep learning to make use of Big Data for their company's advantage.

Due to the big size of data, often called as **data lakes,** deep learning plays a pivotal role in providing big data predictive analytics solutions. Deep learning means a set of machine learning techniques that learn multiple levels of representations in deep architectures.

Deep learning is defined as the machine learning techniques that use supervised and/or unsupervised methods to automatically learn hierarchical representations in deep architectures for classification.

Deep learning is a subset of artificial intelligence field called as machine learning which is predicted on the basic idea of learning from example.

In machine learning, instead of teaching a computer a massive list of rules to solve the complex problem, we give it a model with which it can evaluate examples. Also we give it a small set of instructions to modify the model when it makes a mistake. Please note that we have an expectation that as the time passes, a well suited model would be able to solve the problem more accurately. For example, say our model is defined by a function f(x, θ). The input x is an example expressed in vector form. Like, if x were a gray-scale image, the vector's components would be pixel intensities at each position. The input θ is a vector of the parameters that our model uses. Also note now that it is our machine learning program that tries to perfect the values of these parameters as it is exposed to more and more examples. The conventional learning methods are shallow-structured learning architectures while deep learning is deep-hierarchical leveled learning architecture. It is based on the biological neurons within human brain. Several research domains like speech recognition, Natural Language Processing (NLP), collaborative filtering and computer vision. Big industry giants like Google, Apple and Facebook who work on sheer size of data lakes today have also given vital importance to Big Data Analytics and Web Data Analytics. Google applies deep learning algorithms to massive chunks of messy data obtained from Internet. IBMs brain-like computer uses techniques like deep learning to make available big data available for its betterment. Also note that as the data keeps increasing at an exponential rate, deep learning is playing a key role in providing in big data and web analytics. And that deep learning refers to a set of machine learning techniques that learn multiple levels of representations in deep architectures. Deep learning is the new name for neural networks. Deep learning algorithms have best performance as far as complex problems like pattern recognition are concerned. Practically speaking, even machine learning approaches find it difficult to solve. Theoretically, they can solve any problem. Several libraries also exist for neural nets or deep learning. But deep learning algorithms as an auto-encoder i.e unsupervised deep learning, several parameters and slower deep learning grids are some of the issues to be discussed in this book. These programs may need more hardware.

Big data is at the core of our society today. The need is to process yottabytes (a billion petabytes) of data. Traditional machine learning algorithms are not sufficient as they were designed for data that could be stored in memory. But today data is "big". So, algorithms that can learn from massive amount of data are required now. Large scale deep learning is still in its infancy.

Deep Learning from High Volumes of Data

The data pool available today is a major challenge for deep learning today. The sheer volume of data results in run –time complexity and model complexity. These data lakes often make it impossible to train a deep learning algorithm with a central processor and storage. Hence, distributed machines and parallel machines are preferred. In nutshell, in order to build the future deep learning system scalable to Big Data, we need to develop high performance computing infrastructure-based systems. Also we need **parallel learning algorithms** now.

Another problem with these data lakes is that it results in data incompleteness and noisy labels. **One of the features of deep learning algorithms is that they have the ability to use unlabelled data during training.** So, the presence of large unlabelled data presents many chances for deep learning methods. Advanced deep learning methods are required to handle noisy big data.

Deep Learning from High Variety of Data

One advantage of deep learning is its ability of representational learning with either supervised or unsupervised methods or their combinations. Deep learning can integrate data from different sources. Deep learning can utilize heterogeneous sources for better system performance. In nutshell, *deep learning seems to be well suited to integrate heterogeneous data with multiple modalities due to its capability of learning abstract representations.*

Deep Learning for High Velocity of Data

Conventional neural networks have been used for online learning but still the progress is insufficient. Data is non-stationary i.e. it changes over time. Deep learning algorithm for big data is the ability to learn the data as a stream. So, deep online learning is yet to be explored.

Parallelism in Deep Learning

Recursive decomposition uses **divide** and Conquer strategy

- Parallelism involves trade-offs:
  - Minimal interaction
  - Handling granularity.
  - Inter task communication delay
  - data size.
  - Task size
  - Task decoupling

"The degree of concurrency increases as the decomposition becomes finer".

- Data parallelism is the most common type of multinode deep network training.
- Data Parallel models split large datasets onto different machines.
- Most nodes are workers & have accass to a fraction of the total data used to train the network.

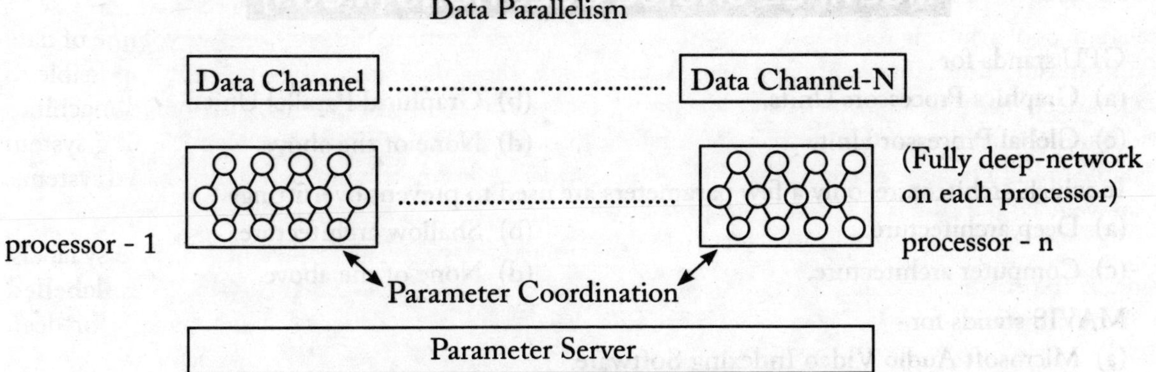

- Each worker node has a complete copy of the model of the model being trained.
- One node is designated as the 'supervisor' that gathers updated weights from the 'workers' at regular intervals & pushes averaged verisons of the weight out to the worker nodes.
- Training DNNs is a **compute** & **data-intensive** task. So, parallelism of data required.
- Delays (d) very high if CPUs are used (communication overheads)
  ∴ GPUs are used. This is improved in our approach
- Parallelization of Training problem over up to 8 GPUs hosted in a single compute node can be considered to be current state of art.
- Gartner says-"By 2020, data will double further". & sequential algorithms are limitations.
  ∴ DL has been accelerated in parallel with GPUs. & clusters.
- Big data can provide large amount of training data set for DL networks. But Training large DL model is expensive & time consuming as it involves several layers.

Summary

In nutshell, big data presents many challenges to deep learning including large scale, heterogeneity, noisy labels and non-stationary distribution etc. Both big data and deep learning have symbiotic relationships. Deep learning is the current area of Machine Learning research with the aim to move machine learning to Artificial Intelligence. Deep learning means learning multiple levels of representation and abstraction that help to make sense of data like images, sound and text. Several libraries do exist for developing deep models like Theano (a Python library).

Deep learning and Big Data are inter-related. Big data refers to the pools of data being generated every second while deep learning is an active research area in the field of machine learning. But as the data is growing at an exponential rate, deep learning is providing big data predictive analytical solutions. According to the report of National Security Agency (NSA), the Internet itself is processing 1,826 Petabytes of data per day. By 2020, the figure will reach 35 Trillion gigabytes. This leads to a remarkable paradigm shift in computer science literature towards data-driven discovery. Today machine learning techniques and newer software, hardware and computational power help in big data as well as web data analytics.

MULTIPLE CHOICE QUESTIONS [MCQs]

1. GPU stands for-
(a) Graphics Processors Units. (b) Graphical Parallel Unit.
(c) Global Processor Unit. (d) None of the above.
2. In which architecture, only a few parameters are used to prevent overfitting-
(a) Deep architecture. (b) Shallow architecture.
(c) Computer architecture. (d) None of the above.
3. MAVIS stands for-
(a) Microsoft Audio Video Indexing Software.
(b) Microsoft Audio Video Indexing System.
(c) Microsoft Audio Video Indexing Service.
(d) None of the above.
4. The learning of a distributed representation for each word is called as-
(a) Word embedding. (b) OLE.
(c) Machine learning. (d) None of the above.
5. Yottabytes refers to a-
(a) Billion petabytes of data. (b) Trillion petabytes of data.
(c) Zetabytes of data. (d) None of the above.
6. A set of machine learning techniques that learn multiple levels of representations in deep architectures-
(a) Shallow learning. (b) Deep learning.
(c) Recurrent learning. (d) None of the above.
7. One of the common applications of deep learning is-
(a) NLP. (b) Data processing.
(c) Language translation. (d) None of the above.
8. 8. Several libraries do exist for developing deep models like
(a) Theano (a Python library). (b) Piano.
(c) Diano. (d) None of the above.
9. One of the benchmarks in computer vision is-
(a) ImageNet. (b) DataNet.
(c) PaperNet. (d) None of the above.
10. Big data has a symbiotic relation with-
(a) Machine learning. (b) Deep learning.
(c) Training of data. (d) None of the above.

Answers:

a	2. b	3. c	4. a	5. a	6. b
7. a	8. a	9. a	10. b		

Conceptual Short Questions with Answers

Q1. Define what is a stacked auto-encoder?

Ans. An auto-encoder is an artificial neural network that is used for efficient coding. The aim is to learn a compressed representation / encoding for a set of data. It means that it was being used for dimensionality reduction or data compression.

Q2. What is transfer learning?

Ans. The ability of a learning algorithm to exploit commonalities between different learning tasks in order to share statistical strength and transfer knowledge across different tasks is known as transfer learning.

Q3. Throw light on some of the recent works in the field of large scale deep learning.

Ans. The following table shows some recent works in the field of large scale deep learning:-

Methods	Computing Power	No. of examples and parameters	Average running time
DBN	280 GPU, 1GB memory	1 million images and 100 million parameters	1 day (approx)
CNN	Two GTX 280 GPUs, 3GB memory	1.2 million high resolution images and 60 million parameters	5-6 days (approx.)
DisBelief	1000 CPUs	1.1 billion audio examples and 42 million model parameters	16 hours (approx.)
Sparse Autoencoder	1000 CPUs with 16,000 cores	10 million pixel images and 1 billion parameters	3 days (approx.)
COTS HPC	64 680 GPUs, each with 4GB memory	10 million images and 11 billion parameters	3 days (approx.)

Q4. Collobert et al. also proposed general deep NN architecture for NLP. It was trained in an end-to-end fashion. What does it state?

Ans. It states that-

1. The input sentence is processed by several layers of feature extraction.
2. The features in deep layers of the network are automatically trained by backpropagation to be relevant to the task.
3. In this structure, the first layer extracts features for each word.

4. The second layer extracts features from the sentence.
5. The following layers are classical NN layers.

Q5. How are machine learning, AI and deep learning related to each other?

Ans. The study of deep learning is sub-field of machine learning which comes under Artificial Intelligence only. It is the current area of research. With the reinvigoration of neural networks (2000s), deep learning has resulted in modern machine learning. Industry giants like MS, Google, Facebook, Deloitte etc. have formed in-house deep learning teams for the same. Present day research papers in this field of deep learning are very rare, scattered and less supportive for deep learning. There seems to be a symbiotic association between Big Data and Deep Learning. The rise of data is exponential. So, the need is to go in for Big Data Analytics and Web Analytics. We define deep learning as a set of machine learning techniques that learn multiple levels of representations in deep architectures. A deep architecture is capable of learning feature representations from both the labelled data and unlabelled data available. We need to do deep learning from this sea of data. Several applications like speech recognition, collaborative filtering, computer vision, Robotics etc use deep learning. Companies giants like Apple, Google, Facebook, Amazon etc. who collect and analyze Big Data on daily basis, have now jumped to deep learning related projects only. Even IBM has used deep learning to make use of Big Data for their company's advantage.

Due to the big size of data, often called as **data lakes,** deep learning plays a pivotal role in providing big data predictive analytics solutions. Deep learning means a set of machine learning techniques that learn multiple levels of representations in deep architectures.

Deep learning is defined as the machine learning techniques that use supervised and/or unsupervised methods to automatically learn hierarchical representations in deep architectures for classification.

Deep learning is a subset of artificial intelligence field called as machine learning which is predicted on the basic idea of learning from example.

In machine learning, instead of teaching a computer a massive list of rules to solve the complex problem, we give it a model with which it can evaluate examples. Also we give it a small set of instructions to modify the model when it makes a mistake. Please note that we have an expectation that as the time passes, a well suited model would be able to solve the problem more accurately. For example, say our model is defined by a function $f(x, \theta)$. The input x is an example expressed in vector form. Like, if x were a gray-scale image, the vector's components would be pixel intensities at each position. The input θ is a vector of the parameters that our model uses. Also note now that it is our machine learning program that tries to perfect the values of these parameters as it is exposed to more and more examples. The conventional learning methods are shallow-structured learning architectures while deep learning is deep-hierarchical leveled learning architecture. It is based on the biological neurons within human brain. Several research domains like speech recognition, Natural Language Processing (NLP), collaborative filtering and computer vision. Big industry giants like Google, Apple and Facebook who work on sheer size of data lakes today have also given vital importance to Big Data Analytics and Web Data Analytics. Google applies deep learning algorithms to massive chunks of messy data obtained from Internet. IBMs brain-like computer uses techniques like deep learning to make available big data available for its betterment. Also note that as the data keeps increasing at an exponential rate, deep learning is playing a key role in providing in big data and web analytics. And that deep learning refers to a set of machine learning techniques that learn multiple levels of representations in deep architectures. Deep learning is the new name for neural networks. Deep learning algorithms have best performance as far as complex problems like pattern recognition are concerned. Practically speaking, even machine learning approaches find it difficult to solve. Theoretically, they can solve any problem. Several libraries also exist for neural nets or deep learning. But deep learning algorithms as an auto-encoder i.e unsupervised deep learning, several parameters and slower deep learning grids are some of the issues to be discussed in this book. These programs may need more hardware.

Exercise Questions

Q1. Explain DSN.

Q2. How is deep learning and big data related?

Q3. List some of the major applications of deep networks.

Q4. Explain the general deep NN architecture for NLP.

Q5. Explain the role of HMM.

9 Deep Learning Survey

9.0 Introduction

In the previous chapters, we have shown how to solve supervised learning problems—how to learn to map one vector to another, given enough examples of the mapping.

Not all problems we might want to solve fall into this category. We may wish to generate new examples, or determine how likely some point is, or handle missing values and take advantage of a large set of unlabeled examples or examples from related tasks.

A shortcoming of the current state of the art for industrial applications is that our learning algorithms require large amounts of supervised data to achieve good accuracy. In this part of the book, we discuss some of the speculative approaches to reducing the amount of labeled data necessary for existing models to work well and be applicable across a broader range of tasks. Accomplishing these goals usually requires some form of unsupervised or semi-supervised learning.

Many deep learning algorithms have been designed to tackle unsupervised learning problems, but none have truly solved the problem in the same way that deep learning has largely solved the supervised learning problem for a wide variety of tasks. In this part of the book, we describe the existing approaches to unsupervised learning and some of the popular thought about how we can make progress in this field.

A central cause of the difficulties with unsupervised learning is the high dimensionality of the random variables being modeled. This brings two different types of challenges-- a statistical challenge and a computational challenge. The **statistical challenge** regards generalization: the number of configurations we may want to distinguish can grow exponentially with the number of dimensions of interest, and this quickly becomes much larger than the number of examples one can possibly have (or use with bounded computational resources). The **computational challenge** associated with high-dimensional distributions arises because many algorithms for learning or using a trained model (especially those based on estimating an explicit probability function) involve intractable computations that grow exponentially with the number of dimensions.

9.1 Representation Learning

As we know that the larger is our input vector, the larger is our model. Also we have discussed that larger models with large number of parameters are better but also they are data hungry. **Please understand that it implies that without large amount of training data, we will overfit or overtrain**

the model. Also note that CNNs help us to deal with the 'curse of dimensionality' by reducing the number of parameters in our models.

We have already discussed about Principal Component Analysis (PCA) as a traditional, classical method of dimensionality reduction. In 2006, Hinton et al. gave a paper on "Reducing the dimensionality of data with neural networks'. It proposes to handle non-linear complexities of neural models unlike PCA. We define **embeddings as low dimensional representations in an unsupervised way. And the process of improving the ability of the autoencoder to generate embeddings that are resistant to noise is known as denoising.** The human ability for perception is resistant to noise.

Basic Principles of denoising: "We corrupt some fixed percentage of the pixels in the input image by setting them to zero".

The problem of Interpretability: Interpretability is the property of machine learning that measures how easy it is to inspect and explain its process and/or output. Deep learning models are not easy to interpret because of the non-linearities and large number of parameters that constitutes that model. This may be problematic here. Like if a machine learning model is predicting that a patient has or does not have Thyroid then the doctor will ask for the explanation to confirm the model's conclusion.

The auto-encoder produces a dense representation i.e. the representation of the original image is highly compresses. But we have many dimensions to work within the representation. So, the activations of the representation will join information from multiple features that are difficult to separate. The result is that as we add components or remove components, the output representation changes in unusual way.

In dimension reduction process, we have rich set of inputs that contain huge noise. In such a scenario, we want to extract this underlying information while ignoring the variations and noise that are external to this fundamental understanding of data. Sometimes we have input representations that say very little about the content that we are trying to capture. Here, the objective is not to extract information rather to gather information from context to build useful representations.

9.2 Transfer Learning

The ability of a learning algorithm to exploit commonalities between different learning tasks in order to share statistical strength and transfer knowledge across different tasks is called as transfer learning.

An approach related to supervised pretraining extends the idea to the context of transfer learning, pretrain a deep convolutional net with 8 layers of weights on a set of tasks (a subset of the 1000 ImageNet object categories) and then initialize a same-size network with the first k layers of the first net.Supervised pretraining for transfer learning is popular (Oquab *et al.*, 2014) for use with convolutional networks pretrained on the ImageNet dataset.

Deep Learning Practitioners publish the parameters of these trained networks for this purpose, just like pre-trained word vectors are published for natural language tasks.

In **transfer learning,** the learner must perform two or more different tasks, but we assume that many of the factors that explain the variations in P1 are relevant to the variations that need to be captured for learning P2. This is typically understood in a supervised learning context, where the input is the same but the target may be of a different nature.

For example, we may learn about one set of visual categories, such as cats and dogs, in the first setting, then learn about a different set of visual categories, such as ants and wasps, in the second setting. If there is significantly more data in the first setting (sampled from P1), then that may help to learn representations that are useful to quickly generalize from only very few examples drawn from P2 . Many visual categories **share** low-level notions of edges and visual shapes, the effects of geometric changes, changes in lighting, etc.

In general, transfer learning, multi-task learning and domain adaptation can be achieved via representation learning when there exist features that are useful for the different settings or tasks, corresponding to underlying factors that appear in more than one setting.

However, sometimes, what is shared among the different tasks is not the semantics of the input but the semantics of the output.

For example, a speech recognition system needs to produce valid sentences at the output layer, but the earlier layers near the input may need to recognize very different versions of

the same phonemes or sub-phonemic vocalizations depending on which person is speaking. In cases like these, it makes more sense to share the upper layers (near the output) of the neural network, and have a task-specific preprocessing.

9.3 Exponential Gains from Depth

We have studied in previous chapters that multilayer perceptrons are universal approximators and that some functions can be represented by exponentially smaller deep networks compared to shallow networks. This decrease in model size leads to improved

statistical efficiency. In this section, we describe how similar results apply more generally to other kinds of models with distributed hidden representations.

Also, we saw an example of a generative model that learned about the explanatory factors underlying images of faces, including the person's gender and whether they are wearing glasses. **The generative model that accomplished this task was based on a deep neural network.** It would not be reasonable to expect a **shallow network, such as a linear network**, to learn the complicated relationship between these abstract explanatory factors and the pixels in the image. In this and other AI tasks, the factors that can be chosen almost independently in order to generate data are more likely to be very high-level and related in highly nonlinear ways to the input. This demands **deep** distributed representations, where the higher level features (seen as functions of the input) or factors (seen as generative causes) are obtained through the composition of many nonlinearities.

It has been proven in many different settings that organizing computation through the composition of many nonlinearities and a hierarchy of reused features can give an exponential boost to statistical efficiency, on top of the exponential boost given by using a distributed representation. Many kinds of networks (e.g., Boolean gates, sum/products) with a single hidden layer can be shown to be **universal approximators.** A model family that is a universal approximator can approximate a large class of functions (including all continuous functions) up to any non-zero tolerance level, given enough hidden units. However, the required number of hidden units may be very large.

Theoretical results concerning the expressive power of deep architectures state that there are families of functions that can be represented efficiently by an architecture of depth k, but would require an exponential number of hidden units (with respect to the input size) with insufficient depth (depth 2 or depth k – 1).

Also we saw that deterministic feedforward networks are universal approximators of functions. Many structured probabilistic models with a single hidden layer of latent variables, including restricted Boltzmann machines and deep belief networks, are universal approximators of probability distributions.

9.4 Challenges of Unstructured Modelling

The goal of deep learning is to scale machine learning to the kinds of challenges needed to solve artificial intelligence. This means being able to understand high dimensional data with rich structure.

For example, we would like AI algorithms to be able to understand natural images, audio waveforms representing speech, and documents containing multiple words and punctuation characters.

Classification algorithms can take an input from such a rich high-dimensional distribution and summarize it with a categorical label—what object is in a photo, what word is spoken in a recording, what topic a document is about. The process of classification discards most of the information in the input and produces a single output (or a probability distribution over values of that single output). The classifier is also often able to ignore many parts of the input. **For example,** when recognizing an object in a photo, it is usually possible to ignore the background of the photo.

It is possible to ask probabilistic models to do many other tasks. These tasks are often more expensive than classification. Some of them require producing multiple output values. Most require a complete understanding of the entire structure. *A natural image is an image that might be captured by a camera in a reasonably ordinary environment, as opposed to a synthetically rendered image, a screenshot of a web page, etc.*

9.5 Using Graphs to explain Model Structure

Structured probabilistic models use graphs (in the graph theory sense of "nodes" or "vertices" connected by edges) to represent interactions between random variables.

Each node represents a random variable. Each edge represents a direct interaction. These direct interactions imply other, indirect interactions, but only the direct interactions need to be explicitly modeled.

There is more than one way to describe the interactions in a probability distribution using a graph. In the following sections we describe some of the most popular and useful approaches. Graphical models can be largely divided into two categories: models based on directed acyclic graphs, and models based on undirected graphs.

I. Directed Models

One type of structured probabilistic model is the **directed graphical model,** otherwise known as the ***belief network* or *Bayesian network*.**

Directed graphical models are called "directed" because their edges are directed, that is, they point from one vertex to another. This direction is represented in the drawing with an arrow. The direction of the arrow indicates which variable's probability distribution is defined in terms of the other's. Drawing an arrow from a to b means that we define the probability distribution over b via a conditional distribution, with a as one of the variables on the right side of the conditioning bar. In other words, the distribution over b depends on the value of a.

Suppose we represented time by discretizing time ranging from minute 0 to minute 10 into 6 second chunks. This would make t0 , t1 and t2 each be discrete variables with 100 possible values. If we attempted to represent p(t0, t1, t2) with a table, it would need to store 999,999 values (100 values of t0 × 100 values of t1 × 100 values of t2, minus 1, since the probability of one of the configurations is made redundant by the constraint that the sum of the probabilities be 1). If instead, we only make a table for each of the conditional probability distributions, then the distribution over t0 requires 99 values, the table defining t1 given t0 requires 9900 values, and so does the table defining t2 given t1. This comes to a total of 19,899 values. **This means that using the directed graphical model reduced our number of parameters by a factor of more than 50!**

In general, to model n discrete variables each having k values, the cost of the single table approach scales like O(kn). Now suppose we build a directed graphical model over these variables. If m is the maximum number of variables appearing (on either side of the conditioning bar) in a single conditional probability distribution, then the cost of the tables for the directed model scales like O(km). As long as we can design a model such that m << n, we get very dramatic savings.

In other words, so long as each variable has few parents in the graph, the distribution can be represented with very few parameters. Some restrictions on the graph structure, such as requiring it to be a tree, can also guarantee that operations like computing marginal or conditional distributions over subsets of variables are efficient.

It is important to realize what kinds of information can and cannot be encoded in the graph. The graph encodes only simplifying assumptions about which variables are conditionally independent from each other. It is also possible to make other kinds of simplifying assumptions.

II. Undirected Models

Directed graphical models give us one language for describing structured probabilistic models. Another popular language is that of **undirected models,** otherwise known as **Markov Random Fields (MRFs) or Markov networks.**

As their name implies, undirected models use graphs whose edges are undirected.

Directed models are most naturally applicable to situations where there is a clear reason to draw each arrow in one particular direction. Often these are situations where we understand the causality and the causality only flows in one direction. One such situation is the relay race example. Earlier runners affect the finishing times of later runners; later runners do not affect the finishing times of earlier runners.

Not all situations we might want to model have such a clear direction to their interactions. When the interactions seem to have no intrinsic direction, or to operate in both directions, it may be more appropriate to use an undirected model.

For example, consider a situation, suppose we want to model a distribution over three binary variables: whether or not you are sick, whether or not your coworker is sick, and whether or not your roommate is sick. Assuming that your coworker and your roommate do not know each other, it is very unlikely that one of them will give the other a disease such as a cold directly. This event can be seen as so rare that it is acceptable not to model it. However, it is reasonably likely that either of them could give you a cold, and that you could pass it on to the other. We can model the indirect transmission of a cold from your coworker to your roommate by modeling the transmission of the cold from your coworker to you and the transmission of the cold from you to your roommate.

In this case, it is just as easy for you to cause your roommate to get sick as it is for your roommate to make you sick, so there is not a clean, uni-directional narrative on which to base the model. This motivates using an undirected model.

As with directed models, if two nodes in an undirected model are connected by an edge, then the random variables corresponding to those nodes interact with each other directly. Unlike directed models, the edge in an undirected model has no arrow, and is not associated with a conditional probability distribution.

9.6 Sampling

Sampling is defined as the process of selecting a few representative instances from data in order to reduce the number of records to mine.

Graphical models also facilitate the task of drawing samples from a model.

One advantage of directed graphical models is that a simple and efficient procedure called *ancestral sampling* can produce a sample from the joint distribution represented by the model.

The basic idea is to sort the variables x_i in the graph into a topological ordering, so that for all i and j, j is greater than i if x_i is a parent of x_j. The variables can then be sampled in this order.

So long as each conditional distribution $p(x_i \mid PaG(x_i))$ is easy to sample from, then the whole model is easy to sample from. The topological sorting operation guarantees that we can read the conditional distributions and sample from them in order. Without the topological sorting, we might attempt to sample a variable before its parents are available.

For some graphs, more than one topological ordering is possible. **Ancestral sampling** may be used with any of these topological orderings.

Ancestral sampling is generally very fast (assuming sampling from each conditional is easy) and convenient.

One drawback to ancestral sampling is that it only applies to directed graphical models.

Another drawback is that it does not support every conditional sampling operation. When we wish to sample from a subset of the variables in a directed graphical model, given some other variables, we often require that all the conditioning variables come earlier than the variables to be sampled in the ordered graph.

In this case, we can sample from the local conditional probability distributions specified by the model distribution. Otherwise, the conditional distributions we need to sample from are the posterior distributions given the observed variables.

These posterior distributions are usually not explicitly specified and parametrized in the model.

Inferring these posterior distributions can be costly. In models where this is the case, ancestral sampling is no longer efficient.

Ancestral sampling is applicable only to directed models only. We can sample from undirected models by converting them to directed models, but this often requires solving intractable inference problems (to determine the marginal distribution over the root nodes of the new directed graph) or requires introducing so many edges that the resulting directed model becomes intractable.

Sampling from an undirected model without first converting it to a directed model seems to require resolving cyclical dependencies. Every variable interacts with every other variable, so there is no clear beginning point for the sampling process. Unfortunately, drawing samples from an undirected graphical model is an expensive, multi-pass process. This simple approach is known as **Gibbs sampling.**

Suppose we have a graphical model over an n-dimensional vector of random variables x. We iteratively visit each variable xi and draw a sample conditioned on all of the other variables, from p (x_i | x–i). Due to the separation properties of the graphical model, we can equivalently condition on only the neighbors of x_i . Unfortunately, after we have made one pass through the graphical model and sampled all n variables, we still do not have a fair sample from p(x). Instead, we must repeat the process and resample all n variables using the updated values of their neighbors.

Asymptotically, after many repetitions, this process converges to sampling from the correct distribution. It can be difficult to determine when the samples have reached a sufficiently accurate approximation of the desired distribution.

9.7 Advantages of Structured Modeling

The main advantage of using structured probabilistic models is that they allow us to dramatically reduce the cost of representing probability distributions as well as learning and inference. Sampling is also accelerated in the case of directed models, while the situation can be complicated with undirected models. The main mechanism that allows all of these operations to use less runtime and memory is choosing to not model certain interactions. Graphical models convey information by leaving edges out. Note that anywhere there is not an edge, the model specifies the assumption that we do not need to model a direct interaction.

A less quantifiable benefit of using structured probabilistic models is that they allow us to explicitly separate representation of knowledge from learning of knowledge or inference given existing knowledge. This makes our models easier to develop and debug. **We can design, analyze, and evaluate learning algorithms and inference algorithms that are applicable to broad classes of graphs.** We can design models that capture the relationships we believe are important in our data. Then we can combine these different algorithms and structures and obtain a Cartesian product of different possibilities. It would be much more difficult to design end-to-end algorithms for every possible situation.

9.8 Deep Learning Approach to Structured Probabilistic Models

Deep learning practitioners generally use the same basic computational tools as other machine learning practitioners who work with structured probabilistic models. However, in the context of deep learning, we usually make different design decisions about how to combine these tools, resulting in overall algorithms and models that have a very different flavor from more traditional graphical models.

Deep learning does not always involve these deep graphical models. In the context of graphical models, we can define the depth of a model in terms of the graphical model graph rather than the computational graph. Consider a latent variable h_i as being at depth j if the shortest path from h_i to an observed variable is j steps. We usually describe the depth of the model as being the greatest depth of any such h_i. This kind of depth is different from the depth induced by the computational graph. **Many generative models used for deep learning have no latent (hidden) variables or only one layer of latent (hidden) variables,** but use deep computational graphs to define the conditional distributions within a model.

Deep learning essentially always makes use of the idea of distributed representations.

Even shallow models used for deep learning purposes always have a single, large layer of latent variables. Deep learning models typically have more latent variables than observed variables. Complicated nonlinear interactions between variables are accomplished via indirect connections that flow through multiple latent variables.

By contrast, traditional graphical models usually contain mostly variables that are at least occasionally observed, even if many of the variables are missing at random from some training examples. Traditional models mostly use higher-order terms and structure learning to capture complicated nonlinear interactions between variables. Latent variables are usually few in numbers.

The way that latent/hidden variables are designed also differs in deep learning. The deep learning practitioner typically does not intend for the latent variables to take on any specific semantics ahead of time. The training algorithm is free to invent the concepts it needs to model a particular dataset. The latent variables are usually not very easy for a human to interpret after the fact, though visualization techniques may allow some rough characterization of what they represent. When latent variables are used in the context of traditional graphical models, they are often designed with some specific semantics in mind like the topic of a document, the intelligence of a student, the disease causing a patient's symptoms, etc. These models are less able to scale to complex problems and are not reusable as deep models.

Another obvious difference is the kind of connectivity typically used in the deep learning approach. Deep graphical models typically have large groups of units that are all connected to other groups of units, so that the interactions between two groups may be described by a single matrix. Traditional graphical models have very few connections and the choice of connections for each variable may be individually designed. The design of the model structure is tightly linked with the choice of inference algorithm. Traditional approaches to graphical models typically aim to maintain the tractability of exact inference. **When this constraint is too limiting, a popular approximate inference algorithm** is used and is named as **loopy belief propagation.** Both of these approaches often work well with very sparsely connected graphs. By comparison, models used in deep learning tend to connect each visible unit v_i to very many hidden units h_j, so that h can provide a distributed representation of v_i.

Distributed representations have many advantages, but from the point of view of graphical models and computational complexity, distributed representations have the disadvantage of usually yielding graphs that are not sparse enough for the traditional techniques of exact inference and loopy belief propagation to be relevant. So, one of the most striking differences between the larger graphical models community and the deep graphical models community is that loopy belief propagation is almost never used for deep learning. Most deep models are instead designed to make Gibbs sampling or variational inference algorithms efficient. **Also note that deep learning models contain a very large number of latent variables, making efficient numerical code essential.**

Finally, the deep learning approach to graphical modeling is characterized by a marked tolerance of the unknown. Rather than simplifying the model until all quantities we might want can be computed exactly, we increase the power of the model until it is just barely possible to train or use. We often use models whose marginal distributions cannot be computed, and are satisfied simply to draw approximate samples from these models.

We often train models with an intractable objective function that we cannot even approximate in a reasonable amount of time, but we are still able to approximately train the model if we can efficiently obtain an estimate of the gradient of such a function. The deep learning approach is often to figure out what the minimum amount of information we absolutely need is, and then to figure out how to get a reasonable approximation of that information as quickly as possible.

9.9 Deep Boltzmann Machines

The learning is a stochastic learning. **A neural net design that is based on this learning is called as Boltzmann learning.** In this learning, the neurons constitute a recurrent structure and they work in binary form. This learning is characterized by an **energy function, E, the value of which is determined by the particular states occupied by the individual neurons of the machine and is given by-**

$$E = -1/2 \; \Sigma_i \; \Sigma_j \; w_{ij} \; x_j \; x_i \; (i \neq j)$$

Where x_i is the state of neuron i and w_{ij} is the weight from neuron i to neuron j.

The value $i \neq j$ means that none of this neurons in the machine has self feedback. The operation of the machine is performed by choosing a neuron at random. The neurons of this learning process are divided into 2 types:-

(a) Visible.
(b) Hidden.

In visible neurons, there is an interface between the network and the environment in which it operates. But in **hidden neurons,** they operate independent of the environment. **The visible neurons might be clamped onto specific states determined by the environment called as clamped condition.** On the other hand, there is a free running condition, in which all neurons are allowed to operate freely.

A method of implementing the pre-training is through restricted Boltzmann machines (RBMS). It uses the learned restricted RBMs to try to regenerate the original input data. **Please note here that the learned feature activations of one RBM are used as input data for training the next layer RBM in the stack.** After pre-training, the RBMs are **unrolled** to create a deep network. **Also note that the stacks of RBMs will create Deep Boltzmann Machines (DBM).** Then use the pre-trained DBM to initialize a deep neural network and train with back propagation as the stacked auto-encoder.

Boltzmann machine is based on a concept of **annealing.** The Boltzmann Machine is a stochastic machine comprising of stochastic neurons. A stochastic neuron resides in one of the two possible states in probabilistic manner. Synaptic connections are symmetric. The objective of **Boltzmann Machine Learning is to produce a neural network that correctly models input patterns according to the Boltzmann distribution.**

The states of the units used in Boltzmann machine are binary values with fixed weights. The weights represent constraints of the problem and the quantity is optimized. It consists of 2D array, a set of units and connection between the pair of units. Units in each row and column are fully interconnected and the weight on each interconnection is –p and there is also a self connection with weight, b, and the units are v_{ij}. It maximizes the consenses function:-

$$C = \Sigma_i \, [\Sigma_j \, w_{ij} \, x_i \, x_j]$$

Maximum consenses can be calculated by changing the units state-

$$\Delta \, c(i) = [1 - 2x_i] \, [w_{ij} + \Sigma_j w_{ij} \, x_j]$$

Where x_i is the current state.

$$\text{And } (1 - 2x_i) = \begin{cases} +1, \text{ if } x_i \text{ is ON} \\ -1, \text{ if } x_j \text{ is OFF} \end{cases}$$

The probability of the net accepting a change is state for unit x_i is-

$$A(i, t) = 1 / 1 + \exp\,[-\Delta e(i) / T]$$

To get maximum consenses, the parameter T is to be reduced.

The weights –p are the penalties for violating the condition that almost one unit should be ON in each row and column b is self connection weight or incentives or bonus to a unit to teun on without making more than one unit ON is a row or column. The net will function properly for p > b.

Steps in Boltzmann Machine:

S1: The weights between v_{ij} is given by:

$$W_{ij} = \begin{cases} -p, \text{ if } i = j \text{ or } j = 1 \text{, not both} \\ b, \text{ otherwise} \end{cases}$$

S2: Initialize weights, control parameters and activation of units.

S3: While stopping condition, steps 3 to 9

S4: Choose integers i,j at random between 1 and n.

S5: Compare the change in consenses.

S6: Calculate the probability of acceptance of the changes.

S7: Reduce the control parameter T(new) = 0.95 T (old).

S8: Test for stopping condition based on temperature.

Applications of Boltzmann Learning

1. It is used to solve the famous TSP (Travelling Salesman Problem).

2. It can be used to recall a stored pattern given the partial input. The partial unit is **clamped** to a suitable visible unit(s) and the network is **annealed to reach equilibrium.** The output state of the visible units at this stage corresponds to the pattern to be recalled. **This is called as pattern completion because we get the desired pattern from a partial pattern.**
3. **Boltzmann Machine** can be used for **pattern association.** During the training process, both the input and the output are given as a pair to visible units. So, **I/O patterns are stored in the network.** The input part is presented and clamped to the visible units. The steps of pattern completion are repeated to give the associated output vector.

In nutshell, BM uses stochastic units. This can reduce the effect of false minima. To reduce error in recall, the weights are updated using the patterns and knowledge of their probabilities. **The learning law involves only local computations and uses simulated annealing according to a schedule.**

9.10 Directed Generative Nets

Directed graphical models make a prominent class of graphical models. While directed graphical models have been very popular within the greater machine learning community, within the smaller deep learning community they have until roughly 2013 been overshadowed by undirected models such as the RBM.

We review some of the standard directed graphical models that have traditionally been associated with the deep learning community.

We have already described deep belief networks, which are a partially directed model. We have also already described sparse coding models, which can be thought of as shallow directed generative models. They are often used as feature learners in the context of deep learning, though they tend to perform poorly at sample generation and density estimation.

Sigmoid Belief Nets

As given by Neal in 1990, Sigmoid belief networks are a simple form of directed graphical model with a specific kind of conditional probability distribution. In general, we can think of a sigmoid belief network as having a vector of binary states s, with each element of the state influenced by its ancestors.

Generative models are used to visualize generative models for representing the process that we believe has created the data.

Differentiable Generator Nets

Many generative models are based on the idea of using a differentiable **generator network.**

The model transforms samples of **latent variables** z to samples x or to distributions over samples x using a differentiable function g (z; θ (g)) which is typically represented by a neural network.

This model class includes **variational autoencoders,** which pair the generator net with an inference net, generative adversarial networks, which pair the generator network with a discriminator network, and techniques that train generator networks in isolation.

Generator networks are essentially just parametrized computational procedures for generating samples, where the architecture provides the family of possible distributions to sample from and the parameters select a distribution from within that family.

9.11 Generative Stochastic Networks

In probability theory, a stochastic process or random process is the counter part to a deterministic process. Error in pattern due to false minima can be reduced if initially the desired patterns are stored at the lowest energy minima of a network. This error can be reduced further by using suitable activation dynamics. It is possible to realistic a transition to **a higher energy state from a lower energy state by using a stochastic update in each unit instead of the deterministic update of the output function as in Hopfield model.**

In **stochastic update,** the activation value of a unit does not decide the next output state of the unit by directly using the output function, f(x). Instead the update is expressed in probabilistic terms. **Please note that following points:-**

1. If the activation value exceeds a threshold, then the probability of firing by the unit is greater than 0.5.
2. If the activation value is less than the threshold, then the probability of firing by the unit is less than 0.5.
3. The probability of firing of an activation value of x is given by:-

$$P(s = 1 \mid x) = 1/\,1 + e^{-(x-\theta)} \mid T$$

The probability function is inversely proportional to the temperature, T. (see figure 9.1)

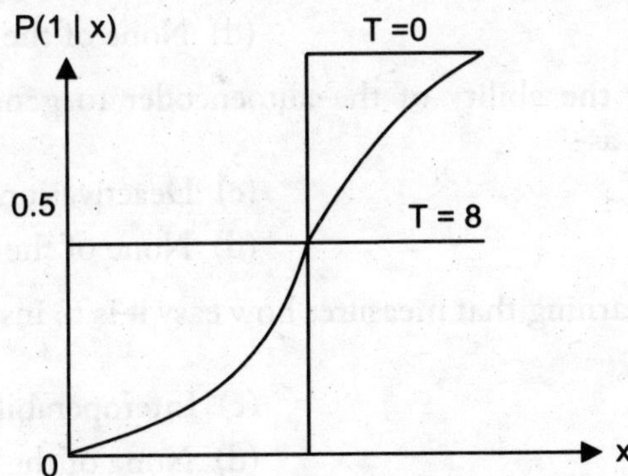

Fig.9.1: The Probability Function

4. From figure 9.1, it is clear that at T=0, the probability function is sharp. As the temperature is increase, the uncertainty in making the update increases and network goes to a higher energy state. At T= ∞, update of the unit does not depend on the activation value, x. The state of a unit changes randomly from 1 to 0 or vice versa.
5. **Equilibrium of Stochastic Networks:** A unit, i, is selected at random for updating:-

$$P(s_i = 1 \mid x_i) = 1/\,1 + \exp(-x_i \mid T)$$

A network with dynamics is called as a stochastic network.

$$S_i = 1/\,1 + \exp(-x_i \mid T)$$

This expression gives **stationary or independent of time.** This can be achieved by **thermal equilibrium. Thermal averaging** will give stability in stochastic networks.

6. **The maximum number of stable states for a stochastic network is called as the capacity of the network.** The capacity is different for different temperature shaded region and shows the existence of stable states i.e. stochastic network exhibits stable states for temperatures below critical temperature.
7. The operation involves **monitoring the trajectory of the states of the feedback network** and studying the features of the resulting random process in terms of probability distributions of states and the relation of these distributions with energy.

Summary

In this chapter, we have seen how deep learning is the current filed of research. It has increasing ramifications everywhere today. Deep learning researchers have worked a lot on deep learning and are still working on it. Terms like deep learning, machine learning, machine intelligence and big data are all inter-related to deep learning. Deep learning is still in its infancy. Many more needs to. be done.

MULTIPLE CHOICE QUESTIONS [With Answers]

1. Low dimensional representations in an unsupervised way are called as-
   (a) Embeddings. (c) Data hidings.
   (c) Dilation. (d) None of the above.
2. The process of improving the ability of the autoencoder to generate embeddings that are resistant to noise is known as-
   (a) Denoising. (c) Deactivations.
   (c) Denormalizations. (d) None of the above.
3. The property of machine learning that measures how easy it is to inspect and explain its process and/or output is known as-
   (a) Interpretability. (c) Interoperability.
   (c) Interdependence. (d) None of the above.
4. The ability of a learning algorithm to exploit commonalities between different learning tasks in order to share statistical strength and transfer knowledge across different tasks is called as-
   (a) Deep learning. (c) Machine learning.
   (c) Transfer learning. (d) None of the above.
5. Multilayer perceptrons are-
   (a) Universal standards. (c) Universal approximators.
   (c) Universal layers. (d) None of the above.
6. Markov networks are-
   (a) Undirected models. (c) Directed models.
   (c) Simple models. (d) None of the above.

7. A neural net design that is based on this stochastic learning is called as-
   (a) Boltzmann learning. (c) Markov Learning.
   (c) Learning by Example. (d) None of the above.
8. Boltzmann learning has been used to solve-
   (a) TSP (Travelling Salesman Problem). (c) Water Jug Problem.
   (c) Barber's Problem. (d) None of the above.
9. A network with dynamics is called as a-
   (a) Stochastic network. (c) Parallel network.
   (c) Computer network. (d) None of the above.
10. The maximum number of stable states for a stochastic network is called as the-
   (a) Coupling of the network. (c) Capacity of the network.
   (c) Commonality of the network. (d) None of the above.

Answers

1.a	2. a	3. a	4. c	5. b	6. a
7. a	8. a	9. a	10. b		

Conceptual Short Questions with Answers

Q1. What is competitive learning rule?

Ans. The basic idea behind this rule is that there are a set of neurons that are similar in all aspects except for some randomly distributed synaptic weights. The output neurons of a neural network compete among themselves to become active.

This rule is suitable for unsupervised network training. The winner neuron during competition is called as **winner-takes-all neuron. The winner-takes-all or the competitive learning is used for learning statistical properties of inputs.**

Q2. What is out star learning rule?

Ans. Rule: "This rule is used to produce the desired response, t from the layer of n neurons". This type of learning is also called as **Grossberg learning.**

Q3. What is Hebb's law?

Ans. Hebb's law states that –**"If two neurons are activated simultaneously then the strength of the connection between them should be increased."**

Q4. Name the four stages of the training algorithm of back propagation.

Ans. It involves four stages:-

(a) Initialization of weights.

(b) Feed forward.

(c) Back propagation of errors.

(d) Updation of the weights and biases.

Q5. State delta rule.

Ans. Rule: "The adjustment made to a synaptic weight of a neuron is proportional to the product of the error signal and the input signal of the synapse".

Exercise Questions

Q1. How is Boltzmann learning rule applied to the travelling salesman problem.

Q2. What do you mean by representation learning? Explain.

Q3. What is transfer learning?

Q4. Explain Deep Boltzmann Machines.

Q5. Write short notes on 'Equilibrium of Stochastic Networks'.

Q6. Explain how the stacks of RBMs will create Deep Boltzmann Machines?

Q7. Explain Deep Generative Models.

Q8. Explain Generative Stochastic Networks with the help of graphs.

Q9. What is Gibb's sampling?

Q10. What are the advantages of structural modelling?

Appendix–A: Glossary

1. **Adaline:** It is an abbreviation for a linear neuron (ADAptiveLINear Element).
2. **Adaptation:** A training method that proceeds through the specified sequence of inputs, calculating the output, error and network adjustment for each input vector in the sequence as the inputs are presented.
3. **Adaptive Learning Rate:** A learning rate that is adjusted according to an algorithm during training to minimize the training time.
4. **Backtracking Search:** A linear search routine that begins with a step multiplier of 1 and then backtracks until an acceptable reduction in the performance is obtained.
5. **Batch:** A matrix of input or target vectors applied to the network simultaneously.
6. **Bayesian framework:** Assumes that the weights and biases of the network are random variables with specified distributions.
7. **Bias:** A neuron parameter that is summed up with the neuron's weighted inputs and passed through the neuron's transfer function to generate the neuron's output.
8. **Bias vector:** A column vector of bias values for a layer of neurons.
9. **Cascade Forward Network:** A layered network in which each layer only receives inputs from the previous layers.
10. **Classification:** An association of an input vector with a particular target vector.
11. **Competitive Learning:** The unsupervised training of a competitive layer with the instar rule or Kohonen rule. Individual neurons learn to become feature detectors.
12. **Conjugate Gradient Algorithm:** In the conjugate gradient algorithm, a search is performed along the conjugate directions which produces generally faster convergence than a search along the steepest descent directions.
13. **Connection:** A one-way link between neurons in a network.
14. **Connection Strength:** The strength of a link between two neurons in a network. It is also called as weight.
15. **Cycle:** A single presentation of an input vector, calculation of output and new weights and biases.
16. **Dead Neurons:** A competitive layer neuron that never won any competition during training.

17. **Delta Rule:** A learning rule used to train single layer linear networks.
18. **Distance:** The distance between neurons that is computed from their positions with a distance function.
19. **Early Stopping:** A technique based on dividing the data into three subsets. The first subset is the training set used for computing the gradient and updating the network weights and biases. The second subset is the validation set. When the validation error increases for a specified number of iterations, the training is stopped and the weights and the biases at the minimum of the validation error are returned. The third sbset is the test set. It is used to verify the network design.
20. **Epoch:** The presentation of the set of training vectors to a network and the calculation of new weights and biases. The training vectors may be represented one at a time or all together in a batch.
21. **Error Jumping:** A sudden increase in a networks sum-squared error during training. This happens due to large learning rate.
22. **Error Ratio:** A training parameter used with adaptive learning rate and momentum training of back propagation networks.
23. **Function Approximation:** The task performed by a network trained to respond to inputs with an approximation of a desired function.
24. **Global Minimum:** The lowest value of a function over the entire range of its input parameters.
25. **Gradient Descent:** The process of making changes to the weights and biases where the changes are proportional to the derivatives of the network error with respect to those weights and biases. This is done to minimize network error. This is done to find the global minimum of error for a network.
26. **Hard limit transfer function:** A transfer that maps inputs greater-than or equal to 0 or 1 and all other values to 0.
27. **Hebb learning rule:** It is the first proposed learning rule for neurons. Weights are adjusted proportional to the product of the outputs of pre and post –weight neurons.
28. **Home Neuron:** A neuron at the center of a neighbourhood.
29. **Learning:** The process by which weights and biases are adjusted to achieve some desired network behaviour.
30. **Local Minimum:** The minimum of a function over a limited range of input values. A local minimum may not be the global minimum.
31. **Mean Square Error Function:** The performance function that calculates the average squared error between the network outputs and the target outputs.
32. **Momentum:** A technique used to make it less likely for a backpropagation networks to get caught in a shallow minima.
33. **Outstar Learning Rule:** A learning rule that trains a neuron's output weight vector to take on the values of the current output vector of the post-weight layer.
34. **Overfitting:** A situation in which the error on training set is driven to a very small value but when new data is presented to the network, the error is large.

35. **Pass:** Each traverse through all of the training input and target vectors.
36. **Pattern Recognition:** The task performed by a network trained to respond when an input vector close to a learned vector is presented. The network recognizes the input as one of the original target vectors.
37. **Perceptron:** A single layer network with a hard-limit transfer function.
38. **Performance:** The behaviour of a network.
39. **Pre-processing:** To perform some transformation of the input or target data before it is presented to the neural network.
40. **Post-processing:** It converts normalized outputs back into the same units that were used for the original targets.
41. **Principal Component Analysis (PCA):** To orthogonalize the components of network input vectors. It also reduces the dimensions of the input vectors by eliminating redundant components.
42. **Resilient Back Propagation:** A training algorithm that eliminates the harmful effect of having a small slope at the extreme ends of the sigmoid squashing transfer functions.
43. **Sigmoid:** Monotonic S-shaped mapping numbers in the interval, to a finite interval such as (-1, +1) or (0, 1).
44. **Sum squared error:** The sum of squared differences between the network targets and the actual outputs for a given input vector or set of vectors.
45. **Update:** To make changes in weights and biases.
46. **Validation Vectors:** A set of input vectors that is used to monitor training progress so as to keep the network from overtraining/overfitting.
47. **Weight Matrix:** A matrix containing connection strengths from a layer's inputs to its neurons.
48. **Widrow-Hoff Learning Rule:** A learning rule used to train single layer linear networks. It is also called as Delta rule.

Appendix–B: Model Question Papers

Q1. What is a neural network? Explain its need.

Q2. Differentiate between single layer and multi-layer neural networks.

Q3. Describe the working of the single layer perceptron neural network.

Q4. Which type of activation function is used:-

(a) In single layer perceptron network.

(b) In multilayer perceptron network.

Q5. Write different steps in backpropagation algorithm.

Q6. Distinguish between feedback and feed-forward neural networks.

Q7. Draw and explain Boltzmann machine in detail.

Q8. Explain unsupervised learning neural networks.

Q9. Distinguish between supervised and unsupervised learning.

Q10. Explain PCA in detail.

Q11. Describe SOMs.

Q12. What are SVMs? Discuss their characteristics.

Q13. What is reinforcement learning? How does the passive reinforcement learning differ from active reinforcement learning?

Q14. Define direct utility estimation.

Q15. Define curse of dimensionality.

Q16. How is big data and deep learning related?

Q17. What do you mean by deep neural networks?

Q18. Illustrate decision trees learning technique with a suitable example.

Q19. Write a short note on Naive Bayes model of statistical learning.

Q20. What is clustering? Explain k-mean clustering technique.

Q21. Compare weights and bias.

Q22. Write a short note on learning rate.

Q23. Which factor improves the performance of bias?

Q24. If the net input to an output neuron is 0.64, calculate its output when the activation function is-

(a) Binary sigmoidal.

(b) Bipolar sigmoidal.

[**Hint:** Net input to the neuron = 0.64

(a) For binary sigmoidal activation function,

$Y = f(netinput) = 1/\ (1+ e^{-0.64}) = 0.6548$

(b) For bipolar sigmoidal actiovation function,

$Y = f(netinput) = 2/\ (1+ e^{-0.64}) = 0.3095$]

Q25. Differentiate between local minima and global minima.

Q26. Explain RNNs.

Q27. What is a confusion matrix?

Q28. Write short note on Learning Vector Quantization (LVQ).

Q29. Describe the basic structure of a biological neuron. How this model has been adapted in ANNs like Pitts model or Perceptron model.

Q30. Differentiate between classification and recognition.

Q31. Construct a feed forward network with 3 neurons in input layer 2 in hidden layer and 2 in output layer. Explain the concept of input vector, connection matrix and activation functions.

Q32. Explain how a neural network can be trained using back propagation? Derive equation for weight modification in a multi-layer perception model. What role is played by learning rate and momentum?

Q33. What is delta learning rule?

Q34. What is overfitting?

Q35. Explain the term 'fully connected'.

Q36. What is beam search? Write its algorithm

Q37. Explain convergence rule for learning.

Q38. What is feature mapping?

Q39. Define generalization. On what factors does it depends?

Q40. Define cross validation.

Q41. Explain early stopping.

Q42. Explain regularization.

Q43. How can overtraining or overfitting be avoided?

Q44. Compare RBN network with MLP.

Q45. What is machine learning? Give an overview of ML with a suitable diagram.

Q46. How is training data set different from testing dataset.

Q47. What are hard margin SVM and soft margin SVM?

Q48. Explain ML approach to Knowledge Acquisition.

Q49. What are the main goals of ML.

Q50. Explain the three step data preparation process in ML.

Q51. Explain LDA.

Q52. Distinguish between generative model and conditional model.

Q53. Explain k-nearest neighbour learning.

Q54. What is inductive machine learning?

Q55. Explain EM algorithm.

Q56. What is LSI? Write its algorithm.

Q57. Explain MDPs.

Q58. Write short notes on- 'Bellman Equation and LQR'.

Q59. Explain Q-Learning for LQR.

Q60. Write a note on POMDPS.

Q61. What is Reinforcement learning? Who gave it? How does it relate to Neuro-dynamic programming? Is RL useful in operations research field? Is it related to Neuroscience?

Q62. Explain the jargon of Q-values, Q-tables and Q-functions.

Q63. What is contingency table? How is it useful?

Q64. What are context units in RNNs? Define unfolding in time and back propagation through time. What are Real-time recurrent learning?

Q65. Is classification a supervised way of learning. Explain.

Q66. Explain Q-learning.

Q67. Explain the value function in context of reinforcement learning.

Q68. Distinguish between shallow learning and deep learning architectures.

Q69. What are deep belief networks?

Q70. With a neat sketch explain CNN architecture.

Q71. Explain the term large scale deep learning.

Q72. Explain the relation between deep learning and the five V's of Big Data.

Q73. What is an auto-encoder?

Q74. Explain deep Boltzmann machines.

Q75. Why is deep learning vital? Explain transfer learning.

Q76. Discuss in details the applications of deep learning and their architectures.

Q77. What is word embedding? Where is it used?

Q78. Explain deep neural network architecture, layerwise.

Q79. Explain noise robustness.

Q80. Explain the term 'Dropout'.

Q81. Explain the following:-

(a) Bidirectional RNNs.

(b) Deep Recurrent Networks.

(c) Recursive Neural Networks.

Q82. Explain the deep learning approach to structured probabilistic models.

Q83. Discuss about H2O tool used in deep learning. What are the minimum requirements for its installation?

Q84. Explain the role of TensorFlow tool in deep learning.

Q85. Explain the following:-

(a) Deep Neural Networks

(b) Deep Machine Learning

(c) Deep Web Intelligence

(d) Deep Big Data

(e) Deep Machine Intelligence.

Q86. What is maxpooling?

Q87. What is sequence analysis? Give some examples from real-life.

Q88. Explain Neural Turing Machines and their architectures?

Q89. What are differentiable neural computers? Explain.

Q90. List down the applications of deep neural networks.

Q91. Explain Capacity, Overfitting and Underfitting.

Q92. Explain the model for sequence analysis.

Q93. Explain the 3-tier architecture for feed-forward neural network.

Q94. What is Gradient Descent?

Q95. How the complete dataset is divided during training?

Q96. Define an Epoch.

Q97. What are hyperparameters of a model?

Q98. With a flowchart, explain the workflow for training a deep learning model.

Q99. What is regularization? Explain mathematically.

Q100. What are the advantages of TensorFlow.

Q101. How do you optimize deep learning models.

Q102. Explain critical points and saddle points.

Q103. What is momentum based optimization?

Q104. What is an ImageNet challenge?

Q105. What is batch normalization?

Q106. Distinguish between local normalized network and global normalized network.

Q107. What are vanishing gradients?

Q108. What are machine learning pipelines?

Q109. RNNs are Turing complete. Explain.

Q110. What is deep reinforcement learning? Explain rewards, action and action terms related to it.

Q111. What is Q-learning and Deep Q-learning?

Q112. Write short notes on DRQN.

Project–1

ACCOUSTIC CRYPTOGRAPHY OF COMPUTER KEYBOARD

ABSTRACT

We show that PC keyboards, notebook keyboards, telephone and ATM pads are vulnerable to attacks based on differentiating the sound emanated by different keys. Our attack employs a neural network to recognize the key being pressed. We also investigate why different keys produce different sounds and provide hints for the design of homophonic keyboards that would be resistant to this type of attack.

Emanations produced by electronic devices have long been a source for attacks on the security of computer systems. Past attacks have exploited electromagnetic emanations as well as optical emanations. Acoustic emanations have also been explored. For example, it is shown that the acoustic emanations of matrix printers can carry substantial information about the text being printed. We investigate acoustic emanations of a PC keyboard. The clicks, to eavesdrop upon what is being typed. This attack is based on the hypothesis that the sound of clicks can differ slightly from key to key, although the clicks of different keys sound very similar to the human ear. Our experiments show that a neural network can be trained to differentiate the keys to successfully carry out this attack.

1 Training ANN & Acoustic Cryptography of Computer Keyboard

INTRODUCTION

Emanations produced by electronic devices have long been a source for attacks on the security of computer systems. Past attacks have exploited electromagnetic emanations [6] as well as optical emanations [10, 13]. Acoustic emanations have also been explored. For example, it is shown in [7] that the acoustic emanations of matrix printers can carry substantial information about the text being printed.

We investigate acoustic emanations of a PC keyboard, the clicks, to eavesdrop upon what is being typed. This attack is based on the hypothesis that the sound of clicks can differ slightly from key to key, although the clicks of different keys sound very similar to the human ear. Our experiments show that a neural network can be trained to differentiate the keys to successfully carry out this attack

This attack is inexpensive and non-invasive. It is inexpensive because in addition to a computer, the only other hardware required is a parabolic microphone. It is noninvasive because it does not require physical intrusion into the system; the sound can be recorded from a substantial distance.

We, therefore, also investigate what can be done to thwart this attack. In addition to the PC keyboards, we also study attacks on notebook computers, touchtone telephones, and ATM keypads. Our experiments suggest that what is being typed on these devices can also be compromised using an attack based on the sounds produced by clicks.

Then we presents the details of the attack. We explain how we extract features from the raw acoustic signal produced by the click of a key on the PC keyboard. These features are then used to train the neural network for differentiating the keys. We first show the effectiveness of the attack in distinguishing two keys and then extend the attack to cover multiple keys. We show that the differences in typing style have little impact on the ability of the network to recognize the keys. This means that the network can be trained on one person and then used to eavesdrop on another person typing on the same keyboard. We also show that it is possible to train the network on one keyboard and then use it to attack another keyboard of the same type, albeit there is a reduction in the quality of recognition.

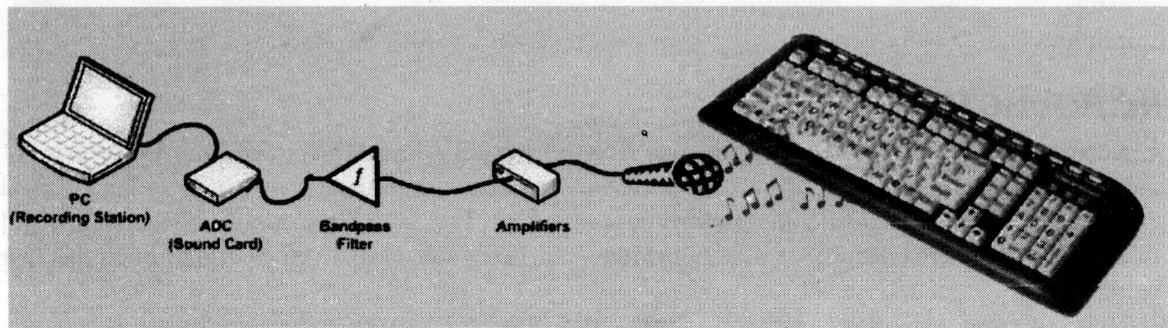

After this we examine the physical characteristics of a keyboard that cause the attack to succeed. Specifically, we determine why different keys produce different sounds. These insights provide clues for the design of homophonic keyboards that would be resistant to this type of attack.

REQUIRED EQUIPMENTS FOR THE ATTACK

We first specify the equipment and the software used in our study.

Keyboards. We used several types of keyboards. Most of PC keyboard experiments were performed with an IBM keyboard S/N 0953260, P/N 32P5100. Experiments with multiple keyboards were performed with three GE Power keyboards HO97798. For experiments with telephones, Siemens RP240 phones (M/N 62001) were used.

Microphones. We used a simple PC microphone for short distances up to 1 meter and a parabolic microphone for eavesdropping from a distance.

Computer omnidirection microphone: serial number 33 – 3026 manufactured by RadioShack; frequency response: 30 Hz–15 kHz; impedance: 1000 ohms ±30%; sensitivity: –68 dB ±3 dB; operating voltage: 1.0 to 10 VDC.

Parabolic microphone: 'Bionic Booster' manufactured by Silver Creek Industries; frequency response 100 Hz-10 kHz (–3 dB response); gain amp. cut off at 90 dB; overall system gain: 40 dB; sensitivity: –46 dB (0 dB = 1 V/Pa).

ADC and FFT. The input was digitized using a standard PC sound card with 44.1 kHz sampling rate. Sigview software v.1.81 was used for recording the sound as well as for calculating time-FFT on 2 ms windows, with the Harming windowing function applied. Window overlap was not available.

Neural Network. We used the JavaNNS neural network simulator [23] to build a backpropagation neural network. The number of input nodes equaled the size of the feature. For example, one value per 20 Hz in the FFT requires 200 input nodes for 0–4 kHz interval. There were 6–10 hidden nodes, depending on the size of the feature and the number of keys. The number of output nodes equaled the number of keys in the experiments with multiple keys. One output node was used in the experiments with two keys.

NEURAL NETWORK

In this case our attack employs a neural network to recognize the key being pressed. We also investigate why different keys produce different sounds and provide hints for the design of homophonic keyboards that would be resistant to this type of attack.

Neural Network

A recognition method aims to classify data (patterns) based on either *a priori* knowledge or on statistical information extracted from the acoustic patterns

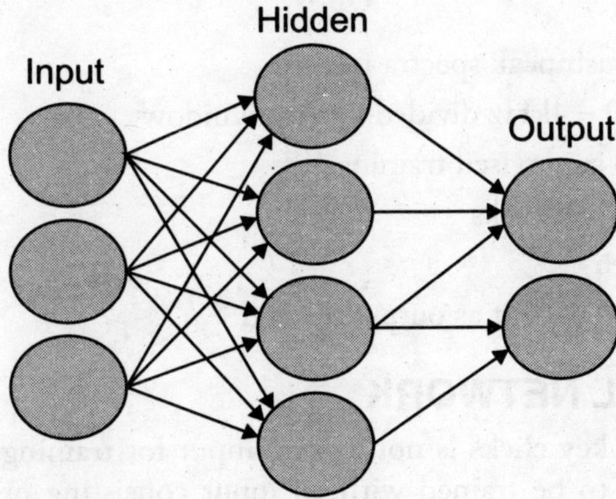

Consist of Neurons in layers, (input, middle, and output)

- Input neurons equal to number of sound features
- Output neurons equal to number of keys in the experiment
- Middle neurons equal to size the feature and number of keys being analyzed.

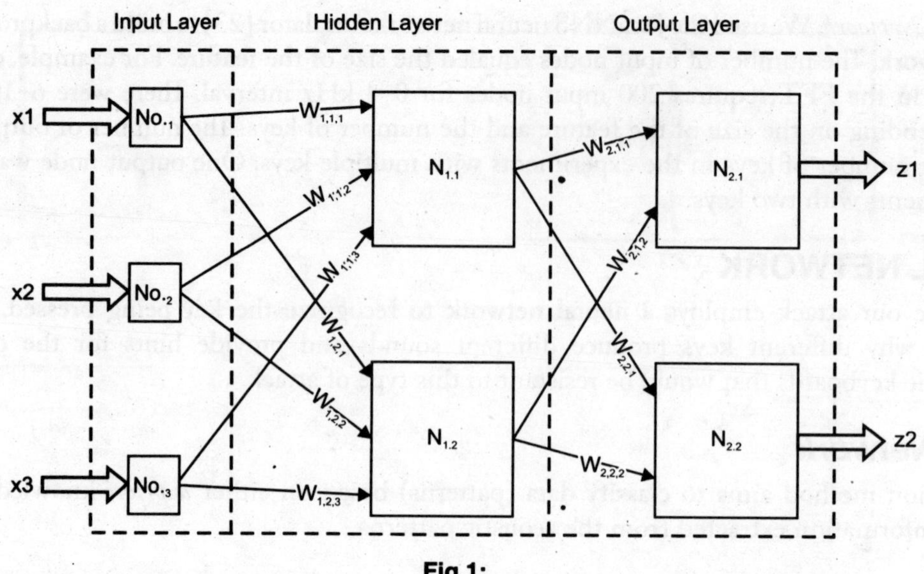

Fig.1:

Input neurons → push peak spectra feature

- FFT value of freq. 0 – 4kHz divided by 2ms window

Trained neurons → supervised training

- sample data of each key clicks
- get the signal pattern
- set the threshold and weight as output desired.

TRAINING A NEURAL NETWORK

The raw sound produced by key clicks is not a good input for training a neural network. Neural networks are recommended to be trained with an input consisting of several dozens to several hundreds of numeric values between 0 and 1, which corresponds to approximately up to 1 kB input. On the other hand, the size of the acoustic signal corresponding to a keyboard click is about 10 kB. We, therefore, extract relevant features from the raw sound.

We want the features that enable the neural network to differentiate between perceptually similar sound samples. The direct frequency spectrum is known to have significant variation for perceptually similar sounds, which makes it particularly attractive for our application. Interestingly, it is this same property of the direct frequency spectrum that causes it not to be used as a feature in the conventional sound classification..

We also need to carefully choose the time at which the spectrum is calculated. For this purpose, an understanding of how the signal of a click looks like is instructive. As shown in Figures 1, 2 and 3, the click lasts for approximately 100 ms, and the acoustic signal has two distinct peaks corresponding to pushing the key and releasing the key. There is relative silence between the push and release peaks.

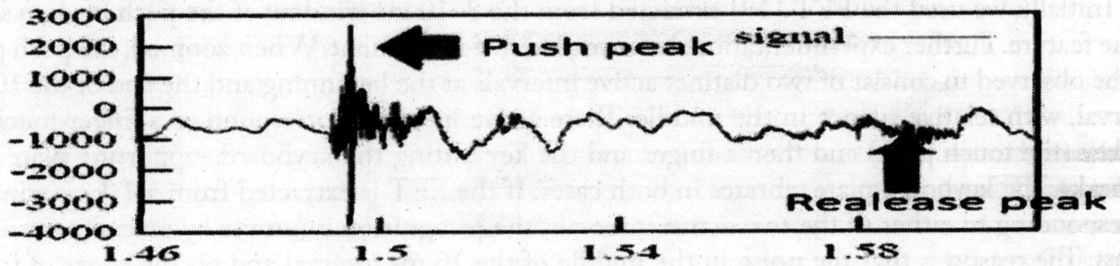

Fig.2: The acoustatic signal of one click.

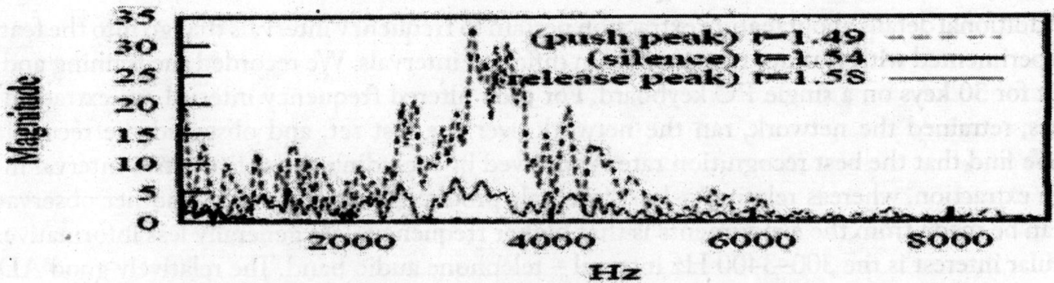

Fig.3: Frequency spectrums corresponding to the push peak, a silence interval, and the release neak.

The frequency distribution is best exposed at the peaks. We calculate the frequency distribution at the time of the press peak because the release peak is considerably lower. After calculating the frequency distribution at the press peak, we normalize the vector so that the values in the spectrum fall in the range [0,1] required for a neural network.

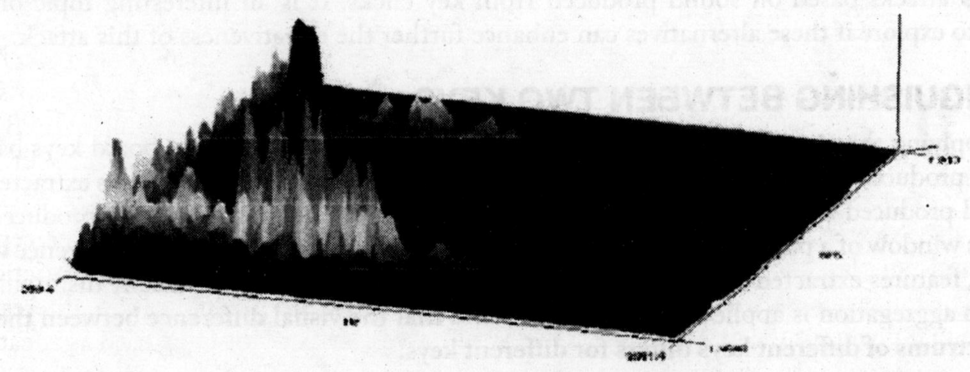

Fig.4: Time FFT of the signal in Figure 1

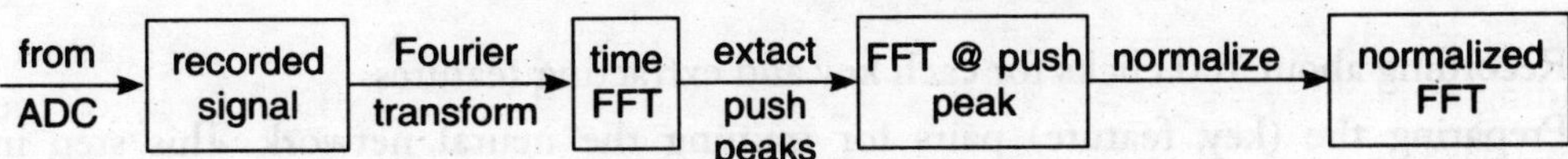

Fig.5: Feature extraction

Initially, we used the FFT [19] extracted from the 8–10 ms window of the push peak to serve as the feature. Further experimentation, however, led to a refinement. When zoomed, the push peak can be observed to consist of two distinct active intervals at the beginning and the end of the 10 ms interval, with relative silence in the middle. These active intervals correspond to a finger touching the key (the touch peak) and then a finger and the key hitting the keyboard supporting plate (the hit peak). The keyboard plate vibrates in both cases. If the FFT is extracted from a 2 3 ms window corresponding to either of the two active intervals, the recognition improves by several percentage points. The reason is that the noise in the middle of the 10 ms interval and on the edges of touch and hit peaks spoil the feature. The touch peak was expressed much better than the hit peak in many of the clicks. We, therefore, use touch peaks to extract features.

Additional details about feature extraction pertain to frequency intervals that go into the feature. We experimented with features extracted from different intervals. We recorded the training and the test set for 30 keys on a single PC keyboard. For each filtered frequency interval, we extracted the features, retrained the network, ran the network over the test set, and observed the recognition rate. We find that the best recognition rate is achieved by including the entire active interval in the feature extraction, whereas relatively short intervals produced poorer results. Another observation that can be made from the experiments is that higher frequencies are generally less informative. Of particular interest is the 300–3400 Hz interval – telephone audio band. The relatively good ADCS for this interval in our experiments suggests that eavesdropping on the clicks over the phone, an attack setting proposed in [12], is potentially possible.

Figure 4 summarizes the sequence of transformations applied to the raw sound of the click for feature extraction. It is conceivable to use alternative feature extraction algorithms. For example, one may use cepstrum instead of raw FFT [19]. As a matter of fact, one can even experiment with a different tvne of classifier such as a support vector machine or a decision tree [14]. As we will see, the current setup was adequate to demonstrate the vulnerability of keyboard and push button devices to attacks based on sound produced from key clicks. It is an interesting topic of future research to explore if these alternatives can enhance further the effectiveness of this attack.

DISTINGUISHING BETWEEN TWO KEYS

Before applying the neural network to the task of distinguishing two PC keyboard keys based on the clicks produced by them, we tried to visualize the difference between the features extracted from the sound produced by the clicks. We applied various aggregations to the features produced from the 10 ms window of a push peak for the two keys, but did not observe significant difference visually. However, features extracted from the 2–3 ms window of a touch peak are visually distinguishable, even if no aggregation is applied (see Figure 5). **Note that the visual difference between the touch peak spectrums of different keys differs for different keys.**

We next report the neural network results. We chose keys k and l on a standard QWERTY keyboard for this experiment. This and most of the further experiments included the following steps:

1. Recording about 100 clicks for each key and extracting features.
2. Preparing the (key, feature) pairs for training the neural network. This step involved recording 100 clicks of each key and extracting the features. Unless noted otherwise, the clicks were recorded from a distance of about 0.5 meter.

3. Training the neural network with pairs {key, feature}
4. Preparing features to test the trained neural network. This step involved recording a set of test clicks (10 clicks per key) and extracting the features.
5. Testing the neural network. In this step, the neural network was provided with a test feature and the output of the network was compared with the identity of the key that was actually pressed.

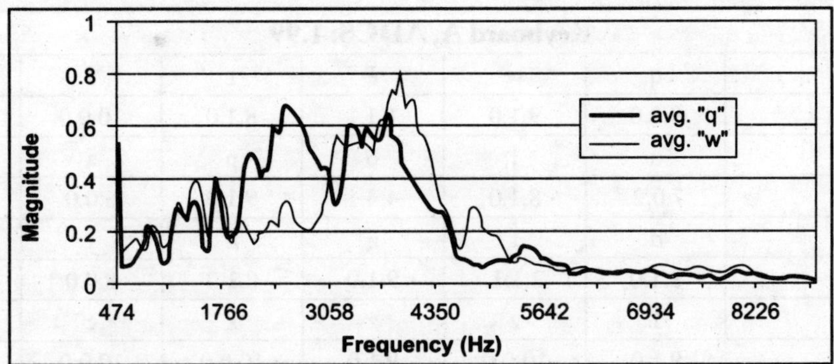

Fig.6: Comparison of the normalized average spectrums (extracted from touch peaks of the clicks).

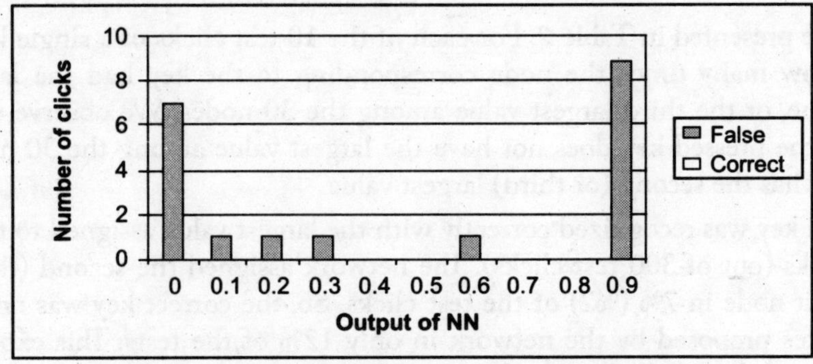

Fig.7: Results of recognizing ten *k* and ten *l* clicks each.

Figure 6 shows a sample experiment of applying a trained neural network to recognize 10 clicks produced by each of the keys k and l. The network recognizes that a click is produced by the key k (1) if it assigns an output node a value between 0 and 0.5 and 1). The histogram displays the number of correct and false recognitions per each 0.1 interval of the output range of the node. In Figure 6, there are no false recognitions, meaning that all 20 clicks were recognized correctly. On average, there were only 0.5 incorrect recognitions per 20 clicks, which shows the exposure of keyboard to the eavesdropping using this attack.

Result with Multiple Keys

We next studied the effect of multiple keys on the quality of recognition.

We trained a network to recognize 30 keys on a keyboard ('q–p', 'a–', 'z–/'). We then recorded 10 test clicks per key. The neural network had 30 output nodes, each node corresponding to one of 30 keys. The network was trained to recognize a key by assigning a unique output node a value close to 1, while other nodes were assigned values close to 0. At the time of testing, a certain key was deemed recognized if the output node corresponding to this key was assigned largest value when the feature corresponding to the key was provided as input to the neural network.

Table 2. The neural network is testes with 300 clicks, 10 clicks per key.

Keyboard A, ADCS: 1.99						
key pressed	q	w	e	r	t	y
recognized	9.0.0	9.1.0	1.1.1	8.1.0	10.0.0	7.1.0
key pressed	u	i	o	p	a	s
recognized	7.0.2.	8.1.0	4.4.1	9.1.0	6.0.0	9.0.0
key pressed	d	f	g	h	j	k
recognized	8.1.0	2.1.1.	9.1.0	8.1.0	8.0.0	8.0.0
key pressed	1	z	z	x	c	v
recognized	9.1.0	10.0.0	9.1.0	10.0.0	10.0.0	9.0.1
key pressed	b	n	m	-	-	-
recognized	10.0.0	9.1.0	9.1.0	6.1.0	8.1.0	8.1.0

The results are presented in Table *2*. For each of the 10 test clicks of a single key we collected three numbers: how many times the node corresponding to the key had the largest value, the second largest value, or the third largest value among the 30 nodes. We observe that if the node corresponding to the pressed key does not have the largest value among the 30 nodes, then with high probability, it has the second (or third) largest value.

In summary, a key was recognized correctly with the largest value assigned to the correct node in 79% of the clicks (out of 300 test clicks). The network assigned the second (the third) largest value to the correct node in 7% (%2) of the test clicks. So, the correct key was not found among the three candidates proposed by the network in only 12% of the tests. This experiment further reinforces the vulnerability of the keyboard to eavesdropping.

EFFECT OF DISTANCE

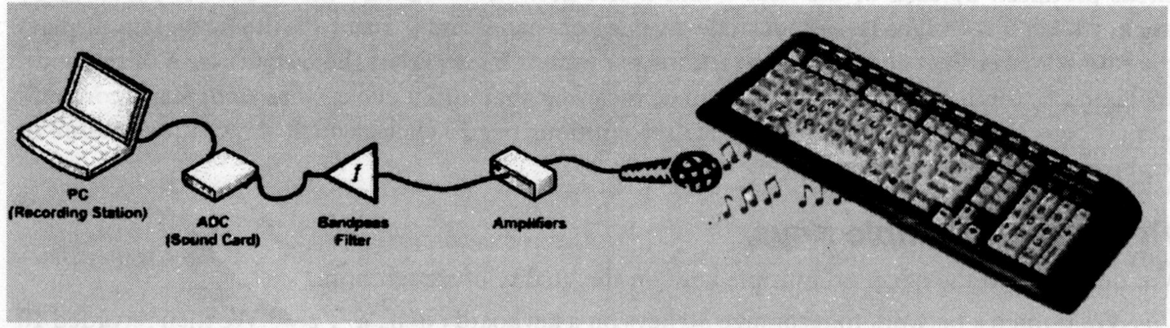

In the above experiment, clicks were recorded from a short distance of less than 1 meter. We repeated the experiment of distinguishing between two keys by recording clicks from different distances to study the influence of the distance on the quality of recognition. We used an inexpensive parabolic microphone to record the clicks. The microphone was placed behind the person typing. The person was sitting in a cubicle in a hall, with substantial background noise.

The maximum distance we experimented with was approximately 15 meters. There was NO decrease in recognition quality even at this distance.

HANDLING DIFFERENT TYPING STYLES

In the previous experiments, all the clicks used in the training set as well as the test set were generated by the same person, using the same finger and approximately the same force. We next studied the effect on recognition if a person types with variable force. Initially, the network was trained on clicks produced with an approximately constant typing force. The results of recognizing the test clicks produced with variable force were poor (Figure 7).

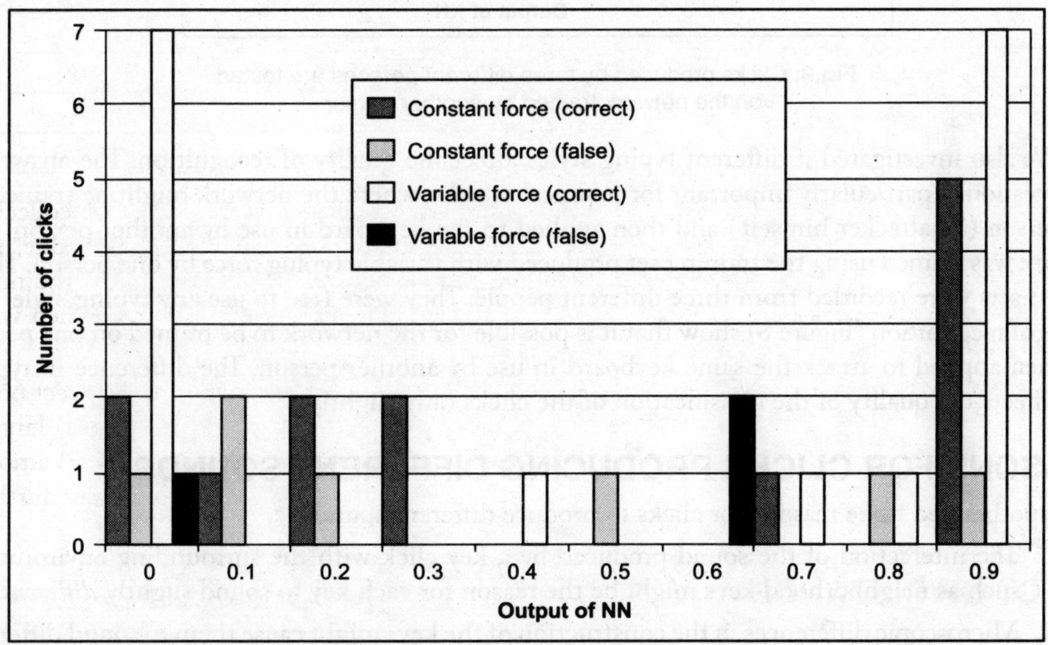

Fig.8: Test clicks produced with variable force are classified by two networks. For one network a constant force was used to produce the training set of clicks. For another network, variable force was used.

Next, we generated a training set in which clicks were produced by typing with a variable force and trained the network again. The testing results (Figure 7) now are as good as in the basic experiment, meaning that the network can be trained to recognize the clicks produced with different forces. Other experiments show that the same conclusion is valid for typing with one vs. many fingers. Namely, if trained with one finger only, the clicks produced by different fingers are recognized with high error rate. But a network trained with many fingers is as good as the basic one in recognizing the clicks: approx. 1 click (out of 20 clicks) is recognized incorrectly.

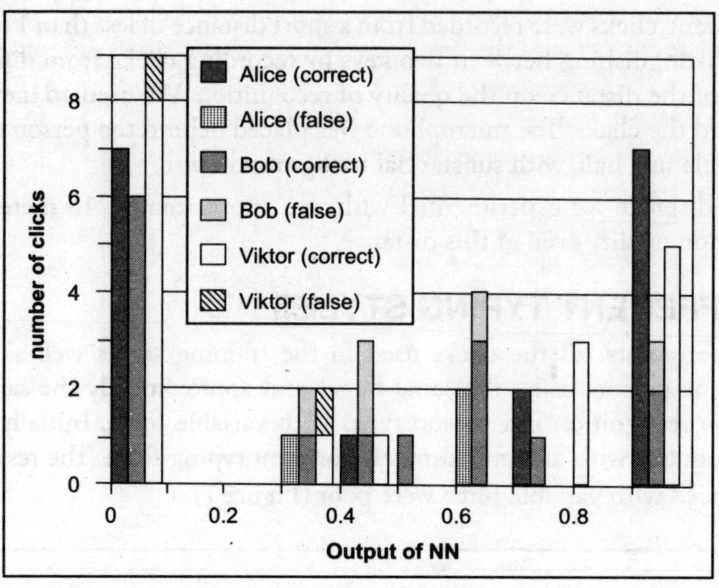

Fig.9: Clicks produced by three different persons are tested on the network trained by another person.

We also investigated if different typing styles affect the quality of recognition. The answer to this question is particularly important for practical attacks, where the network might be trained by one person (an attacker himself) and then applied to the keyboard in use by another person. The network was trained using the training set produced with variable typing force by one person. Then, the test sets were recorded from three different people. They were free to use any typing style. The results of recognition (Figure 8) show that it is possible for the network to be trained on one person and then applied to attack the same keyboard in use by another person. The difference in typing style affects the quality of the classification of the clicks only slightly.

REASONS FOR CLICKS PRODUCING DIFFERENT SOUNDS

We hypothesized three reasons for clicks to produce different sounds

1. The interaction of the sound produced by a key click with the surrounding environment such as neighborhood keys might be the reason for each key to sound slightly *different.*
2. Microscopic differences in the construction of the keys might cause them to sound different.
3. Different parts of the keyboard plate might produce different sounds when the nearby key is pushed. By analogy with a drum, striking a key at different locations on the plastic plate provides different timbres.

The first hypothesis was ruled out by the following experiment. After the neural network was trained to distinguish between two keys, the surrounding environment was changed by removing several neighborhood keys on the keyboard. This modification should have changed the way the clicks sound if the environment is the underlying reason. However, the recorded test clicks were successfully classified by the trained network, invalidating the hypothesis.

To check the second hypothesis, we trained the network to recognize two keys: k and l. We then interchanged them on the keyboard plate and recorded their test clicks. The network identified the test clicks of the k element as l, and the test clicks of the l element as k (Figure 10).

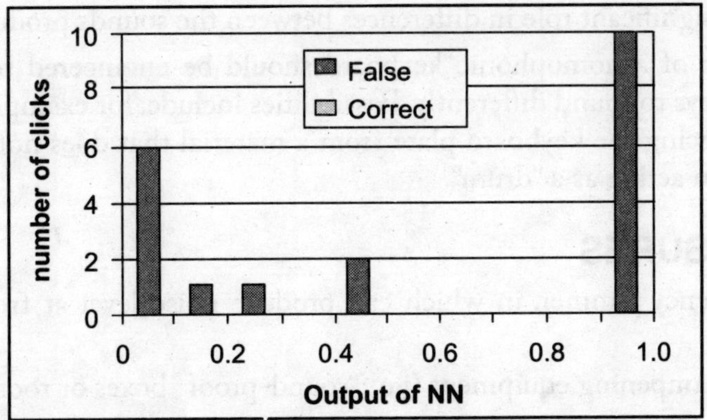

Fig.10: Results of recognizing two keys exchanged on the keyboard. First 10 clicks are produced by the *l* key element, the next 10 clicks are produced by the k key element. The network is trained to recognize k with 0 and f with *l* before the keys were exchanged.

This experiment led us to conclude that the second hypothesis can be ruled out: The microscopic differences in key elements play no or minor role in making the clicks to sound different. This conclusion does not reject the obvious observation that macroscopic differences play role in causing the keys to sound different. For example, the space key may sound different from a standard key partially because of the difference in size between the keys.

To check the third hypothesis we cut out several pieces of the keyboard plate with one key in each piece using a milling machine. Obviously, this operation should render the third hypothesis irrelevant, because there is not any notion of the position of the keys on the keyboard plate. If the third hypothesis were true, we expect the network not to be able to distinguish between clicks produced by the keys mounted in these pieces. Indeed, after we trained the network, the network was unable to recognize the keys based on the test clicks (Figure 11), thus supporting our third hypothesis.

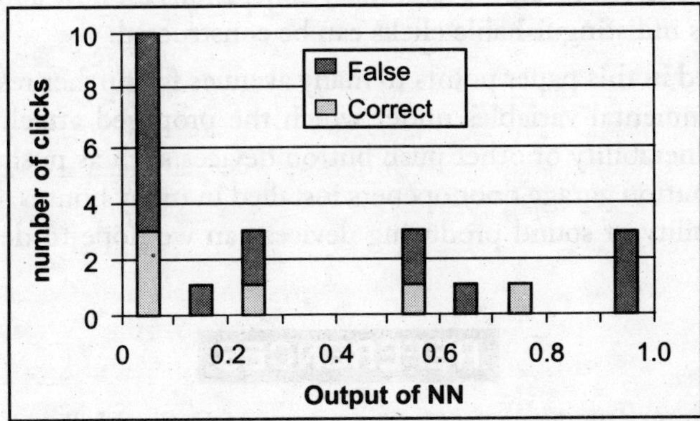

Fig.11: Results of recognizing two keys cut out of the keyboard plate. The network was trained to recognize the keys after the keys were cut out.

These experiments suggest that the clicks sound different because the keys are positioned at different positions on the keyboard plate. Knocking at different positions on the plate makes different sounds. Neither microscopic differences between the key elements nor a surrounding environment plays a significant role in differences between the sounds produced by different keys.

The construction of a homophonic keyboard should be engineered to obliterate the above identified cause for keys to sound differently. Possibilities include, for example, not placing the keys in one plate, or producing the keyboard plate from a material that does not conduct vibrations to prevent the plate from acting as a "drum".

COUNTERMEASURES

- Use a frequency jammer, in which can produce noise level at frequency range of keys sounds
- Use sound dampening equipment (i.e., "sound-proof" boxes or rooms)
- Use keyboard based on a touch screen or touchstream technologies
- Use of specific keyboard with different keys structure

CONCLUSION

- Acoustic cryptanalysis attack relies on a very specific object's structure and behavior
- Acoustic attack is a natural attack which efficient and simple. No need to implement deep mathematical equations to reveal important information.
- Acoustic emanations analysis is based on the signal patterns produced by object being observed

We explored acoustic emanations of keyboard-like input devices to recognize the content being typed. After providing a detailed description of the basic attack on a PC keyboard, we successfully applied this attack to other types of push button input devices, such as notebook keyboards, telephone pads, and ATM pads.

A sound-free (non-mechanical) keyboard is an obvious countermeasure for the attack. However, it is neither comfortable for users nor cheap. We identified possible reasons that cause the keys to sound slightly different to draw preliminary conclusions on how a homophonic mechanical keyboard that produces indistinguishable clicks can be constructed.

The work presented in this paper points to many avenues for further research. One can explore to quantify the environmental variables under which the proposed attack can succeed. One can also investigate the vulnerability of other push button devices such as push button locks found on many doors and push button garage door openers installed in many houses. Only by measuring and analyzing the vulnerability of sound producing devices can we hope to develop countermeasures and make them secure.

REFERENCES

1. P.Kocher, "Timing attacks on implementations of Diffie-Hellman, RSA, DSS, and other systems", at www.cryptography.com/resources/whitepapers/TimingAttacks.pdf

2. J.F. Dhem, F. Koeune, P.-A. Leroux, P. Mestre, J.-J. Quisquater, and J.-L. Willems, "A practical implementation of the timing attack", at www.cs.jhu.edu/~fabian/courses/CS600.624/Timing-full.pdf
3. A. Shamir and E. Tromer, Acoustic cryptanalysis, On nosy people and noisy machines, http://www.wisdom.weizmann.ac.il/tromer/acoustic/
4. en.wikipedia.org/wiki/Acoustic_cryptanalysis
5. www.win.tue.nl/~aserebre/2IF03/2008/papers/Adi.pdf
6. www.freshersworld.com/resources/sp/cs_seml34.htm
7. Acoustic cryptanalysis On nosy people and noisy machines http://people.csail.mit.edu/tromer/acoustic/

Project–2
CRYPTOGRAPHY USING ANNs

ABSTRACT

A Neural Network is a machine that is designed to model the way in which the brain performs a task or function of interest. It has the ability to perform complex computations with ease. The objective of this project is to investigate the use of ANNs in various kinds of digital circuits as well as in the field of Cryptography. During this project, we will study different neural network architectures and training algorithms.

A comparative study will be done between different neural network architectures for an Adder and their merits/demerits will be discussed. Using a Jordan (Recurrent network), trained by back-propagation algorithm, a finite state sequential machine was successfully implemented. The sequential machine thus obtained was used for encryption with the starting key being the key for decryption process. Cryptography was also achieved by a chaotic neural network having its weights given by a chaotic sequence.

1 Introduction

1.1 Artificial Neural Network

Work on artificial neural network has been motivated right from its inception by the recognition that the human brain computes in an entirely different way from the conventional digital computer. The brain is a highly complex, nonlinear and parallel information processing system. It has the capability to organize its structural constituents, known as neurons, so as to perform certain computations many times faster than the fastest digital computer in existence today. The brain routinely accomplishes perceptual recognition tasks, e.g. recognizing a familiar face embedded in an unfamiliar scene, in approximately 100-200 ms, whereas tasks of much lesser complexity may take days on a conventional computer.

A neural network is a machine that is designed to model the way in which the brain performs a particular task. The network is implemented by using electronic components or is simulated in software on a digital computer. A neural network is a massively parallel distributed processor made up of simple processing units, which has a natural propensity for storing experimental knowledge and making it available for use. It resembles the brain in two respects:

1. Knowledge is acquired by the network from its environment through a learning process.
2. Intemeuron connection strengths, known as synaptic weights, are used to store the acquired knowledge.

Neural networks, with their remarkable ability to derive meaning from complicated or imprecise data, can be used to extract patterns and detect trends that are too complex to be noticed by either humans or other computer techniques. Other advantages include:

1. **Adaptive learning:** An ability to learn how to do tasks based on the data given for training or initial experience.
2. **Self-Organization:** An ANN can create its own organization or representation of the information it receives during learning time.
3. **Real Time Operation:** ANN computations may be carried out in parallel, and special hardware devices are being designed and manufactured which take advantage of this capability.

1.2 Cryptography

There are many aspects to security and many applications, ranging from secure commerce and payments to private communications and protecting passwords. One essential aspect for secure communications is that of cryptography.

Cryptography is the science of writing in secret code and is an ancient art; the first documented use of cryptography in writing dates back to circa 1900 B.C. when an Egyptian scribe used non-standard hieroglyphs in an inscription. Some experts argue that cryptography appeared spontaneously sometime after writing was invented, with applications ranging from diplomatic missives to war- time battle plans. It is no surprise, then, that new forms of cryptography came soon after the widespread development of computer communications. In data and telecommunications, cryptography is necessary when communicating over any untrusted medium, which includes just about *any* network, particularly the Internet.

Cryptography, then, not only protects data from theft or alteration, but can also be used for user authentication. There are, in general, three types of cryptographic schemes typically used to accomplish these goals: secret key (or symmetric) cryptography, public-key (or asymmetric) cryptography, and hash functions, each of which is described below. In all cases, the initial unencrypted data is referred to as *plaintext*. It is encrypted into *ciphertext*, which will in turn (usually) be decrypted into usable plaintext.

1.3 Chaotic Neural Network

Chaotic neural networks offer greatly increase memory capacity. Each memory is encoded by an Unstable Periodic Orbit (UPO) on the chaotic attractor. A chaotic attractor is a set of states in a system's state space with very special property that the set is an attracting set. So the system starting with its initial condition in the appropriate basin, eventually ends up in the set. The most important, once the system is on the attractor nearby states diverge from each other exponentially fast, however small amounts of noise are amplified.

1.4 Chaos

Chaos is statistically indistinguishable from randomness, and yet it is deterministic and not random at all. Chaotic system will produce the same results if given the same inputs, it is unpredictable in the sense that you can not predict in what way the system's behavior will change for any change in the input to that system. A random system will produce different results when given the same inputs.

1.5 Cryptography using chaotic neural networks

A new chaotic neural network for digital signal encryption and decryption was studied in this project. According to a binary sequence generated from a chaotic system, the biases and weights of neurons are set. The chaotic neural network can be used to encrypt digital signal. The network's features are as follows:

1. High Security
2. No distortion
3. Suitable for system integration.

The MATLAB simulation results are also included for demonstration. It indicates that the integration of the proposed system and MPEG2 for TV distribution, communication, and storage is practicable.

Among the proposed encryption techniques, the basic ideas can be classified into three major types:

1. **Position permutation:** The position permutation algorithms scramble the positions of original data.
2. **Value transformation:** The value transformation algorithms transform the data value of the original signal.
3. **The combining form:** Finally, the combining form performs both operations. The encryption scheme belongs to category of value transformation. Based on a binary sequence generated from the 1-D logistic map, the biases and weights of neurons are set in each iteration.

2 Application of Neutral Network

2.1 Sequential Machine

A "sequential machine" is a device in which the output depends in some systematic way on variables other than the immediate inputs to the device. These "other variables" are called the *state variables* for the machine, and depend on the *history or state* of the machine. For example, in a counter, the state variables are the values stored in the flip flops. The essence of a state table can be captured in a state diagram. A state diagram is a graph with labeled nodes and arcs; the nodes are the states, and the arcs are the possible transitions between states.

In the project we have used the fact that the output of the sequential machine depend on the state of the machine as well as the input given to the sequential machine. Therefore we have used a Jordan network in which a few outputs are used as inputs, these outputs denote the states. A multilayered neural network is designed on this basis whish has a hard limiter in the output layer as a transfer function. The network has 3 layers an input layer, a hidden layer and an output layer. The size of the input layer depends on the number of inputs and the number of outputs being used to denote the states. The learning algorithm used for this network is back propagation algorithm and the transfer function in the hidden layer is a sigmoid function. For implementation of sequential machine a serial adder and a sequential decoder is used.

2.2 Serial Adder

The serial adder accepts as input two serial strings of digits of arbitrary length, starting with the low order bits, and produces the sum of the two bit streams as its output. (The input bit streams could come from, say, two shift registers clocked simultaneously.) This device can be easily described as a state machine.

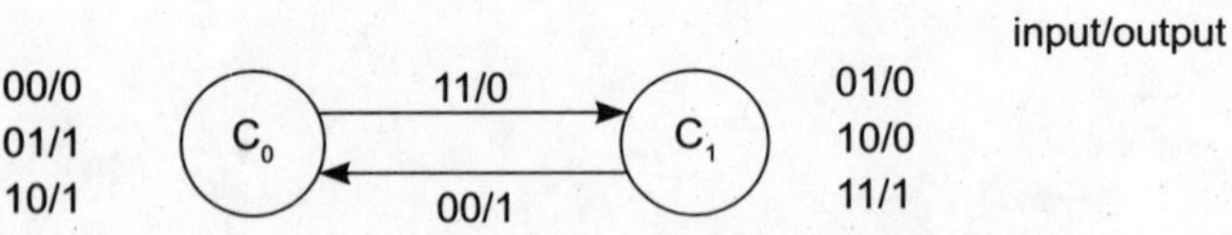

Fig.1: State diagram of Serial Adde.

2.3 Sequential Detector

A state machine is required which outputs logic 1 whenever a particular sequence is detected in the input data stream, and which outputs a zero otherwise. The input is supplied serially, one bit at a time. The following is an example input sequence and output sequence:

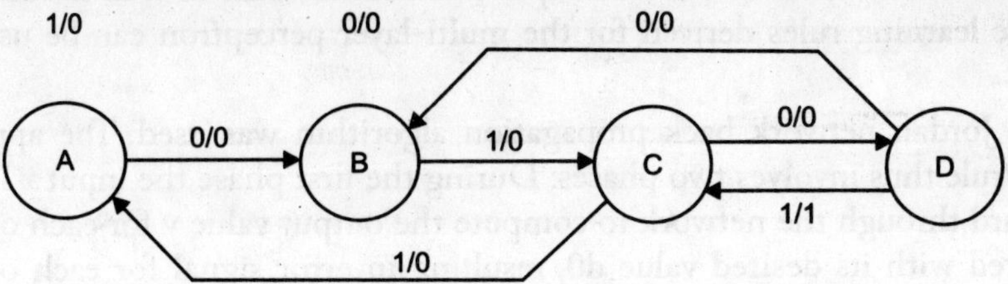

Fig.2: State diagram

The following is a state table corresponding to the state diagram. We can derive a state table from the state diagram as follows:

Present state	Inputs		Next state	Output
C_0	0	0	C_0	0
C_0	0	1	C_0	1
C_0	1	0	C_0	1
C_0	1	1	c,	0
C_1	0	0	C_0	1
C_1	0	1	C_1	0
C_1	1	0	C_1	0
C_1	1	1	C_1	1

2.4 Sequential Machine Implementation

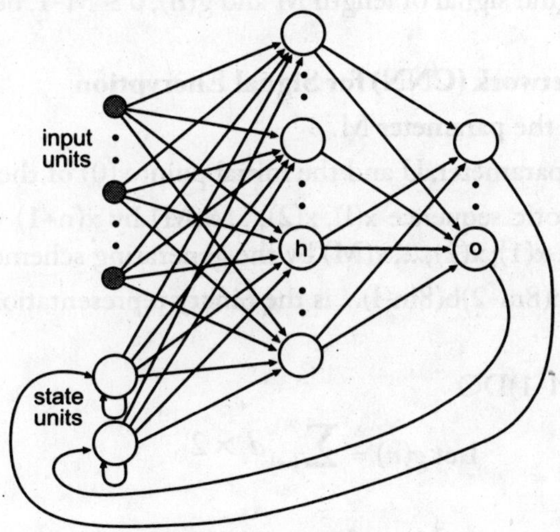

Fig.3: Jordan Network

A finite state sequential machine was implemented using a Jordan network is used. In the Jordan network, the activation values of the output units are fed back into the input layer through a set of extra input units called the state units. There are as many state units as there are output units in the network. The connections between the output and state units have a fixed weight of+1 and learning takes place only in the connections between input and hidden units as well as hidden and output units. Thus all the learning rules derived for the multi-layer perceptron can be used to train this network.

To train the Jordan network back propagation algorithm was used. The application of the generalized delta rule thus involves two phases: During the first phase the input x is presented and propagated forward through the network to compute the output value y for each output unit. This output is compared with its desired value d0, resulting in error signal for each output unit. The second phase involves a backward pass through the network during which the error signal is passed to each unit in the network and appropriate weight changes are calculated.

For the implementation of the sequential machine the state table is used as input and the outputs as well as next states are used as the combined output for the Jordan network. Depending upon the size of the dataset the size of the hidden layer is changed as the complexity of the sequential machine increases.

In sequential logic two implementations are done namely:

1. Serial adder
2. Sequence detector

Both of the examples can be represented by a simple state diagram. The state table is made and the neural network is trained for the above stated examples of sequential logic. The weights after training obtained represents a network trained according to the sample data.

2.5 Cryptography using Chaotic Neural Network

A network is called a chaotic neural network if its weights and biases are determined by a chaotic sequence. Let g denote a digital signal of length M and g(n), 0 ≤ M-1, be the one-byte value of the signal g at position n.

The Chaotic Neural Network (CNN) for Signal Encryption

Step 1: Set the value of the parameter M.

Step 2: Determine the parameter, U and the initial point x(0) of the 1-D logistic map [SI.

Step 3: Evolve the chaotic sequence x(l), x(2),..., x(M) by x(n+1) = μ(n)(1-x(n)), and create b(O), b(1),.,., b(8M-1) from x(1), x(2),..., x(M) by the generating scheme that

0.b(8m- 8)b(8m-7)..... b(8m-2)b(8m-l)... is the binary representation of x(m) for m = 1,2,... .,M.

Step 4: FOR n:0 TO(M-1)DO

$$\text{Let } g(n) = \sum_{i=0}^{7} d_i \times 2^i$$

For i = 0 TO 7 DO 1

$$\begin{cases} 1 & \text{if } j = i \text{ and } b(8 \times n + i) = 0, \end{cases}$$

$$w_p = \begin{cases} -1 & \text{if } j = i \text{ and } b(8 \times n + i) = 1, \\ 0 & \text{if } j \neq i \end{cases}$$

j (0,1,2,3,4,0,6,7)

END

For

i = 0 TO 7 DO

$$\theta_i = \begin{cases} -\tfrac{1}{2} & \text{if } b(8 \times n + i) = 0, \\ \tfrac{1}{2} & \text{if } b(8 \times n + i) = 1, \end{cases}$$

Where f(x) is 1 if x *2* 0 and 0 otherwise,

END

Step 5: The encrypted signal g" is obtained and the algorithm is terminated.

The decryption procedure is the same as the above one except that the input signal to the decryption CNN should be *g '(n)* and its output signal should be *g "(n)*.

In case of a image, pixels are processed by neurons according to (3.11). The desirable result of the encrypted image being completely disorder can be obtained. In the decryption phase of CNN, according to the same chaotic system and its initial state, i.e. the same chaotic binary sequence, the original image can be found by decrypting CNN.

Hence, the chaotic binary sequence is unpredictable. It is very difficult to decrypt and encrypt image correctly by making exhaustive search without knowing x(0) and μ. Hence, CNN is one of the guaranteed high security.

SYSTEM DESIGN

RESULTS AND CONCLUSION

Cryptography Using Chaotic Neural Network

A chaötic network is a neural network whose weights depend on a chaotic sequence. The chaotic sequence highly depends upon the initial conditions and the parameters, x(0) = 0.75, and μ = 3.9 are set. It is very difficult to decrypt an encrypted data correctly by making an exhaustive search without knowing x(0) and μ..

Here a sequence of ten numbers is used for encryption and the initial parameters for the chaotic network are used as mentioned. The output or the encrypted data is then used for decryption. It can easily be seen that the output is in a chaotic state.

Depending upon the chaotic sequence a weight matrix and a bias matrix is obtained and the net input is obtained. Then a hard limiter is applied as a transfer function in order to obtain the digital encrypted data. For decryption the same network is used and the same initial value is used to generate the chaotic sequence and for decrypting the data successfully. The CNN here used can also be used to encrypt and decrypt data such as images by converting it into a single vector. Hence, CNN is one of guaranteed high security.

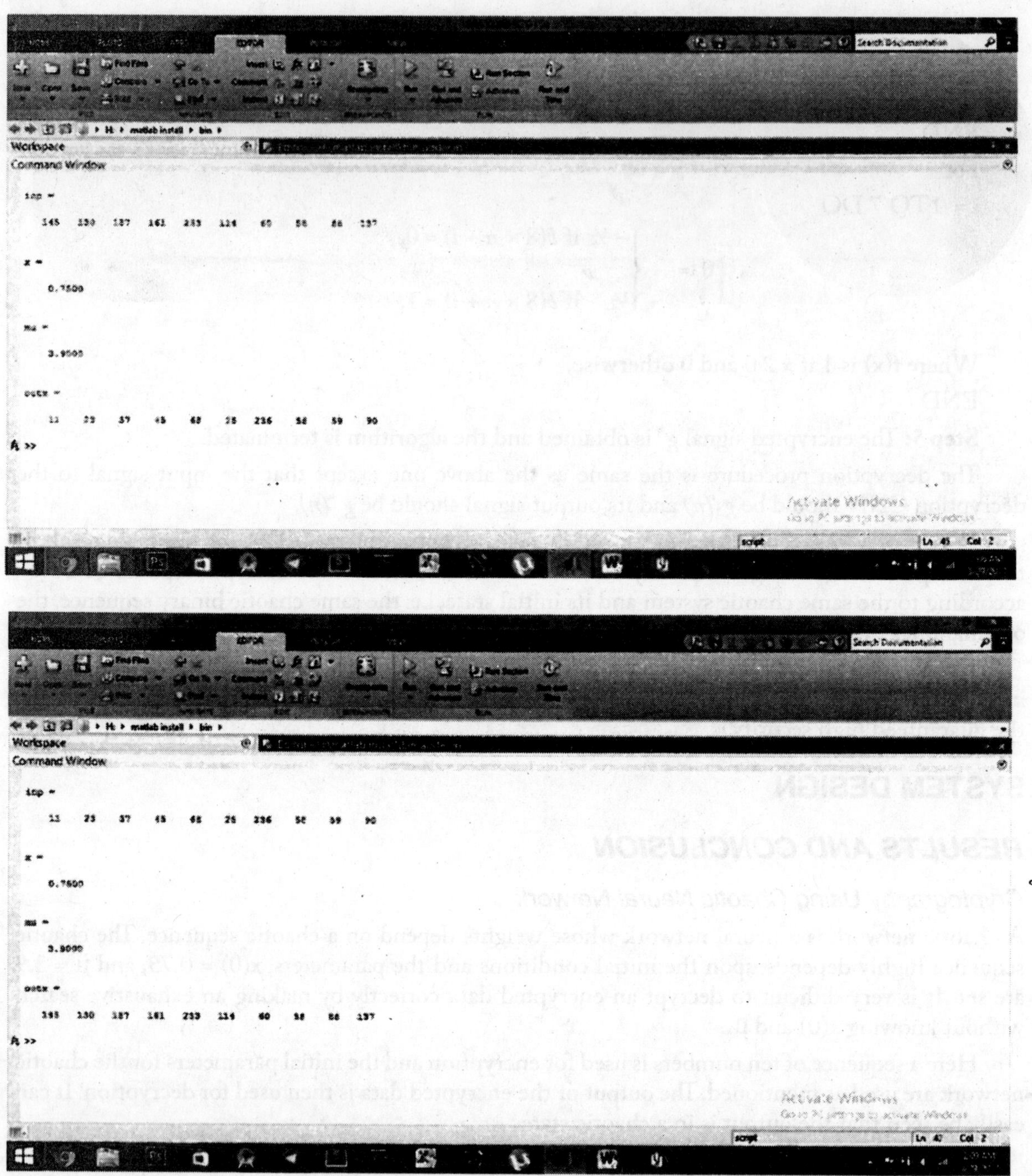
EDITOR
Search Documentation
Workspace
Command Window
inp =
145 130 187 161 233 114 60 58 88 137
x =
0.7500
mu =
3.9900
outx =
11 23 37 45 68 25 236 58 59 90
>>
Activate Windows
EDITOR
Search Documentation
Workspace
Command Window
inp =
11 23 37 45 68 25 236 58 59 90
x =
0.7500
mu =
3.9000
outx =
145 130 187 161 233 114 60 58 88 137
>>
Activate Windows

References

1. http://wwwjjarcsms.com/docs/paper/volume2/issuel 1/V2I11-0095.pdf
2. http://www.nnw.cz/doi/2014/NNW.2014.24.01 l.pdf
3. http://ccis2k.org/iajit/PDF/vol.9,no.2/9-1508.pdf
4. http://www.scs-europe.net/conf/ecms2012/ecms2012%20accepted%20papers/is_ECMS.0113.pdf
5. http://www.iarjset.com/upload/2015/april-15/IARJSET%2019.pdf

Appendix

Sequential machine code:

```
clc;
closeall;
inputs_x=input('enter the no of inputs');
output_x-input('enter the no of output');
statx=input('enter the no of states');
% no of bits for states
fortem=l:100
if2^tem>=statx
states=tem;
break
end
end
hls=5;%2^(inputs_x+output_x+2); % size of the hidden layer
% weight initialization————————
wl =rand(hls,(inputs_x+states+1));
w2=rand((output_x+states),hls+l);
neta=l;
a=l;
sx=0;
p=U;
fortex=l :(2^(inputs_x)*statx);
trainmg_setx(tex,:)=input('enter input and state');
training_outx(tex,:)=input('enter output and state¹);
end forx=i:7000
```

```
training_set=training_setx(a,:);
training_out=training_outx(a,:);
% output hidden layer—————————
inputu=[1 training_set];
sum_h=(w1 *(inputu)')';
o_h= 1./(1 +exp(-sum_h));

% output layer ————————
input_h=[1 o__h];
sum_out=(w2*(input_h)')';
out=17(1+exp(-sum_out));
% delta ----------------
delta_out=(out*(1-out)).*(training_out - out);
delta_h=(delta_out*w2).*input_h.*(1-input_h);

% update of weight ---------------
% output layer ---------------
for t=1:(output_x+states)
w2(t,:) = w2(t,:) + neta*delta_out(t)*input_h;
end
% hidden layer ---------------
fort=1:hls
w1(t,:) = w1(t,:) + neta*delta_h(t+1)*inputu;
end
for t=1 :(output_x+states)

ifout(t)>=0.7
out1(t)=1;
elseifout(t)<=0.2
out1(t)=0;
else out 1(t)=out(t);
end

end
p=[p sum(out-training_out)];
```

```
if outl ==training_out
a=a+l;
sx=sx+l;
end

if a > ((2^inputs_x)*statx)
a=a-((2^inputs_x) * statx);
end
end
plot(p);
% testing the program
statx=zeros(l,states);
zaz='y';
forxz=l:10
ipo = input('enter the input');
ipox=[ipostatx];
inputp=[l ipox];
sum_h=(wl *(inputp)')';
o_h= 1./(1 +exp(-sum_h));

% output layer ---------------
input_h=[l o_h];
sum_out=(w2*(input_h)')';
out= 1./(1 +exp(-sum_out));

for t=l:(states+output_x)

ifout(t)>=0.7
outl(t)=l;
elseifout(t)<=0.2
outl(t)=0;
else outl(t)=out(t);
end

end
```

```
out1
statx=outl( (outputjt + l);(output_x+states));
end
inputs_x=input('enter the no of inputs');
training_setxm=[];
training_outxm=[];
forcl=0:l
for inxl=0:2^(inputs_x)-l
for inx2=0:2^(inputs_x)-l
temp=inx 1 +inx2+c 1;
training^outxm=[training_outxm; bitget(temp,inputs_x+l>l:l)];
training_setxm=[training_setxm;bitget(inxl,inputs_x:-l:l)
bitget(inx2,inputs_x:-l:l) cl];
end
end
end

training_setx=[];
training_outx=[];
hls=[4 3 1];% size of the hidden layer
% weight initialization---------------
for vl=l:inputs_x+l

ifvl =inputs_x+l
wl=rand(hls(vl),2*(vl-l)+2);
else
wl=rand(hls(vl),2*vl+2);
end
w2=rand(l,hls(vl)+l);
neta=0.5;
a=l;
sx=0;
p=[];
if vl == inputs_x+l
training_setx=training_setxm;
else
```

```
training_setx=[training_setxm(: ,inputs_x- v 1+1 :inputs_x)
training_setxm(:,2*inputs_xvl+l:2*inputs_x+l)];
end

training_outx=[training_outxm(: ,(inputs_x+1)-v 1+1)];

forx=l:15000
train ing_set=training_setx(a,:);
training_out=training_outx(a,:);
% output hidden layer----------
inputu=[l training_set];
sum Ji=(w 1 *(inputu)')';
o_h=1./(1 +exp(-sum_h));
% output layer ----------
input_h=[l o_h];
sum_out=(w2*(inputji)')';
out=l./(1 +exp(-sum_out));
% delta ---------
delta_out=(out.*(l-out)).*(training_out - out);
delta_h=(delta_out*w2).*input_h.*(l-input_h);
% update of weight ---------
% output layer ---------

w2 = w2 + neta*delta_out*input_h;
% hidden layer---------
fort=l:hls(vl)
wl(t,:) = wl(t,:) + neta*delta_h(t+l)*inputu;
end
fort=l:l
ifout(t)>=0.7
outl(t)=l;
elseifout(t)<=0.2
out 1(t)=0;
else outl(t)=out(t);
end
end
```

```
p=[p mean((out-training_out).^2)];
if outl—training_out
a=a+l;
sx=sx+l;
end
ifa>((2^(inputs_x))^2)*2
a=a-((2^(inputs_x))A2)*2;
end

end
figure;
plot(p.*p);
end
```

Multilayer single output feed-forward Adder

```
clc;
clear all;
close all;
inputs_x=input('enter the no of inputs');
training_setxm=[];
training_outxm=n;
forcl=0:l
for inxl=0:2A(inputs_x)-l
    for inx2=0:2A(inputs_x)-l
temp=inx 1 +inx2+c 1;
training_outxm=[training_outxm ; bitget(temp,inputs_x+l:-l:l)];
training_setxtn=[training_setxm; bitget(inxl,inputs_x:-l:l)
bitget(inx2,inputs_x:-l:l)
cl];
end
end
    end
training_setx=[]; training_outx=[]; hls=[4 3 1 j;% size of the
hidden layer
% weight initialization ————————
for v 1=1 :inputs_x+l
```

```
    if vl ==inputs_x+l
    wl=rand(hls(vl),2*(vl-l)+2);
    else
    wl=rand(hls(vl),2*vl+2);
    end
    w2=rand(l,hls(vl)+l);
    neta=0.5;
    sx=0;
    P=[];
    if vl s==inputs_x+l
    training_setx=training_setxm;
    else
training_setx=[training_setxm(:,inputs_x-vl+l:inputs_x)
training_setxm(:,2*inputs x-vl+l:2*inputs_x+l)];
end
training_outx=[training_outxm(:,(inputs_x+l)-vl+l)];
for x=l: 15000
training_set=training_setx(a(:);
training_out=training_outx(a, : );
% output hidden layer ----------
inputu=[l training_set];
sum_h=(w 1 *(inputu)')T;
o_h=l./(l+exp(-sum_h));
% output layer ----------
input_h=[l o_h];
    sum_out=(w2*(input_h)')';
out=l ./(! +exp(-sum_out));
% delta ----------
    delta_out=(out.*(l-out)).*(training_out - out);
    delta_h=(delta_out*w2).*input_h.*(l-input_h);

% update of weight ----------
% output layer ----------
    w2 = w2 + neta*del layout *input_h;
% hidden layer ----------
    fort=l:hls(vl)
```

```
wl(t,:) = wl(t,:) + neta*delta_h(t+l)*inputu;
    end
    fort=l:l
    ifout(t)>=0.7
    out l(t)=l;
elseifout(t)<=0.2
outl(t)=0;
else outl(t)=out(t);
    end
    end
p=[p mean((out-training_out).^2)];
    if outl=training_out
    a=a+l;
    sx=sx+l;
    end
    ifa>((2^(inputs_x))^2)*2
    a=a-((2^(inputs_x))^2)*2;
    end
    end figure;
    plot(p.*p);
end
```

Multilayer multiple output feed-forward Adder

```
clc;
clear all;
    close all;
inputs_x=input('enter the no of inputs');
training_setx=[]; training_outx=[];
forcl-0:l
for inxl=0:2^(inputs_x)-l
    for inx2=0:2^(inputs_>0-l
    temp=inx 1 +inx2+c 1;
training_outx=[training_outx ; bitget(temp,inputs_x+l:-l:l)];
training_setx=[training_setx ; bitget(inxl,inputs_x:-l:l)
bitget(inx2,inputs_x:-l:l) cl];
    end
```

```
end end

hls=12;% size of the hidden layer
% weight initialization——————————————————
wl=rand(hls,2*inputs_x+2);
w2=rand(inputs_x+1 ,hls+1);
neta=0.5; a=l; sx=0; p=[];
for x=l: 15000
training_set=training_setx(a,:);
training_out=training_outx(a,:);
% output hidden layer——————————————————
inputu=[l training_set];
sum_h=(w 1 *(inputu)')';
o_h=l./(l+exp(-sum_h));
% output layer——————————————————
input_h=[l o_h];
sum_out=(w2*(input_h)')';
out= 1./(1 +exp(-sum_out));
% delta ——————————————————
delta_out=(out.*(l-out)).*(training_out - out);
delta_h=(delta_out*w2).*input_h.*(l-input_h);

% update of weight——————————————————
% output layer——————————————————
for t=l :(inputs_x+l)
w2(t,:) = w2(t,:) + neta*delta_out(t)*input_h;
end
% hidden layer——————————————————
fort=l:hls
wl(t,:)=wl(t,:)+neta*delta_h(t+l)*inputu;

    end
for t=l:inputs_x+l
    if out(t)>=0.7
    outl(t)=l;
    else
```

```
ifout(t)<=0.2
    outl(t)=0;
elseoutl(t)=out(t);
    end
        end
p=[p mean((out-training_out).ˆ2)];
        if out 1 =training_out
    a=a+l;
    sx=sx+l;
end
    ifa>((2ˆ(inputs_x))ˆ2)*2
    a=a-((2A(inputs_x))A2)*2;
    end
        end
plot(p.*p);
```

Encryption using chaos neural network

```
clear all;
    close all;
clc;
% input --------------------
inp=[l 1 23 37 45 68 25 236 58 59 90]
fori=l:length(inp)
    inpx(i,:)=bitget(inp(i),8:-l:l);
end
% generating a chaotic sequence -------------------
l=length(inp);
x(l)=0.75mu=3.9

for i=2:l
x(i)=mu*x(i-1)*(1-x(i-1);

end
    x=uint8(((x-min(x))/max(x))*255); b=[] ;
fori=l:l
    b(i,;)=bitget(x(i),8:-1:1);
```

```
end
temp=0;
    outx=zeros(1,length(inp));
% network ------------------------
forc=1:length(inp)
    fori=1:8
    forj=1:8
    if(b(c,i)==0)&(i==j)
        weight(ij)=1;
    elseif(b(c,i)==1)&(i==j)
        weight(ij)=-1;
        elseif i-=j
            weight(i,j)=0;
        end
    end
        if(b(c,i)==0)
        theta(i)=-1/2;
    elsetheta(i)=1/2;
        end
    end
    fori=1:8
        dx(c,i)=hardlim(sum(weight(i,:).*inpx(c,:))+theta(i));
            end
    for i=1:8
        outx(c)=outx(c)+uint8(dx(c,i))*(2^(8-i));
    end end
    outx
```

Decryption using chaos neural network

```
clear all;
close all;
clc;
% input ----------------------------
inp=[145 130 187 161 233 114 60 58 88 137]
fori=1:length(inp)
    inpx(i,:)=bitget(inp(i),8> 1:1);
```

```
end
% generating a chaotic sequence -----------------

l=length(inp);
x(l)=0.75mu=3.9
for i=2:l
end
x=uint8(((x-min(x))/max(x))*255);
b=[];
fori=l:l
end temp=0;
outx=zeros( 1 Jength(inp));
% network -----------------------------------
for c=l :length(inp)
    fori=l:8
        forj=l:8
            if(b(c, i)==0)&(i==j)
        weight(i,j)=l;
    elseif(b(c,i)==l)&(i==j)
        weight(i,j)=-l;
    elseif i~=j
weight(i,j)-0;
    end
end
if(b(c,i)==0)
        theta(i)=-l/2;
    else theta(i)=l/2;
    end
    end
fori=l:8
    dx(c,i) = hardlim(sum(weight(i,:).*inpx(c,:))+theta(i));
    end fori=l:8
outx(c)=outx(c)+uint8(dx(c,i))*(2^(8-i));
    end
end
        outx
```

Project–3

DATA VISUALIZATION TOOL (DVT)

ABSTRACT

Graphite (Data Visualisation Tool), is basically a tool which delivering the power of data visualisation to a non-technical user as Analysis of data is a process of inspecting, cleaning, transforming, and modelling data with the goal of discovering useful information, suggesting conclusions, and supporting decision-making. It is a tool, with a simple GUI, in which different types algorithms are used to implement analysis on any type of data.

The purpose of analysing data is to obtain useful information. The analysis, irrespective of whether the data is qualitative or quantitative, may:

- Describe and summarise the data
- Identify relationships between variables
- Compare variables
- Identify the difference between variables
- Forecast outcomes

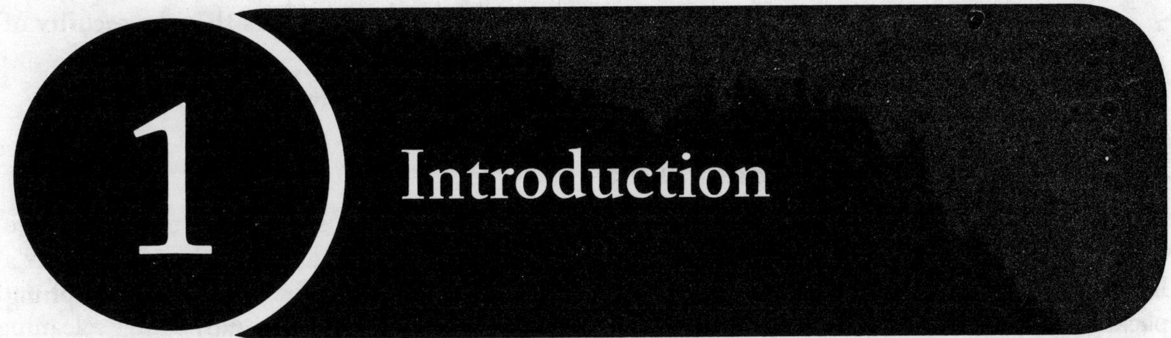

1 Introduction

1.1 Introduction to Java

Java is a high-level, third-generation programming language like C, FORTRAN, Perl and many others. It is a platform for distributed computing – a development and run-time environment that contains built-in support for the World Wide Web.

Java Features

Some of the important features of Java are as follows:

- Simplicity
- Orientation
- Platform Independence
- Security
- High Performance
- Multi-Threading
- Dynamic linking.
- Garbage Collection.

One of the most important features of Java is platform independence, which makes it famous and suitable language for World Wide Web.

Java Virtual Machine (JVM)

The client application or operating system must have a Java byte-code interpreter to execute byte-code instructions. The interpreter is a part of a larger program called the JVM. The JVM interprets the byte code into native code and is available on platforms that support Java. When the user runs a Java program, it is up to the JVM to load, possibly verify, and then execute it. The JVM can perform this function from within a browser or any other container program or directly on top of the operating system.

When a browser invokes the JVM to run a Java program, the JVM does a number of things:

- It validates the requested byte-code, verifying that they pass various formatting and security checks.

- It allocates memory for the incoming Java class files and guarantees that the security of JVM is not violated. This is known as the class loader module.
- It interprets the byte code instructions found in the class files to execute the program.

1.2 Introduction to R Programming

R is a language and environment for statistical computing and graphics, similar to the S language originally developed at Bell Labs. It's an open source solution to data analysis that's supported by a large and active worldwide research community. But there are many popular statistical and graphing packages available (such as Microsoft Excel, SAS, IBM SPSS, Stata, and Minitab).

R has many features to recommend it:

- Most commercial statistical software platforms cost thousands, if not tens of thousands of dollars. R is free! If you're a teacher or a student, the benefits are obvious.
- R is a comprehensive statistical platform, offering all manner of data analytic techniques. Just about any type of data analysis can be done in R.
- R has state-of-the-art graphics capabilities. If you want to visualize complex data,
- R has the most comprehensive and powerful feature set available.
- R is a powerful platform for interactive data analysis and exploration. From its inception it was designed to support the approach.
- Getting data into a usable form from multiple sources can be a challenging proposition.
- R can easily import data from a wide variety of sources, including text files, database management systems, statistical packages, and specialized data repositories. It can write data out to these systems as well.
- R provides an unparalleled platform for programming new statistical methods in an easy and straightforward manner. It's easily extensible and provides a natural language for quickly programming recently published methods.
- R contains advanced statistical routines not yet available in other packages. In fact, new methods become available for download on a weekly basis. If you're a SAS user, imagine getting a new SAS PROC every few days.
- If you don't want to learn a new language, a variety of graphic user interfaces (GUIs) are available, offering the power of R through menus and dialogs.
- R runs on a wide array of platforms, including Windows, Unix, and Mac OS X. It's likely to run on any computer you might have.

1.3 Modules Used

- Data Exploration: The aim pursued with Data exploration is to give an overview of the data and to allow users to interactively browse through different portions of the data.. In this sense, Data exploration can be understood as an undirected search for relevant information within the data. To support users in the search process, a high degree of interactivity must be a key feature of Data exploration techniques.

- Clustering: The task of grouping a set of objects in such a way that objects in the same group (called a cluster) are more similar (in some sense or another) to each other than to those in group
- Classification: It is the way to identifying to which of a set of categories a new observation belongs, on the basis of a training set of data.
- Neural Network Analysis: Neural Networks are computational models inspired by biological neural networks (the central nervous systems of animals, in particular the brain) and are used to estimate or approximate functions that can depend on a large number of inputs and are generally unknown. Artificial neural networks are generally presented as systems of interconnected "neurons" which can compute values from input.
- Time Series Decomposition: A time series is a sequence of data points, typically consisting of successive measurements made over a time interval. Time Series Decomposition is to decompose a time series into trend, seasonal, cyclical and irregular components. The trend component stands for long term trend, the seasonal component is seasonal variation, the cyclical component is repeated but non-periodic fluctuations, and the residuals are irregular component
- Seasonal Analysis: To estimate the trend component and seasonal component of a seasonal time series, This helps in predicting the future component and is widely used for seasonal planning of programs for the enterprise

2 Software Requirements Specification

2.1 Introduction

Purpose

The purpose of our project is to analysing data is to obtain usable and useful information. The analysis, irrespective of whether the data is qualitative or quantitative, may describe and summarise the data, identify relationships between variables, compare variables, identify the difference between variables, forecast outcomes

Scope

3S's of the future of Data Analysis tool:

- Small: Data is Big but the solution should be small. Reducing the scope of the product to the one magical thing that could solve a potential use case.
- Simple: Complexity sells but as a service and not as a product. This tool could be used to transform complex data into simple facts.
- Scale: A good system should be able to grow with the company it is helping to grow. This tool can be used in making the data scalable, i.e., grow with data.

Overview

The SRS constitute of all the details of the project. Every minute detail of the specific things like which action is performed on a particular mouse click is explained. Along with these specifications, the information about the software requirement, the platform used, the environment used. In addition, hardware requirements that enables our software to run efficiently. The attributes like security and portability are all as discussed below.

2.2 The General Description

Product Perspective

Our product is made using Java and R Programming. It is used because it is platform independent and can run on any operating system.

System Interfaces

The computer on **which** our product will be used should have operating system and also it should fulfil all the hardware and software requirements.

Interfaces

The user while using our product will feel comfortable with the main interface of our product because it is very easy to use. All the buttons and the function they perform are very user friendly.

Hardware Interfaces

- Our product essentially requires a 80GB of hard disk
- IGB RAM or above.
- Pentium 4 processor 2GHz or above..

Software Interfaces

The various software requirements are as follows:

- Operating System : Windows XP or above.
- Tools used :My Eclipse

Memory Constraints

The product requires a minimum of 128 MB of primary memory i.e. RAM and alongside 40 GB of secondary memory i.e. hard disk will indeed serve the purpose of the optimal working of the product.

Operations

The various features provided by our product are:

i. Clusters

ii. Classify

iii. Neural Network

iv. Time Series Decomposition

v. Seasonal Analysis

User Characteristics

In our product, even the naTve user can use our product with ease. Just by a click using any pointing device the user can access various functionalities.

2.3 Specific Requirements

External Interfaces

The main external input is from the datasets which will be choose by user itself.

Functions

The purpose of our project is to analysing data is to obtain usable and useful information. The analysis, irrespective of whether the data is qualitative or quantitative, may describe and summarise the data, identify relationships between variables, compare variables, identify the difference between variables, forecast outcomes.

Performance Requirements

Any number of users can be added in our System.

Design Constraints

The coding part of the designing of the software is done very carefully because such loops are avoided in which memory used is high. Thus coding is done in a very efficient and optimized way.

Software System Attributes

The main concern while designing the software was that the software should be reliable, easy to maintain and portable so that it can be carried from one place to another and thus handling becomes easy. One more attribute is that it is secured. Thus it cannot be altered in any way.

3 System Design

3.1 Definition

System design is simply the design of systems. It implies a systematic and rigorous approach to design—an approach demanded by the scale and complexity of many systems problems. Today, ideas from design methods and systems design may be more relevant to designers than ever before—as more and more designers collaborate on designing software and complex information spaces. Frameworks suggested by systems design are especially useful in modelling interaction and conversation. They are also useful in modelling the design process itself.

3.2 Input Design

Input facilities the entry of data into the computer system. Input design involves the selection of the best strategy for getting data into the computer system at the right time and as accurately as possible. This is because the most difficult aspect of input design in accuracy. The use of well-defined documents can encourage users to record data accurately without omission. Input design must capture all the data that the system needs, without introducing any errors. Input errors can be greatly reduced when inputting directly by using appropriate forms for data capture and well designed computer screen layout.

3.3 Output Design

Output design involves specifying how production of on screen results will occur. Output may occur to database or file for storing information entered or also for use by other systems.

3.4 Logical Design

The depiction of the conceptual design on a certain data structure (e.g. relational, object-oriented, network, transfer format). The part of the design phase of the SDLC in which all functional features of the system chosen for development in analysis are described independently of any computer platform.

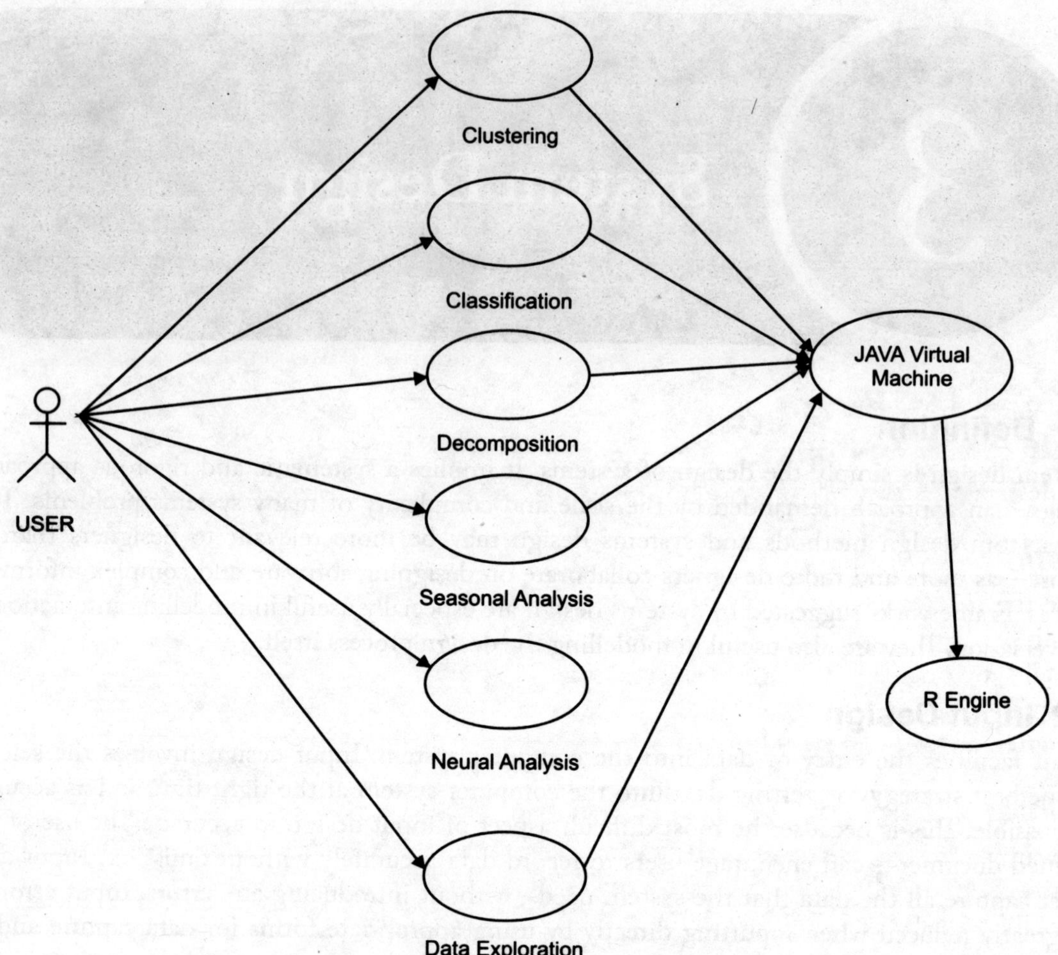

Fig.1: Use Case Diagram of Graphite.

4 Conceptual View

Code Generation

The design is translated into a machine-readable form using some programming tools.

Testing

Once the design is converted into machine-readable form the program testing phase starts. The testing process on our software mainly focused on the logical internals of the software, ensuring that all statements have been tested properly, and on the functional externals. Through testing we mainly intended to uncover errors and ensured that the defined input produces the desired results that agree with required results in the specification.

Maintenance

Software will undoubtedly undergo change after it is delivered to the customer. Change will occur due to either errors have been encountered or the software have been adapted to accommodate in its external environment or the customer requires functional or performance enhancements. Software support/ maintenance re-apply each of the preceding phases to an existing program rather than a new one. The linear nature of the classic life cycle worked perfect without any "blocking states" as the project is to be developed by me and my team member only & hence we started the next phase as soon as the current phase is finished without waiting for anyone else.

5 Algorithms Used

Algorithms Used

Data Exploration

Data exploration is an informative search used by data consumers to form true analysis from the information gathered. Often, data is gathered in a non-rigid or controlled manner in large bulks. For true analysis, this unorganized bulk of data needs to be narrowed down. This is where data exploration is used to analyze the data and information from the data to form further analysis.

Some people believe these terms are synonymous, while others see a technical difference between them. Data mining generally refers to gathering relevant data from large databases. Data exploration, on the other hand, generally refers to a data user being able to find his or her way through large amounts of data in order to gather necessary information.

Data exploration is a common process in data warehouses which are characterized by large bulks of data coming from disparate systems. Since these systems can have data in different formats and sources also, when data converge in a central data warehouses, it may be a very difficult task to get the relevant data needed for statistical reporting as well as trend and pattern spotting.

In this method we implemented two type of plots:

Pie Chart: A pie chart (or a circle chart) is a circular statistical graphic, which is divided into sectors to illustrate numerical proportion. In a pie chart, the arc length of each sector (and consequently its central angle and area), is proportional to the quantity it represents. Pie charts are very widely used in the business world and the mass media. However, they have been criticized, and many experts recommend avoiding them, pointing out that research has shown it is difficult to compare different sections of a given pie chart, or to compare data across different pie charts. Pie charts can be replaced in most cases by other plots such as the bar chart.

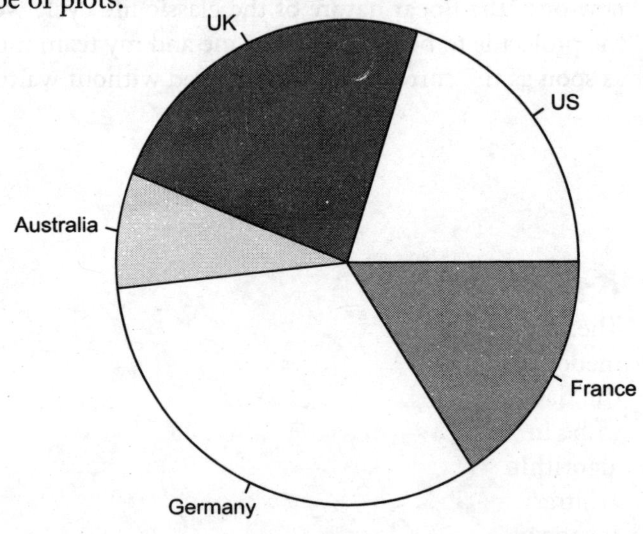

Fig.2: Pie Chart

Scatter Plot: A scatter plot, scatterplot, or **scattergraph** is a type of mathematical diagram using Cartesian coordinates to display values for two variables for a set of data.

The data is displayed as a collection of points, each having the value of one variable determining the position on the horizontal axis and the value of the other variable determining the position on the vertical axis. This kind of plot is also called a *scatter chart,* scatter gram, *scatter diagram,* or *scatter graph.*

A scatter plot is used when a variable exists that is below the control of the experimenter. If a parameter exists that is systematically incremented and/or decremented by the other, it is called the *control parameter* or independent variable and is customarily plotted along the horizontal axis. The measured or dependent variable is customarily plotted along the vertical axis. If no dependent variable exists, either type of variable can be plotted on either axis and a scatter plot will illustrate only the degree of correlation (not causation) between two variables.

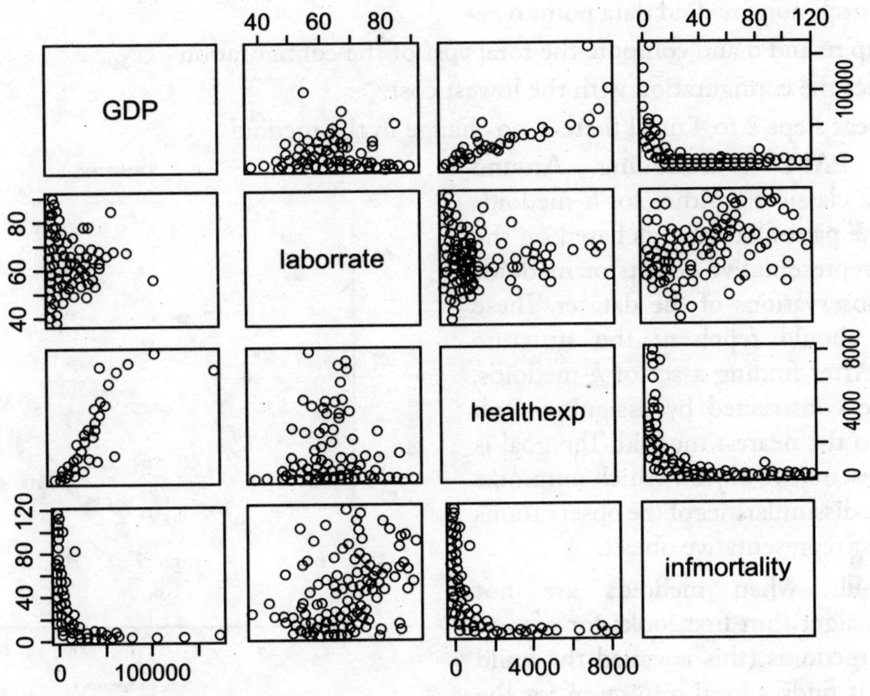

Fig.3: Scatter plot

K-medoids Clustering

The A-medoids algorithm is a clustering algorithm related to the *k*-means algorithm and the medoidshift algorithm. Both the *k*-means and &-medoids algorithms are partitional (breaking the dataset up into groups) and both attempt to minimize the distance between points labelled to be in a cluster and a point designated as the center of that cluster. In contrast to the *k*-means algorithm, *k*-medoids chooses datapoints as centers (medoids or exemplars) and works with an arbitrary matrix of distances between datapoints instead of '11'. This method was proposed in 1987 for the work with '11' norm and other distances.

k-medoid is a classical partitioning technique of clustering that clusters the data set of *n* objects into A: clusters known *a priori. A.* useful tool for determining *k* is the silhouette. It is more robust to noise and outliers as compared to *k*-means because it minimizes a sum of pairwise dissimilarities instead of a sum of squared Euclidean distances. A medoid can be defined as the object of a cluster, whose average dissimilarity to all the objects in the cluster is minimal i.e. it is a most centrally located point in the cluster.

The most common realisation ofA-medoid clustering is **the Partitioning Around Medoids (PAM)** algorithm and is as follows:

Initialize: randomly select (without replacement) *k* of the *n* data points as the medoids Associate each data point to the closest medoid. ("closest" here is defined using any valid distance metric, most commonly Euclidean distance, Manhattan distance or Minkowski distance)

- For each medoid m
- For each non-medoid data point o
- Swap m and o and compute the total cost of the configuration
- Select the configuration with the lowest cost.
- Repeat steps 2 to 4 until there is no change in the medoid.

In R, PAM (Partitioning Around Medoids) is a classic algorithm for k-medoids clustering. The pam-algorithm is based on the search for k representative objects or medoids among the observations of the dataset. These observations should represent the structure of the data. After finding a set of *k*-medoids, *k* clusters are constructed by assigning each observation to the nearest medoid. The goal is to find *k* representative objects which minimize the sum of the dissimilarities of the observations to their closest representative object.

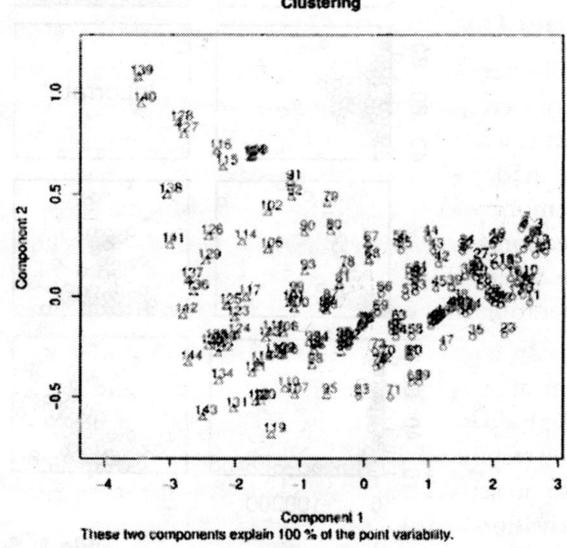

Fig.4: Clusters

By default, when medoids are not specified, the algorithm first looks for a good initial set of medoids (this is called the build phase). Then it finds a local minimum for the objective function, that is, a solution such that there is no single switch of an observation with a medoid that will decrease the objective (this is called the swap phase). When the medoids are specified, their order does *not* matter; in general, the algorithms have been designed to not depend on the order of the observations.

Neural Networks

Neural networks mimic the human brain by learning from a training dataset and applying the learning to generalize patterns for classification and prediction. These algorithms are effective when the data is shapeless and lacks any apparent pattern. The basic unit of an artificial neural network is modelled after the neurons in the brain. This unit is known as a node and is one of the two main structures of the neural network model. The other structure is the link that corresponds to the connection between neurons in the brain.

A neural network (NN) model is very similar to a non-linear regression model, with the exception that the former can handle an incredibly large amount of model parameters. For this reason, neural network models are said to have the ability to approximate any continuous function.

Neural network is very good at learning non-linear function and also multiple outputs can be learnt at the same time. However, the training time is relatively long and it is also susceptible to local minimum traps. This can be mitigated by doing multiple rounds and pick the best learned model.

Neural networks use learning algorithms that are inspired by our understanding of how the brain learns, but they are evaluated by how well they work for practical applications such as speech recognition, object recognition, image retrieval and the ability to recommend products that a user will like. As computers become more powerful, Neural Networks are gradually taking over from simpler Machine Learning methods. They are already at the heart of a new generation of speech recognition devices and they are beginning to outperform earlier systems for recognizing objects in images.

How Do Neural Networks Differ From Conventional Computing?

To better understand artificial neural computing it is important to know first how a conventional 'serial' computer and it's software process information. A serial computer has a central processor that can address an array of memory locations where data and instructions are stored. Computations are made by the processor reading an instruction as well as any data the instruction requires from memory addresses, the instruction is then executed and the results are saved in a specified memory location as required. In a serial system (and a standard parallel one as well) the computational steps are deterministic, sequential and logical, and the state of a given variable can be tracked from one operation to another.

In comparison, ANNs are not sequential or necessarily deterministic. There are no complex central processors, rather there are many simple ones which generally do nothing more than take the weighted sum of their inputs from other processors. ANNs do not execute programed instructions; they respond in parallel (either simulated or actual) to the pattern of inputs presented to it. There are also no separate memory addresses for storing data. Instead, information is contained in the overall activation 'state' of the network. 'Knowledge' is thus represented by the network itself, which is quite literally more than the sum of its individual components.

What Applications Should Neural Networks Be Used For?

Neural networks are universal approximators, and they work best if the system you are using them to model has a high tolerance to error. One would therefore not be advised to use a neural network to balance one's cheque book! However they work very well for:

- capturing associations or discovering regularities within a set of patterns;
- where the volume, number of variables or diversity of the data is very great;
- the relationships between variables are vaguely understood; or,
- the relationships are difficult to describe adequately with conventional approaches.

What Are Their Limitations?

There are many advantages and limitations to neural network analysis and to discuss this subject properly we would have to look at each individual type of network, which isn't necessary for this general discussion. In reference to backpropagational networks however, there are some specific issues potential users should be aware of.

- Backpropagational neural networks (and many other types of networks) are in a sense the ultimate 'black boxes'. Apart from defining the general archetecture of a network and perhaps initially seeding it with a random numbers, the user has no other role than to feed it input and watch it train and await the output. In fact, it has been said that with backpropagation, "you almost don't know what you're doing". Some software freely available software packages (NevProp, bp, Mactivation) do allow the user to sample the networks 'progress' at regular time intervals, but the learning itself progresses on its own. The final product of this activity is a trained network that provides no equations or coefficients defining a relationship (as in regression) beyond it's own internal mathematics. The network 'IS' the final equation of the relationship.
- Backpropagational networks also tend to be slower to train than other types of networks and sometimes require thousands of epochs. If run on a truly parallel computer system this issue is not really a problem, but if the BPNN is being simulated on a standard serial machine (i.e. a single SPARC, Mac or PC) training can take some time. This is because the machines CPU must compute the function of each node and connection separately, which can be problematic in very large networks with a large amount of data. However, the speed of most current machines is such that this is typically not much of an issue.

What Are Their Advantages Over Conventional Techniques?

Depending on the nature of the application and the strength of the internal data patterns you can generally expect a network to train quite well. This applies to problems where the relationships may be quite dynamic or non-linear, ANNs provide an analytical alternative to conventional techniques which are often limited by strict assumptions of normality, linearity, variable independence etc. Because an ANN can capture many kinds of relationships it allows the user to quickly and relatively easily model phenomena which otherwise may have been very difficult or impossible to explain otherwise.

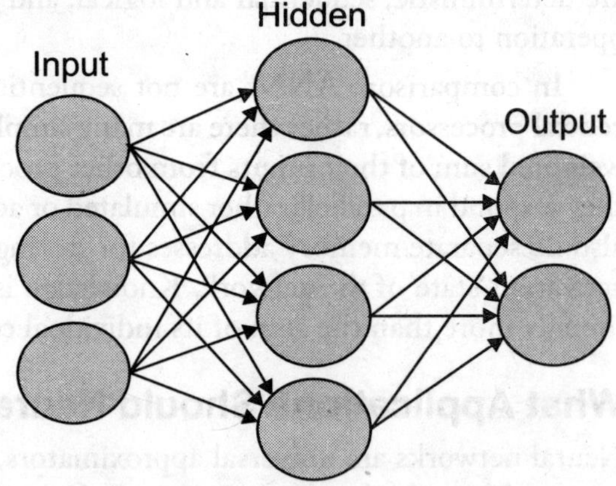

Fig.5: Neural Networks

Seasonal Analysis

A seasonal time series consists of a trend component, a seasonal component and an irregular component. Decomposing the time series means separating the time series into these three components: that is, estimating these three components.To estimate the trend component and seasonal component of a seasonal time series that can be described using an additive model, we can use the "decompose ()" function in R. This function estimates the trend, seasonal, and irregular components of a time series that can be described using an additive model. The function "decompose()" returns a list object as its result, where the estimates of the seasonal component, trend component and irregular component are stored in named elements of that list objects, called "seasonal", "trend", and "random" respectively.

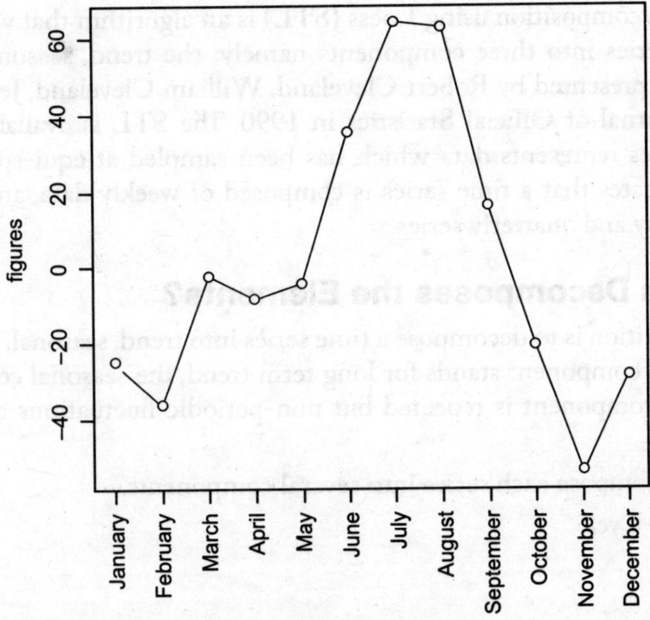

Fig.6: Seasonal Analysis

By plotting the seasonal component we can observe the patterns being followed over the course of time for the particular year .This helps in predicting the future component and is widely used for seasonal planning of programs for the enterprise.

```
>#  R-Code
> # decompose time series
> apts<- ts(AirPassengers, frequency=l 2)
>/<- decompose(apts)
> # seasonal figures
>fSfigure
HI -24.748737 -36.188131 -2.241162 -8.036616 -4.506313 35.402778
63.830808
18] 62.823232 16.520202 -20.642677-53.593434 -28.619949
> piot(f$figure, type="b", xaxt="n", xlab="")
> #get names of 12 months in English words
```

```
>monlhNames <- months(ISOdate(20H,l;12,l))
> # label x-axis with month names
>#la$is set to 2 for vertical label orientation
> axisfl, at=l:12, labels=monthNames, las=2)
```

Time Series Decomposition

The Seasonal Trend Decomposition using Loess (STL) is an algorithm that was developed to help to divide up a time series into three components namely: the trend, seasonality and remainder. The methodology was presented by Robert Cleveland, William Cleveland, Jean McRae and Irma Trepanning in the Journal of Official Statistics in 1990. The STL is available within R via the **stl** ftinction.Time series represents data which has been sampled at equi-spaced points in time. A frequency of 7 indicates that a time series is composed of weekly data, and 12 and 4 are used respectively for monthly and quarterly series.

How Time Series Decomposes the Elements?

Time Series Decomposition is to decompose a time series into trend, seasonal, cyclical and irregular components. The trend component stands for long term trend, the seasonal component is seasonal variation, the cyclical component is repeated but non-periodic fluctuations and the residuals are irregular component.

We propose to decompose each series into several components.

- T Ct ~ Trend-Cycle
- St ~ Seasonal
- Rt ~ Random

By identifying the various components, our aim is to separate the Random component from the other components of the series. This way we hope to be able to eliminate the noise and isolate the true signal.

The method for evaluating the trend of a time series is to use nonparametric regression techniques (which in fact can be seen as a special case of linear filters). The function stl( ) performs a seasonal decomposition of a given time series Xt by determining the trend Tt using "loess" regression and then calculating the seasonal component St (and the residuals et) from the differences Xt -Tt performing the seasonal decomposition for the time series. The data is firstly fed into r and then "Transformed". This "transformation" is required for most of the time-series functions, since a time series contains more information than the values itself, namely information about dates and frequencies at which the time series has been recorded.

```
> # R-Code
> # decompose time series
> apts <- ts(AirPassengers, frequency=12)
>/<- decompose(apts)
>plot(f)
The additive model used is:
```

```
Y[t]=T[t] + S[t]+e[t]
The multiplicative model used is:
Y[t] = T[t]*S[t]*e[t]
```

The function first determines the trend component using a moving average (if filter is NULL, a symmetric window with equal weights is used), and removes it from the time series. Then, the seasonal figure is computed by averaging, for each time unit, over all periods. The seasonal figure is then centered. Finally, the error component is determined by removing trend and seasonal figure (recycled as needed) from the original time series

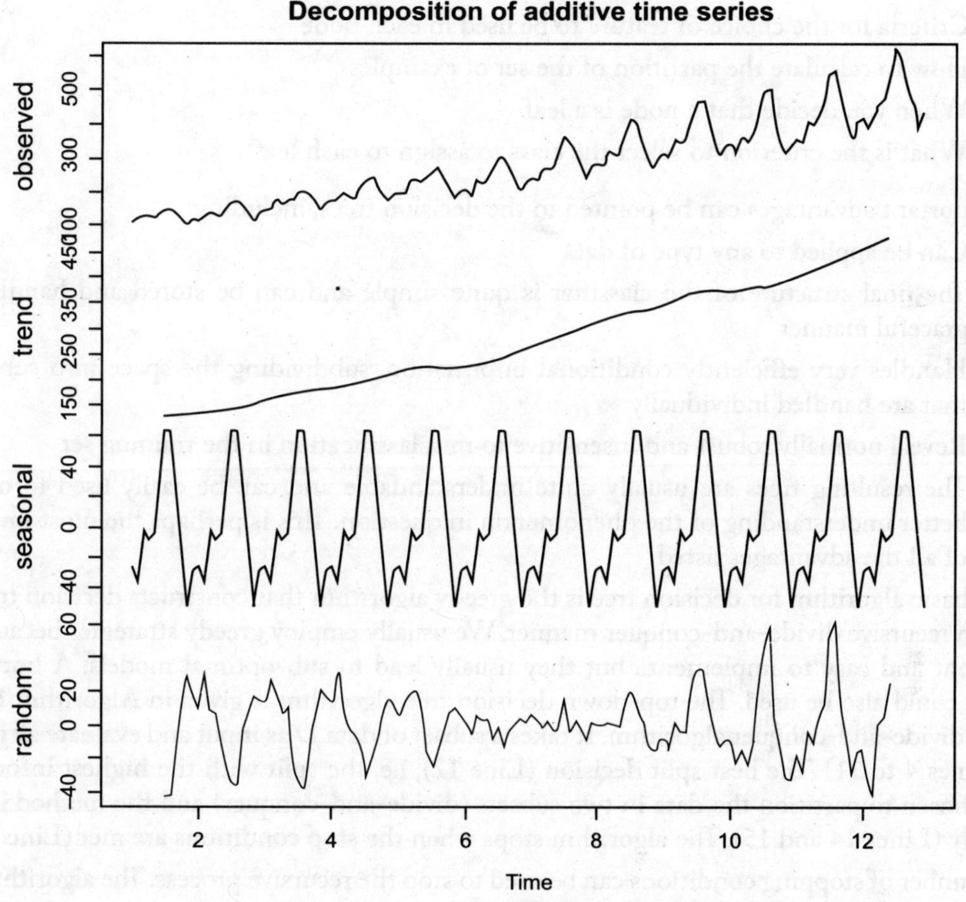

Fig.7: Time Decomposition

Classification-Decision Trees

The philosophy of operation of any algorithm based on decision trees is quite simple. In fact, although sometimes containing important differences in the way to do this or that step, any algorithm of this category is based on the strategy of divide and conquer. In general, this philosophy is based on the successive division of the problem into several subproblems with a smaller number of dimensions, until a solution for each of the simpler problems can be found. Based on this principle, the classifiers based on decision trees try to find ways to divide the universe into successively more subgroups (creating nodes containing the respective tests) until each addressing only one class or until one of the classes shows a clear majority do not justifying further divisions, generating in this situation a leaf containing the class majority. Obviously, the classification is only to follow the path dictated by the successive test placed along the tree until it found a leaf containing the class to assign to the new example.

Although the basic philosophy of all the classifiers based on decision trees is identical, there are many possibilities for its construction. Among all the key points in the selection of an algorithm to build decision trees some of them should be highlighted for their importance:

- Criteria for the choice of feature to be used in each node
- How to calculate the partition of the set of examples
- When you decide that a node is a leaf
- What is the criterion to select the class to assign to each leaf

Some important advantages can be pointed to the decision trees, including:

- Can be applied to any type of data
- The final structure of the classifier is quite simple and can be stored and handled in a graceful manner
- Handles very efficiently conditional information, subdividing the space into sub-spaces that are handled individually
- Reveal normally robust and insensitive to misclassification in the training set
- The resulting trees are usually quite understandable and can be easily used to obtain a better understanding of the phenomenon in question. This is perhaps the most important of all the advantages listed

The basic algorithm for decision tree is the greedy algorithm that constructs decision trees in a top-down recursive divide-and-conquer manner. We usually employ greedy strategies because they are efficient and easy to implement., but they usually lead to sub-optimal models. A bottom-up approach could also be used. The top-down decision tree algorithm is given in Algorithm 1. It is a recursive divide-and-conquer algorithm. It takes a subset of data D as input and evaluate all possible splits (Lines 4 to 11). The best split decision (Line 12), i.e. the split with the highest information gain, is chosen to partition the data in two subsets (divide-and-conquer) and the method is called recursively (Lines 14 and 15). The algorithm stops when the stop conditions are met (Line 1 to 3).

A number of stopping conditions can be used to stop the recursive process. The algorithm stops when any one of the conditions is taie:

- All the samples belong to the same class, i.e. have the same label since the sample is already "pure"
- Stop if most of the points are already of the same class. This is a generalization of the first approach, with some error threshold
- There are no remaining attributes on which the samples may be further partitioned
- There are no samples for the branch test attribute

Rpart

The rpart package found in the R tool can be used for classification by decision trees and can also be used to generate regression trees. Recursive partitioning is a fundamental tool in data mining. !t helps us explore the structure of a set of data, while developing easy to visualize decision rules for predicting a categorical (classification tree) or continuous (regression tree) outcome. The rpart programs build classification or regression models of a very general structure using a two stage procedure; the resulting models can be represented as binary trees. The tree is built by the following process: first the single variable is found which best splits the data into two groups ('best' will be defined later). The data is separated, and then this process is applied separately to each sub-group, and so on recursively until the subgroups either reach a minimum size (5 for this data) or until no improvement can be made. The resultant model is, with certainty, too complex, and the question arises as it does with all stepwise procedures of when to stop. The second stage of the procedure consists of using cross-validation to trim back the full tree.

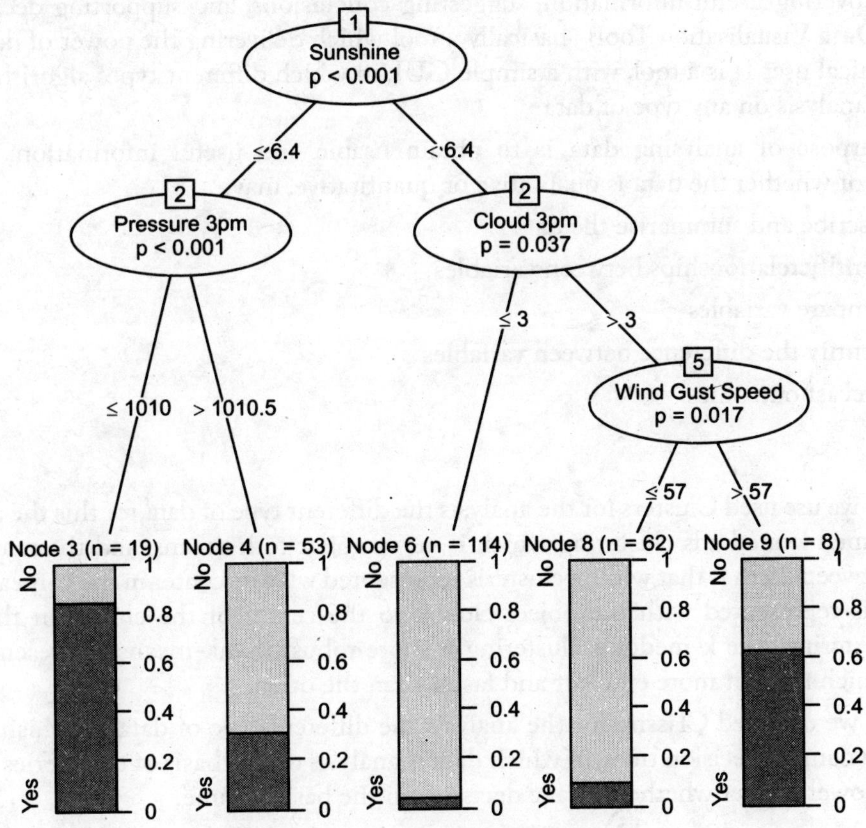

Fig.8: C tree (Classification)

6 Summary

Summary

Analysis of data is a process of inspecting, cleaning, transforming, and modelling data with the goal of discovering useful information, suggesting conclusions, and supporting decision-making. **Graphite(Data** Visualisation Tool) , basically a tool which delivering the power of data analysis to a non-technical user It is a tool, with a simple GUI, in which different types algorithms are use to implement analysis on any type of data.

The purpose of analysing data is to obtain usable and useful information. The analysis, irrespective of whether the data is qualitative or quantitative, may:

- describe and summarise the data
- identify relationships between variables
- compare variables
- identify the difference between variables
- forecast outcomes

Benefits

- As we use used Clusters for the analysis the different type of data,for this the algorithm use named k-medoids clustering which is very similar to k-means, and the major difference between them is that while a clusteris represented with its center in the k-means algorithm, it is represented with the object closest to the center of the cluster in the k-medoids clustering. The k-medoids clustering is more robust thank-means in presence of outliers ,which make it more efficient and faster than the other.
- As we use used Classify for the analysis the different type of data, for this the algorithm use named Decision trees, in which data is analysis on the basis of time series as it is giving a power to user whether to take decision on the basis of time.
- As we use used Neural Network for the analysis the different type of data, for this w used algorithm neuralnet, as the name suggest, the working of this is same as the working of neurons of the brain as it found what is logic used for different type of data.
- As we use used Seasonal Analysis for the analysis the different type of data, for the seasonal analysis algorithm is used, it is kind of dynamic algorithms as it used time intervals for

making analysis & even if a data is not having time constraint then it dynamically by round off some values it make analysis. This helps in predicting the future component and is widely used for seasonal planning of programs for the enterprise.

- As we use used Time Series Decomposition for the analysis the different type of data, for the Time Series Decomposition algorithm is used in which time is decomposed in such a way thorugh which it make analysis on the data.

7 Conclusions & Future Scope

Conclusions & Future Scopes

'Graphite' has been developed in Java & R Programming, keeping in mind the specification of the system.. Overall the project teaches us the essential skills like:

- many analysis algorithms are implemented
- working with R programming

Future Scopes

3S's of the future of Data Analysis tool and Why?

- Small: Data is Big but the solution should be small. Reducing the scope of the product to the one magical thing that could solve a potential use case. Data analysis tool shall do the same.
- Simple: Complexity sells but as a service and not as a product. Simple solutions are often understood quickly and therefore meet easy adoption, hence better sales. This tool could be used to transform complex data into simple facts.
- Scale: A good system should be able to grow with the company it is helping to grow. This tool can be used in making the data scalable, i.e. grow with data.

Practical Scopes

- Maximize return on investment in future mailings.
- Predictive problems include forecasting bankruptcy.
- Analysis of retail sales data to identify seemingly unrelated products that are often purchased together.
- Fraudulent credit card transactions.

8 References

References

1. Snijders, C., Matzat, U., & Reips, U.-D. (2012). 'Big Data': Big gaps of knowledge in the field of Internet. *International Journal of Internet Science,* 7, 1-5. http://w\vw.iiis.net/iiis7 l/ijis7 l editorial.html
2. Micheal Milton/"Data Analysis", Head First, Paperback, Edition 2009
3. John Hopkins University, "Data science specialization", Cousera.com, -https://www.coursera.org/specialization/ihudatascience/l
4. John W. Tukey, "Data Analysis" ,Wikipedia- http://en.wikipedia.org/wiki/Data analvsis
5. Yanchang Zhao, "R and Data Mining: Examples and Case Studies", RDM, Edition 2013
6. Yanchang Zhao, "Introduction to Data Mining with R and Data Import/Export in R" -http://www.rdalamining.com/docs/RDataMining-slides-introduction-data-import-export.pdf
7. Bart, "Using neural networks for credit scoring: a simple example" , http://www.r-bloRgers.com/using-neural-networks-for-credit-scoring-a-simple-example/
8. Justin Esarey, "Neural Networks" ,
   https://www.youtube.com/ watch?v=US9 wP20Wiw
9. CRAN Project, "rJava: Low-level R to Java interface", http://cran.r-project.org/vveb/packages/rJava/index.html
10. R: rJava package install failing, http://stackovcrflow.com/questions/3311940/r-riava-package-install-failing
11. Ghost4j script and jar, http://dl.ghost4i.org/ghQSt4i-0.5.1.zip
12. Tips Thought Notes- "How to resolve issue - Unable to load library 'gsdll64' ?"-http://tipsthQughtsnotes.wordpress.com/2014/IO/2I/how-to-rcsolve-issue-unable-to-lQad-Iibrarv-gsdll64/
13. Java/R Interface , "JRI" , http://rforge.net/JRi/index.html
14. R Plots, "Saving Plots in R", http://www.stat.berkeley.edu/~sl33/saving.html
15. RWeka, "Package 'RWeka'", http://cran.r-proiect.org/web/packages/RWeka/RWeka.pdf

16. Stephen Turner, "Google Developers R Programming Video Lectures", http://www.r-bloggers.com/google-developers-r-programming-video-lectures/
17. Datasets, "The R Datasets Package"- https://stat.ethz.ch/R-manual/R-devel/library/datasets/html/OOlndex.html
18. Sander Mak, "Data Science with R for Java developers", http://www.slideshare.net/SanderMak/data-science-with-r-for-java-d
19. Rosuda, "Class Rengine" , http://www.rosuda.org/rosuda/JRI/Renginc.html

SCREEN SHOTS

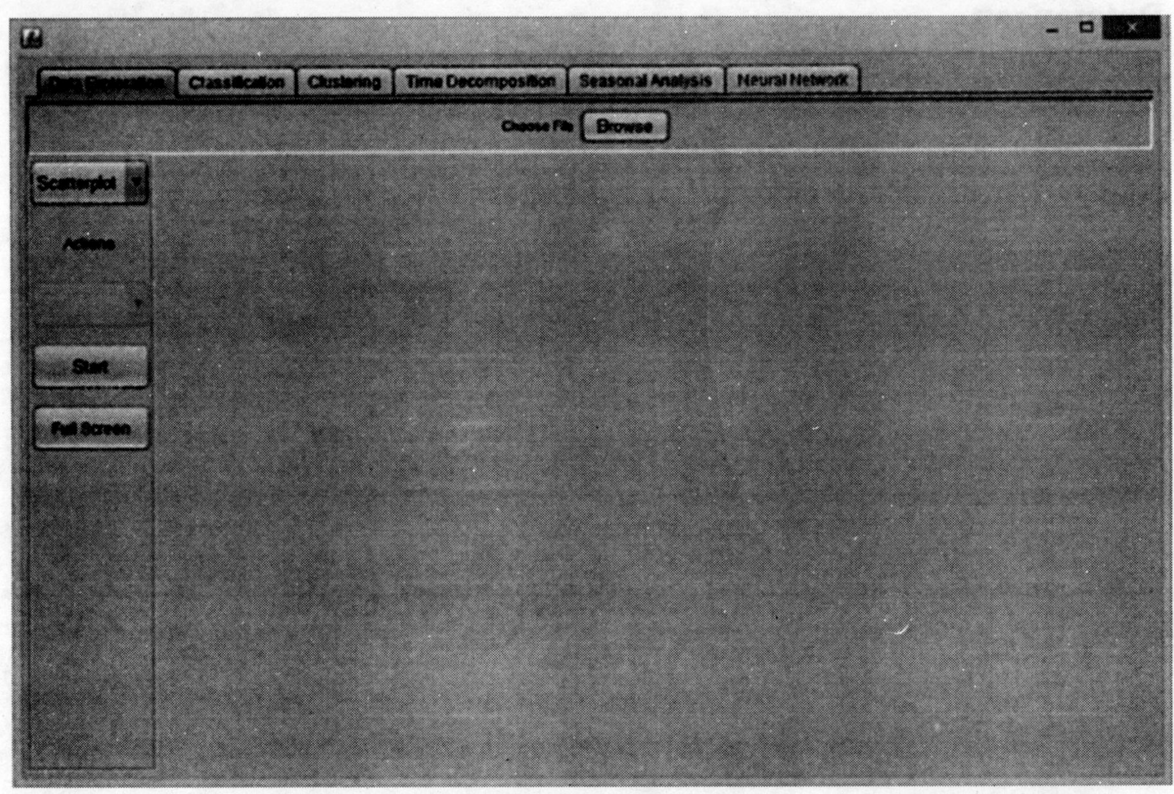

Fig.9: Data Exploration Window

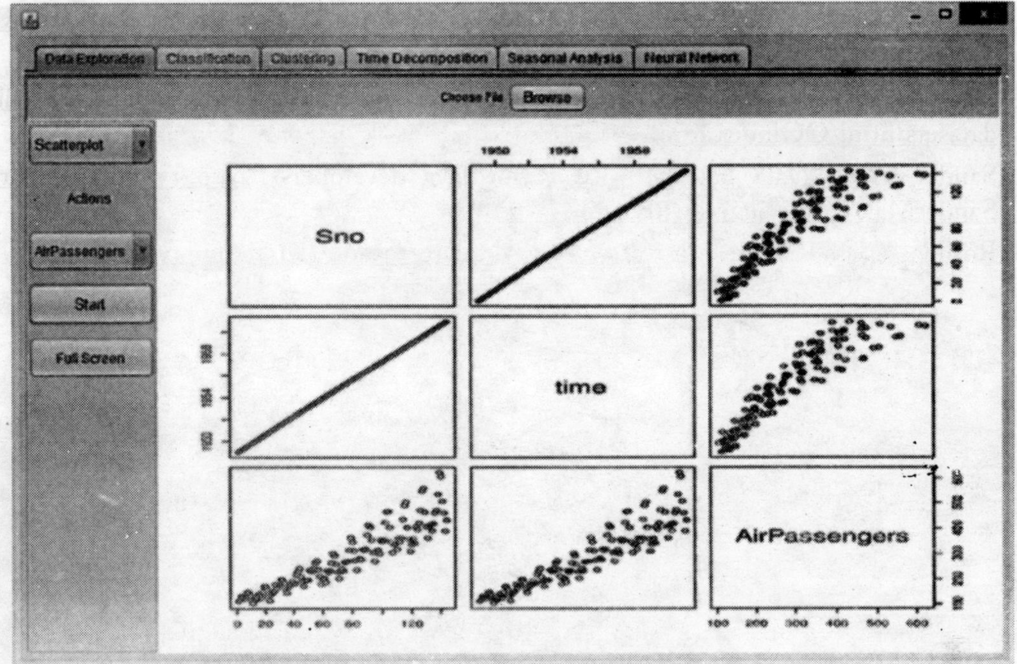

Fig.10: Data Exploration Scatter Plot

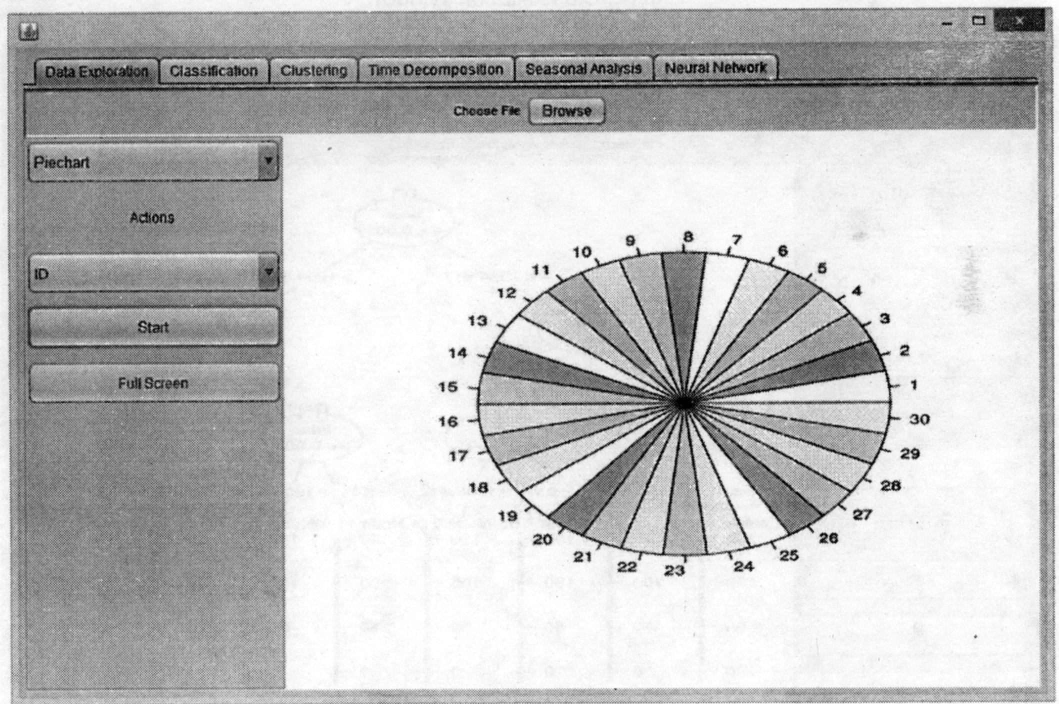

Fig.11: Data Exploration Pie Chart

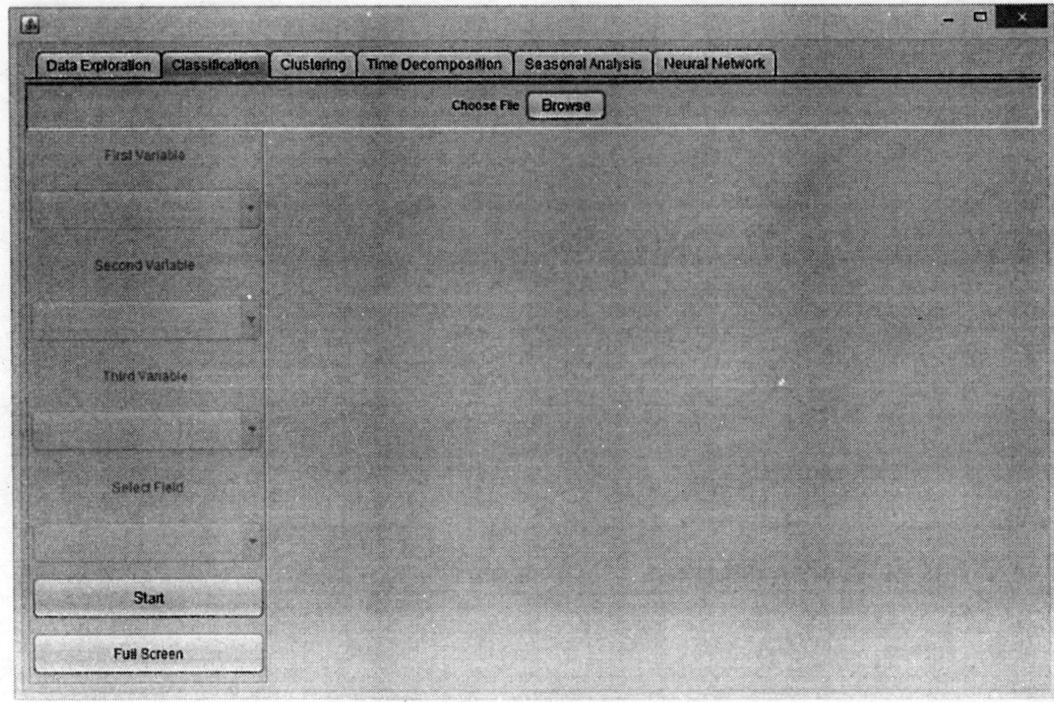

Fig.12: Classification Window

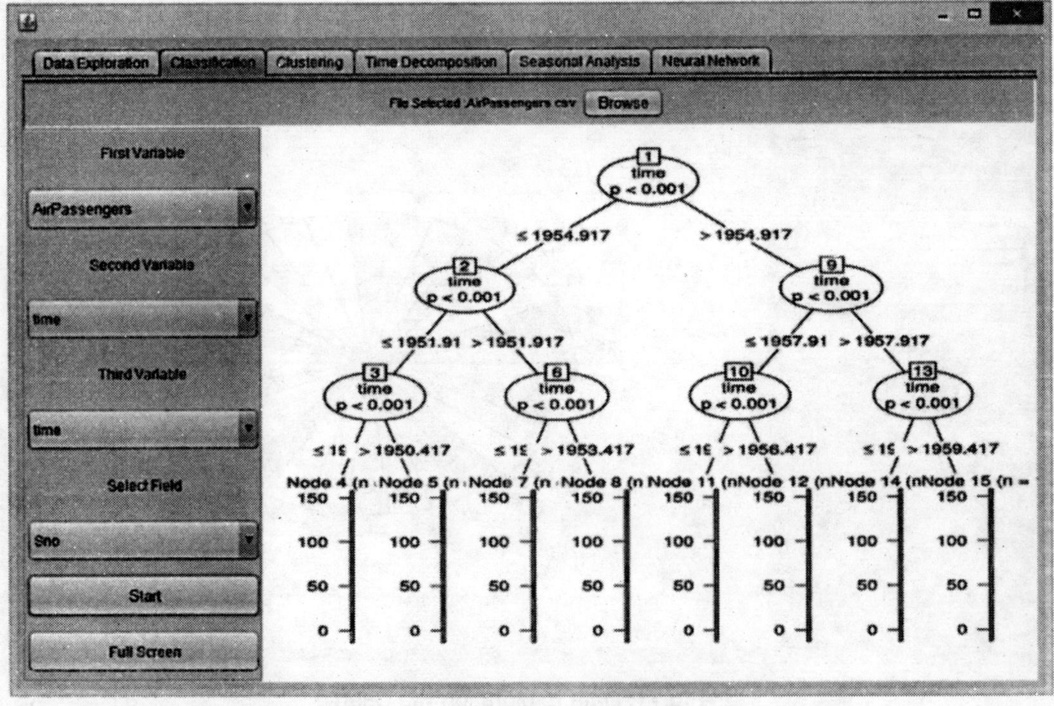

Fig.13: Classification Operation

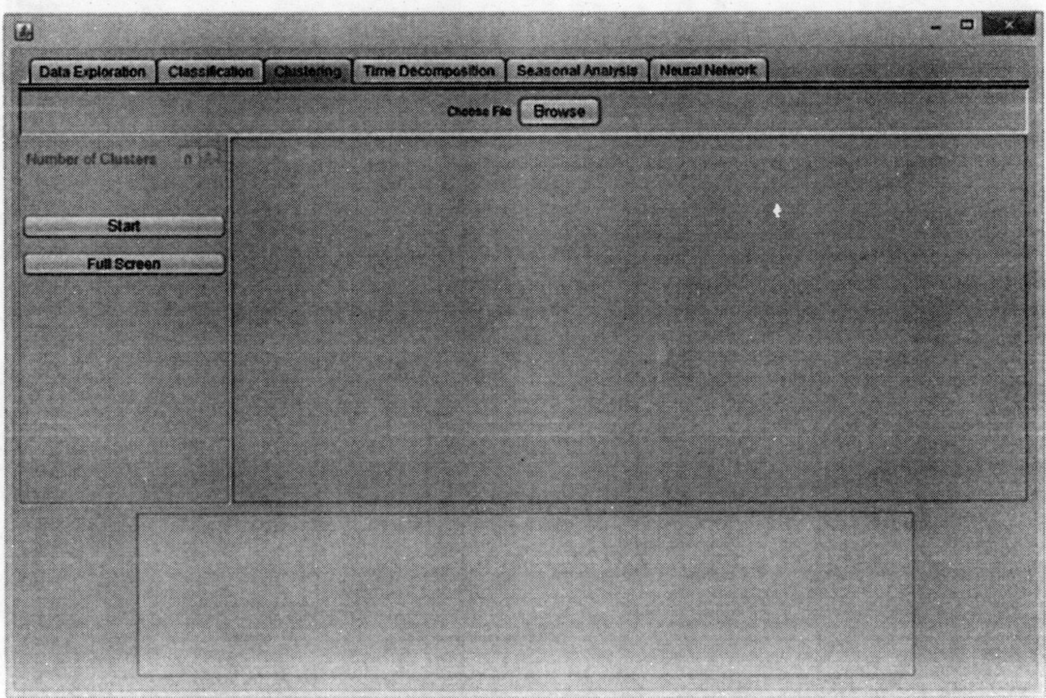

Fig.14: Clustering Window

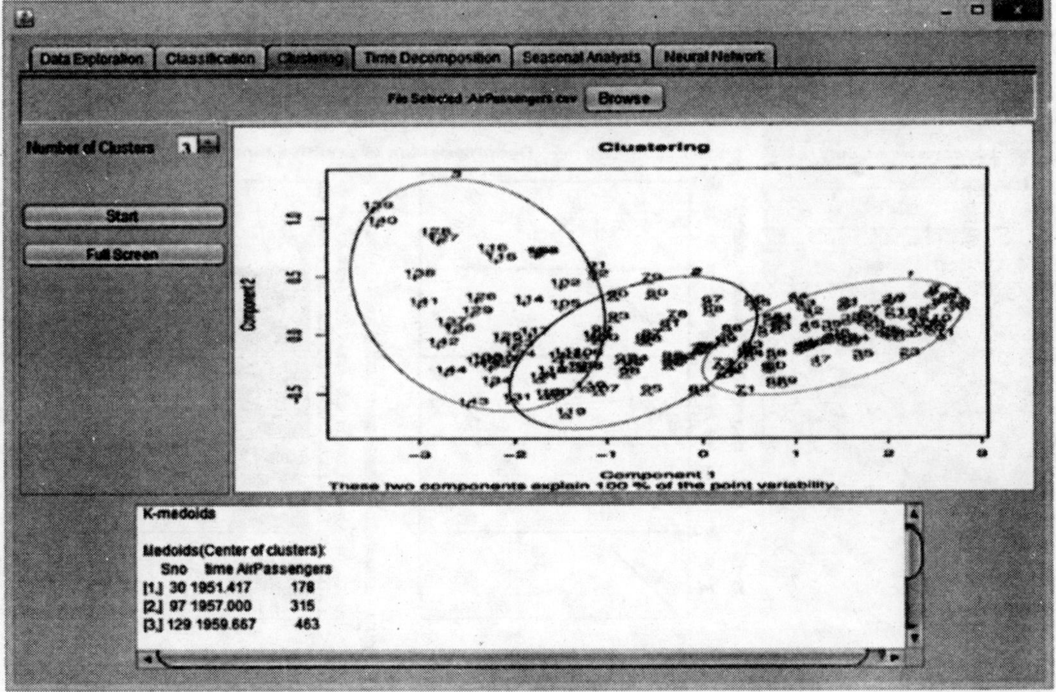

Fig.15: Clustering Operation

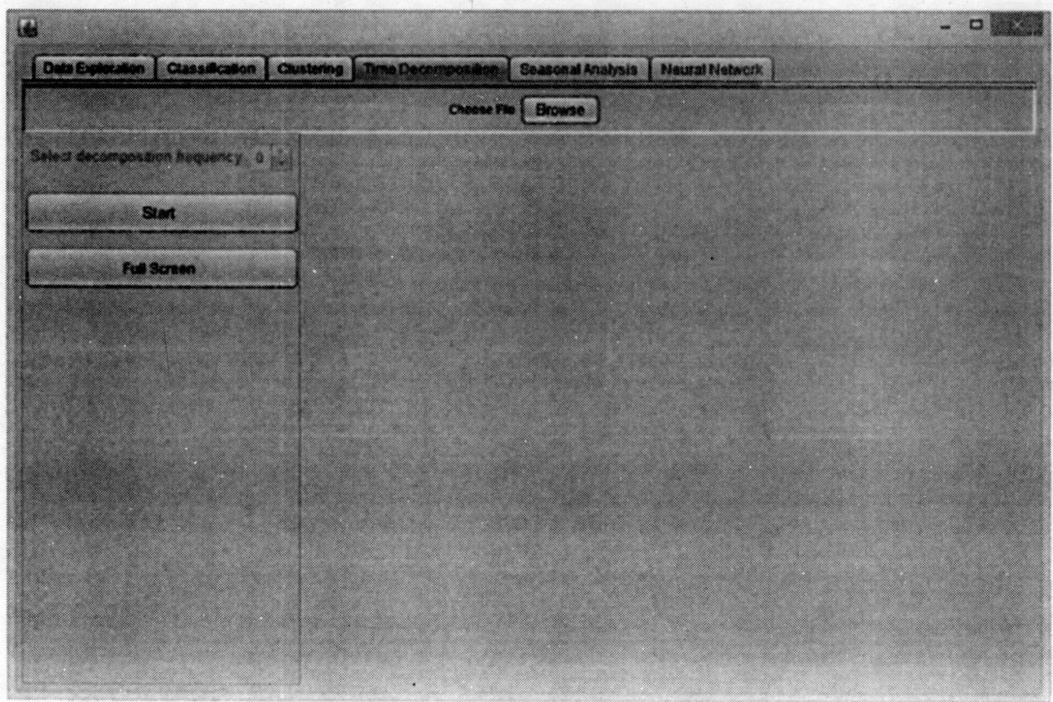

Fig.16: Time Decomposition Window

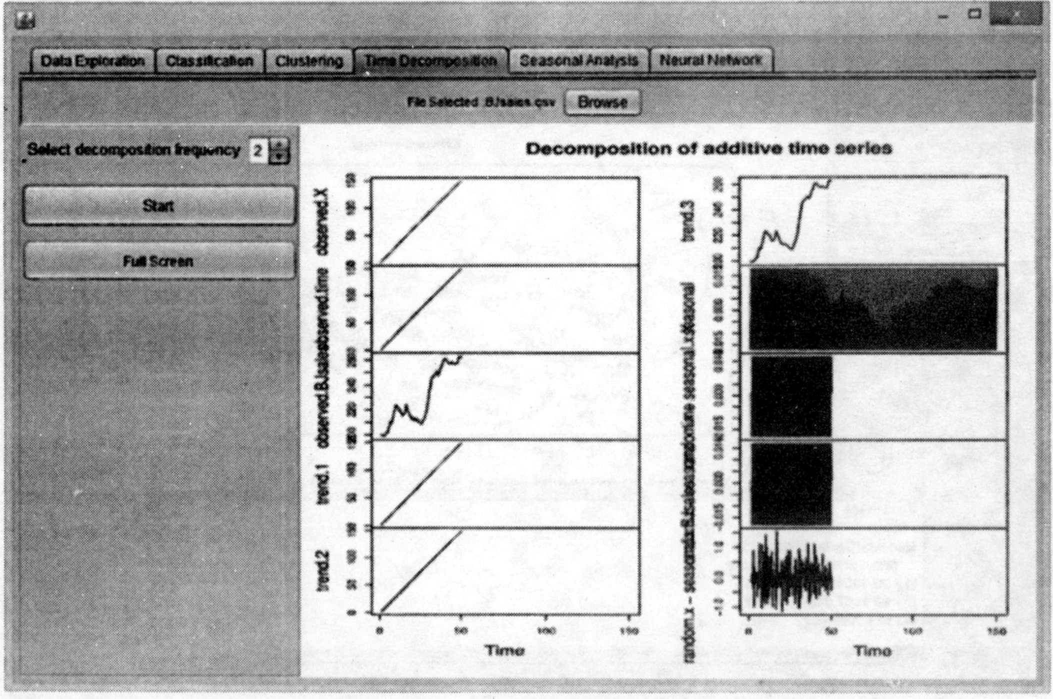

Fig.17: Time Decomposition Operation

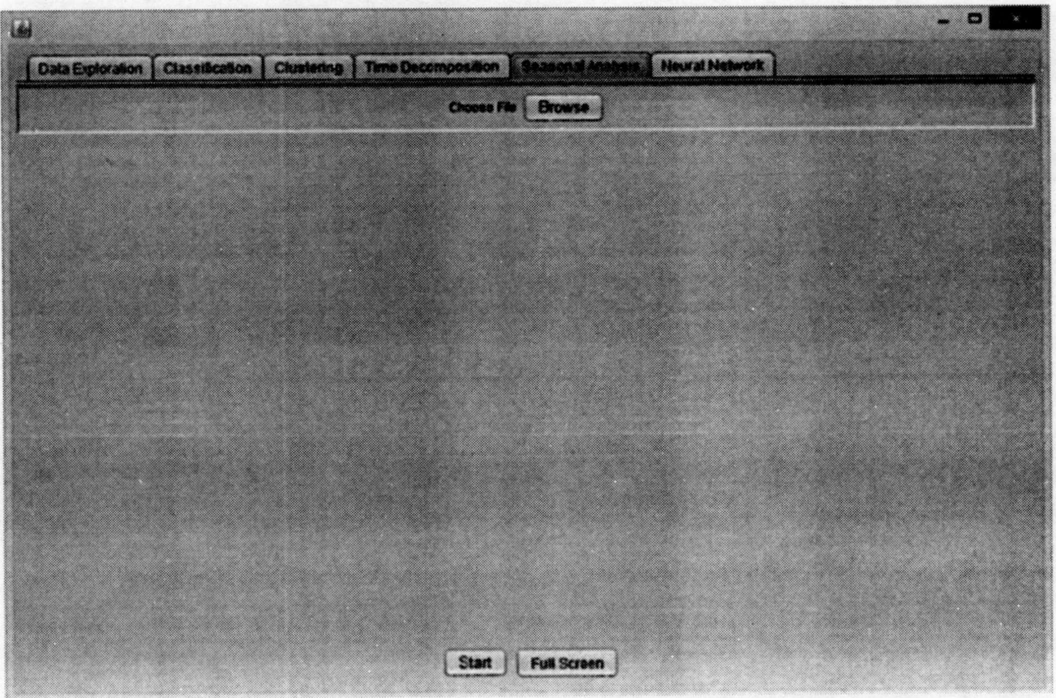

Fig.18: Seasonal Analysis Window

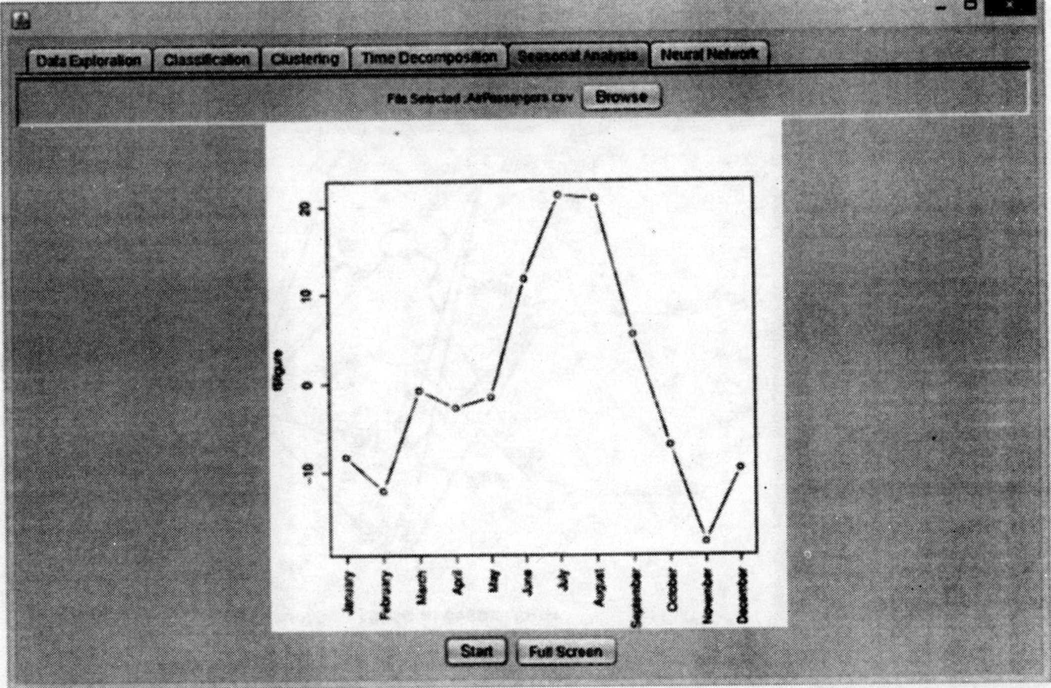

Fig.19: Seasonal Analysis Operation

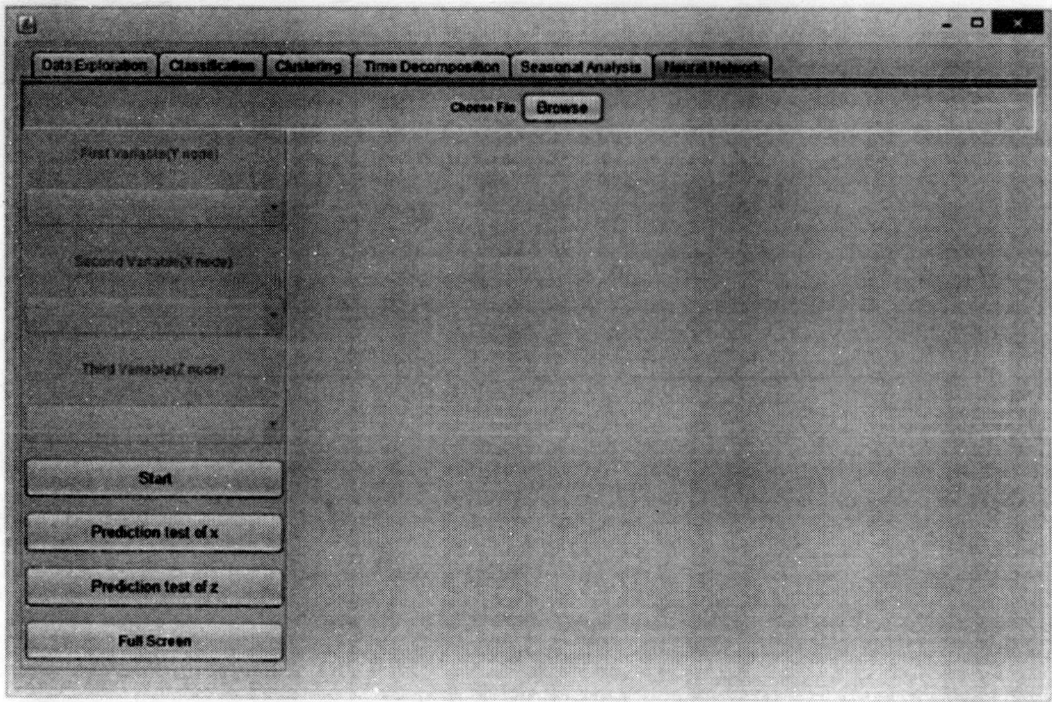

Fig.20: Neural Network Window

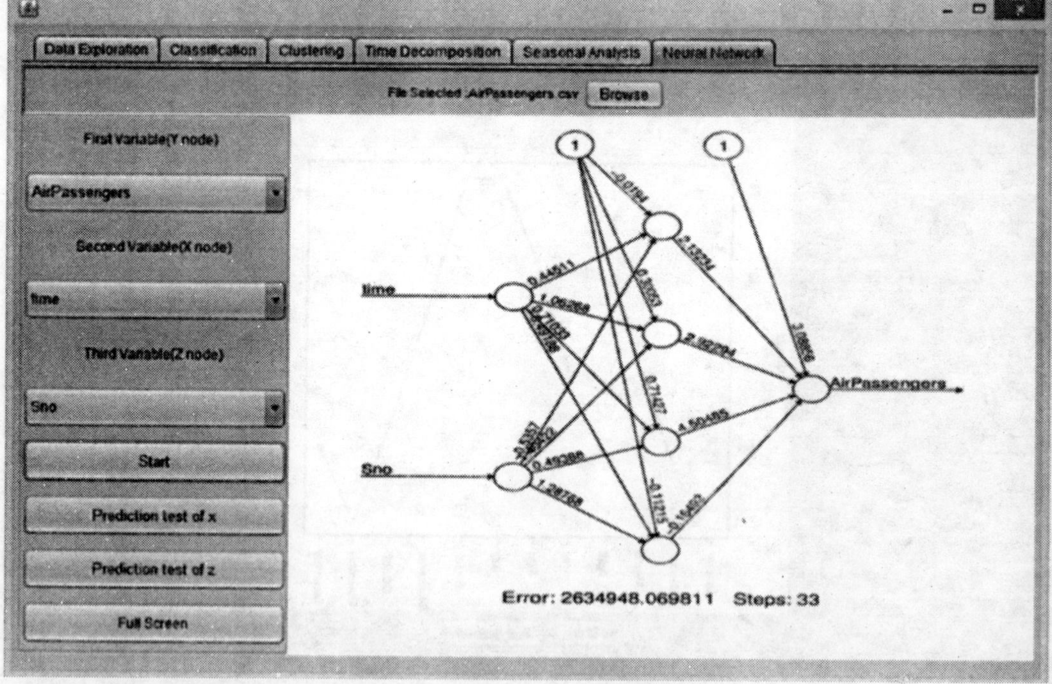

Fig.21: Neural Network Operation

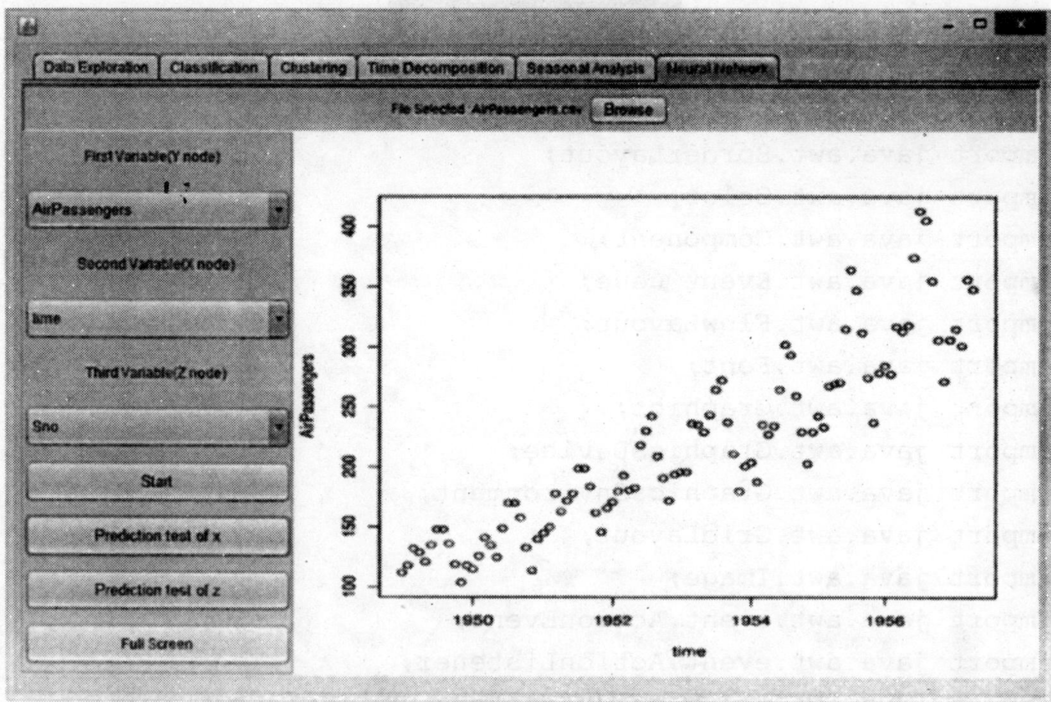

Fig.22: Neural Network Prediction of X node

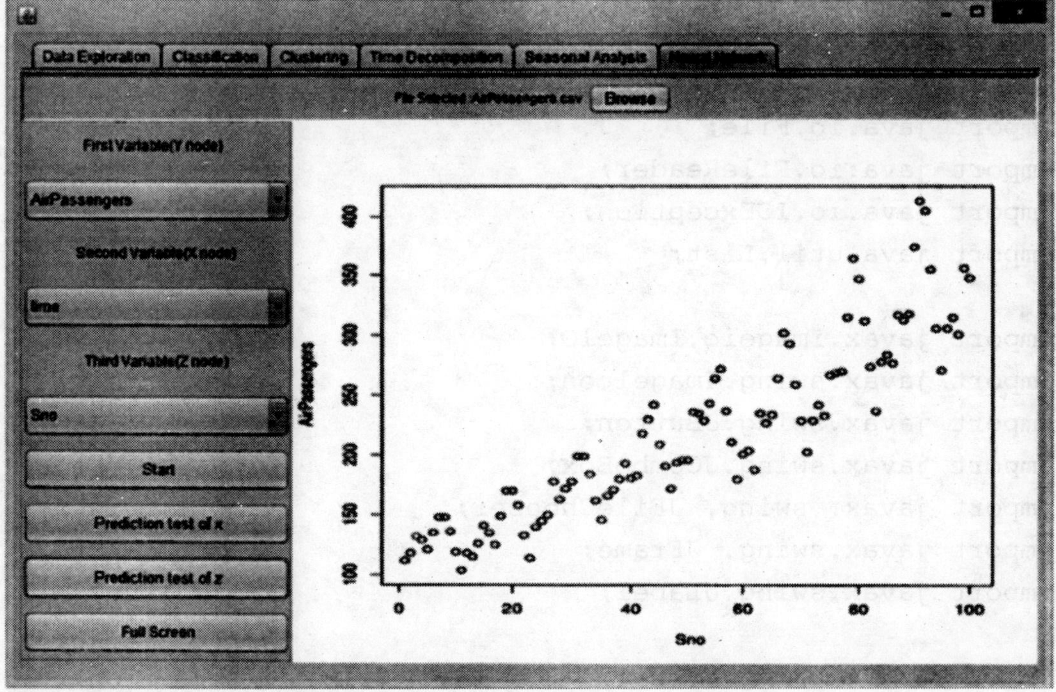

Fig.23: Neural Network Prediction of Z node

SOURCE CODE

```
package data;

import java.awt.BorderLayout;
import java.awt.Color;
import java.awt.Component;
import java.awt.EventQueue;
import java.awt.FlowLayout;
import java.awt.Font;
import java.awt.Graphics;
import java.awt.GraphicsDevice;
import java.awt.GraphicsEnvironment;
import java.awt.GridLayout;
import java.awt.Image;
import java.awt.event.ActionEvent;
import java.awt.event.ActionListener;
import java.awt.event.MouseAdapter;
import java.awt.event.MouseEvent;
import java.awt.image.Bufferedlmage;
import java.awt.image.Renderedlmage;
import java.io.BufferedReader;
import java.io.File;
import java.io.FileReader;
import java.io.IOException;
import java.util.List;

import javax.imageio.ImagelO;
import javax.swing.Imagelcon;
import javax.swing.JButton;
import javax.swing.JComboBox;
import javax. swing. JFileChooser;
import javax.swing. JFrame;
import javax.swing.JLabel;

import javax.swing.JPanel;
import javax.swing.JScrollPane;
```

```
import j avax. swing J Spinner;
import javax.swing.JTabbedPane;
import javax.swing.JTextArea;
import j avax. swing. S wingConstants;
import javax.swing.UIManager;
import javax.swing.border.BevelBorder;
import javax.swing.border.EmptyBorder;
import javax.swing.border.EtchedBorder;

import java.awt.BorderLayout;
import java.awt.Color;
import java.awt.EventQueue;
import java.awt.FlowLayout;
import java.awt.Font;
import java.awt.GridLayout;
import java.awt.Image;
import org.rosuda.JRLREXP;
import org.rosuda.JRI.Rengine;
import javax.swing.SwingConstants;
//import org.eclipse.wb.swing.FocusTraversalOnArray;
import org.ghost4j.document.PDFDocument;
import org.ghost4j.renderer.SimpleRenderer;
import java.io.IOException;
import java.util.List;

//import org.eclipse.wb.swing.FocusTraversalOnArray;
import org.ghost4j.document.PDFDocument;
import org.ghost4j.renderer.SimpleRenderer;
import org.rosuda.JRLREXP;
import org.rosuda.JRI.Rengine;
public class Main extends JFrame {
static Rengine re;
static REXP x;
private JPanel contentPane;
JFileChooser fileDialog;
File file;
```

```
BufferedReader br;
String hd[],ln,wd;
JComboBox combof;
JLabel Ib,lbl,lb2;
J Spinner spinner;
JPanel clus_north,cluster_panel,clus_west,clus_south;
private JTextArea textArea;
private JLabel label;
Image img,imgl;
JScrollPanejp;
JFrame fm;
private JButton btnFullScreen,btnFullScreenl,
btnFullScreen2,btnFullScreen3,btnFullScreen4;
private JPanel Classify_panel;
private JPanel Classifyjnorth;
private JLabel label_l;
private JButton button,button2;
private JPanel Classify_west,neural_panel,neural_north,neural_
west;
private JComboBox comboBoxl;
private JButton button_l;
private JLabel labell ,labell 1;
private JLabel Iabel2,label_21,label21;
private JComboBox comboBox,comboBoxl 1,comboBox21,cornboBox31;
private JLabel Iabel3,label31,label41;
private JComboBox comboBox2;
private JLabel Iabel4;
private JPanel TimeDecompose;
private JPanel panel;
private JLabel Iabel_2;
private JButton button_2;
private JPanel Decompose_west;
private JButton button_3;
private JPanel panel_2;
private JLabel IblSelectDecompositionFrequency;
private JSpinner spinner_l ;
```

```
private JLabel labelS;
private JPanel panel_3;
private JPanel panel_4;
private JLabel label_3;
private JButton button_4;
private JPanel panel_5;
private JButton button_5;
private JLabel mylabel;
private JLabel Ibel;
private JComboBox comboBox_l ;
/**
* Launch the application.
*/
public static void main(String[] args) {
try{
UIManager.setLookAndFeel("com.sun.java.swing.plaf.nimbus.Nim-
busLookAndFeel");
} catch (Throwable e) {
e.printStackTraceQ;
}
re=new Rengine(args, false ,new TextConsoleQ);
EventQueue.invokeLater(new RunnableQ {
public void run() {
try{
Main frame = new MainQ;
frame.setVisible(true);
} catch (Exception e) {
e.printStackTraceQ;
/**
* Create the frame.
*/
public MainQ {
setDefaultCloseOperation(JFrame.EXIT_ON_CLOSE);
setBounds(100, 50, 900, 600);
contentPane = new JPanelQ;
contentPane.setBorder(new EmptyBorder(5, 5, 5, 5));
```

```
contentPane.setLayout(new BorderLayout(0, 0));
setContentPane(contentPane);
JTabbedPane tabbedPane = new JTabbedPane(JTabbedPane.TOP);
contentPane.add(tabbedPane, BorderLayout.CENTER);
cluster_panel = new JPanelQ;
tabbedPane.addTab("Clustering", null, cluster_panel, null);
cluster_panel.setLayout(new BorderLayout(0, 0));
clus_north = new JPanel();
cms_north.setBorder(new BevelBorder(BevelBorder.LOWERED, null,
null, null, null));
cmster_panel .add(clus_north, BorderLayout.NORTH);
clus_west = new JPanel();
clus_west.setBorder(new EtchedBorder(EtchedBorder.LOWERED,
null, null));
clus_west.setToolTipText("Arguments");
cluster_panel.add(clus_west, BorderLayout.WEST);
clus_west.setLayout(new GridLayout( 10,1,10,10));
JPanel cluswestl = new JPanelQ; cms_west.add(cluswest 1);

Ibl = new JLabel("Number of Clusters ");
lbl.setFont(new Font("Arial", Font.PLAIN, 13));
Ibl .setEnabled(false);
cluswestl.add(lbl);
spinner - new JSpinner();
spinner.setEnabled(false);
cluswestl .add(spinner);
JPanel cluswest2 = new JPanel();
clus_west.add(cluswest2);
Ib2 = new JLabel("Choose Field for cluster Evaluation");
lb2.setEnabled(false);
lb2.setFont(newFont("Arial", Font.PLAIN, 13));
//cluswest2.add(lb2);

combof = new JComboBoxQ;
combof.setEnabled(false);
combof.setFont(new Font("AriaT, Font.PLAIN, 13));
```

```
//combof.setMaximumRowCount(20);
//clus_west.add(combof);


clus_south = new JPanel();
cluster_panel.add(clus_south, BorderLayout.SOUTH);
clus_south.setLayout(new FlowLayout(FlowLayout.CENTER, 5, 5));


textArea = new JTextAreaf);
text Area. setRows(5);
text Area. setCoIumns(90);
jp-new JScrollPane(textArea);
textArea. setEnabled(false);
text Area. setEditable( false);
label^new JLabelQ;
jp=new JScrollPane(label);
cluster_jpanel.add(jp, BorderLayout.CENTER);
label.setlcon(null);
label.setBackground(Color.WHITE);
label.setSize(clus_center.getWidth(), clus__center.
getHeight());
Ib - new JLabel("Choose File");
lb.setFont(new Font("Arial", Font.PLAIN, 11));
clus_north.add(lb);
fileDialog = new JFileChooserQ;
JButton btnl = new JButton("Browse");
btnl.setFont(new Font("Arial", Font.PLAIN, 13));
btnl.addActionListener(new ActionListener() {
public void actionPerformed(ActionEvent e) {
int returnVal = fileDialog.showOpenDialog(clus_north);
if (returnVal == JFileChooser.APPROVE_OPTION) {
file = fileDialog.getSelectedFileQ;
```

```
lb.setText("File Selected :"+ file.getName());
try{
combof.removeAllItems();
br=new BufferedReader(new FileReader(file));
ln=br.readLine();
hd=ln.split(",");
for(int i-0;i<hd.length;i++){
combof.addltem(hd[i]);
}
combof.setEnabled(true);
Ib.setEnabled(true);
Ibl .setEnabled(true);
lb2.setEnabled(true);
spinner.setEnabled(true);
textArea.setEnabled(true);

textArea.setEditable(false);
}
catch(Exception er){
System.out.println(er);
}}});
clus_north.add(btnl);
JButton startbtn - new JButton("Start");
startbtn.setFont(new Font(ltArial", Font.PLAIN, 13));
startbtn. add ActionListener(new ActionListener() {
public void actionPerformed(ActionEvent argO) {
try{
System.out.println(file.getAbsolutePath());
String str=file.getAbsolutePath();
str=str.replaceAll("\\\\", "/");
int noc=(Integer)spinner.getValue();
System, out. println(noc);
    re.eval("library(fpc)");
re.evalC'libraryCcluster)");
re.eval(ttdf<-read.csv(\""+str+"\")");
if(noc<=l){ re.evalC'pamk.resulK-pamkCdf)1');
```

```
}
else{ re.eval(tlpamk.result<-pamk(df;i+noc+")");
}
String cbvar^(String)combof.getSelectedItem();
x=re.eval("table(pamk.result$pamobject$clustering,dfS"+cbv
ar+")tr);
textArea.setText(re.eval("table(pamk.
result$pamobject$clustering,
dfT+cbvar+'TO-toStringO);
wd=re.eval("getwd()").toString();
re.eval("pdf(Temp.pdf)");
    re.eval("layout(matrix(c(l,2),l,2))");
re.eval("clusplot(pamk.result$pamobject,main=\"Clustering\",la
bel^2)");
re.eval("dev.off()");

PDFDocument document = new PDFDocumentQ;
String wdl =wd.replaceAll("/", "\\\\");
String part[]=wdl.split("Vnt);
System.out.println(part[l]+''\\Ternp.pdf');
document.load(new File(part[l]+"\\Temp.pdf'));
SimpleRenderer Tenderer = new SimpleRendererQ;
renderer.setResolution(300);
List<Image> images = renderer.render(document);
try{
for (int i = 0; i < images.sizeQ; i++) {
ImageIO.write((RenderedImage) images.get(i), "png",new File((i
+ 1) + ".png"));
}
} catch (lOException e) {
System.out.printlnfERROR: " + e.getMessageQ);
}
Imagelcon ic=new Imagelcon(part[l]+"\\l.png");
img=ic.getlmage();
img=img.getScaledInstance(label.getWidth(), label.
getHeight(),
```

```
java.awt.Image.SCALE_SMOOTH);
label.setlcon(new Imagelcon(img));
}catch(Exception e){
System.out.println(e);
}
}
});
clus_west.add(startbtn);
btnFullScreen - new JButton("Full Screen");
clusjwest.add(btnFullScreen);
btnFullScreen.addActionListener(new ActionListener(){
public void actionPerformed(ActionEvent argO) {
fm=new JFrame();
fin . setUndecorated(true) ;
try{

fm.getContentPane().add(new ComponentQ {
String wdl=wd.replaceAll("/", "\\\\");
String part[]=wdl .split("\"");
Bufferedlmage img = ImagelO. read (new File(part[l]+"\\l.
png"));
©Override
public void paint(Graphics g) {
super.paint(g);
g.drawlmage(img, 0, 0, getWidthQ, getHeight(), this);
});
} catch (lOException e) { e.printStackTrace();
}
fm.addMouseListener(new MouseAdapter() {
public void moused icked(MouseEvent e) {
fin.disposeQ;;
}
});
GraphicsEnvironment ge = GraphicsEnvironment.getLocalGraphic-
sEnvironment();
GraphicsDevice gs = ge.getDefaultScreenDevice();
```

```
gs.setFullScreenWindow(fm);
fm.validate();
}});
//Classify code next -------------------------------

Classify_panel = new JPanel();
tabbedPane.addTab("Classification", null, Classiry_panel,
null);
Classify_panel.setLayout(new BorderLayout(0, 0));
Classiiy_north = new JPanelQ;
Classify_north.setBorder(new BevelBorder(BevelBorder.LOWERED,
null, null, null, null));
Classify _panel.add(Classify_north, BorderLayout. NORTH);
label_l = new J Label ("Choose File");
label_l.setFont(new Font("Arial", Font.PLAIN, 11));
Classify_north.add(label_l);
Classify_west = new JPanelQ;
Classify_west.setToolTipText("Arguments");

Classify_west.setBorder(new EtchedBorder(EtchedBorder.LOWERED,
null, null));
Classify_panel.add(Classify_west, BorderLayout.WEST);
Classify_west.setLayout(new GridLayout(10, 1,10, 10));
label1 = new JLabel(" First Variable ");
labell.setHorizontalAlignment(SwingConstants.CENTER);
label l.setEnabled(false);
Classify_west.add(label 1);
comboBoxl = new JComboBoxQ;
comboBoxl.setMaximumRowCount(30);
comboBoxl.setFont(new Font("Arial", Font.PLAIN, 13));
comboBoxl .setEnabled(false);
Classify_west.add(comboBoxl);
Iabel2 = new JLabel("Second Variable ");
label2.setHori2ontalAlignment(SwingConstants.CENTER);
labe!2.setEnabled(false);
Classify__west.add(label2);
```

```
comboBox = new JComboBoxQ;
comboBox.setEnabled(false);
Classify_west.add(comboBox);
button = new JButton("Browse");
button.addActionListener(new ActionListenerQ {
public void action?erformed(ActionEvent argO) {
int returnVal = fileDialog.showOpenDiaIog(CIassify_north);
if (returnVal == JFileChooser.APPROVE_OPTION) {
file = fileDialog.getSelectedFile();
label_l.setText("File Selected :"+ file.getName());
try{
comboBox.removeAHItems();
comboBoxl .removeAHItems();
comboBox2.removeAHItems();
comboBox_l .removeAHItems();
br=new BufferedReader(new FileReader(file));
ln=br.readLine();
hd-ln.split(",");

for(int i=0;i<hd.length;i++){
comboBox.add!tem(hd[i]);
comboBoxl.add!tem(hd[i]);
comboBox2.add!tem(hd[i]);
comboBox_l .addltem(hd[i]);
}
comboBox . setEnabl ed(true);
comboBoxl .setEnabled(true);
comboBox2.setEnabled(true);
comboBox_J .setEnabled(true);
labell .setEnabled(true);
labe!2.setEnabled(true);
label3.setErtabled(true);
Ibel.setEnabled(true);
}
catch(Exception er){
System.out.println(er);
```

```
}

}
}});
button. setFont(new FontfArial”, Font.PLAIN, 13));
Classify_north.add(button);
Iabel4 = new JLabel();
Classify_panel.add(label4,BorderLayout.CENTER);
button_l = new JButton(“Start”);
button_l.addActionListener(new ActionListener() {
public void actionPerformed(ActionEvent argO) {
try{
String str=file.getAbsolutePath();
str=str.replaceAll(“\\\\”, “/”);
re.eval(“library(party)”);
re.eval(“df<-read.csv(\””+str+”\”)”);
String cbvar2^(Stnng)comboBox.getSe]ectedItem();

String cbvar3=(String)comboBoxl .getSelectedltem();
String cbvar4=(String)comboBox2.getSelectedItem();
String cbvars=(String)comboBox_l .getSelectedltem();
if(cbvar2==””)
{
cbvar2=” “;
}
String strl ^file.getName(),namestr^””;
chare;
for(int i=0;i<strl.length()&& strl.charAt(i)!=V;i++)
{
c=strl.charAt(i);
namestr+=c;
}

re.eval(“df_ctree <- ctree(“+cbvars+” ~ +”+cbvar2+”
+”+cbvar3+”+”-t-cbvar4+” , data=df)”);
re.eval(“pdf(Temp.pdf)”);
```

```
re.eval("plot(df_ctree)");
re.evalC'dev.offO");
wd=re.eval("getwd()").toString();
String wdl=wd.replaceAll("/lt, "\\\\");
String part[]=wdl.split("\mt)
PDFDocument document = new PDFDocumentQ;
document.load(newFile(part[l]+"\\Temp.pdf'));
SimpleRenderer Tenderer = new SimpIeRenderer();
render er.setResolution(300);
List<Image> images = Tenderer. render(document);
try{
for (int i = 0; i < images. sizeQ; i++) {
ImageIO.write((RenderedImage)images.get(i),"png",new
File(i+1)+".png"));
}
} catch(IOException e) {
System.out.println("ERROR: " + e.getMessage());
}

Imagelcon icl=new ImageIcon(part[l]+"\\Lpng");
img=icl .getlmage();
img=img.getScaledInstance(label4.getWidth(),label4.
getHeight(),
java.awt.Image.SCALE_SMOOTH);
Iabel4.setlcon(new Imagelcon(img));
}catch(Exception e){
System . out. println(e) ;
}}});
label3 = new JLabel("Third Variable");
label3.setHorizontalAlignment(SwingConstants.CENTER);
labe3.setEnabled(false);
Classify_west.add(label3);
comboBox2 = new JComboBox();
comboBox2.setEnabled(false);
Classify_west.add(cornboBox2);
Ibel = new JLabel(" Select Field");
```

```
Ibel.setHorizontalAlignment(SwingConstants.CENTER);
Ibel.setEnabled(false);
Classify_west.add(lbel);
comboBox_l = new JComboBox();
comboBox_l .setEnabled(false);
Classify_west.add(comboBox_1);
button J.setFont(newFont(MAriaT, Font.PLAIN, 13));
Classify_west.add(button_1);
btnFullScreenl = new JButton("Full Screen");
Classify_west.add(btnFullScreenl);
btnFullScreenl. addActionListener(new ActionListener() {
public void action? erformed(ActionEvent argO) {
fin-new JFrameQ;
frn.setUndecorated(true);
try{
frn.getContentPane().add(new Component() {
String wdl=wd.repiaceAH("/", "\\\\");

String part[]=wdl .splitf"/");
Bufferedlmage img = ImageIO.read(new File(part[l]+"\\l.png"));
@Override
public void paint(Graphics g) {
super.paint(g);
g.drawlmage(img, 0, 0, getWidth(), getHeight(), this);
}});
} catch (lOException e) {
e.print S tackTrace( ) ;
}
fm.addMouseListener(new Mouse Adapter() {
public void mouseClicked(MouseEvent e) {
fm.dispose();;
}
});
Graphic sEnvironment ge =
GraphicsEnvironment.getLocalGraphicsEnvironment();
GraphicsDevice gs = ge.getDefaultScreenDevice();
```

```
gs . setFul 1 ScreenWindow (fm);
fm.validate();

//Time Decompose -----------------------------------------
--
TimeDecompose = new JPanel();
tabbedPane.addTab("Time Decomposition", null, TimeDecompose,
null);
TimeDecompose. setLayout(new BorderLayout(0, 0));
panel = new JPanelQ;
panel. setBorder(new BevelBorder(Bev el Border. LOWERED, null,
null, null, null));
TimeDecompose.add(panel, BorderLayout.NORTH);
panel.setLayout(new FlowLayout(FlowLayout.CENTER, 5, 5));
label_2 = new JLabel("Choose File");
label_2.setFont(new Font("Arial", Font.PLAlN, 11));
panel. add(label_2);
button_2 = new JButton("Browse");

button_2.addActionListener(new ActionListener() {
public void actionPerformed(ActionEvent arg()) {
int retumVal = fileDialog.showOpenDialog(clusjnorth);
if(returnVal == JFileChooser.APPROVE_OPTION) {
file = fileDialog.getSelectedFile();
label_2.setText("File Selected :"+ file.getNameQ);
try{
br=new BufferedReader(new FileReader(file));
ln=br.readLine();
hd=ln,split(","); label_2 .setEnabl ed(true) ;
spinner_l .setEnabled(true); IblSelectDecompositionFrequency.
setEnabled(true);
}
catch(Exception er){
System.out.println(er);
}}
}});
```

```
button_2.setFont(new Font("AriaT, Font.PLAIN, 13));
panel.add(button_2);
Decompose_west = new JPanel();
Decompose_west.setToolTipText("Arguments");
Decompose_west.setBorder(new EtchedBorder(EtchedBorder.LOW-
ERED, null, null));
TimeDecompose.add(Decompose_west, BorderLayout.WEST);
Decompose_west.setLayout(new GridLayout(10, 1, 10, 10));
panel_2 = new JPanel();
Decompose_west.add(panel_2);
IblSelectDecompositionFrequency = new JLabel("Select decompo-
sition frequency");
    lblSelectDecompositionFrequency.setFont(new Font("Arial",
Font.PLAIN, 13));
IblSelectDecompositionFrequency.setEnabled(false);
panel_2.add(lblSelectDecompositionFrequency);
spinner_1 = new JSpinner();
spinner_1 .setEnabled(false);
panel_2.add(spinner_1);

label5 = new JLabel();
TimeDecompose.add(label5, BorderLayout.CENTER);
button_3 = new JButton("Start");
button_3.addActionListener(new ActionListener() {
public void actionPerformed(ActionEvent arg()) {
try{
String str=file.getAbsolutePath();
str=str.replaceAll("\\\\", "/");
intnoc=(Integer)spinner.getValue();
S ystem. out .println(noc);
String strl=file.getName(),namestr="";
chare;
for(int i=0;i<strl .length()&& strl.charAt(i)!=V;i++)
{
c=strl .charAt(i);
namestr+=c;
```

```
}
System.out.println(namestr);
re.eval("library(fpc)");
re.eval("df<-read.csv(\""+str+"\")");
if(noc==0){
re.eval("apts <- ts(df, frequency=12)");
}
else{
re.eval("apts <- ts(df,frequency="+noc+")");
re.eval("f <-decompose(apts)");
}
textArea.setText(re.eval("f<-decompose(apts)").toString());
wd-re.eval(Mgetwd()").toString();
String wdl-wd.replaceAll('V", "\\\\");
String part[]=wd 1 .split("/"");
System.out.println(part[l]);
//re.eval("png('Temp.png')");
re.evalC'pdfCTemp.pdf)");

re.evalflayout(matrix(c(1,2),1,2))");
re.eval("plot(f)");
re.eval("dev.off()");
PDFDocument document = new PDFDocument();
document.load(newFile(part[l]+"\\Temp.pdf'));
SimpleRenderer Tenderer = new SimpleRenderer();
renderer.setResolution(300);
List<Image> images = renderer.render(document);
try{
for (int i = 0; i < images. si ze(); i++) {
ImageIO.write((RenderedImage)images.get(i),"png",new
}
} catch(IOException e) {
System.out.println("ERROR: " + e.getMessage());
}
Imagelcon icl=new Imagelcon(part[l]+"\\1.png");
System.out.println(icl.toString());
```

```
Image imgl=icl .getlmage();
imgl=imgl.getScaledInstance(label5.getWidth(),labeI5.
getHeight(),java.awt.Image.SCALE_SM
OOTH);
Iabel5.setlcon(newlmagelcon(imgl));
}catch(Exception e){
System.out.println(e);
}}});
Decompose_west.add(button_3);
button_3.setFont(new Font("Arial", Font.PLAIN, 13));
btnFullScreen2 = new JButton("Full Screen");
Decomposejwest.add(btnFuIlScreen2);
btnFullScreen2.addActionListener(new ActionListenerQ {
public void actionPerformed(ActionEvent argO) {
rm=new JFrame();
rm .setUndecorated(true) ;
try{
frn.getContentPane().add(new Component(){
String wdl=wd.replaceAll('V", "\\\\");
String part[]=wdl.split("/");
Bufferedlmage img = ImageIO.read(new File(part[l]+"\\l.png"));
@Override
public void paint(Graphics g) {
super.paint(g);
g.drawlmage(img, 0, 0, getWidthQ, getHeightQ, this);
}});
} catch (lOException e) {
// TODO Auto-generated catch block
e.printStackTraceQ;
}
fm.addMouseListener(new Mouse Ad apter() {
public void mouseClicked(MouseEvent e) {
fm.dispose();;
}});
Graphics Environment ge =
GraphicsEnvironment.getLocalGraphicsEnvironment();
```

```
GraphicsDevice gs = ge-getDefaultScreenDevice();
gs.setFullScreenWindow(fm);
frn.validate();
}
});
//Seasonal Analysis ------------------------------------------
-----
panel_3 = new JPanel();
tabbedPane.addTab("Seasonal Analysis", null, panel_3, null);
panel_3.setLayout(new BorderLayout(0, 0));
panel_4 = new JPanelQ;
paneM.setBorder(new BevelBorder(BevelBorder.LOWERED, null,
null, null, null));
panel J3 .add(panel_4, BorderLayout. NORTH);
label_3 = new J Lab el ("Choose File");
label_3.setFont(new Font("Arial", Font.PLAIN, 11));
panel_4.add(label_3);
button_4 = new JButton("Browse");
button_4.addActionListener(new ActionListener() {
public void actionPerformed(ActionEvent argO) {
int returnVal = fileDialog.showOpenDialog(clus_north);
if (returnVal == JFileChooser. APPRO VE_OPTION) {
file = fileDialog.getSelectedFileQ;
label_3.setText("File Selected :"+ file.getName());
try{
combof. remove All It em s();
br=new BufferedReader(new FileReader(file));
ln=br.readLine();
hd=ln.split(M,");
}
catch(Exception er){
System, out. println(er);
}
}
}});
button_4.setFont(new Font("Arial", Font.PLAIN, 13));
```

```
panel_4.add(button_4);
panel_5 = new JPanel();
panel_3.add(panel_5, Border Layout. SOUTH);
button_5 = new JButton("Start");
button_5.addActionListener(new ActionListenerQ {
public void actionPerformed(ActionEvent argO) {
try{
String str^file.getAbsolutePath();
str=str.replaceAIl("\\\\", "/");
String strl =file.getName0,namestr=" ";
char c;
for(int i=0;i<strl.length() && strl.charAt(i)!='.';i++)
{
c=strl.charAt(i);
namestr+=c;
}
System . out.println(namestr) ;

re.eval("library(rpc)");
re.eval("df<-read.csv(\""+str+"/")");
re.eval("apts <- ts(df, frequency=12)");
re.eval("f <- decompose(apts)");
re.eval("fS figure");
re.eval(npdf('Temp.pdf)");
re.eval("plot(fSfigure,type="+""b"+")xaxt="+1Mn"t4-",
re.eval("monthNames <- months(ISOdate(2011,1:12,1))");
re.eval("axis(l, at=l:12, labels=monthNames, las=2)");
textArea.setText(re.eval(Ilf$figure"+"monthNames <-
months(ISOdate(2011,1
at=l:12, labels=monthNames, las=2)").toString());
re.eval("dev.off()");
wd=re.eval("getwd()").toStringO;
String wdl=wd.replaceAll('7", "\\\\");
String part[]=wdl.split('/");
PDFDocument document = new PDFDocument();
document.load(new File(part[l]+"\Temp.pdf'));
```

```
SimpleRenderer renderer = new SimpleRenderer();
renderer.setResolution(300);
List<Image> images = renderer.render(document);
try{
for (int i = 0; i < images.size(); i++) {
ImageIO.write((RenderedImage)images.get(i),"png",new File((i +
1)+"
}
} catch(IOException e) {
System.out.println("ERROR: " + e.getMessage());
}
Imagelcon icl=new Imagelcon(part[1]+"\\1.png");
img=icl .getlmage();
img=img.getScaledInstance(mylabel.getHeight(), mylabel.
getHeight(),
java.awt.Image.SCALE_SMOOTH);
mylabel.setlcon(new Imagelcon(img));
} catch(Exception e){
System.out.println(e);

}}});
button_5.setFont(new Font("Arial", Font.PLAIN, 13));
panel_5.add(button_5);
mylabel = new JLabel();
mylabel.setHorizontalAlignment(SwingConstants.CENTER);
panel_3.add(mylabel, BorderLayout.CENTER);
btnFullScreen3 = new JButton("Full Screen");
panel_5.add(btnFullScreen3);
btnFullScreen3.addActionListener(new ActionListenerQ {
public void actionPerformed(ActionEvent argO) {
fin=new JFrame();
ftn.setUndecorated(true);
try {
frn.getContentPane().add(new Component() {
String wdl=wd.replaceAll("/", "\\\\");
String part[]=wdl.split("\"");
```

```
BufferedImage img = ImageIO.read(new File(part[1]+"\\1.png"));
@Override
public void paint(Graphics g) {
super.paint(g);
g.drawImage(img, 0, 0, getWidth(), getHeight(), this);
}});
} catch (IOException e) {
e.printStackTrace();
}
fm.addMouseListener(new MouseAdapter()
public void moused icked(MouseEvent e) {
fm.dispose();;
}
});
GraphicsEnvironment ge = GraphicsEnvironment.getLocalGraphic-
sEnvironment();
GraphicsDevice gs = ge.getDefaultScreenDevice();
gs.setFullScreenWindow(fm);
fm.validate();

}
});
//Seasonal Analysis over -------------------------------
-----
neural_panel = new JPanel();
tabbedPane.addTab("Neural Network", null, neural_panel, null);
neural_panel.setLayout(new BorderLayout(0, 0));
neural_north = new JPanel();
neural_north.setBorder(new BevelBorder(BevelBorder.LOWERED,
null, null, null, null));
neural_panel.add(neural_north, BorderLayout.NORTH);
label_21 = new JLabel("Choose File");
label_21 .setFont(new Font("Arial", Font.PLAIN, 11));
neural_north.add(label_21);
neural_west = new JPanel();
neural_west.setToolTipText("Arguments");
```

```
neural_west.setBorder(new EtchedBorder(EtchedBorder.LOWERED,
null, null));
neural_panel.add(neural_west, BorderLayout.WEST);
neural_west.setLayout(new GridLayout(10, 1, 10, 10));
label 11 = new J Label ("First Variable(Y node) ");
label 11 .setHorizontalAlignment(SwingConstants.CENTER);
labell 1 .setEnabled(false);
neural_west.add(labell 1);
comboBoxll = new JComboBoxQ;
comboBoxl 1 .setMaximumRowCount(30);
comboBoxll.setFont(new FontC'Arial", Font.PLAIN, 13));
comboBoxl 1 .setEnabled(false);
neural_west.add(comboBoxl 1);
Iabel21 = new J Label ("Second Variable(X node) ");
Iabel21 .setHorizontalAlignment(SwingConstants.CENTER);
Iabel21 .setEnabled(false);
neural_west.add(labe!21);
comboBox21 - new JComboBoxQ;
comboBox21 .setEnabled(false);
neural_west.add(comboBox21);
labeBl - new JLabel("Third Variable(Z node)");

Iabel31 .setHorizontalAlignment(SwingConstants.CENTER);
labe!31.setEnabled(false);
neural_west.add(labe!31);
comboBox31 = new JComboBox();
comboBox31 ,setEnabled(false);
neural_west.add(comboBox31);
button2 = new JButton("Browse");
button2.addActionListener(new ActionListener() {
public void actionPerformed(ActionEvent arg0) {
intreturnVall = fileDialog.showOpenDialog(neural_north);
if(retumVall = JFileChooser.APPROVE_OPTION) {
file = fileDialog.getSelectedFile();
label_21.setText("File Selected:"+ file.getName());
try{
```

```
comboBox21 .removeAllItems();
comboBoxl 1 .remove All Items();
comboBox31 .removeAHItems();
br=new BufferedReader(new FileReader(file));
ln=br.readLine();
hd=ln.split(",");
for(int i=0;i<hd.length;i++){
comboBox21 .addltem(hd[i]);
comboBoxl 1 .addltem(hd[i]);
comboBox31 .addltem(hd[i]);
}
comboBox21 .setEnabled(true);
comboBoxl1 .setEnabled(true);
comboBox31 .setEnabled(true);
label 11 .setEnabled(true);
Iabel21 .setEnabled(true);
Iabel31 .setEnabled(true);
}
catch(Exception er) {
System.out.println(er);

}
}}});
button2.setFont(new Font("Arial", Font.PLAIN, 13));
neural_north. ad d (button_2);
button_2 - new JButton("Start");
button_2.addActionListener(new ActionListener() {
public void actionPerformed(ActionEvent arg0) {
try{

String str=file.getAbsolutePath();
str=str.replaceAll("\\\", "/");
re.eval("library(neuralnet)");
re.eval("dataset<-read.csv(\""+str+"\")");
Stringcbvar21 =( String) comboB ox 11.getSelectedItem();//y
node
```

```
String cbvar31=(String)comboBox21.getSelectedItem();//x node
String cbvar41=(String)comboBox31.getSelectedItem();//z node
if (cbvar21=="")
{
cbvar21="";
}
String str2=file.getName(),namestr="";
charcl;
for(int i=0;i<str2.1ength()&& str2.charAt(i)!=V;i++)
{
cl=str2.charAt(i); namestr+=cl;
}
re.eval("trainset <- dataset[l:100, ]");
re.eval("creditnet <- neuralnet("+cbvar21+" ~ "+cbvar31+" +
"+cbvar41+" ,trainset, hidden - 4,
lifesign = 'minimal', linear.output = FALSE, threshold =
0.1)");
    wd=re.eval("getwd()").toString();
String wdl=wd.replaceAll("/", "\\\\");
String part[]=wdl.split("\"");

re.eval("pdf(Temp.pdf)");
re.eval("plot(creditnet, rep = 'best')");
re.eval("dev.off()");
PDFDocument document = new PDFDocument();
document, load (new File(part[l]+"\\Temp.pdf'));
SimpleRenderer Tenderer = new SimpleRenderer();
renderer.setResolution(300);
List<Image> images = renderer.render(document);
try{
for (int i = 0; i < images.sizeQ; i++) {
ImageIO.write((RenderedImage)images.get(i),"png",new
File(i+1)+".png"));
}
} catch(IOException e) {
System.out.println("ERROR: " + e.getMessage());
```

```
}

Imagelcon icl=new Imagelcon(part[l]+"\\l.png");
imgl =icl .getlmageQ;
imgl=imgl.getScaledInstance(label41.getWidth(), label41.
getHeight(),
java.awt.Image.SCALE_SMOOTH);
Iabel41 .setlcon(new Imagelcon(imgl));
}
catch(Exception e){}
}});
Iabel41 = new JLabel();
neural_panel.add(labe!41,BorderLayout.CENTER);
button_2.setFont(new Font("Arial", Font.PLAIN, 13));
neural_westadd(button_2);
JButton testx,testz;
testx = new JButton("Prediction test of x");
testx.addActionListener(new ActionListener() {
public void actionPerformed(ActionEvent arg0) {
try{
String cbvar21=(String)comboBox 11 . getSelectedItem();//ynode

String cbvar31=(String)comboBox21,getSelectedItem();//x node
String cbvar41=(String)comboBox31.getSelected!tern();//z node
wd=re.eval("getwd()").toString();
String wdl=wd.replaceAll("/", "\\\\");
String part[]=wdl.split("\"");
re.eval("pdf('neuraltestx.pdf)");
re.eval(cbvar31+".test<-seq(from=0, to=l, by=0.01)");
re.eval(cbvar21+".fit<-compute(creditnets
covariate^matrix(c("+cbvar31+".test, rep(0.5,
Iength("+cbvar31+".test))), nrow-length("+cbvar31+".test),
ncol=2))$net.result");
re.eval("plot("+cbvar21+"~"+cbvar31+", trainset)");
re.eval("lines("+cbvar21+".fit-"+cbvar31+".test, type=T, col-
ored1, lwd=2)");
```

```
re.eval("dev.off()");
PDFDocument document = new PDFDocument();
document.load(new File(part[ 1 ]+"\\neuraltestx.pdf ));
SimpleRenderer renderer = new SimpleRenderer();
Tenderer. setResolution(3 00);
List<Image> images = renderer.render(document);
try{
for (int i = 0; i < images.sizeQ; i++) {
ImageIO.write((RenderedImage)images.get(i),"png",new File((i +
l)+".png"));
}
} catch(IOException e) {
System.out.println("ERROR: " + e.getMessage());
}
labeI41 .removeAll();
Imagelcon icl=new Imagelcon(part[l]+"\\l .png");
imgl=icl.getlmage();
imgl=imgl.getScaledInstance(label41.getWidth(), labeI41.
getHeight(),
java.awt.Image.SCALE_SMOOTH);
label41.setlcon(new Imagelcon(imgl));
}
catch(Exception e){}
}});
testx.setFont(new Font("Arial", Font.PLAIN, 13));

neural_west. add(testx);
testz = new JButton("Prediction test of z");
testz.addActionListener(new ActionListener() {
public void actionPerformed(ActionEvent arg0) {
try{
String cbvar21 =(String)comboBox 11 .getSelectedItem();//y
node
String cbvar31 =(String)comboBox21 .getSelected!tem();//x node
String cbvar4i=(String)comboBox31.getSelectedItem();//z node
   wd=re.eval("getwd()").toString();
String wdl-wd.replaceAllC1/", "\\\\");
```

```
String part[]=wdl.split("\"");
re.evalfpdfCneuraltesty.pdf)");
re.eval(cbvar41+".test<-seq(from=0, to=l, by=0.01)");
re.eval(cbvar21+".fit<-compute(creditnet,
covariate^matrix(c(rep(l,
Iength("+cbvar41+".test)),"+cbvar41+".
test),nrow=length(1f+cbvar41+".test),
ncol=2))$net.result");
re.eval(Hplot("+cbvar21+"~"+cbvar41+", trainset)");
re.eval("lines("+cbvar21+".fit~"+cbvar41+".test, type=T, col-
ored1, lwd=2)");
re.eval("dev.off()");
PDFDocument document = new PDFDocument();
document.load(new File(part[l]+"\\neuraltesty.pdf});
SimpleRenderer Tenderer = new SimpleRenderer();
renderer.setResolution(300);
List<Image> images = renderer.render(document);
try{
for (int i = 0; i < images.sizeQ; i++) {
ImageIO.write((RenderedImage)images.get(i),"png",new
File((i+1)+".png"));
}
} catch( IO Excepti on e) {
System.out.println("ERROR: " + e.getMessage());
}
Iabel41 .removeAH();
Imagelcon icl=new Imagelcon(part[l]+"\\1.png");

imgl=icl .getlmage();imgl =imgl .getScaledInstance(labe!41
.getWidthQ, Iabel41 .getHeight(),
java.awt.Image.SCALE_SMOOTH);
Iabel41.setlcon(new Imagelcon(imgl));
}
catch(Exception
}
});
testz.setFont(new Font("Arial", Font.PLAIN, 13));
```

```
neural_westadd(testz);
panel_2 = new JPanel();
neural_panel.add(panel_2, BorderLayout.SOUTH);
panel_2.setLayout(new FlowLayout(FlowLayout.CENTER, 5, 5));
btnFullScreen4 = new JButton("Full Screen");
neural_west.add(btnFullScreen4);
btnFullScreen4.addActionListener(new ActionListener() {
©Override
public void actionPerformed(ActionEvent arg()) {
fm=new JFrame();
frn.setUndecorated(true);
try{
rm.getContentPane().add(new Component() {
String wdl=wd.replaceAll(7", "\\\");
String part[]=wdl.split("\"");
Bufferedlmage img = ImageIO.read(new File(part[l]+"\\l.png"));
@Override
public void paint(Graphics g) {
super.paint(g);
g.drawlmage(img, 0, 0, getWidth(), getHeight(), this);
}
});
} catch (lOException e) {
e.printStackTrace();
}
fm.addMouseListener(new MouseAdapter() {

public void mouseCHcked(MouseEvent e) {
ftn.dispose();;
}
});
GraphicsEnvironment ge -
GraphicsEnvironment.getLocalGraphicsEnvironment();
GraphicsDevice gs = ge.getDefaultScreenDevice();
gs.setFullScreenWindow(frn);
fm.validate();
}});}}
```

1. Plant disease Classifier.
2. Road sign identificaltion (Belgian traffic dataset)
3. Transportation analysis showing travel times
4. Matching algorithm for finding a compatible data.
5. Leaf classification from images.
6. Face recognition using CNN.
7. Image classification using CNN.
8. Stock market Price Predictor.
9. Diamond Price Predictor.
10. Building Gaming Bot
11. E-commerce Recommendation System.
12. Text Summarization.
13. Job Recommendation System.
14. Real-time object Recognition App.
15. Developing chatbots.
16. NLP using DL.

References

1. http://sciencemag.org/content/293/5539/2425.
2. Ethem Alpaydin, "Introduction to Machine Learning", Third Edition, PHI learning.
3. Rajiv Chopra, "Web Engineering", First Edition, PHI learning.
4. Nikhil Buduma, "Fundamentals of Deep Learning", O' Reilly, Delhi.
5. Rajiv Chopra, "Cloud Computing: An Introduction", First Edition, Mercury Learning and Info., USA, 2018; listed in Library Catalogue, USA.
6. E. Crego et al., "Big Data and Deep Learning", Business Online, 2013.
7. G. Hinton, "A Practical Guide to Training Restricted Boltzmann Machines", Department of Computer Science, Univ. Toronto, Canada, 2010.
8. Rajiv Chopra, "Testing Web Applications: The state of art and future trends", First Edition, Cambridge International Science Publishing, UK.; listed in British Catalogue Library, UK.
9. K. Uma Rao, " AI and Neural Networks", First Impression, Pearson Education, 2011.
10. S. Balamurugan, "A practical approach for machine Learning and Deep Learning Algorithms", Ist Edition, BPB Publications, 2019.
11. Bharath Ramsundar, "Tensor Flow for Deep Learning", Shroff Publishers, I[st] Indian Reprint 2018.
12. Valentino Zocca etc. al, "Python Deep Learning" Packt Publishing, Ist Edition, 2017.
13. Rajiv Chopra, "Machine Learning", Khanna Publications, 2nd Edition, 2019-2020.

Index

D

E

F

G

H

I

K

L

M

N

O

P

U

V

W

DEEP LEARNING

(A PRACTICAL APPROACH)

RAJIV CHOPRA

FEEDBACK FORM

1. Which topics from your examination point of view are inadequately or not covered in this book?

____

____

2. Is there any misprints/ mistakes/ factual inaccuracy in this book? If so, please specify.

____

____

3. What is your assessment of this book as regards the presentation of the subject-matter, expression, precision and price in relation to the other recommended books available on this subject?

____

____

4. Which competing books you regard as better than this? Please mention their author and publishers.

____

____

5. Any further suggestions/comments you would like to make for the improvement of the book?

____

____

PS: If needed, please attach a separate sheet.

Name : ____________________

College : ____________________

Address : ____________________

Email : ____________________

Mobile : ____________________

Please mail the feedback form at:

KHANNA BOOK PUBLISHING CO. (P) LTD.

4C/4344, Ansari Road, Daryaganj, New Delhi-110002

You can also email this feedback form at contact@khannabooks.com or Whatsapp at +91 – 99109 09320

BEST FEEDBACK WILL BE REWARDED SUITABLY